Gaucho Laird

The Life of
R. B. Cunninghame Graham –
"Don Roberto"

by

Jean Cunninghame Graham

[Lady Polwarth]

The Long Riders' Guild Press

www.horsetravelbooks.com

ISBN: 1-59048-179-8

Cover painting, *Don Roberto*, by Sir John Lavery, reproduced by permission of the Museo Nacional del Bellas Artes, Buenos Aires, Argentina.

DEDICATION

To Basha and CuChullaine O'Reilly
Founders of The Long Riders' Guild.

www.horsetravelbooks.com

All extracts from family letters came from the private collection of Jean Cunninghame Graham on her succession as Literary Executor to her great-uncle, Robert Cunninghame Graham. She has now given the whole collection to the National Library of Scotland, in Edinburgh, where they can be seen by the public on request.

J. C. G.
(Lady Polwarth)
2004

www.horsetravelbooks.com

AUTHOR'S INTRODUCTION

I first started to research my grand-uncle's life forty years after he had died. I remembered him well, and I had been brought up in his home on the Clyde, Ardoch – the house he moved to, built by one of his forebears at the end of the eighteenth century, with some help from his friends, the Adam brothers. Robert Bontine Cunninghame Graham sold the family estate of Gartmore in 1901. Many Scottish lairds, in his day, were forced to dispose of their large estates due to falling agricultural rents from their farms as the industrial revolution took hold.

Fortunately for me, Uncle Robert had taken as many of his possessions as he could cram in to the smaller house of Ardoch – and this was where I found his hoard of family letters, a life's worth of correspondence from the days before mobile telephones. Letters from his mother and father, letters from his two brothers, and letters from his many friends and relations. Gradually they began to form the picture at the end of the jigsaw puzzle – my grandfather's deeply loved elder brother – Robert!

I must admit that the thought of writing about his life was rather daunting – there seemed to be so *much* of it. But I made a start.

Then a rather extraordinary thing happened which gave my task an added impetus – I was told that, if I did not write the book I should be haunted by a certain person until I did. That person was a very erudite and amusing lawyer I met in Dallas, Texas. What an unlikely ghost! His name was Henry Coke, and his grandfather had been a Governor of Texas.

I had gone with my husband, Harry, on a business trip to Texas, where he was the British non-executive director of a world-wide company, travelling two or three times a year to their headquarter in Dallas. A lunch-party was given for us, to meet the other directors and their wives.

I found myself sitting next to an elderly lawyer, who immediately turned to me with a smile, and said, "You are a Cunninghame Graham, aren't you?"

I was astonished! How could he possibly know my maiden name? Why did he seem to be so interested in it? I expressed my surprise, and he told me that he had all of my Uncle Robert's published books – all thirty of them. It was because of his love of Joseph Conrad's books that he turned to reading Conrad's great friend Robert's in turn, finding them quite fascinating.

Henry and his English wife were to become very close friends of ours, on our many visits to Dallas. I loved prowling round Henry's huge and varied library. Every time I went to their home, Henry would ask me, "And how is the book coming along?" Then he would say, "If you don't finish it, I will haunt you after I'm dead."

He has died, and I *did* eventually finish it. So, thank you for continuing to haunt me after you died, dear Henry.[*] This book is for you and for another Henry, my inspiration – Harry (Lord Polwarth) my beloved husband.

J.C.G. (J.P.)

---

[*] You can stop now!

www.horsetravelbooks.com

ACKNOWLEDGEMENTS

First of all I must thank all the people who wrote those letters to Uncle Robert and brought him alive for me, especially as they probably could not read *his* answers to *them* due to his totally illegible handwriting – the nightmare of all printers' compositors.

Then I must thank various people who have helped me to edit my first attempt, which was eight hundred pages long! It has taken two or three of them to achieve this miracle – the best of all being dear Basha O'Reilly.

Sarah Macnab, my step-daughter, typed out my first "marathon" for which she deserves several medals. Thank you Sarah! (It was a very long time ago, perhaps you have forgotten it?)

My printers, Creeds, from Broadoak near Bridport, have tidied up my manuscript quite wonderfully, photocopying and binding the result so that The Long Riders' Guild received something fairly manageable for publication in due course.

Finally, I must thank the many, many people (and some total strangers) who encouraged me to tell the true story of the life of Robert Bontine Cunninghame Graham (1852-1936).

J.C.G.

www.horsetravelbooks.com

Principal Characters in *Gaucho Laird*

"Missy" (Robert's mother)	Anne Elizabeth Elphinstone – daughter of Admiral The Hon. Charles Elphinstone Fleeming (second son of the 10th Lord Elphinstone). He had to take the second namd of Fleeming – or Fleming, they spelt it *both* ways – when he inherited Cambernauld House and estate from his Fleming grandmother, daughter of the Earl of Wigton, just as the Grahams of Gartmore had to take the second name of Cunninghame when Nicol Graham of Gartmore married Lady Margaret Cunninghame, daughter of the Earl of Glencairn – the Cunninghames.
"Willy" (Robert's father)	William Cunninghame Graham Bontine (Major in the Scots Greys). He too had to take an extra name, Bontine, as the eldest son of Robert's grandfather – another Robert Cunninghame Graham – who was Laird of Gartmore. The Cunninghame Grahams were the only "commoners" to have an entail on the estate of Ardoch, in which the eldest son inherited the estate and lived on its income while his father was still alive and the Laird of Gartmore. He had to use the name Bontine while he owned Ardoch, as it came to the family from a Bontine heiress who married a Graham in the 17th Century. All very complicated but family names and lands, in Scotland, are inextricably linked. In 1851 Willy married Missy.
Doña Catalina Paulina Alessandro	Missy's mother, who married Admiral Fleming when she was 15 (and he was about 40)! They had a very happy marriage and had five children, Missy being the youngest. Catalina was born in 1801 in Cadiz, where her family were "merchant adventurers" trading with the New World. They considered themselves to be Spanish, but in the 16th Century their ancestors had come from Ancona, in

	north-east Italy.
Admiral Fleming	Doña Catalina's husband, the admiral, died in his final "retiring job" as Commander-in-Chief of Greenwich Hospital.
Admiral Katon	Catalina's second husband.
Missy's siblings	Carlota, John (later to scuceed his uncle as Lord Elphinstone), Clementina, "Keithy" (Mary Keith, called after her father's uncle, Admiral Lord Keith) and Anne Elizabeth – "Missy."
Willy's family	His younger brothers and sisters were: Archie, Margaret, Annie, Douglas and Bob (Robert). His cousin was another Annie, married to his grand-mother' brother – "Aunt Annie Speirs."

PROLOGUE

On 24th May 1852 the eldest son of the Laird of Gartmore, William Bontine Cunninghame Graham, wrote a note to his Spanish mother-in-law, Doña Catalina, to tell her that her grandson had arrived safely.

5, Cadogan Place
London

(To Ryde, Isle of Wight)

24th May 1852

"My dear Mum,

Thank God it is all over. A young gentleman appeared at one o'clock this morning, Monday. Poor Missy is doing well, but has had a dreadfully severe trial. I had to give her 'cloroform' [sic] for nearly half an hour. The Doctor says she is very well and quite out of danger, but for some time the case appeared very serious. She has suffered a great deal, poor child.

Give my love to Katon, yours affectionately,

William Bontine."[1]

Baby Robert was born on Queen Victoria's thirty-third birthday, and that morning guns firing the Royal Salute boomed out from Hyde Park. As a direct descendant of King Robert II of Scotland, William and Missy decided the salute had, in fact, been to greet the birth of their son and heir.

The new little family of three returned soon to Scotland after the birth, to settle into their home, Finlaystone, on the banks of the River Clyde downstream from Glasgow.

Eighteen months later, on 1st January 1854, Robert's younger brother, Charles Elphinstone Fleeming Cunninghame Graham, was born in Edinburgh. Robert had only been give one name at his christening – the name of a Scottish king – but Charles was to be called after his maternal grandfather, Admiral the Honourable Charles Elphinstone Fleeming, and was destined from the start to be a sailor, and a chip off the old block; fortunately he was not to disappoint his mother. Robert may have been

---

[1] Letters were far formally signed in the 19th Century; the writer always used his full name as a signature, even as a son or son-in-law.

jealous of the new baby at first, but by the time they were eight and six (which is when the first photograph was taken of them) they had already formed an indestructible partnership.   In the picture Robert looks fearlessly ahead, while Charlie seems to depend totally on his brother for support.

As they grew older, the relationship was sometimes to be reversed, and Robert often called on his younger brother to help him sort out his problems.   When they were old enough to write letters to each other, their total devotion to each other soon became evident; especially if they had been temporarily parted for some reason or other, for they never ceased asking their mother for news of each other, or to comment on some new accomplishment the other had achieved.

"I have not heard from Charlie yet, but I suppose he is all right?" anxiously from Robert;   or "Robert bowled four of the best players!" from Charlie and again, with pride, "Robert is doing Xenophon, Horace, and Homer."

Robert was later to refer to Charlie as "my Pylades," and Charlie often helped him to disentangle himself when his enthusiasm for life had involved him in a particularly fraught situation.

Their characters were so totally different that they were always to complement each other.   Robert, with his dark red hair, was all fire and ardour from an early age, while Charlie took life as it came.   Robert's temper was uncontrollable when things went wrong;   Charlie was placid and philosophical.

In 1860 a third son was born, to named after a fifteenth century Graham ancestor and Earl of Menteith – Malise.   He was full of fun, like his brothers, but his life was to be a short one due to the dreaded scourge of the nineteenth century, tuberculosis.   He was to die of it when he was 25.

As small children, Robert and his brothers Charlie and Malise were looked after by "Ninny," the old nurse, paying visits to their parents in the drawing-room after tea, dressed in white muslin dresses with coloured sashes.   This was still the era when small children were dressed alike (whether they were boys or girls) until they reached the age of four or five.   The first drawing of Robert and Charles shows them similarly attired, with bare shoulders and very pink and white complexions, resembling small blond angels.

That they were far from angels in their early childhood came to light in a letter to Willy from his brother-in-law, William Hope, son of the Lord Justice Clerk. Knowing the Bontines had just been on a visit to Gartmore, he wrote to ask Willy if they had "all arrived in a satisfactory state, and that Robt and Charlie had committed no very aggravated assaults upon any fellow passengers or railway officials?"

It is also recorded that Robert's favourite prank was to leapfrog over a grown-up sitting in a chair, to the intense alarm of his 'victim.'

According to Missy, Robert started life as a very plain baby, but he must have put on weight quite quickly and had soon become an attractive 'Podge,' by which pet name he was to be known for the first two years of his life.

Missy went from Finlaystone to lodgings at 3, Coates Crescent in Edinburgh, to await the arrival of her second child, and Robert had accompanied her as a baby of not quite two. She wrote to her uncle, Mountstuart Elphinstone, her father's youngest brother, who had just returned from India where had been Governor of Bombay.

"'Podge' and I are much admired on our daily walks, perhaps because we are the ugliest specimens of our respective kind to be seen. Podge is rather improved in looks, and is of a dreadfully inquiring mind, which shows itself in trying to abstract coals from out of the fire, and other experiments of that kind."

Little did his mother realise that she had made an astonishingly prophetic comment. Robert was indeed to try to abstract hot coals from many fires throughout his adventurous life.

Eight years later, the Bontine family were to spend a happy Christmas together at Finlaystone, unaware that it was to be the last before they moved to the estate of Gartmore, the beautiful Perthshire house which had been the family home of the Grahams of Menteith since it was built in the early seventeenth century.

GRAHAMS OF GARTMORE
FAMILY TREE

Relationship to Don
Roberto

Great-great-grandfather	6th Laird of Gartmore – Robert Graham of Gartmore (son of Nicol Graham of Gartmore and Margaret Cunninghame) – "Doughty Deeds."
Great-grandfather	7th Laird of Gartmore – William Graham of Gartmore – "The Swindler."
Grandfather	8th Laird of Gartmore Robert.
Father	9th Laird of Gartmore – William.

PART I
BOYHOOD – 1862-1870
CHAPTER I

Robert's most vivid childhood memory was always to be his last Christmas at Finlaystone in 1862. The yew trees were frosted white and a sprinkling of snow had covered the lawn. The river was shrouded with mist. Piping waders trod delicately on a skin of ice at the water's edge. The old house of Finlaystone, the seat of the Earls of Glencairn, stood sombre and grey beside the Clyde, its harling dulled by the white snow.

Young Robert had been told that John Knox had once celebrated communion, in Reformation days, under these same yews, as he cast his yoke of Calvinism over Scotland. He also knew that Robert Burns had drunk fine claret with his patron, Robert's Cunninghame ancestor, James, 14th Earl of Glencairn, here, as he tried to lift that same yoke off the shoulders off his countrymen with his lighthearted verse.

Warmth and light shone from the windows between the long velvet curtains, and log fires burned cheerfully.

In the drawing room, Papa and Mamma were lighting thousands of candles on the German tree, while Charlie stood nearby with a sponge on a long pole in case of a holocaust. Baby Malise had been brought in by Ninny to see the pretty lights and to collect his parcels off the tree. Then Robert and Charlie, aged ten and eight, had been allowed to open their own presents.

Best of all was his Spanish grandmother, Catalina's, present, the new Kingston's *Annual for Boys* for 1863, full of exciting adventure stories. Robert had spent the rest of Christmas day curled up on the sofa, reading the story of a boy called Tom Bainbridge, who had sailed to the Americas, where he had been involved in every sort of hair-raising adventure, and had been chased across the chaparral, in Texas, by Apache Indians as they galloped after him on their mustangs, or *mestenos*. (Robert had already learnt a little Spanish from his mother, so he knew the word meant "the wild ones.") Having inherited his maternal grandfather's love of horses, he could think of nothing more exciting than a life spent riding over the prairies just like Tom Bainbridge in the story.

He had another vivid memory of that day, for Papa had told him at dinner, while he gobbled sugar plums, that he would have to go away to school at the end of January. It had been a day of intense contrasts, great happiness followed by total misery. He had not wanted to go away to school. He wanted to stay in Scotland and go to the village school like the tenants' bairns. Why did he have to go to a grand private school in England, anyway? Couldn't Charlie go with him? He was near to tears, but Mamma put her arm round him to comfort him, and reminded him how much he always liked seeing new places and having new things to do.

Papa was very gentle with him, too, and told him how much he would enjoy the great Latin and Greek epics he would learn at his new school. The minister at Langbank had already given him some grounding, but now he would have the mysteries of Pliny and Virgil, Xenophon, Horace and Homer revealed to him. There would be football and cricket, too, and plenty of good fellows for companionship. He was to lodge with Dr. Bickmore at Hill House, Budbrooke Park, and he would be quite near to the great horsewoman of his family, Aunt Helen Speirs, at Leamington, who would invite him often to her house, and perhaps even to *ride*!

Robert left Finlaystone on a cold January day in 1863. It was years later that he came to write down some memories of his last days in his childhood home on the Clyde.

"I remembered the old house in Scotland, perched on a rock above the Clyde and set about with trees, the avenue winding about through woods and crossing a little stream on bridges to Upper and Lower Paradise, as parts of the garden wre known, and made the most of by landscape-gardener's art. I saw the yew-trees under which John Knox is said to have preached and dealt with heresy and superstition, like the man he was, driving out all that kindly paganism which is mingled with the Catholic faith, and planting in its stead the stern, hard, hyper-Caledonian faith which bows the knee before its God in a temple like a barn, and looks upon the miserable east end of Glasgow as a thing ordained by God. The tulip-tree, the yellow chestnut, and the laurels tall as houses all came back to me, the little garden with its curious stone vases and the tall hollyhocks. I saw the river with the steamers passing between the fairway marks, saw Dumbarton Castle on its rock and wondered how it could have been the seat of Arthur's Court, as wise men tell. Again I recollected that one day upon the sands I found the outside covering of a cocoa-nut and launched it on the Clyde just opposite to where the roofless house of Ardoch stood, and watched it vanish into nothing, after the fashion of an Irish peasant woman on the quay at Cork watching the vessel take her son away, and just as sure as she of his return."

Robert vividly remembered for the rest of his life, the day he arrived at Hill House. Dr. Bickmore showed him into his study, and sat him down in a comfortable chair, while his wife bustled in with cups of tea and slices of seed-cake. He remembered that he could not swallow the seed-cake for he was feeling rather sick. Perhaps it was the long train journey from London, where his grandmother, Doña Catalina, had seen him off.

"Now, young man," Dr. Bickmore had said cheerfully, "what are we goin' to call you, I wonder? It seems that your Papa is Major Bontine, and you are Mr. Graham? Is that correct?"

It was not something they had ever discussed at home. Robert knew there was some complication about the entail of Ardoch, which had come to them through a Bontine heiress, and that the eldest son of a Graham of Gartmore usually had to take the name Bontine while his father was still alive. Perhaps when Grandpapa died he would have to call himself Bontine, and Papa would revert to Cunninghame Graham. It was all very confusing, but Dr. Bickmore solved it for him.

"We'll stick to Graham, I think. Much easier all round. Do you agree, young man?"

Robert nodded his head emphatically.

"Well, that settles it. Graham it shall be," said Dr. Bickmore.[2]

At that moment there was a knock at his door.

"Come in!" called Dr. Bickmore, and round the door came a mop of fair curls and a freckled face with a cheerful grin.

"Ah, Villiers. I sent for you to take Graham to show him where he is to sleep, help him unpack his box, and please look after him generally."

---

[2] In that era, boys at private schools were always called by their surnames.

"Yes, sir," said Villiers, turning to inspect Robert.

Robert thought he looked very friendly, and his heart began to lift. Perhaps school was not going to be so bad after all.

"Now, off you go, you two boys!" said Dr. Bickmore, dismissing them and picking up a pile of Latin exercises to correct.

Robert followed Villiers out of the door with a grateful glance at his new Headmaster; he had not made him finish that horrid seed-cake after all.

Out in the long passage with its chocolate brown walls and linoleum floor, Villiers said, "We're not supposed to run down this passage, but there's no-one around, so let's sprint."

Flying down the long passage behind Villiers did a lot to relieve Robert's pent-up feelings.

"Is this a decent place?" he asked his new friend.

"Pretty decent!" smiled Villiers.

Even in his old age, Robert was to remember his friend Villiers' cheerful welcome, on that first night away from home.

* * * * * *

Much later in his life Robert was to hear the dreadful story which explained why his great-grandfather was called "The Swindler." In Florence, where William Cunninghame Graham had taken his family to avoid financial difficulties in Scotland, his wife's son by her first marriage, Allen Bogle, met and made friends with an unscrupulous young Frenchman called de Bourbel. This young man had already been known to have conducted fraud for financial gain, although young Bogle was quite unaware of this.

It was de Bourbel who discovered that the London bankers, Glyn, Hallifax, Mills and Company had begun to issue 'Circular Letters of Credit' for the convenience of their customers travelling abroad. The letters were signed by one of the Bank's partners and addressed to the Bank's correspondents abroad. Allen Bogle had mentioned that his stepfather, William Cunninghame Graham, had invented an engraving machine at Gartmore, and he thought he had brought it to Florence with him.

de Bourbel's evil brain went into action. All he had to do was get a signature of the partner who had signed the Letter of Credit, and ask Allen to get a copy off his step-father's engraver, then – hey presto! – they would have a method of obtaining almost limitless money on the Continent.

Allen was obviously very simple, or else very bad. He immediately agreed to do it for de Bourbel. On 26th May 1840 a printer employed by The Times, one John Lawson, published an account of a judicial inquiry in Brussels into the forgeries that had been discovered. Allen Bogle promptly sued for libel.

Whether William Cunninghame Graham, the 7th Laird of Gartmore, had himself been involved in the fraud was never discovered. But not only had his name been dragged in the mud by his stepson, but he was to end his life in disgrace and penury. William had learnt to gamble when his father sent him to Switzerland as a very young man as part of his education. William was soon addicted to gambling, and gradually lost all the family wealth to pay his debts; every stick of furniture and a priceless collection of pictures, acquired by his father, Robert Graham of Gartmore (known to the family as "Doughty Deeds," from a famous poem he had published) had to be sold.

His "men of affairs" were able to arrange a small annual allowance for him, provided he lived abroad.

Robert could never believe that the misdeeds of one of his apparently honourable forbears could have happened in such a way, causing the Cunninghame Grahams such a great financial loss in one fell swoop. They still had plenty of land, but he knew his father was very short of "real money."

As often happens with the swing of the pendulum, William's eldest son Robert (to be the 8th Laird of Gartmore from 1845) was to be a paragon of virtue and kindness. He brought up his eight children partly at Finlaystone and partly on the Continent – first in Frankfurt and subsequently in Brussels – while the scandal raged. It was only on the death of his father in 1845 that he moved back to Gartmore, to find the house empty of furniture and pictures, for nearly everything had been sold by William to pay his creditors.

It was because of this unfortunate episode in the family history that the Grahams of Gartmore lost their valuable collection of pictures, including a large number of Poussins, Claudes and other French masterpieces, as well as "The Flight into Egypt" by Rubens. Mercifully, family portraits by Reynolds and Raeburn were saved.

When his eldest son, Robert moved to Frankfurt, the grandsons, Willy and his younger brother, Archie, were sent to the Grammar School at Market Bosworth, near Nuneaton, a famous old school that had been founded in 1320. The new Headmaster was a distinguished Welshman called Arthur Benoni Evans, who had been a professor of classics and history at the Royal Military Collage at Sandhurst. At the end of the Napoleonic Wars, when the army was gradually being disbanded, the Military College had to reduce its students and its staff, and Evans was out of a job. In 1827 Evans decided to apply for the Headmastership of Rugby, but there was an unfortunate delay in getting necessary testimonials from Sandhurst, and the post went to Dr. Thomas Arnold.

At this point, the Vice-Provost of Eton came to his aid and got him appointed as Master of the Free Grammar School at Market Bosworth, an appointment that was in the hands of the Visitor, the Bishop of Lincoln. Evans immediately introduced a new scheme to the school which would limit the number of free places for local boys to sixty, and he advertised for boarders from all over the country, hoping to turn the old Grammar School into a minor public school, modelled on Rugby, but with much lower fees.

As money was in short supply when the Graham family first moved to the Continent, Willy's father, Robert, was delighted to be able to take advantage of Dr. Evans' new scheme for his two eldest sons, for he could not possibly afford to send them to Eton, Harrow, Winchester or Rugby. Added to this, Evans' close connection with the Royal Military College at Sandhurst was another benefit for both Willie and Archie were destined for the army when they left school.

The final year of Willy's education was spent learning languages and fencing under the consular chaplain in Brussels, where his parents and his five younger brothers and sisters had moved from Frankfurt. Willy's final six months of "formal" education were spent in Weimar, where he also learned German at the court of the Grand Duke, and fell in love for the first time with none other than Göthe's grand-daughter.

At Weimar he got to know Liszt, and Madam Shroeder Devrian, a great singer who looked after the Grand Duke's private theatre, while Liszt arranged the music and opera at the court of Weimar. Willy also recorded in his diary that it was here that he met the young Emperor Alexander of Russia, who was married to the Archduke's sister, and that they had all played "blind man's bluff" after dinner. The Archduke of Austria (who was "a good deal stiffer than Alexander," according to Willy's diary) also paid several visits to Weimar while Willy was there.

When Willy (later to be the 9th Laird of Gartmore) returned to England with his family, his grandfather's death must have come as a blessing in disguise for them all, lifting a dark veil from the lives of the Cunninghame Grahams. Willy joined his father for their first season of hunting, in Warwickshire, from a rented house in Leamington Spa, where they settled until Gartmore was habitable. On 2nd March 1845 Willy's father wrote to his friend and family lawyer in Edinburgh, Arthur Campbell, "I do not say I shall go to live at Gartmore, but to rough it." They hoped to go there for the shooting the following autumn.

In 1846 the two elder boys, Willy and Archie, went into the Army; Willy as an ensign, to join his regiment, the 15th Regiment of Foot, to quell an uprising in Ireland during the Potato Famine. Archie, being three years younger, attended the Royal Military College at Sandhurst as a cadet. In both cases, their military careers were to end in tragedy. In October 1846, Willie received a serious and permanent head injury, and by 1855 his adored younger brother, Archie, had died of a fever whilst on military service in India.

Willy's head injury occurred when he was dealt a blow on the head by an Irish rebel, and was not considered too serious at first. The army doctor assured him that he would feel no ill-effects for many years to come. He transferred to a cavalry regiment, the Scots Greys, in 1848 and enjoyed a further two years soldiering in Ireland. The rebellion was almost over and Willy tells in his diary that his head-wound had ceased to bother him, and he was enjoying hunting and taking part in local race-meetings on his horse. In 1850 the Scots Greys left Ireland and marched

south from Liverpool to Canterbury, where they were to be stationed in
the Barracks for the coming three years.

At Canterbury Cricket Week in 1850 he was fortunate to meet Anne
Elizabeth Elphinstone Fleeming – always known by her family as
"Missy" – at a Ball. She was introduced to him by her uncle, The
Honourable Mountstuart Elphinstone, with whom she was staying on his
recent return from many years in India with the East Indian Company.
There he had risen to be Governor of Bombay and a notable
administrator, much loved by the Indians for his sensitive handling of his
responsible role. He was Missy's father's younger brother.

His eldest sister, Keithy, had married Erskine of Cardross, the next
estate to Gartmore, beside the Lake of Menteith. He knew Willy Bontine
from the shoots at Gartmore to which he was often invited, and Willy
remembered meeting Missy's elder sisters and her brother when they
spent two years with their aunt while their father and mother had been
away in Venezuela.

It was love at first sight. Willy was now twenty-five, and Missy was
twenty-two.

They were married in June 1851 and set off for a long wedding trip to
the Continent, during which Missy quickly became pregnant. She gave
birth to her eldest son, Robert, in May 1952. Eventually he would
become the 10th Laird of Gartmore, some thirty years into the future.

* * * * * *

Anne Elizabeth was born on 10th February 1828 on board her father's
flagship, H.M.S. Barham, between Jamaica and Venezuela. The Royal
Navy had sent him to keep an eye on the situation in South America
during the mood for Independence. She was to spend her first three years
with her mother and father, living in a colonial house near to the
cathedral in Caracas.[3] The two distinguished "Liberators," Simon
Bolivar and José Antonio Paez, were their neighbours and friends.

The four older children wrote regularly from Cardross House in
Perthshire, where they were staying with their Elphinstone aunt during

---

[3] Author's personal note: My eldest grandson, Jeremy Jauncey, was also born in
Caracas in 1984!

their parents' absence abroad. In these letters they told their parents how much they were missing them, and inquired after their baby sister, whom they were all longing to see. It had been her Venezuelan nursery-maid who first starting calling the baby, "Yitty Missy."

"How sensible 'Yitty Missy' must be!" wrote the twelve-year-old Carlota in 1830. "I am surprised to hear she speaks so well already. She will be quite a companion for Mary Keith, though she is much younger." Mary Keith was six by the time three-year-old 'Missy' returned to their own home in 1831.

Cumbernauld, the Fleeming property, was their father's inheritance from his great-aunt, the heiress of the 6th Earl of Wigtown. Mary Keith bore the name Keith, like her aunt, Lady Erskine, in honour of her distinguished great-uncle, the Viscount Keith, Admiral of the White, who was the 10th Lord Elphinstone's younger brother.

The return to Cumbernauld from South America must have been quite a spectacle, for the Fleemings were laden with parting presents from the great Liberator, José Antonio Paez, and from their other South American friends, including two pacing ponies ("Tony" and "Caballero"), several brightly coloured macaws which flew about in their chilly aviary screeching furiously, and a peculiar South American rodent called a "Chirhuiri" which promptly went to ground under the dining-room table at Cumbernauld and lived on a diet of chewed lace from the ladies' petticoats. The lively Fleeming children shrieked with delight, while the macaws shrieked even louder: never had there been such a noisy, happy reunion. Naturally 'Yitty Missy' was everyone's darling, and had always been a particular favourite of her Uncle Mount's (Mountstuart Elphin-stone) as well, since her father, the Admiral, his elder brother, had died when Missy was only twelve. He kept a very kind eye on his brother's children for the rest of his life.

Uncle Mount was home from India where he had been Governor of Bombay until 1828. The Duke of Wellington proposed that he should be made Governor-General of India, but Elphinstone was to turn the job down, partly because of ill-health and partly in order to write an important "History of India." He was fifty-five on his retirement.

The friendship that began between his youngest niece and himself in 1831 continued until his death in 1859, and their letters show how alike they must have been, with their love of music, books, liberal politics and people. At a time when girls received little or no education, Missy was fortunate to have such a "tutor" as her adored uncle. And he was to play an important role in her life when her father died of an influenza epidemic, simultaneously with his eldest daughter, Carlota, in 1840, during his final Naval appointment as Governor of Greenwich Hospital.

Missy was only twelve at the time of her father's death, and Uncle Mount became like a second father to her until nine years later, in 1849, when her mother remarried. Her new husband was a captain in the Royal Navy, James Katon, who had been a shipmate and friend of her first husband. Strangely enough, James Katon, serving on board H.M.S. Barham as a young boy, had been midshipman of the watch on the very day the Admiral's wife had given birth to her youngest daughter.

He too was to fill a very important role in his young stepdaughter's life, and she was always to be his special favourite. It was Missy who started calling her mother, Catalina, and stepfather "the two Cats," after their marriage; and James Katon soon became "Khat" to the children as they imitated their mother's Spanish pronunciation of his nickname.

* * * * * *

"The child that is born on the Sabbath Day
    Is bonny and blithe and good and gay!"
This was the rhyme Missy's brother Johnny and her sisters Carlota, Clementina and Mary Keith used to sing to her when she was little, for the day of her birth had indeed been a Sunday, and her sunny character gave credence to the nursery rhyme.

Missy did not recollect much of her Naval upbringing, though she would tell her children how she used to hide in a large cupboard in the hall at Admiralty House at Sheerness, where her father was the Commander-in-Chief from 1834 to 1837, to watch the grand people coming down to dinner. The memory was particularly vivid because one night the glass cupula over the staircase shattered and glass came pouring down the staircase to the door of her hiding-place, which gave Missy a bad fright.

After Sheerness, her father became Commander-in-Chief at Portsmouth. His final appointment was as Governor of Greenwich Hospital in 1839. This hospital was founded to take care of elderly and infirm men who had served in the Royal Navy. It was run on Naval lines, and there was always an Admiral, usually one about to retire, as its Commander-in-Chief.

The family made its home in the beautiful Queen's House that went with the job. Missy's older sisters had "come out"[4] by now, and she used to help them dress for Balls and to curl their hair for them. When a Ball was held in their own house at Greenwich, Missy would peep through the banisters to see the splendid young Naval Officers in their evening dress, smothered in gold lace, paying court to her older sisters.

Sometimes the family went with their father to the hunting-box he owned in Warwickshire called Atherstone Hall. He was a great horseman and had taken several couple of hounds to Gibraltar from Cumbernauld when the Calpe Hunt was formed and he was serving there during the Peninsular War.

The three older Elphinstone girls had all inherited their mother's striking Spanish looks, but Missy's brown hair and fair complexion showed that she was much more of an Elphinstone – nevertheless she soon learnt to speak Spanish as fluently as her sisters as she spoke with her mother, Doña Catalina. Like her sisters, Missy was educated at home by their governess, Miss Partridge.

The Fleemings' stay at Greenwich was cut tragically short when her father died. But, fortunately for Missy, she was to be invited back to Greenwich regularly; for her father's Scottish shipmate and friend, Admiral Sir Charles Adam, succeeded him as Governor of Greenwich Hospital on his death, and his daughter, Mary Adam, had always been Missy's greatest childhood friend.

Missy's early life had been full of romps and fun, as was shown by the letters the family wrote to each other. An early letter from her brother from Cumbernauld said, "Mama and 'Cota' (Carlota) were at the fancy ball in Edinburgh some time ago. 'Cota' was dressed as a Catalan, and Mum as Madame de Sevigné – they both looked very ugly!" (The

---

[4] The term "to come out" refers to the practice of young ladies becoming debutantes, meeting the King or Queen, and entering society.

young Elphinstones wrote in the same style as their mother, with frequent underlinings, and with plenty of criss-crossings, to save paper.)

Missy herself wrote long letters to her two childhood friends, one being Mary Adam and the other Blanche Stanley, a daughter of the Earl of Derby who was later to become the Countess of Airlie.

"Here is a riddle," Missy writes to Mary, "why is a sculptor likely to die a very shocking death? – Because he makes faces and busts!"

To "dearest Buzzard" (Blanche) Missy writes, "You told me in your letter to tell you when all our birthdays are: Mum's is on 26th June and I think Pups' is on the 16th but I am not sure, and I do not think that he knows when it is himself Clemmy's is on the 1st of June and Keith's on the 1st of May. Cota's is on the 11th November and Johnny's on the 11th December, does not this look strange."

Mary goes on to mention her eldest sister's illness, so although the letter is not dated, it becomes apparent that it was written when Missy was twelve years old. (The letter-head shows a charming engraving of Greenwich in 1840.)

Missy never put any punctuation in her letters at this age, any more than her eldest son was to do at the same age. Young Robert's lack of punctuation continued well into his teens, and they were both to write their letters in a great rush, as though they were carrying on a conversation rather than a literary exercise. Robert's writing was almost a replica of his grandfather Fleeming's, both totally illegible.

Robert was undoubtedly to inherit many qualities from his mother's Elphinstone relations. They had all been distinguished administrators and most of them were highly individual. Her father, the Admiral, as a young man in command of H.M.S. "Tartar," had the poop of his ship cut off while in harbour in South America, on the Pacific coast, because he found his ship would "neither sail nor stay." As he had not referred the matter to the Admiralty before taking action, the Board called upon him for an explanation of his "surgery" on one of His Majesty's vessels. Whereupon Captain Fleeming replied to the effect that, although he had "not hitherto given himself the trouble to draw his pay, if their Lordships insisted in requesting explanations about 'a mere poop' he would find himself under the disagreeable necessity of claiming so many thousands of pounds from the Paymaster-General," adding that it was of course "for their Lordships to select their alternative." He, and his friend Cochrane, were later to be great admirals, but were always considered *enfants terribles* by their Lordships at the Admiralty.

In the sad years after her husband's premature death, Doña Catalina entertained her children with many stories of her happy marriage to their father. The children particularly loved to hear about their unusual honeymoon, when her dashing husband had hired a funeral coach in which to take his bride to the Derby, being unable for love or money to find a more conventional form of transport! The sixteen-year-old Catalina from Cadiz felt just like an Infanta of Spain as the team of plumed black horses sped her to the races that June day in 1816 on her first visit to England.

Another more alarming event had taken place a few years later, when she was travelling by coach with her husband the Admiral across the great plateau to Madrid, after climbing the Sierra Nevada from Malaga. A band of robbers suddenly galloped up to their coach but, instead of ordering them out of the vehicle to ride off with their money and possessions, as they had expected, the seven men formed a guard of honour and rode in two columns either side of the coach all the way to the outskirts of Madrid. At this point the leader bowed politely to the admiral, explaining that the reason his men had provided the *Almirante* and his charming wife with such an escort was because the admiral had once saved his life by selecting him and setting him free one Easter Day, in Malaga, from a bunch of convicts in the galleys, as part of the Easter celebrations. "We are *Los Siete Ninos!*" he cried, as he bowed once more and galloped off with his men.

Doña Catalina had heard this strange name before, and realised to her horror that their guard of honour were the most dangerous bandits in Spain. Missy knew the story well, and often told it to Robert, Charlie and Malise, who loved to hear it, later at Finlaystone.

After her husband's death, Doña Catalina moved with her family to a house at Harbledown, a small village on a hill overlooking Canterbury, where they were able to keep in touch with many naval friends from their Sheerness and Greenwich days.

Grandpapa Cunninghame Graham's death on 23rd January 1863 came only a week after Robert had arrived at school in Warwickshire. His mother wrote to give him the sad news, and to tell him of a strange occurrence at Gartmore the night the old Laird died in London. His daughter, Margaret (known to them all as Meg, or Aunt Maggie) had been staying there with her soldier husband, Uncle William Hope, who had won the VC[5] in the recent Crimean War; the factor was coming home late from a local ceilidh[6] and, as he passed the "Big Hoose" he was amazed to see lights blazing from every window of the house. His immediate thought was that the house was on fire, and he ran up the long drive to hammer on the door, shouting "Fire! Fire!"

Colonel Hope had been the first to waken, and he hurried downstairs in his dressing-gown, calling to the factor to tell him where the fire had started. Opening the heavy front door, he found the man standing apologetically outside, murmuring that he must have been mistaken. There was no sign of the blazing illuminations that had shone from the house only minutes before. Colonel Hope returned to bed, convinced that the factor must have taken a dram too many at his ceilidh.

Next morning the telegram announcing the old Laird's death in London arrived, and the local people nodded wisely to each other as they told of the factor's strange experience: it was always the same when a Laird of Gartmore died, they said, the phenomenon of the blazing lights had been known down the ages, they had been told about it when they were bairns, for their grandparents and great-grandparents minded it well.

Robert Cunninghame Graham, young Robert's grandfather, was laid to rest in the family burial ground at Gartmore on a day of cold winds and heavy rainstorms, with three of his four sons (one having died as a young soldier in India) to bear his coffin down the drive, aided by the many tenants and employees from the great estate, who followed the funeral procession in genuine sadness. He had been a good Laird, they murmured to each other, and it had been through no fault of his own that he had been unable to live at Gartmore in the style of his wealthy forebears. The one he used to talk about most of all was his great-

---

[5] Victoria Cross, the highest award for bravery in Great Britain.
[6] An Irish or Scottish social gathering with traditional music, dancing, and storytelling.

grandfather, an earlier Laird of Gartmore, the one they called "Doughty Deeds."

The nickname had come about because of a beautiful poem he had written to his lady-love in Jamaica, who was later to become his adored wife, Annie. The first line started, "If doughty deeds my ladye please, right soon I'll mount my steed." Young Robert's mind ran on horses for most of the time so he thought this was a splendid sentiment. When he grew up, he, too, would like to perform "doughty deeds" on horseback for beautiful ladies, he decided, like his great-great-grandfather "Doughty Deeds."

Charlie wished Robert had been able to come back to Scotland for their grandfather's funeral, but it was too soon after the beginning of term, and Missy knew it would be dreadfully unsettling for him. Uncle Archie Speirs of Edlersley was there, in his tall tube hat, and the old Graham great-aunts, Aunt Anne Erskine, Aunt Charlotte Woodmass, both widowed, and wearing fur capes and mourning bonnets; and the other Graham aunts and the two young uncles, Bobby and Douglas Cunninghame Graham, aged twenty-one and nineteen, home on compassionate leave from their cavalry regiments.

Eccentric Uncle Tom Speirs was there too, and Aunt Helen, his sister, from Leamington, and their sister-in-law Aunt Annie Speirs. It was a great family gathering. At last it was all over, and Willy piled Missy and Charlie into the carriage to drive back to Finlaystone. As soon as the worst of the wintry weather was over, they would move to Gartmore, for Willy was now the Laird.

Robert's mother was oppressed with sadness at the thought of leaving Finlaystone after eleven happy years on the shores of the Clyde. She felt a strange premonition of unhappy events to come, but her husband brushed them away with his cheerful talk. He was elated by the thought that he would soon be able to take his family to live at Gartmore. He was having a temporary respite from his habitual headaches, and was feeling better than he had felt for months. Life at Gartmore was going to be very pleasant.

Robert did not hear about the frightening event at Finlaystone till much later in his life. It had happened only a few days after the funeral of his grandfather. Back at Finlaystone again, Willy awoke with a blinding headache. Missy suggested to his Italian valet, Sigismondo Oliviere, that he should pull down the blinds and make a tisane for his master. Later in the morning they heard a great commotion and William Hope – who had been staying with them, with his wife, Willy's sister Margaret, since the funeral – went to the foot of the main staircase to see the terrifying sight of Willy rushing at him with a drawn sabre, clad only in his nightshirt, crying out for more "reinforcements."

Knowing that Willy enjoyed practical jokes, his brother-in-law started to laugh; but he soon realised that Willy was in earnest, and did not seem to have the slightest idea that his behaviour was odd in the extreme. He was obviously hallucinating, and thought himself back with his regiment in Ireland, where he had served during the Potato Famine. William Hope jumped aside just in time to avoid being slashed by his brother-in-law's sabre, managing to knock the weapon out of his hand as he did so. Oliviere had followed his master down the stairs and had soon caught hold of him and persuaded him to go up to his bedroom again.

Willy was now like a child who had walked in his sleep, the anger had left him, and he looked at his valet in total bewilderment. Oliviere had stayed with him until the doctor was fetched. A nurse was soon brought from the local asylum, and laudanum prescribed, but Dr. Horsburgh shook his head sadly, murmuring that the case seemed pretty hopeless. Missy and her sister-in-law Margaret were distraught; worst of all, Willy did not seem to recognise them.

It had been a sudden and severe brainstorm, the result of the head injury Willy had suffered as a young officer in the Fifteenth Regiment of Foot at Waterford in October 1846.

Aunt Annie Speirs arrived the next day and Missy could have cried with relief, for somehow Aunt Annie was one of those special people who always appear at exactly the right moment. Having sized up the situation, Aunt Annie sent Charlie, ,Malise and Ninny, their nurse, to her house at Moffat. Then she set about comforting Missy and suggested that she should go south for a few days to her elder sister, Clementina (Clemy), married to Lord Hawarden and living in London, to get over the shock.

There was no need for the Hopes to stay at Finlaystone, for Aunt Annie was quite prepared to remain there in charge of the fierce nurse from the asylum, whom she suspected was being unkind to Willy. Aunt Annie (a Grant of Kilgraston) had always thought of Willy as the son she never had. He had spent his early schooldays at Merchiston Castle in Edinburgh, living with her, before her husband, Robert Speirs, the Sheriff Principal, had died, and she was devoted to him.

Aunt Annie was firm but kind, and Missy eventually agreed to her plan, realising that there was not much point in staying with Willy if he did not even recognise her. She would travel to London with Maggie and William Hope. Once everything was settled, Aunt Annie sent for Dr. Horsburgh to find out if he felt he could manage the case, or whether a specialist should be summoned. When she discovered that the local doctor seemed to know nothing whatsoever about the effects of brain-damage, she dismissed both him and the fierce nurse, knowing that she, and Willy's devoted valet, Sigismondo, could nurse him perfectly well together. A few days later Missy was delighted to find her husband was nearly back to his old self again, and well enough for Aunt Annie to feel able to join Charlie and Malise at Moffat.

It soon became apparent that Willy's mother, old Mrs. Cunninghame Graham, was trying to get him away from his wife's care. Missy was not sure whether this might not be a scheme to get herself re-installed at Gartmore, or perhaps she even intended to have her son living with her in London.

Missy quickly wrote to Arthur Campbell, the family lawyer, for advice, explaining that she only had a very limited knowledge of the law, and also of the 'family money.' In Campbell's reply he explained that, under the circumstances of Willy's illness, a 'Curator Bonis' could be appointed who would take over all Willy's financial and legal affairs. He went on to say, "... it is very desirable that no relation of the family should hold the office, but that some professional, hitherto totally unaquainted with the family and its affairs, should be selected. If a man at the top of his profession were selected, the expense would be very considerable, but if some younger, though experienced man were chosen, the expense would be much lessened."

Missy had also asked in her letter about such aspects as "the guardianship of the children, and pecuniary matters." Missy was always to be practical and level-headed, as future events were to prove, but obviously her mind must have been in a turmoil as she began to think what the future might hold in store for herself and her children, if her beloved husband's state worsened. She was relieved to receive several helpful and reassuring letters from the lawyer.

She was even more cheered by Robert's first letter home, written on 3rd February 1863:

"My dear Mamma, I hope you are quite well. Have you received my letter which I wrote on Saterday? [sic] I liked the day I spent at Brighton very much. And I liked the pantomine [sic] I saw very much also. I am afraid you will have some difficulty in reading my other letter if you get it. Give my love to Papa and Charlie and Grandmamma and Kat and Mal. I have received your letter this morning and I fear by it you have not got mine. I thank you for sending for my desk.

I am your affectionate son,
        R. C. Graham."

The handwriting was deplorable, but, most surprisingly, it actually contained some punctuation! Robert had obviously been under supervision when he wrote it, and it is conceivable that the reason his mother never received "the letter which I wrote on Saterday" was because the school, in its wisdom, had decided against sending on the first epistle, which she would have "difficulty in reading." In fact, Missy, like all mothers parted from their children, would probably have treasured the letter in spite of its ink blots and illegible handwriting.

Meanwhile Charlie, staying with Aunt Annie Speirs at Moffat, also wrote to his mother.

"My dear Mama, I hope you are quite well. I like Moffat very much. Uncle Tom has given me a fishing rod and I have fished twice in the Annan but caught nothing. We drove to Loch Wood and I looked into the dungeon, there was a wood of fine old Oaks round the ruins. I wrote to Robert and told him that his poney had a foal. When I go to Gartmore is my poney to go with me? – (as I cannot ride Robert's)? – Aunt Anne told me that if I am good till Thursday she will give me half-a-crown. Give my love to Papa,

I am your affect. Son, C.E.F.C. Graham."

Charlie, aged just nine, took more pains with his writing than his elder brother; it was quite clear that Robert hated writing letters. There were far too many other diversions at Hill House; football, skating, sailing boats, swimming in the Leamington baths, going to lectures, concerts, and "panorarmas" [*sic*] (a specially good one was "of the American Civil War," he wrote), and collecting stamps. In addition, he had already made friends with plenty of "good fellows" at his new school. On the whole, he was enjoying life.

At Finlaystone everything had quickly returned to normal, and Willy seemed quite unaware of the fright he had given his family. Oliviere still looked after his master with touching devotion, and gradually the tension relaxed and the terror of Willy's attack receded. Charlie and Malise came back from Aunt Annie; and while Charlie did lessons in the mornings and rode his pony in the afternoons, they all began to look forward to the imminent move to Gartmore and Robert's return from Hill House for the Easter holidays. Missy knew the two events would cheer Willy up and do him a lot of good. There was a great deal to do, which was fortunate, as it meant that Missy did not have time to worry about Willy's health.

Robert was not told much about his father's frightening illness, but he knew that his mother had gone on an unexpected visit to London. He wrote an anxious and unpunctuated letter on 18th February 1863:

"My dear Mamma,

I hope you are quite well how is Charlie why did you go to London? I have bought a frame for Papa's picture how is Papa give my love to Grandmama.

I am your affec. son Old Bob Ridley."

("Old Bob Ridley" probably came from a music-hall song or an anecdote which had amused his family, and Robert loved to give himself odd nicknames. Later, when he was using the Spanish language in his everyday life, he would often sign his letters "Roberto el Bobo". The Spanish dictionary translates "el bobo" as "a dunce, dolt or fool, simpleton, ninny, easily cheated" – this would have appealed greatly to Robert's sense of humour, for he was always to love best of all the jokes against himself.)

Meanwhile, Willy was like an impatient schoolboy as the final days at Finlaystone were accomplished. He could not wait to get back to Gartmore, to show his sons the flighting pond, the thick fir woods which sheltered the roe deer, the deep peaty pools where large trout lay, and the heather-covered Menteith hills where scarlet-eyed grouse swept low, calling urgently, "Come back! Come back! Come back!" Soon he would be able to take Robert and Charlie up to the high tops to shoot ptarmigan, or deep into the old pines of the Caledonian Forest to flush capercailzie.

He hoped the Lake of Menteith would freeze over the next winter so that the boys could learn the "Roarin Game," the art of curling, with big stones which birled across the glistening ice, as the local men wielded their brooms to smooth the path shouting "Soop, soop, soop!" Perhaps there would then be a "Bonspiel" – the great curling match on the Lake of Menteith, that took place after a long freeze between all the local villages, when the "wee refreshments" that were passed around wiped out all former feuds and made everyone happy and full of bonhomie.

CHAPTER II

In April Robert arrived home for the Easter holidays to find his family already installed at Gartmore. It was an exciting time for the two older boys. They spent most of the first few days at Gartmore riding their ponies round the huge estate, on the edge of the Highlands. Robert had now been given a lively mare, having outgrown his Shetland, who had been passed on the Charlie.

The Gartmore servants and their father's employees and tenants were delighted to have a young family living at Gartmore once more. It was more than thirty years since the place had been a real family home, when children had brought the "big hoose" to life with their shouts and laughter. Gartmore was an idyllic place for small boys to grow up in, surrounded by hills and heather, burns and lochs, trees to climb and rocks to scramble over. The district of Menteith had once been a Royal Forest, where the kings of Scotland had hunted; it had also been a battleground, a controversial frontier between Lowlands and Highlands, where men lived to raid their neighbours, or gain an advantage over them, like a geographical game of chess.

Rob Roy had been the famous freebooter of the area, a sort of highland "Robin Hood," who stole from the rich to give to the poor. He had instituted a form of blackmail, or protection money, forcing the local Lairds to pay. The Grahams, the Drummonds, the Murrays, the Macnabs, and the MacGregors all feuded with each other, and some of them married each other – usually in order to gain a handsome "tocher" from their bride's father, and even more lands. Many were the tales of knightly chivalry or dastardly treachery that could be told of the families that lived in the Menteith Lands on the Highland Line.

The young Grahams liked best of all the silver waters of the Lake of Menteith, rowing across to the wooded islands of Inchmahome and Inch Talla, where they played hide-and-seek amongst the ruins of the thirteenth century Augustinian priory and castle. Robert and Charlie played ducks and drakes among the yellow water-lilies, where deep peaty water washed translucent over shining pebbles. They inspected the stone effigy of a crusader ancestor with his legs crossed – an ancestor who had gone with other Scottish knights to join the French king, Louis IX, on his crusade to the Holy Land in 1249.

Then, during a sudden warm spell, which often comes to Scotland in late April, the older boys would be joined by their little brother Malise as they paddled on the shallow sands at the "Fairy Strand," the place they knew as Arnmauk, where the fairies were supposed to have woven a web of sand from the shores of the lake to the island of Inchamahome. Beside the Lake of Menteith, at Port of Menteith, they played with the two young daughters of Mr. Macgregor who kept the inn, and on Sundays they went with their parents to the church at Port of Menteith to sit snugly in their family pew, with a coal fire to warm their toes, hidden from the congregation so that they could indulge unseen in "the sermon game," to alleviate their boredom.

Best of all, they used to visit David and Horatia Erskine, their young Elphinstone and Erskine cousins. The Erskines had only been married for a mere three years, and had recently moved to Cardross House. David and Horatia were in their early twenties but they already had two baby boys. Horatia's father, Sir George Seymour, had become the Ranger of Windsor Park after retiring from a distinguished diplomatic career, and Horatia had been brought up in court circles, attending tea-parties with Queen Victoria's elder children. Robert and Charlie loved riding with her in her phaeton and hearing her stories of court life.

At the flighting pond they could hear the throaty quacks of mallard, and the whistling of teal in the air above. From the wood they collected red and white spotted toadstools for little Mallie's delight. As a small boy he was always called "Mallie," as will become apparent. Over rocks and heather the boys liked to find the few remaining rowan berries for their pea-shooters. They rode their ponies to the little grove called Barbadoes [sic], planted by "Doughty Deeds" and named in memory of his own West Indian idyll. With the King Charles spaniel "Clytie" chasing wild fowl through birches and over green moss, they wandered as far as the eerie Flanders Moss, the strange "blood-stone" at the centre, haunted by curlews who remembered that in prehistoric times the huge North Sea breakers had once rolled up the Forth Valley to the foot of the Menteith hills.

Sometimes, on stormy days, Robert and Charlie would curl up in comfortable chairs in the book-room, while their father told them about the many "gallant Grahams" of the past. They especially liked to hear about the forty-two Grahams who founded a regiment, later to be known as the "42nd" Highland Regiment. Many of the estate workers and the villagers were descendants of men who had fought with the Grahams at Bannockburn; one in particular, Andrew Wood, a huge man of six foot four or five tall, had scores of tales to tell the boys of how his forebears feuded and fought the Macfarlanes and the Macgregors from across the Highland Line.

At Gartmore, across the gravel sweep of the front drive, behind more trees, lay the stables, in which Robert was to spend more time than anywhere else. By the age of ten he was already a natural horseman: Robert and his mare made a good pair as they galloped across the rushy parks, the boy with his dark red curly hair like an aura, and his back straight as a young *hidalgo*. Missy loved to watch her eldest son setting off on a ride; most of the time he did everything with Charlie, but riding he seemed to enjoy best by himself. Robert simply had to be alone from time to time – it seemed to be as necessary to him as food and drink.

Charlie was more gregarious, and liked to walk round the "policies"[7] with his father, carrying his prized possession, his four-ten, tucked under his arm. He was already a good shot, his father noted as they potted at pigeons together.

On sunny days a popular picnic place was the island of Inchmahome on the Lake of Menteith. The trip across from the Port of Menteith was a special delight as the sun sparkled on the wavelets, and the water slapped gently against the side of the boat. William Bontine and Robert each took an oar, Charlie steered from the stern, and Mrs. Bontine sat with the picnic basket at her feet and Mallie firmly clasped on her lap.

Leaving their mother to spread the picnic on the soft green grass by the pebbly shore, and Mallie happily throwing stones into the loch, Robert and Charlie went with their father to the ruined Priory, where the effigies of Walter and Mary, the mid-thirteenth century Earl and

---

[7] In Scotland the estates were – and still are – known as "the policies."

Countess of Menteith, carved with their arms about each other, lay love-making into eternity, their children and dogs at their feet.

The boys loved the little boxwood bower where Mary Queen of Scots had played with her dolls, with her four Maries, in the safety of Inchmahome before sailing for France.[8] From there they could see the 'Isle of Dogs,' Inch Cuan (Gaelic for Isle of Dogs) where the Earls of Menteith kept their deer-hounds and "earthe dogges." Water-hen scuttled and ducks quacked between the islands of Inchmahome and Inch Talla. No wonder the last Countess of Menteith decided to move off to Edinburgh after her husband died, because she could not bear the noise of the frogs in the reeds round the island. It was later that her daughter married Sir William Graham of Polder and they built the beautiful house of Gartmore not far from the Lake of Menteith. There had been Grahams for seven hundred years or more, and their descendants still owned the same lands.

Robert started to look up the family history in the library at Gartmore, and found out that his forebears had been the Graham earls of Menteith since 1427. An earlier Malise Graham, a descendant of Robert the Bruce, was made Earl of Menteith (with descent through "heirs male") by his cousin, King James I of Scotland. This was a cunning move to take away from him the royal earldom of Strathearn, which he had inherited from his grandmother, Euphemia, Countess Palatine of Stathearn. This Malise had been married, during his imprisonment in England as a supplementary hostage for the Scots King's ransom, to Lady Anne Vere, daughter of the Earl of Oxford, by whom he had three sons, Alexander, John and Walter. The Grahams of Gartmore were descended from this line through his son John, known as "Sir John of the Bright Sword."

The first mansion-house of Gartmore, built in the 1660s, was beautifully simple. (The earldom had become dormant.) Nicol Graham added to the house in 1740, putting classical touches here and there, with the help of a Kirkcaldy builder's son, later to be the distinguished

---

[8] Little Mary Queen of Scots went to France in 1548 when she was six years old to be affianced to the little Dauphin. She was accompanied by four small Scottish children, the daughters of noblemen, all called Mary --Mary Carmichael, Mary Seton, Mary Beaton and Mary Fleming.

architect William Adam. In 1779 Nicol's son, Robert Graham of Gartmore ("Doughty Deeds") made further improvements with the help of the architect John Baxter. Ceilings were decorated by itinerant Italian plasterers, columns were added, porticos adorned the new doorways and the house took on an altogether grander appearance.

The Earls of Menteith would have been astonished if they could have seen this new civilised aspect of their Graham descendants. The old castle on the little island of Inch Talla in the quiet waters of the Lake of Menteith had been their home until the last Earl of Menteith died.

Robert loved the smaller island of Inch Talla. It belonged to him in a very special way, part of his inheritance, so many of the families who had lived here had been his ancestors. Set like a jewel in the sparkling waters of the lake, surrounded by the great Bens – Ledi, Venue, Vorlich, Mhor, Stobinian and Lomond, it had been safer to surround yourself with water in those lawless days, especially if you had a strong claim to the throne of Scotland, as had the Earls of Menteith. You might not want to take up that claim, but you would always have jealous enemies, who considered you a rival, clamouring at your door.

William Bontine was now the ninth Laird of Gartmore. He had no wish to prove publicly his descent from King Robert the Bruce, nor to set the cauldron bubbling that had remained unstirred since the Union of the Crowns; he did not even want to claim the dormant earldom of Menteith. He had named his eldest son Robert, for the Bruce, and for the Grahams of Gartmore; Charles for his wife's noble family, the Elphinstones and for his Speirs grandmother's family, the Fitzwilliams; Malise was named for the Earls of Menteith, because it was Malise who had become the first Graham Earl of Menteith in 1427. There were some who said he should have been given back his grandfather's title, Earl of Strathearn, with its hint of royal succession, Malise's father, Patrick Graham, having married Euphemia, only daughter of King Robert II's son, David.

Young Robert liked the drawing-room best of all the rooms at Gartmore: he was later to write a description of the room, mentioning the plaster ceiling, painted in delicate colours to show up the beautiful Adam decoration, curving at one end to a sweep of huge windows which looked out across the terrace to the Flanders Moss, and to Stirling Castle.

There were chairs with needlework seats, depicting the Cunninghame and Graham coats of arms. A large grand piano always stood covered by a thick paisley shawl; and, that spring, a table with barley-sugar legs stood in front of the window, laden with china bowls filled with sweet-smelling hyacinths and pot-pourri.

A Meissen clock ornamented the chimney-piece, which was flanked by a Boulle escritoire on one side, and a comfortable sofa on the other. At the opposite end to the windows, the room ended in an alcove with classical pillars. Basket-seated Empire chairs, decorated in black and gold, with green silk cushions, were arranged in groups about the room at the far end, and a Queen Anne walnut settee stood against the wall.

Malise liked to sit on it to look at picture books, when he came down with Ninny in his muslin dress after tea, and his favourite game was to slide off the slippery horse-hair seat on to a furry rug at his feet, with shrieks of joy. When Mamma told him to sit still, he complained that there were black prickles from the horse-hair seat, which stuck into his bare legs. He loved to hear his mother playing the piano, and sometimes she would let him sit on the shiny wooden piano stool beside her to sing nursery rhymes. Missy was convinced that little Malise was going to be very musical. Charlie was learning to play the 'cello and loved music too, but she knew that Robert would be far too impatient to take the trouble to learn to play an instrument. Anyway, when he was at home, he thought of nothing but horses.

Charlie was to join Robert at Hill House for the summer term, and he was longing to go to school with his elder brother. The Easter holidays seemed to end far too quickly, and they were soon packing their boxes for school. They went off in May for the summer term. Willy was having a respite from his ill-health, so he started to plan a new cricket pitch at Gartmore as a surprise for the older boys when they came home again. Willy knew that his youngest son, Malise, missed his brothers intolerably; at three years old Malise loved the fun and romps with his two older brothers, and he liked all the noise they made, clattering round the huge old house. Their voices seemed to fill the house with life and jollity. Now it seemed to Mallie far too quiet without them, although he still had old Ninny for company, and his mother's German maid, Homer, Mrs. Boss the Cook, and the maids, Jeannie and Jemima, to play with.

Robert's letter arrived first – he was growing out of all his clothes.

"I hope I am going into long trousers next holidays," he said in his brief, badly-written letter. He also confirmed that he and Charlie had arrived safely and that his brother was settling in happily.

Robert was getting quite tall, and his Spanish looks seemed even more pronounced. Thin, energetic and wiry, he had intelligent eyes and a broad forehead. He had a strongly developed sense of humour, and always found a great deal to laugh about. Acutely observant, he seemed to breathe the world in through his skin. His hair was darker now, but still tinged with red, and his eyes were brown. His deportment was the really striking thing about him, and his grace and dignity and self-assurance combined to give him the air of a young Spanish *hidalgo*. His moods swung almost too readily, however, and when things went wrong he flew into ungovernable rage. His impatience, too, led him into several scrapes.

After the older boys left for school, Mallie caught the whooping cough; but by the middle of May he had thrown it off. Aunt Annie Speirs came to the rescue once more and took the three-year-old Malise, with old Ninny, to Troon, hoping the sea breezes would put some roses back into the little fellow's cheeks.

Charlie's first letter from school arrived soon after Robert's. In his large, clear, round handwriting, it said:

"My dear Mamma, We arrived here quite safe about three o'clock. There are only six boys in my form counting myself. I rigged my boat today and it sailed very well. I have begun Caesar."

Robert was overjoyed to have his brother with him at Hill House, and they were both delighted to think there would be no more separations for the time being. Charlie's clear handwriting put Robert to shame, and he suddenly began to take more trouble with his writing. Missy smiled when she got the second letter in his new tidy and legible handwriting; she had always known that Robert was perfectly capable of writing properly if he tried. He just could not be bothered, and was always in far too much of a hurry to take trouble.

The two Graham boys both entered wholeheartedly into school life, as was apparent from their letters home: they told of the new wall bars which had been put up, that they went swimming to the baths in

Leamington, and that they had even gone to the Grand Annual Steeple Chase, to see the horse "Emblem" win – "the ground was very unfavourable, and there were a good many falls," wrote Robert.

They went out to dinner with Aunt Helen Speirs, and to "Aunt Woodmouse" (Willy's aunt Charlotte, the widow of a Mr. Woodmass) – and they wrote to ask Papa for stamps for their collections, money to mend a broken watch, photographs and frames, and all the things that every small boy through the ages has required at his preparatory school. They worked hard, and they played even harder. They could write of nothing but cricket and, very occasionally, a brief mention of work. Cricket had become Robert's real passion and he told his parents that he was to play in his first school match in the first week in July. On 22nd June he wrote, "Is Papa going to play many more matches? ... sorry to hear from your letter that the Stirling were licked by the Glasgow. Are the ponies all quite well. I am very glad Charlie is so much taken up with cricket."

But he also liked to hear what was going on at Gartmore.

"Is the cricket ground finished yet? Is it to be as big as the old one? It is to be much better than the old one, is it not? Is the billiard room built yet? I am sorry to hear that the wood is all cut down. There will not be many roe (deer) left. Does not Papa say he intends to have the fir hill cut down next year?"

Missy was glad that Robert seemed so interested in everything to do with Gartmore, especially as, being the eldest son, he might well have to help Papa with the estate after leaving school. Charlie would go into the Navy, and Malise into the Church, for that was the way these things were arranged amongst the gentry of their day.

Later in the term Robert sent his parents an essay he had written, for which he had received very high marks:

"Cruelty is a very demoralising thing," he had written, "It is a sure sign that a nation is getting weak, when it delights in wild beast fights and gladiatorial combats like the ancient Romans. Cruelty and cowardice often go hand in hand together: thus the boy who delights in tormenting animals is almost always a coward. Cruelty shows itself in all ages and is always attended with the same results. Often armies and states have mutinied through the cruelty of their leaders and kings. It would seem likely that when people see cruelty in others, they would avoid it themselves, but it often takes a directly different course and people who are accustomed to see cruelty generally practice it themselves. Nothing is so hard to eradicate as cruelty and the person who is cruel in his youth frequently in spite of all correction grows up to be very cruel and cowardly when he is a man."

Dr. Bickmore had been impressed by this thoughtful essay, written by a lively, intelligent boy. If he could think and write like that at ten years old, young Graham would have a bright future ahead of him, the Headmaster predicted.

On 29th June Robert wrote about Warwick College's regatta on the Avon:

"There were two or three good races. There was a tub race in which one boy's mop broke and he won the race with his handle. A man threw himself into the water and would not be taken out, one of the boats went clean over him, he was quite tipsy! Some of the coxswains were not nearly so big as Charlie."

The two boys arrived back at Gartmore in July for the summer holidays, and at the end of July the new tutor, Mr. Gulliver, arrived. He had been recommended to Mrs. Bontine by a friend as being "… a very nice fellow indeed, the only son of a Naval officer, a very good scholar and, above all, a gentleman." He was 19 years old, and had been an Exhibitioner[9] at Cambridge. Very tall, his enormous appetite, especially for dessert, had him immediately nicknamed "Big Pudden." Equable and kind, he soon infected the boys with his passion for cricket and fishing.

Robert was thrilled that Mr. Gulliver also shared his passion for Sir Walter Scott's books, and they read them together. Sir Walter had written parts of "The Lady of the Lake" at Gartmore, and had known the Grahams well, purchasing from great-grandfather William, who was always short of funds, the claymore that had belonged to the Marquis of Montrose, for his Abbotsford armoury.

On Sundays, the whole family went to the Presbyterian church at the Port of Menteith. Sermons tended to be long and the boys were glad that Papa did not make them go to the Free Kirk built by Grandpa in

---

[9] A sort of scholarship.

Gartmore village, where the services were even longer, and they sang only psalms, never tuneful hymns.

After Sunday lunch, Mrs. Bontine would take the children calling in the dog-cart. There were many pleasant neighbours and the young attractive Bontines were becoming very popular. There was to be a great Ball at nearby Cardross House, across the Lake, for their cousin David Erskine's coming-of-age at 25.[10] David's mother was Missy's aunt, having been Admiral Fleeming's[11] younger sister.

The tutor soon settled in at Gartmore with the Grahams, and Gulliver decided Robert was pretty quick on the uptake. He was going to enjoy these two lively boys. He took them fishing and showed the boys how to put their thumbs in the trout's mouth, when they caught one, and push its head back with a quick jerk until the neck snapped. Charlie and Robert both felt rather squeamish about the whole affair at first, but before long they were happily skewering worms and removing hooks from fishes' gills, covering the trout with soft green ferns to keep them cool until Mrs. Boss grilled them for supper. Robert decided life was going to be fun now that old "Pudden" had arrived.

Missy often looked into the boys' bedrooms on her way to bed. It was usually past nine o'clock and still light. She loved the long evenings of the Highlands, and she only wished they did not have to pay for them during the winter months, when daylight only came between nine in the morning and four in the afternoon. She had once looked at a map of the world, and was amazed to see how near the Arctic Circle they lived. Tracing the latitudes round with her finger she found that Glasgow was on the same line as Ketchican or some of the small fishing communities in the south of Alaska. No wonder it got so cold in the winter, and no wonder they were compensated, in the summer, with their own version of the "midnight sun."

Sometimes she would find Robert still lying awake as she put her head round the door. She would go in and sit on his bed, and they would

---

[10] 25 was the "legal majority" in those days; this meant you could inherit an estate and run your own life.

[11] It is usually spelt "Fleming" but the old spelling was Fleeming.

talk far into the night about all the things that had been happening at Gartmore.

While they were fishing in the burn with their trout rods, the new tutor told them amusing stories about his own boyhood in Dorset, and about his rambles over the downs where the Cerne Abbas Giant, a huge naked man holding a club, was carved out of the turf by primitive man. The figure was a bit like Jack the Giant Killer, said Mr. Gulliver, and Robert joked that, if it was Mr. Gulliver who had found him, the figure was more likely to be like one of the Brobdignag giants.

Robert's thoughts were often occupied with Gartmore, even at school. Robert thought Gartmore was the best place in the whole wide world, and he was utterly happy to spend his entire holidays riding round the estate on his beautiful black mare. Missy knew that her son would grow up to be the most enthusiastic laird that Gartmore had ever had – everything suddenly seemed to be falling into place.

Gulliver liked to see Robert sprinting straight off to the stables and to watch him trot off on horseback up the drive a few minutes later. The boy was a fine young horseman, thought Gulliver as he saw him galloping across the park, like a young centaur – boy and mare seemed to have become inextricably one. Robert would always be totally content as long as there was a horse to ride, the tutor was soon to discover.

During their holidays at Gartmore the boys spent their time fishing and helping on the farms. Soon all the Gartmore people knew them, and welcomed the Laird's sons into their cottages for a "jeely piece"[12] or a hot scone straight off the griddle. Robert and Charlie began to hear all the local gossip, and to learn the folklore of the area. Missy encouraged the boys to visit the Gartmore people, for this was the best possible way for them to soak up their heritage. Scottish lairds had nearly always been on friendly terms with their estate workers, feeling them to be equals; there was none of the English "feudal" relationship which produced the patronising breed of landowners that were sometimes found in the South.

They had all settled in so happily at Gartmore, and two years passed by. Although Willy had been so well since his attack in January 1863, the doctors were still keeping a close watch on him, and they suggested

---

[12] A piece of bread spread with jam.

to Missy that she should persuade him to spend the winter of 1866 abroad. He had been working hard to set the estate of Gartmore to rights. He also had to visit his Dunbartonshire estate, Ardoch (the Bontine property), on the opposite side of the Clyde, as often as possible. Recently there had been the heart-ache of the sale of Finlaystone, but he knew that one of the estates had to go if they were to be able to go on living at Gartmore. All this had meant more responsibility than he had been used to, and the doctors told Missy confidentially that stress of this sort might well precipitate another brainstorm. To spend the winter abroad would give Willy a rest from the burden of his new duties as Laird of Gartmore, which he was performing so well.

Missy was delighted; she had never liked the winter in Scotland. Her early childhood in Venezuela, where her father, the Admiral, was Commander-in-Chief, West Indies, had made her susceptible to the cold, and she was convinced that her Spanish and Italian blood, inherited from her mother, Doña Catalina, ran thin in this northern climate. Willy and Missy became as excited as children; they decided to take a house in Florence (where large numbers of their English friends congregated each winter) from November 1865 to March 1866. This would give them a real change of scene.

But first of all they would take Robert and Charlie travelling with them. The boys were of an age where they would benefit from some broadening of the mind, and besides, Willy was longing to show his sons some of the places in Belgium and Germany where he had spent his boyhood in the early 1840s with his parents and his large family of brothers and sisters.

CHAPTER III

At the end of July, 1866, a very happy family party crossed the Channel from Dover, accompanied by the brother of Willy'' Italian valet as their courier. Malise had been left with Aunt Annie Speirs, as usual, with Ninny to look after him. This arrangement suited both the elderly widow and the small boy, who had become devoted to each other. Malise aged five was too young to travel abroad, added to which he suffered from a weak chest, and Missy was frightened of subjecting him to the possible threat of cholera or typhus, which were still very real hazards on the continent. Robert and Charlie were healthy young animals, and she was sure that they, at least, would survive.

The boys had now left Hill House, with sad farewells to all their masters and chums. Robert was particularly pleased that both Charlie Bickmore (the Headmaster's son) and Villiers were moving on to Harrow with him, for their first term in September. Charlie would be there too, for the first year between leaving Hill House and being accepted for the Royal Navy, when he would be fourteen. He would spend the first year after leaving Harrow at a crammer at Alverstoke which specialised in getting boys into the Navy.

For the moment, the plan was that they would spend their summer holidays with their parents on the continent, and Mr. Gulliver would come to fetch them from Hamburg in time to take them to Harrow in September. They would also join their parents again in Florence for Christmas.

As they crossed the Channel to start their great adventure, they all four travelled abroad together for the first time, and it would also be the first time that they had spent their holidays out of Scotland. As small children they had often been to England to stay with their Spanish grandmother on the Isle of Wight, and sometimes to Uncle Mountstuart Elphinstone at Hookwood. They had also stayed with their Hope cousins and their Maude cousins in London but, apart from Charlie's one short trip to Homburg with his parents after Robert had gone away to school, they had always been at Finlaystone and Gartmore for their holidays.

As their coach clattered over the cobbles of Brussels, Robert began to feel that he would like to go on travelling forever. The stimulation of new sights, sounds, and even smells, gave him a feeling of elation that he had never experienced before.

In Brussels their father showed them the school in Rue Sans Souci where he had been educated in the years 1841 and 1842, and the house that had been his family home at the time, outside the Port de Namur. From Brussels they moved on to Cologne to see the huge cathedral, and on to the craggy rocks round the Closter Lac, high up at a thousand feet in its basaltic mountain, where they saw the quarries which produced millstones for the whole of Germany.

Then to Coblenz, with a short trip up the Moselle to look at a fairy-tale castle, followed by a sail up the Rhine past the famous Lorelei, where sailors were supposed to be lured to their death.[13] Willy teased his sons, telling them that the Lorelei would be more interested in them in a few years' time when they had become handsome young gentlemen.

Willy then took his family on to Frankfurt. Here Willy became more nostalgic than ever, for he had spent many happy years there with his family, and he still had several old friends to visit, and to whom he must introduce his wife and sons. While they were staying at the comfortable Hotel Russie, Willy paid a special visit to his old family doctor, Dr. Speiss. The old German doctor had looked after Willy and his large family of younger brothers and sisters, the youngest of whom had been born in Frankfurt. Willy was anxious to know whether he would ever regain his full health. Dr. Speiss knew all about Willy's head injury, and told him that there was no reason why he should not continue in good health, as long as he kept to moderation in all things, and tried to live a quiet and peaceful life.

But Missy knew that her husband was no longer the same cheerful, healthy young man she had married fourteen years earlier; recently he had often seemed depressed, and at other times even hilarious and over-excited. She also knew he frequently gambled. Then he had those

---

[13] The German legend says that there was once a beautiful young maiden, named Lorelei, who drowned herself in the river in despair over a faithless lover. After she died she was transformed into a siren, and from then on she could occasionally be heard singing on a rock in the Rhine River. Her seductive music lured sailors to their death.

frightening fits of temper, and became irritable over the least little thing. His condition was like a see-saw, swinging from one extreme to the other – the frightening word that Missy hardly dared to use, even to herself, was "unbalanced." She prayed that their winter in Florence might help to stabilise her husband, and she was glad to know that the old doctor in Frankfurt would always be ready to give advice if he was needed. German doctors were always so clever, she knew, and much more ready to treat the mind as well as the body.

The boys were quite unaware of their parents' preoccupations in Frankfurt, and were longing to move on to Wiesbaden which was to be their next destination. They were thoroughly enjoying themselves and were beginning to pick up a few words of German, to add to the Spanish and French they had learned to speak since their early childhood. It was considered most important for children of landed families to speak French and German, and many English families made a point of having French and German nursery governesses, just as the high-born French and German families had English nannies. In Robert's and Charlie's case they had always spoken Spanish, since they were very young, with their grandmother Doña Catalina, and with their mother.

Before leaving Frankfurt, Willy introduced his family to his old friend the Grand Duke of Nassau, who had a house quite near to where the Cunninghame Grahams had lived in the early 1840s. Willy told his sons that the Duke used to take the waters with them at Bad Ems, and in later years had invited Willy's sisters (their aunts Maggie, Char and Annie) to Court Balls at the Hague. Robert and Charlie were most impressed by their first introduction to a member of a European royal family, but surprised that he was such a quiet, unassuming, friendly old man. They had been convinced that he would be wearing a crown, or perhaps a crimson robe trimmed with ermine. His snuffy[14] jacket did not seem at all in keeping with royalty.

After a quick visit to both Wiesbaden and Hamburg, the family moved on to Muggendorfe, where they stayed with another old friend, Baron von Autsees, and went trout fishing. The boys were most intrigued to find that they were accompanied by two men with spades,

---

[14] Snuffy was a word often used to described someone who took snuff and spilled it over his clothes!

who dug small tanks on the riverbank into which they dropped the fish they caught. It was apparently considered very poor form to kill your trout in the way Mr. Gulliver, their tutor, had taught them at Gartmore. The German game-keepers explained that the trout tasted better if they were kept alive in fresh water until they were taken to the kitchen. That night, at dinner, Robert and Charlie knew the keepers had been right -- they had never tasted such delicious trout, even from the peaty waters of the upper reaches of the River Forth at Gartmore.

When their host heard that they were to travel on to Bayreuth he looked grave, and told them that a great fuss was brewing up over the Schleswig-Holstein affair, and that there was already talk of a possible war between Prussia and Austria. They might easily find Bayreuth full of troops, and perhaps they would be wise to change their plans. The death of the Danish king, Frederick VII, two years earlier in 1863 had caused the Danish-German dispute to escalate swiftly, and now there was talk that the duchies of Schleswig and Holstein were being filled with Austrian and Prussian troops, and there was a real danger that the two duchies would be annexed to Prussia.

Like all small boys, the idea of a war with real soldiers and guns seemed irresistible to Robert and Charlie, and they begged their father to take them on to Bayreuth. Willy hated to disappoint his sons, and the Baron agreed that it was unlikely that events could move so quickly that they would be subjected to any real danger. The latest move in the situation had sinister implications, however, for there had just been a meeting at Biarritz between Napoleon III of France and the great Prussian statesman, Bismarck, at which Napoleon had announced his intention of remaining neutral in the event of an Austro-Prussian war.

Everyone knew that Bismarck's greatest ambition was to annex the duchies and to unite Germany as a whole, and it was a nervous time for the old feudal families. It was also known that the French emperor was a sick man, and that Bismarck could easily outmanoeuvre him. Nevertheless, Willy decided to take his family on to Bayreuth, and from there to Dresden, to spend their last two weeks in Willy's favourite place of all, Weimar, where he had spent the final year of his education at the court of the Grand Duke, before joining the army.

In Bayreuth there were, as the Baron had predicted, large numbers of troops, and sentries were posted outside the family's bedroom doors at their hotel. Robert and Charlie were immensely impressed by this evidence of political unrest, and hoped the shooting would start before they left the town. But, to their parents' relief, they managed to get off to Chemnitz the next day without a single warlike incident occurring; the boys were dreadfully disappointed.

They soon cheered up, however, when they reached Weimar. Willy's old friend Colonel Rhein, their host, was a most genial man, and amused them greatly by reminiscing about Willy's wild escapades when he had stayed with the Grand Duke's head forester in 1844, when he was nineteen. Colonel Rhein remembered Herr Schwendler forcing Willy to smoke a clay pipe, remarking, "What! – Not smoke, Herr Graam? You will never get on at Weimar until you learn to smoke!" Colonel Rhein also told them about their father's preoccupation with the attractive young Fräulein Göethe; and how he had learnt to love music, encouraged by the brilliant Hungarian pianist and composer, Franz Liszt.

It had been a happy time for Willy, and his sons could tell how much he was enjoying the opportunity to relive it all. The boys' holiday ended with several partridge shoots which were laid on specially for them by Colonel Rhein, at which, Willy was glad to see, his sons performed honourably. They had both had plenty of practice at Gartmore, shooting pigeons and rabbits with their four-tens. Charlie's early promise was developing into real prowess, a skill which was ultimately to earn him a place at the great royal shoots at Sandringham and Balmoral in the 1880s and 1890s.

Robert enjoyed riding round the huge estates with Colonel Rhein best of all, and was complimented on his superb horsemanship. It had been a good holiday, and their parents were proud to find that their sons could cope just as naturally and easily with the grand style of life amongst the "hochgeboren"[15] at Weimar as they did in their simpler home on the edge of the highlands in Scotland.

---

[15] "High-born."

From Weimar the boys travelled by train to Hamburg, where their tutor, Mr. Gulliver, had arrived to escort them to England for their first term at Harrow.

CHAPTER IV

After the novelty of the first two weeks at Harrow had worn off, Robert found that he had made two enemies. One was the Headmaster, Dr. Butler, who was an awe-inspiring man, more like a God from Mount Olympus, Robert thought; and the other was his fag-master,[16] Edward Marjoriebanks, son of the first Lord Tweedmouth.

Dr. Butler had formed a system of strict discipline to forge the boys in his care into a mould that would turn them out as officers and gentlemen. In 1865 the British Empire was at its most glorious, and Queen Victoria had been on the throne for nearly thirty years. Great administrators were needed to maintain her vast Empire, and good soldiers were needed to keep an eye on the trouble-spots.

Dr. Butler's system was to expose his boys to all the exigencies of the life they were going to have to lead, with its unfairness, bullying, exploitation, and every form of human vice and weakness. The idea was that, if the boys got used to all these things at school, nothing would ever seem so terrible to them again, and they would be able to cope with every situation they encountered. With the year divided into three terms, the boys would have the holidays in which to go home and lick their wounds before returning for the next dose of discipline.

It was a hard system, but it worked, on the whole, although a small minority were broken by it. But Robert made the mistake of showing quite clearly that he thought Dr. Butler's system was inhumane. Its main disadvantage was that there was apt to be a certain type of boy, or sometimes even a master, whose brutal instincts were released in the process, making him into a total bully. Such a boy was Marjoriebanks. As Marjoriebanks' fag, Robert's life became a perpetual form of slavery.

The crunch came towards the end of Robert's first term. While he was sleeping peacefully one night, Marjoriebanks crept silently into his room and indulged in the age-old torment of shutting up his fag in his folding bed. Robert awoke in terror to find that he was standing on his head in the dark with a terrible choking sensation. Fortunately a new

---

[16] A "fag" in this context refers to the old public-school system wherein the younger boys perform menial chores for older pupils.

friend, Reuter, heard his muffled cries and quickly opened the bed out again. Marjoriebanks was seen tiptoeing away down the passage, so there was no doubt as to who his assailant had been. The Christmas holidays began two days later, to Robert's relief.

The Christmas holidays in Florence passed all too quickly. Mr. Gulliver was unable to come with them, so they travelled out with a young man called Owen Whiteside who was going to Africa to become Sir Garnet Wolseley's ADC. Robert and Charles did not like him very much, and when they reached Florence they were relieved to find that he was to be succeeded by another tutor, Mr. Cook, whom they liked much better. Christmas was fun for both parents and children alike, with skating, riding and parties amongst the Bontines' new-found friends in Florance. They were amused to find that their Italian friends called them "the Bontinis," being unable to get their tongue round the name "Cunninghame Graham," and therefore using their father's "entailed" surname.

Mallie was still in Scotland with Ninny, in the care of Aunt Annie, and he sounded very happy. The old nurse, Ninny, was like a mother to him; she had brought up all three boys and was very much a part of the family.

The day after Charlie's twelfth birthday, New Year's Day 1866, Robert wrote a letter to Doña Catalina to tell her about their holidays in Florence.

"2nd January 1866

My dear Ganama

I like Florence very much. We have been to lots of parties and things. On Sunday we went to the Opera. It was not well done, but there was a very good ballet. Tomorrow we are going to a picture gallery. We have seen two other galleries. There has been a week of skating, and a hunt. Papa has such a pretty little grey Arab called 'Tommie' which he rides in the park. There was a review, but we did not see it. There are such pet[17] little ponies here. Mamma calls them 'Smouches'! They go at a tremendous pace. Our house looks out on the river Arno. I have had a

---

[17] Robert's use of the word 'pet' came from his Spanish grandmother's own vocabulary. She often used English words in their wrong sense, and they became incorporated into the Bontine family's 'private language.'

cold but it is nearly well now. Mummie and Puppie and Charlie send their love. Please give my love to dear Kat.
    I remain, your affectionate gd'son,
            R. C. Graham."
    Back at Harrow for their second term, Robert found to his utter joy that Marjoriebanks had been sacked. He wrote joyously to his parents in Florence:
    "I have a very nice room now, and Marjoriebanks has really left! When it was known through the house that he was not coming back, there was a shout. Charlie took the third fourth, which is not bad at all. I have taken the fourth shell, which is a very good remove. Out of sixteen boys who came to Dr. Butler's, I and another fellow are equal third. I like Harrow very much now. I was very stupid not to like it before. The only thing I do not like is that one day the work is very easy and short, and another day it is very long and hard. Charlie also likes it very much. We play racquets[18] a good deal. Of all the masters I like Hutton best, and Butler[19] worst. Give my best love to dear Papa,
    I remain,
            Your affectionate son, R. C. Graham."
    Missy had suspected that Robert had been miserable at Harrow during his first term, for he had often seemed nervy and morose during the holidays in Florence. At the end of the holidays he was particularly strung up and touchy. Now she knew what it was all about; reading between the lines, Robert had been terrorised by the awful Marjoriebanks. She hoped he would now start to do really well at school. It was a great relief to know that he had settled down at last.
    A second letter arrived a few days later in which Robert reiterated his new-found enthusiasm for Harrow.
    "I like Dr. Butler's house a great deal better now that Marjoriebanks is gone. I have got a very nice room with a very nice fellow. Villiers is in the same form as I am. He is getting on very well, and so is Charlie Bickmore."
    Robert was now nearly fourteen years old, and Charlie twelve. Robert was in the Headmaster's house. Charlie was in "Small Houses,"

---

[18] An old ball game, played in an enclosed court like squash.
[19] The Headmaster of Harrow; Robert was in his House.

a special house for younger boys, because he was to be at Harrow for only a year before going on to the school at Alverstoke to be coached for the Admiralty Board's examination for the Royal Navy.

Villiers, Robert's greatest friend at Hill House, had come to Harrow the same term, and was in Mr. Vaughan's house. Together they learnt, during their first term, the new words of the strange Harrow "language," and found their way about the school; from School Buildings to the Speech Room, from "Duck Puddle" (the swimming pool) to the football fields, and from Chapel to the old Schools. They were taught not to trespass on Middle Walk, where only the 'bloods' were allowed, to carry their umbrella unfolded, and to wear their straw boaters straight, as a new-boy should.

They were shown where to "tub" and where to "tosh," and always to wear their "bluers" buttoned. This applied to all the boys who had been in the school for less than three years. They learned to call the maths masters "teak-beaks" and their armchairs "a frowst."

They were also initiated into the delights of the "Tudor Creameries," a fashionable tuck-shop in the main street. A speciality sold there in the summer term was a gorgeous concoction called a "dringer" made of strawberries, sugar, cream and ice cream, all squashed into a jam-pot, to be purchased for the princely sum of 6d.[20]

Robert's third letter to his parents in Florence announced: "I am doing very well in form as yet, and I have been top a great many times, and I hope I shall keep so. I have not heard from Charlie lately, but I suppose he is all right. It is very wet here today. There is to be a confirmation here soon."

He was able to report after a week or two, "I and another fellow are equal, being third in form."

A few days later he received a letter from his father from Florence.

"My dear Robert,

I am delighted to hear that you and Charly are getting on so well. I saw an excellent motto over the door of a house here the other day, 'Dominus cum Fortibus'[21] – old Palmerston[22] was a striking

---

[20] 6d. means six pennies. In the pre-decimal British currency, there were twelve pennies to the shilling and twenty shillings to the pound.
[21] 'Rule with Strength.'

exemplification. It is an excellent motto if a man can follow it up without becoming a bully.

As to fencing, of course learn it. It is the best exercise in the world and gives a man confidence. If you want foils write to Uncle Bobby (2 Leicester Street, Regent Street) to get them for you, if you can't get them at Harrow. Stick to Racquets. Remember in playing Racquets a correct eye and a quick hand is worth a dozen pair of legs. Only bad players are always running over the court.

Don't forget in your zeal for fencing and racquets that, in our family crest, the Eagle holds in his other claw a pen!

Give my love to Charly and tell him he has only one boy to beat as he is second.

Your affec. Father.

W. C. Bontine."

As Robert strolled about the grounds of Harrow with Villiers he thought about its past – he had been told about the merchant, John Lyon, who had founded the school in 1571, and he had already learned the words of some of the school songs. Apparently they would all join in singing them, in a great roar, at "Speecher."[23]

He found himself strangely inspired by the words of a new song called, "Forty years on." It had just been written by a young classics master, Edward Bowen, who had been kind to him. Bowen held most interesting radical views, and was a great admirer of Garibaldi.[24] The song was quite rousing, and Robert liked the bit about "fights for the fearless and goals for the eager." It reminded him of the great poem of his kinsman, Montrose:

"He either fears his fate too much
    Or his deserts are small

---

[22] Henry John Temple, 3rd Viscount Palmerston was Foreign Secretary three times (1830-34, 1825-41 and 1846-51) and twice Prime Minister (1855-58 and 1859-65).

[23] The famous end of term "sing-song," often referred to by Winston Churchill, famous Old Harrovian.

[24] Guiseppe Garibaldi (1807-1882) was the foremost military figure and popular hero of the age of Italian unification, he is deemed one of the creators of modern Italy.

Who dare not put it to the touch
To win or lose it all."

Bowen was writing articles for the Saturday Review, and hoped to launch a new curriculum at Harrow which would teach the boys more history, modern languages, and science, but no Greek. He insisted that the boys in his house should wear red shirts for football, as a mark of respect for the guerilla leader, Garibaldi. He rapidly became Robert's hero, and Robert enjoyed nothing more than listening to Bowen's radical talk.

By the summer term, the Graham boys were beginning to gain prestige as budding athletes. They were both strong and wiry, and they both had a quality of endurance which Robert was sure they had inherited from their Moorish ancestors, in the dim, distant past. Robert soon won a coveted place in the house cricket eleven, along with two of his friends, Digby Cobden and Matthews. He played cricket and racquets, swam in "Ducker" and went for long rambles with Villiers down the green lanes of Harrow Weald and Roxeth. Together they peeped through the gates of Bentley Priory, the property of the Duke of Abercorn and Chandos. Villiers, who loved music, told Robert that Handel had once been the Duke of Chandos's chapel organist.

Returning home they liked to pop into "the Creameries" to stand themselves the famous "dringer," and they were sometimes joined by Robert's other great friend, Reuter, whose father had become the first foreign correspondent to "The Times" newspaper. Those were halcyon days, and the sun seemed to shine day after day. Robert won cups for long-distance running, and for jumping, and his prestige increased day by day.

But at the end of the summer term disaster struck: Dr. Butler sent a letter to Robert's parents to complain about Robert. On July 12th Robert wrote to his mother in deep contrition:

"My dear Mamma,

I am very sorry that I have been doing so badly. I will work up very hard in 'trials.' I shall certainly get my remove this quarter and have some chance for a double. I can't make out why Butler said that I was not reverend in chapel, for I never did anything that I know of. It is only a fortnight next Tuesday to the Holidays.

I remain, your affec. son, R. C. Graham.
(N.B. I will really work in trials!)"
Two weeks later Robert and Charlie arrived back at Gartmore. Missy gave Robert a serious talking to, and he promised to do better the following term. Willy was surprisingly gentle with his son and made several helpful suggestions which made Robert all the more anxious to please dear "Puppy."

The first half of the holidays went by as quickly as ever, while Robert and Charlie rode, shot, fished, boated and bathed at Gartmore. Mallie was now six, and he loved to join in some of his older brothers' expeditions. Sometimes they helped with the haymaking on the home farm;   Mallie rode on the hay-bogie[25] while Robert led the great Clydesdale horses, and Charlie walked behind to gather up fallen armfuls of hay as the bogie bounced over rutted fields.

Half way through the holidays Robert and Charlie caused great alarm by disappearing for more than twenty-four hours. The boys had thought up a scheme to portage their boat from the Lake of Menteith to the nearby Goodie Burn, and thence to the river Forth. All went well until they started to glide under the old bridge at Stirling, past the Abbey of Cambuskenneth, towards the tidal waters of the Firth of Forth. Here the current swept them downstream so quickly that they could not row the boat upstream again.

Finding they were benighted, they pulled the boat up on the bank and slept the night under an old willow tree. It did not occur to them that, finding the boat had vanished from the waters of the Lake of Menteith, their family would be convinced that they had both gone to a watery grave. Missy was distraught; she knew that Robert and Charlie were drowned, and she was already in agonies of remorse over her sharp lecture to poor darling Bob at the beginning of the holidays. Nothing would calm her. Willy tried to reassure her and persuade her that the boys were probably having a huge adventure and enjoying themselves thoroughly, spending the night in some hideout. Willy seemed to be the only person among the wailing women at Gartmore who was quite certain that the boys were still alive and well.

---

[25] A cart with pairs of wheels that swivel.

Eventually it transpired that the two young daughters of Mr. MacGregor, from the hotel at Port of Menteith, knew all about the expedition but had been sworn to secrecy by their heroes, the Graham boys. They had not dared tell their father for fear that Master Bob and Master Charlie would never talk to them again. But eventually, when they heard talk of dragging the waters of the Lake for the missing boat, they knew they must divulge their secret. All was told, and their father rode post-haste to Stirling, to find that the police had already sighted the boys on the banks of the River Forth.

By dinner-time Robert and Charlie were back at Gartmore, and Missy remarked that she now knew exactly what that wretched Prodigal Son's parents felt like! They all burst out laughing, and Willy treated his sons to a glass of port each. It was a particularly happy evening. None of them realised that this was to be the last family dinner they would ever have together.

Next day Willy fell seriously ill. This time the attack lasted longer than before, leaving him totally bewildered and unaware of his surroundings. At one moment he was found wandering round the garden on a cold night in his nightshirt. Another time he managed to get into the night nursery where Malise was sleeping peacefully and Ninny, hearing footsteps, found him lifting the child out of bed. It was all very alarming.

Missy sent the boys south to her mother in Ryde on the Isle of Wight for the final weeks of their holidays, where Doña Catalina and their step-grandfather tried to keep them cheerful and to reassure them about the nature of their father's illness. Willy's younger brother, Bobby, came to Gartmore, and he and Missy reluctantly decided that the time had come to arrange for a house where Willy could live alone, looked after by his devoted and reliable Italian valet, to prevent him from harming his family during one of his violent brain-storms.

Doctors were consulted and they all agreed that Willy's condition was deteriorating, and that it was Missy's duty to keep him away from his children. The running of the estate should also be taken out of his hands. Aunt Annie Speirs came to their rescue once again to tell them that she had heard of a delightful shooting lodge in Dumfriesshire, not far from Moffat at Penpont, called Eccles House. It could be rented from the

Duke of Buccleuch and Willy could live there quietly with his servant. Aunt Annie spent a good deal of the time at Moffat these days, so she and her brother-in-law, Tom, would keep an eye on Willy so that he would not feel a total outcast.

There was to be another enormous advantage in the plan, for Dumfries boasted a particularly talented doctor who specialised in nervous diseases and brain injuries, one of the very few in the world. His name was Sharpe. The family lawyer, Arthur Campbell, entirely agreed with this arrangement, and encouraged Mrs. Bontine to go ahead and take the house for her husband. He also told her that it looked as though they must now appoint a 'Curator Bonis' to look after their affairs. He knew just the man, a young Edinburgh accountant called George Auldjo Jamieson.

Bobby decided to go to Dumfriesshire with Willy, to help settle his elder brother into his new home. He had managed to rent some shooting from the Duke of Buccleuch (whose own castle, Drumlanrig, lay near to Eccles), and Willy was delighted to hear that Bobby was taking him shooting and they would stay in an attractive lodge in the Dumfriesshire hills overlooking the river Annan.

Missy was grateful to her young brother-in-law for his help, and for the clever way he had got Willy away from Gartmore. The Italian valet also proved invaluable, and she knew he would look after Willy faithfully and well. He was the only man who seemed to be able to keep his master calm and tranquil.

Missy's heart was breaking as she left Gartmore to take a small house in London, where she and her boys could live. She had lost her husband, her home, and her security, at a stroke. Gartmore was to be let to a shooting-tenant, and now they were virtually homeless. Her whole world had collapsed in ruins. Poor darling Willy – her dearest husband, how lonely he would be. But she dared not stay with him, for the doctors had told her that a man in his state very often tried to kill the person who was dearest to him. His mind was unhinged, and he often had no idea what he was doing. Worst of all, she was in the seventh month of a new pregnancy.

Before leaving Gartmore Missy had looked through the accounts with Mr. Jamieson, and had begun to realise that she could not even afford to keep Robert on at Harrow. It was an accepted practice of the day for less wealthy families to send their sons to the Continent, just as his grandfather had done for Willy, where they received a very useful and considerably cheaper education. Missy knew that Robert would be delighted to be released from Harrow and from the boys he described as "sprigs of the nobility," whom he seemed to dislike so much.

She was also quite glad to remove him from the influence of Edward Bowen, about whom Robert talked ceaselessly, for she feared that her son was being thoroughly indoctrinated with this progressive schoolmaster's radical ideas. He would have to leave at Easter, she decided.

At Ryde, Robert and Charlie had shaken off their sense of shock. There were the usual walks with "Khāt" (as their Spanish grandmother always called her second husband) along the esplanade, striding out to keep pace with the sailor's deceptively rapid, decided gait which made him look as though he half expected the esplanade at any minute to pitch like the deck of a ship.

Sometimes Khāt took the boys through the arcade in Ryde, in which glass bottles, filled with sand from Alum Bay, jostled shell baskets; toy boats (which fell helpless on their broadsides as soon as they were launched) lay next to pin-cushions, and tape measures in which the tape was hidden in a shell. Then there was the jeweller who had his shop at the first corner of the main street, on the left going up it from the pier, and in his window hung, for all time, a red enamel watch, with a dog in rather brassy gold, which Robert coveted. The boys were fascinated by these seaside shops, so different from the general store in Aberfoyle.

On Sundays Robert and Charlie accompanied their grandparents to the Anglican church and listened to Khāt and other old sailors and soldiers of his kind repeating their responses fervently in voices of command. Khāt was a churchwarden, so he always went to church wearing what he called his "jimmy-swinger" – a well-cut frock coat. Devoutly he looked into his hat for a few moments when he entered church, then, after taking his Prayer Book out of a hassock, with a practical front that opened, composed himself for the service.

All was well until the sermon began. Then he would look critically at the clergyman until the time came to carry round the collection plate, at which moment he would step busily into the aisle, looking unfeignedly relieved, doing his duty as an officer and a gentleman, and crossing his fellow churchwardens to and fro as they wove in and out in a sort of dignified square dance. Robert would murmur to Charlie, "Cross over Jonathan; figure in Jemima," in the words of an old negro song, as the churchwardens performed their ritual dance up and down the aisles with their collecting plates, and Charlie would stuff his handkerchief into his mouth to stifle his laughter. Bob was always so funny, he thought, looking sideways at his brother, who had resumed a dead-pan expression.

Next day, Khāt was due to sit on the bench as a local magistrate, and Robert was thought to be old enough to attend in the public gallery. Fortunately his grandmother was not aware that the case before the court that day concerned a woman charged with prostitution. The old sailor had been at sea since the age of twelve and had known the basic facts of life for as long as he could remember, and it did not occur to him that the case of the "poor whore," as he called her, should be unsuitable for his young step-grandson's ears. Walking home to lunch afterwards he commented to Robert that he had let her off lightly for, "after all, it took two people to commit the fault." Robert was always to remember this piece of wisdom, and in late years he was to write stories on the subject that were considered finer than those of Maupassant.

Khāt was the only man who was close enough to Robert at this time to influence his developing ideas about life, and the old sailor was to be just like a real father to the three Graham boys as they grew older. In the evenings, at Ryde, Robert enjoyed talking Spanish with his grandmother and hearing about their Spanish relations, some of whom still lived in Cadiz and Gibraltar. He hoped that he would be able to visit them all one day.

Robert was told that his father would be going to live near Moffat, and therefore quite close to Aunt Annie Speirs and Uncle Tom . At least he had not been sent to a lunatic asylum. He could hardly believe that the wise father who had talked so kindly to him about his problems at Harrow should now be so ill that he could not stay in his own home.

In their new little house in Wilton Place, London, his mother tried to explain to him that, amongst their other problems, Papa seemed to have inherited his grandfather William's "gambling streak" and had been spending a great deal too much money lately, so it was far better for him to be away from Gartmore in the circumstances.

Robert went to spend the final week of the holidays with the Speirs at Moffat before going back to Harrow. Travelling by train from Euston, he changed onto the little branch line at Beattock junction, and Aunt Annie met him at Moffat Station. (This journey was to inspire the best short story Robert was ever to write, well known as "Beattock For Moffat.")

But when they went to visit Papa at Eccles House, he did not seem to know his son. Aunt Annie and Uncle Tom took Robert quickly back to their house, and for a picnic to the Devil's Beeftub[26] to try to cheer him up. But nothing would take Robert's mind off his father's sad condition. Worst of all was the knowledge that Gartmore had been let for shooting, and that their new home was now in London. He could hardly bear it.

Back at Harrow, Robert moped inconsolably, and Dr. Butler began to wonder if the boy should be sent home to his mother. But Missy was otherwise occupied, and Robert was never to know that his mother had given birth to a stillborn daughter that December, although he often wondered why he and his brothers had seen so little of her during that autumn term.

---

[26] A "beeftub" was a natural, steep "hole" where stolen cattle were often kept hidden.

CHAPTER V

Charlie passed his examination for the Navy in May 1867 when he was thirteen, and joined the training ship, H.M.S. Britannia. At the same time Robert, who was now 15, left Harrow and went to Brussels, to the Consular Chaplain's educational establishment in 116 rue Sans Souci where Papa had been tutored more than twenty years earlier.

It was the best thing that could have happened to him in the circumstances, and his natural exuberance soon returned. This was to be his first real adventure away from his family and he could hardly conceal his excitement. Brussels was an exhilarating place at any time, and to Robert it seemed the most sophisticated city in the world.

He could already imagine himself lolling in a smart restaurant with a cigar in his mouth and a cognac at his elbow; but when he got the measure of his tutor, Mr. Jenkins, it became all too apparent to him that his new master would be intent on keeping the boys' noses to the grindstone, with a full programme of classes and no time to get up to mischief.

Robert was frustrated at first, but soon started to enjoy himself when he realised that the language classes were more interesting than at Harrow, and it would be useful when he started to travel about the world to be able to speak French and Spanish really fluently. He was also making a lot of new friends, and found that his fellow-pupils were splendid fellows.

He enjoyed the fencing classes most of all, and soon became the most promising pupil, winning several contests with grace and ease. His teacher declared that he was a "natural," and Robert began to realise why his father had felt that every boy should learn to fence; it taught concentration, quickness of decision, and made the body supple and strong. Robert had never enjoyed anything so much in his life before as this exciting combination of dancing and fighting.

Robert suggested that Charlie should come out for a visit during his leave from the "Britannia." So, in the middle of June 1867 the two brothers were reunited once more and Robert wrote to tell his mother about Charlie's visit:

"116 rue Sans Souci, Brussels. June 17th.

My dear Mamma

Charlie and I have had great fun, we went to Waterloo and everywhere else. I heard from 'Pudden' the other day but he said nothing except that his holiday would be soon. Shall I come home today week, or tomorrow week? Almost everyone will be going about that time. I am going in for some athletics this evening. 'Tarlee' will give particulars. I hope he will be able to get some more leave. I am sorry 'Tarlee' is going because I have enjoyed his visit so much.

I remain your affec. son, R. C. Graham."

He did not mention in his letter that he had been to a Ball, nor that he had fallen madly in love, for the first time in his life, with pretty Miss Cogswell, who had been his dancing partner.

Missy smiled over the letter. How typical it was. He never managed to tell her any news. And there was the same devotion to Charlie, or 'Tarlee' as he still called him, adopting Mallie's first babyish name for his brother.

What would Robert do without his brother when Charlie finally went to sea? And what career should Robert follow when he left Brussels next year? Missy supposed he ought to start managing Gartmore for Willy, but surely he must be allowed to sow a few wild oats first? At least she had managed to persuade Willy that Robert was not at all suited for the Brigade of Guards. Her brother-in-law, William Hope, had suggested he should go into an Indian Cavalry Regiment, like Skinner's Horse, but she knew Robert was far too much of an individual for the army.

She was convinced that he was quick, and highly intelligent, and this was why he did not have the patience to learn from his methodical school-masters. He was unlikely to show academic brilliance, but he had a keen, observant eye, and an abundance of energy. Robert would do something wonderful with his life, if he was allowed to pursue it in his own way, she was sure.

In July, Robert joined his old tutor, Gulliver, for a holiday in Switzerland before he returned to England. During the rest of the holiday Missy took her three boys on a round of visits to their relations, and before he returned to Brussels at the end of September Robert spent a week with the Fitzwilliam cousins in their huge pile, Wentworth, Yorkshire, for the cubbing.[27] He was lent a striking mare called "Luna."

Back in Brussels, Robert worked hard at his Spanish and wrote to his mother to say, "I go three times a week to my Spanish master now, and I am learning to write letters in Spanish, but I cannot do a thing to my name (the 'Rubrico,' & those long flourishes) which the man insists on. I have a fencing master twice a week. I actually heard from Charlie the other day, but he said nothing but 'scuppers, booms and halliards.' I had a splendid walk the other day to a place called Villers le Ville, where there is an old ruined Abbey."

In December Charlie was due for some leave before joining H.M.S. Ariadne for a Mediterranean cruise. They were to take the Prince of Wales on a cruise to Greece and Turkey. Robert decided to come home for Charlie's final leave before his brother went to sea as a fully fledged midshipman.

"I think I will come by Ostend," he wrote to his mother, "because the sea is so dreadful in winter." Robert had already discovered on his channel crossings that he was a 'bad sailor,' and he did not intend to tempt Providence. "I had a swim yesterday," he went on, "it was not very pleasant, but I want to bathe in every month of the year!"

Missy spent Christmas 1867 with her three sons in Southsea, where she had managed to rent a house for the boys' holidays. She wanted to have them completely to herself for the last time, and was not even prepared to share them with her mother at Ryde.

Charlie was still very small, and looked far too young, in his midshipman's uniform, to be going to sea for the first time. She was delighted to hear that another midshipman, who was his best friend, would be going too. He was a charming young German prince called Louis of Battenberg. Charlie told her that some of the cadets had been pretty beastly to Louis, "because he's a German, and a Prince. It's jolly rotten of them. After all, how can he help being either of thse things?" asked Charlie angrily.

Charlie did not realise at the time how his championship of young Prince Louis was to bear fruit in his later life, and that the German Prince

---

[27] (Fox) cub-hunting.

was to become his lifelong friend. One day Charlie would become a courtier to both King Edward VII and to King George V, entirely thanks to his friendship with Prince Louis. He would also be given a most interesting job, as an inspector in the Lifeboat Service, as a result of Prince Louis writing a glowing reference for him after he left the Navy. But at the time Charlie only knew that he had made friends with an exceptionally splendid young fellow, and he was delighted that they were to be shipmates on their first cruise together.

Some of the Graham and Speirs relations wanted to give Charlie presents to celebrate his elevation from cadet to midshipman. Charlie thought he would like a revolver, but his mother was horrified at the idea and told her younger son that he really could not ask one of his maiden aunts for such a thing. Robert thought the idea was very funny; he was sure Aunt Annie, at least, would think it a tremendously good present. But his mother refused to agree, and promptly wrote to Aunt Helen suggesting that what Charlie really needed was a reliable watch.

But Aunt Helen decided in the end to give him a telescope; when it arrived they were sure she had bought it in an antique shop in Leamington, for it had a great many more sections than any telescope they had ever seen before. Charlie was delighted with it, however, and strutted about like an admiral on his quarterdeck, tucking it casually under his arm. Missy, Robert and Malise became quite hilarious, making up silly rhymes about "Tarlee's wonderful magic telescope."

Charlie sailed in H.M.S. Ariadne on 4th January 1868, three days after his fourteenth birthday, and Missy took Robert and Malise back to the horsey Fitzwilliam cousins in Yorkshire for some more hunting. Robert found the chase very exciting, but felt unhappy about the poor fox. Somehow he did not think he had inherited Admiral Elphinstone Fleeming's passion for riding to hounds.

He also found that he disliked the snobbish people he encountered in the field, who were rather like the arrogant boys he had left behind at Harrow. But he had to admit that he loved the hunt, with the sensation of a fast gallop, senses tingling and the feeling that he and the great grey horse "Barebones" were one and the same. Sadly he was not allowed to ride the beautiful "Luna" on this visit, for she had now become a brood mare.

Malise, too, went out hunting several times and managed neither to fall off his small pony nor to disgrace himself in the hunting field. When Mallie went back to school, Robert returned to Brussels and was soon absorbed once more in his French and Spanish classes. He was enjoying his fencing lessons more than ever, and his social life was becoming full and entertaining.

For another year Robert worked hard, but came home from Brussels at regular intervals to see as much as possible of his mother and youngest brother. He knew how lonely his mother had become, and the news of Papa was far from good.

In the spring of 1869 Robert fell seriously in love. He and his mother had been on a visit to an old friend of his mother's, Lady Langdale, whom they had met in Florence. Her pretty daughter was married to a Hungarian, Count Teleki. Robert fell head over heels in love with the beautiful young Countess, seeing her as often as he could, while their mothers drank tea together.

Robert poured out all his hopes and fears to the sympathetic young Countess and confided in her his longing to travel to South America, where he would like to gallop over the pampas in Argentina. The young Countess teased him gently by calling him "the Gaucho." She admired this good-looking boy greatly and enjoyed going for rides with him; but she laughingly told his mother that she had preferred him before he became a "spoony[28] gaucho." The love-sick Robert was an entirely new person to Missy, and she wished he had not fallen in love with a married woman, who was undoubtedly leading him on.

Countess Teleki was always setting out on adventures, and the last time Robert was to see her was just before she left for a trip to Egypt and Damascus. She wrote to him from Cairo, to tell him about the pyramids, and how she had been hoisted up so that she could get inside some of the secret chambers. She also told him about some monks who were swimming naked in the Nile and tried to board their ship.

After that there was a long silence. Robert could hardly believe it when his mother told him gently that his beautiful young countess had died of a fever in Damascus. She had been so lively and vivacious, it

---

[28] Sentimental.

was extraordinary to think that she was no longer alive. Robert was heart-broken and could not get her out of his head. He carried her photograph everywhere with him.

What he did not know was that she had recently terminated an affair with a brother of Sir Redvers Buller, who had shot himself shortly after her departure for Egypt, convinced that his life would be totally empty now that she had left him for ever.

Her mother having been one of her greatest friends, it was Missy who had to comfort Lady Langdale in her deep distress. She was shown a copy of the suicide note left by the Countess's lover, and also the lawyer's letter which had informed the young woman harshly that he had "died of a broken heart." Perhaps Countess Teleki had, in turn, died of a broken heart too, as the result of this terrible chain of events.

She had left Missy her pearls in her will, but Robert's mother could not bear to wear them – the whole affair was too utterly distressing. The Countess had been so lovely and so amusing, but these qualities had unwittingly caused much havoc among her many admirers. Robert had never before felt such overwhelming grief, young as he was. It was even worse than hearing that Papa had been sent to Eccles, he thought miserably.

Early in 1869, to help him forget his grief, Missy planned a visit with Robert to Cortachy, in Forfarshire, to stay with the Countess of Airlie. As Blanche Stanley, the daughter of the Earl of Derby, she had been Missy's dearest childhood friend and they had always kept in touch. The two women talked about Robert's future, and Robert found Lady Airlie to be kind and sympathetic, and totally understood his reaction to his Uncle William Hope's suggestion that he should join an Indian Cavalry Regiment. Robert would hate military discipline, she laughed, *any* son of Missy's was bound to be a rebel!

"What about South America?" she suggested. Her husband had some young Ogilvy cousins running an estancia in Entre Rios in Argentina, about a hundred miles from Buenos Aires. They seemed to be enjoying the life and she was sure they would be glad of another young partner on their estancia, especially so good a horseman as Robert. Robert could hardly believe his ears, here was his mother's friend suggesting the very place to which he had always wanted to go; and she could even provide him with a contact in Argentina! He almost threw his arms round her neck – *dear* Lady Airlie. Missy was delighted that Blanche had been able to help Robert with his future plans. She was sure South America would be just the right place for him, with its strong Spanish influence. How lucky it was that he already spoke Spanish so fluently.

Next day the Ogilvys of Balnaboth, her husband's cousins, were summoned to meet Robert. They were a huge family and the younger sons had gone out to the Argentine to work there because they knew there was not enough work to go round on the family estate near Kirriemuir.

One of them was home on leave, and Robert was left with James Ogilvy, talking in the garden together, while Blanche took Missy for a drive. When the two friends got home they found that everything had been arranged to the young men's satisfaction. Robert would sail to South America when James returned at the beginning of May 1870, and the Ogilvy brothers would be delighted to have an extra pair of hands on their estancia in Entre Rios – with some minimal investment for their ranching project. Missy was sure the Curator Bonis would agree to that.

Robert's immediate future was suddenly assured, and Missy felt enormously relieved. She could see, too, how excited he was at the proposal. He had been dreadfully morose of late, and his mother knew it was just because he was so bored: Robert was so full of energy that he could not bear to sit still and liked to be active every moment of the day. He would be a very long way away from her if he went to South America, but the most important thing of all was for him to be usefully occupied and happy.

She would write to Mr. Jamieson at once for funds for his journey, and for new clothes. She could see by the look in Robert's eyes that he was convinced he was about to find his "El Dorado" – how clever of Blanche to think of it! Robert had suddenly come alive again, *properly* alive, for the first time since his father had been removed to Eccles House, since they had all had to leave Gartmore, and since his first love, the beautiful Countess Teleki, had died.

The next few months passed by in a whirl as Robert fitted himself out for his new life in South America. He rushed from Edinburgh to Glasgow, and then south on the train to London. There he went to

Whistler's the gunmaker; and then for fittings with Runciman the Bootmaker, Chapman and Moore the hatters, and both Thornton Hume and Edward Bax for waterproof clothing.

His passage to Buenos Aires would cost £35; Mamma told him he would be given another £20 for the voyage, with £50 to lodge with a bank in Argentina or Uruguay when he arrived. He bought a saddle for £8.5.6[29] from Andrew Watt in Edinburgh, and spent £30 on shirts, underwear, socks and nightshirts at Bowring and Armadale in London.

Once his purchases had been made Robert made a final round of visits to his relations, and a specially long one to 'Ganama' Catalina and Khāt. Robert told them all about his new clothes for his adventure in South America, and Khāt promptly made a pen-and-ink sketch of "Bob as he will appear when ready for the road," with spurs, gaucho-knife, broad-brimmed hat, and two pistols stuck through his belt. Doña Catalina was thrilled that her favourite grandson was setting out for South America, where she had been so happy nearly forty years before. She was glad, too, that he would have the chance to use the Spanish she had taught him.

Gazing admiringly at him, she knew that she had managed to burnish the "hidalgo" in this very Spanish-looking boy, who had inherited so many of her own characteristics and her own outlook on life. He had so much of her dear Charles, his grandfather Elphinstone Fleeming, in him too; how proud Catalina's first husband would have been of this adventurous grandson, and how she wished he could have lived long enough to have known his beloved little Missy's eldest son Robert – or "Robertito," as she always called him.

---

[29] Eight pounds, five shillings and sixpence.

CHAPTER VI

Robert sailed from Liverpool to Buenos Aires on 13th May 1870 in S.S. Patagonia, the ship in which James Ogilvy was returning to South America. The boys had agreed to meet up on board the ship, for Robert knew his mother would want to see him off, and he felt rather embarrassed to be seen so obviously untying the apron strings of his youth in public, on the quay. But he knew Mamma would be dignified, and was unlikely to burst into tears or cause an emotional scene as she bid her son farewell. Homer, her German maid, accompanied them and was to see her mistress safely back to London once the ship had sailed. Robert and his mother walked up the companionway and were shown into the tiny cabin which was to be Robert's home for the next four or five weeks.

The first port of call was Coruña, where Robert watched between three and four hundred Galician[30] emigrants swarming on board with their pathetic bundles. One of them even carried a bird-cage, with a small brown bird singing its heart out. They spoke no English and Robert was much in demand as interpreter to assist the ship's crew when things had to be explained in Spanish.

He could not help thinking that they looked terribly like the cattle at the Falkirk Tryst, huddled into pens as the farmers brought them to market, moved from their own calf-lands to new and strange pastures, or, indeed, to end in the slaughter house. There eyes had the same frightened look, the whites showing uncertainty, and fear manifest in furtive movements.

Robert had tried to reassure them, and to pass on to them his own certainty that life would have much to offer on the far side of the Atlantic. They were pathetically grateful to him, and were often to appeal to this young boy in their own language when life on board ship oppressed them too greatly. There was to be much life and death on that long journey: babies were born, several of the immigrants died, and nearly all were ill.

---

[30] Galicia is a region of north-west Spain.

Robert seemed to be the only passenger who could help these unfortunate peasants. Perhaps it was because they reminded him of the Gartmore people that he was able to build up the same rapport, so uniquely common to Scots and Spaniards --who have the individualism and dignity that puts man and master on an equal footing.

James Ogilvy was no help at all. His idea of the voyage was that it should be one long orgy of drinking. Robert only hoped that the bottle would start to play a less important role in his life once they sailed up the River Plate. For the time being James remained in his small cabin surrounded by empty bottles, and shouting obscenities. To make matters worse, he had handed over his dog, Curd, to be looked after by Robert.

In Lisbon Robert went off on his own to explore the beautiful old city on the banks of the Tagus. Then the sails were hoisted once more and they started the long crossing to the American Continent. Most of the time the little "Patagonia" pitched and tossed, but sometimes she rolled simultaneously in a sickening corkscrew motion, and Robert wished he was dead. The Irish steward, Pat, was kind and cheerful throughout, bringing dry biscuits and soup to Robert's cabin, persuading him to eat, like a mother coaxing a sick child.

On quieter days Robert lay reading "The Faery Queen," with Curd curled up at his feet. He delighted in Spenser's beautiful language and soaked himself in this masterpiece of literature with all the joy that reading would always give him.

After sighting the Cape Verde Islands there was a week or two of total calm, to Robert's intense joy, and to the Captain's frustration, as he walked the decks whistling for the wind. The weather was idyllic for the traditional "crossing the line"[31] ceremonies, and the passengers felt that life was good once more, as they laughed at the antics of the crew who had transformed themselves into fearsome attendants at King Neptune's Court. Suddenly there was a feeling of fiesta about the old ship and everyone began to sing and dance.

Robert sat on deck talking to the Galicians and watching shoals of flying fish leaping iridescent from the cerulean blue waters. The sea appeared glassy and burning and he remembered the Ancient Mariner's

---

[31] Equator.

despairing words as he gazed out upon the painted sea with the sun blazing down forever.[32]

At last the wind filled the sails once more and the blessed respite from seasickness continued for several days as the "Patagonia" sliced through rippling waters with a convoy of dolphins playing in her wake.

The first sight of land off the great Continent of South America was the spectacular island of Fernando de Noronha, with its volcanic peaks rising steeply out of the sea like a mirage. Robert could smell a spicy aroma blowing off the island as he gazed rapturously at the waving palm trees. His promised land was coming nearer every day. It was the 24th May 1870, his eighteenth birthday.

Two days later they sighted the bay of Rio. Robert had risen early from his bunk to watch the ship making landfall. In the shimmering early-morning light lay the most beautiful bay he had ever seen, with its sugar-loaf hills, myriad islands and the wide sweep of a sandy beach. The misery of the voyage had been a small price to pay for such a sight as this. He could not wait to get ashore to see the people who lived in the beautiful Portuguese houses, warm-blooded people who had been nurtured on bright sunshine and the brilliant colours of flowering tropical trees. He felt himself unfolding in the hot sunshine like an opening bud. He could cope with anything in this climate, he knew. Something that had lain dormant throughout his Scottish upbringing was coming alive – the blood was racing in his veins. It must be his Spanish heritage, the genes he had inherited from Doña Catalina, his grandmother.

Joining some friends, Robert went ashore for a few hours in a small sailing vessel. To set foot at last on the soil of South America was almost a sacramental act for him. He felt hot tears in his eyes, as though his Scottish reserve was melting away. It was strange to hear nothing but Portuguese in his ears, but he found he could understand some of the words quite well, and was sure that he would soon be able to speak another new language. After all, several of the immigrants had spoken it on board the "Patagonia," so it was not entirely unfamiliar to him.

The "Patagonia" sailed again that same evening, heading once more for the open sea and for the final leg of the voyage to Monte Video and

---

[32] "The Rime of the Ancient Mariner," by Samuel Taylor Coleridge.

Buenos Aires. Robert was soon back in his bunk again as great rollers tossed the small ship like a cork.

"Always nasty, this bit," said Pat the steward gloomily as he bustled in with a mug of soup. James Ogilvy's dog was curled in a shivering heap, as usual on Robert's feet. The poor beast obviously thought he was destined to be a canine Flying Dutchman, sailing the seven seas for evermore. His master had spent the voyage on one huge drinking spree and scarcely ever emerged from the whisky fumes of his cabin.

At last, on the 2nd June, they reached Monte Video and Pat popped his head round the cabin door to announce, "Land Ahoy!" Robert was soon out of his bunk and on deck to join the immigrants as they crowded the rails, with Curd at his heels.

The harbour at Monte Video was a scene of great activity that morning. Robert leant over the rail of the ship, lost in thought as he recalled the exciting events of the past weeks. How astonishingly quickly he had crossed the great gulf from schoolboy to man. He had never thought it would be so easy!

In the distance he could see a small boat, bulging with officials, coming out to meet them. An hour later, after partaking of the Captain's hospitality, the officials emerged once more to descend the companion-way to their boat and return to the shore. Robert hurried to see the Captain, to ask if they might go ashore.

"I think it would be unwise, Mr. Graham," said the Captain lugubriously. "I've just been told they're at each other's throats once more. There's a new revolution in these parts between the Colorados and the Blancos. General Urquiza, the Gauchos' favourite leader, has been murdered and everyone is up in arms. There's fighting going on throughout the northern part of the country, from the Banda Oriental to Corrientes. So, no sightseeing this trip, young feller-me-lad! Never mind, we'll not be delayed long and you'll soon be put ashore at Buenos Aires once this wretched *pampero* has blown itself out."

Robert had noticed a blustery, cold wind blowing. It was mid-winter here in the southern hemisphere, being June, but even so the wind seemed uncommonly strong. A *pampero*! That's what it was called! He felt a shiver of exhilaration. That meant it blew from the pampas; there was something romantic about that thought. He could imagine wild horses snorting in the wind and galloping as though to race it, with manes and tails flying.

That evening he had a pleasant surprise when Don Rodrigo, a Spanish passenger with whom he had made friends, announced that they could go ashore together, as he was landing here and had obtained a special permit for Robert to accompany him. He would put him up in a hotel for the night so that he could attend a birthday party that was being held in Monte Video for his niece, Emiliana Bravos, with whom Robert had made friends on board. She was the first girl to attract him since his beloved Countess had died.

Robert was overjoyed to leave the ship, if only for one night, and soon found himself luxuriously installed in the Hotel Oriental. After changing his clothes, Robert went to the house of his Spanish host, where the dancing party was in progress in honour of his very pretty niece. Next morning, before returning to the ship, Robert posted a letter to his mother to tell her about the party, and to give her the good news of his safe arrival in the River Plate.

"My dear Mamma,

We arrived this afternoon to my tremendous joy, as I was sick up to the time we entered the River Plate. There is a revolution here, and one in Entre Rios, so we are rather uncertain as to our movements.

The last time I wrote to you I was entering the harbour at Rio de Janeiro. I don't think I ever saw so magnificent a view; you go in between high hills through a sea of islands covered with tropical vegetation. I don't think the first view of Rio is to be compared. I came ashore in a sailing boat. 'Le Petit Faust' was going on in Rio but as I had heard it three times, I withstood the temptation.

I'm afraid Entre Rios will be in a very bad condition after Urquiza's death, as they say he was about the only man who could rule the Gauchos. The rebels have been driving off the cattle from the Estancias, I believe.

Ogilvy's dog had a very rough time of it on board but is now all right.

Monte Video is very quiet and abominably cold. The landing from the steamer was perfectly dreadful as there was a *pampero* blowing. The rooms here in the hotel are alarmingly palatial, being about as big as ordinary dining-rooms in England! I have just been to the house of a

Spanish gentleman who came here in the steamer and have been dancing and eating and drinking. As the girls only danced polkas and I only danced valses, there was a pretty cursed difficulty, but we got on alright and my Spanish was fine. (I have a great talent for Portuguese! – this I think facilitated partly by my knowledge of Spanish.)

Give my love to all, and, Believe me, your affectionate son, R. B. C. Graham."

Two days later, the passengers were allowed to disembark at Buenos Aires.

The *Patagonia* had sailed the thirty miles across the great River Plate and now she lay off the town of "pleasant airs" (as the Spaniards had named it), in the thick yellow waters of the great estuary. Whale boats plied to and fro with the passengers and their baggage; once shallow water was reached they were transferred to carts drawn by three horses, with a man riding the near horse; or oxen-carts which splashed between the shoals to dry land. Most of the boatmen or porters were either Genoese or Basque, previous immigrants who had settled in the New World with their families.

At this point James Ogilvy tottered out of his cabin, blinking in the unaccustomed sunshine after his incarceration of four weeks or more, and soon it was the turn of Robert, James and Curd to descend the companion-way with their baggage, and to step into a high-wheeled cart drawn by oxen to be taken to the shore.

A horse-drawn cab took Robert, James and their luggage to Claraz's hotel, Hotel Universal, at the corner of the streets called Twenty-fifth of May and Calle de Cangallo. It was a busy spot with the life of Buenos Aires flowing round it like an eddying river. Only three squares away were the two great plazas with the Casa Rosada, the President's Palace, and the barracks; the Stock Exchange was close by, the mole[33] a stone's throw, and up the deep-cut Calle de Cangallo stood several of the principal hotels, including the best of them all, The Plaza.

The hotel Robert was taken to was run by a Swiss, who provided shelter in Buenos Aires for all his friends from "the camp." It was built all round a courtyard, with a great archway, over which were the rooms

---

[33] A long pier for shipping.

where Claraz kept his saddlery, his books and his natural-history collections, and in which he generally lived to be away from noise. The rest of the building, one storey high, looked out across the River Plate to La Colonia, thirty miles away on the opposite bank, which could only be seen on a particularly clear day.

Claraz was tall, black-haired and well-educated, with a scientific bent. He was a naturalist who frequently explored the hinterland, and had lost a finger as a result of an attack by a jaguar, or a "tiger" as it was called in these parts. Running a hotel was only a sideline to finance his botanical expeditions.

His guests were nearly all sheep-farmers and cattle-farmers, who strode into the place with Basque porters carrying their saddles, took off their pistols, hung them on their bedpost, and called loudly for drink, stamping about the brick courtyard in their long riding-boots and spurs. As all the rooms looked out onto the yard, the fashion was to leave the doors wide open and to converse, whilst lying on their beds, with anyone they knew.

In some respects the place was not unlike a school and Robert was at first reminded of Harrow – though he soon found his companions to be a great deal more stimulating than the boys he had got to know at his public school.

Emerging from his room, Robert was buttonholed by Kincaid from Patagonia who asked him if he happened to have an old copy of "The Glasgow Herald" about him, for he was "fair starved of news about the activities of the Free Church in Scotland," under which discipline he had been raised.

A few minutes later Benitez Wilson introduced himself; half-Argentine, half-English, he told how he had been sent to England to be educated, but had returned more determined than ever to carry out his lifelong ambition – to run a pulperia, or bar, in the south camp.

It was not long before Robert had discovered that this word "camp" had nothing to do with tents, but came from the Spanish word "campaña" which meant plain, or level country.

Benitez was thin, slight and dark, with long, brown hands, and feet eternally imprisoned in tight patent-leather boots, and Robert was told that he was a master of the art of throwing empty bottles when a fight arose in his frontier drinking-shop, or *pulperia*. He was also an expert in the science of gaucho racing on the flat, three squares or fifty, bare-backed and owners up. It was said that no-one from Tres Arroyos or Tandil was more cunning in the innumerable false starts and other Gaucho tricks of the race-course.

Byrne, a Porteño (the word used to describe an inhabitant of Buenos Aires) came stamping in carrying his saddle on his back, stout and highly-coloured, dressed in great thigh-boots and baggy breeches, a black silk handkerchief tied loosely round his neck, a black felt hat upon his head and a great silver watch-chain, with a snaffle bridle in the middle of it. This contrasted oddly with his broad pistol belt, with its old silver dollars for a fastening.

He was followed by a tall dark man dressed in semi-native clothes, another Porteño of Irish stock, whose original name, Docherty, had been changed by his companions to the more Castilian sounding "Duarte."

Two brothers called Witham came from Ayrshire originally, and were delighted to greet a fellow Scot. They introduced their friends Eduardo Peña, Congreve, and Eustaquio Medina, all of whom were neighbours, and had come to town for some revelry from their ranchos on the great River Yi. This was near Durazno, in the Banda Oriental, the name used for Uruguay. The conversation was all of revolution and of how the Reds and Whites were at it again, causing terrible destruction as they swept through the country engaged in their own form of guerrilla warfare.

Robert became quite confused as more and more *estancieros* hailed the two newcomers with friendly greetings. That night Robert was warned by Claraz, "Don't read too long by candle-light. The favourite sport of some of my gentlemen when they have imbibed too freely is to shoot out the candles of their fellow guests!"

Robert laughed. "Don't worry, I shall sleep like a log tonight! It's the first time for weeks that I have had a bed that keeps *still*!"

"I'm glad to have you here, Mr. Graham," said Claraz warmly, "please let this be your pied à terre whenever you come in from the camp – it's supposed to be the best club in town!"

In his own little bedroom, Robert gazed about him; an iron bed on a tiled floor, a chair, a cracked mirror, and a chest of drawers; and out in the courtyard all the company he could ever wish for. He certainly would not be lonely. Robert felt excited; his adventures were beginning, he had reached his destination at last.

Next morning the two young men boarded the river steamer for Entre Rios. All day and night the little steamer ran between islets and sandbanks and sometimes it seemed impossible that she could thread her way between the mass of floating weed which clogged the channel. Now and then the branches of the tall trees on the banks swept the deck as the vessel hugged the shore.

The river was an enormous yellow flood, flowing between high banks of rich alluvial soil, chunks of which were ever slipping with a dull splash into the stream. On every side, thought Robert, nature seemed to be overwhelming man and making him feel his insignificance. Sometimes wild horses came into sight and snorted as the steamer passed; or a gaucho, wilder than the horse he rode, with flowing hair and floating poncho, cantered along the plain where the banks were low, his horse galloping like a piece of clockwork.

In the slack water, under the lee of the islands, alligators lay like tree trunks and basked. Waterhogs called *corpincho* swam to the banks to disappear into the woods known as *montes* as the steamer approached. In the trees, flocks of green parrots chattered, and the wild cry of the strange bird known as the *chajá* sounded as it rose in the air, flapping its great wings.

In the evening the air became full of the filmy white cobweb-like filaments which, Robert was told, the north wind always brought with it, clinging from every rope and piece of rigging like cotton.

Occasionally Robert saw some deer or ostriches disappearing fast across the great brown plains; or a flock of sheep, close-herded by a small boy on a horse, because of the revolution. A party of gauchos on the steamer had told Robert that the revolution had caused the cattle to become as fierce as buffaloes. Several times he saw herds of tame mares which had run half wild, their tangled manes and tails, all knotted up with burrs, streaming out in the wind as they snorted and made off at the approach of the steamer.

Soon they reached the point where the two great rivers divided. The left fork was the Paraná, heading for Corrientes; the right-hand fork the

Uruguay, making its way towards Brazil. The area known as the "Banda Oriental," or Uruguay, lay on its right bank. The lands in between the two great rivers were called Entre Rios. It would be another twenty-four hours before they reached journey's end and the estancia of Santa Anita. James, who had sobered up considerably, sat in a deck chair smoking black cigarettes.

"We should get off the steamer by dawn tomorrow," he announced, "and the diligence[34] usually comes to meet us, so that takes care of our baggage. We'll probably stay our first night at the hotel in Gualeguaychú. That will give us time to send a message to Santa Anita to announce our arrival."

Robert knew that James really meant it would give his brothers time to sober up to greet their new partner, for he was beginning to guess that the bottle played an essential part in the lives of most of the Scots and English *estancieros*.

The steamer was now gliding from the yellow waters of the River Plate into a narrow channel over-arched with trees, which almost swept the deck. A thick white mist rose from the stream which shrouded both banks and rose half-way up the masts and funnel, leaving the tops of trees hanging like islands in the air. Upon their highest branches cormorants and vultures sat asleep, awaking as the boat past, screaming and dropping into the mist.

Over their heads hung the Southern Cross and the moon was slowly rising. Robert thought the stars seemed far more luminous and gleamed more yellow and phosphorescent than ever they did in the Northern Hemisphere.

Moths, large as humming birds, hung round the binnacle, making the helmsman curse, although his compass was a sinecure: it was the pilot who, from the bow, sounded with a cane and guided the vessel up the stream. The night was very quiet and nothing was heard but now and then the pilot's nasal cry as the stream shoaled, or the faint distant neigh of some wild stallion gathering up his mares.

Hours, which seemed as long as days, went past and still the steamer struggled with the current, pressing on into the night. At times she ran

---

[34] Stagecoach.

her nose against the bank and from the trees the mist, congealed upon the leaves, came pouring down like rain upon the awnings and the shrouds. Sometimes she grounded on a sandbank, backed, and was helped by all the crew, pushing her off with poles; shivering, she swung into the stream, strove for a minute with the hurrying water, and once more glided through the mist. The gauchos, asleep on their saddles, or *recados*, on the lower deck, stirred in their sleep, and moved a hand to reach unconsciously for their *facónes*, or knives, then fell into oblivion once more, while mosquitoes whined round their heads.

At last the mist grew lighter and the moon, sinking below the trees, showed that morning was at hand. The stars waxed paler and the air more chilly, and some of the passengers drew their ponchos close or sat up and lighted cigarettes, the white dew glistening on their blankets and their hair.

As the dawn brightened, and the star Capella fell behind the trees, the ship's whistle sounded, echoing through the woods. The vessel edged into the bank, as if by instinct, and her sides rubbed against a pier made of rough planks, almost level with the stream.

Some sleepy soldiers, smoking cigarettes, came through the mist like spectres. A man dressed in uniform stepped from the pier onto the deck, went down below, and in a little while came up again, wiping his lips with an air of having done his duty to the State.

They had arrived at Robert's destination – Gualeguaychú in Entre Rios.

PART II
GAUCHO! – 1870-1871
CHAPTER VII

Robert never forgot the first moment of disillusionment. He and James finally trotted through the great wooden gates of the Ogilvy's estancia, a few miles from Gualeguaychú in Entre Rios, Argentina, at midday the following day. If Robert had expected a warm welcome from his new partners he was to be disappointed. The place seemed to be totally deserted. There was no sign of life anywhere. Broken-down carts lay without axles, rusty cans rolled in the dust as a gentle wind blew in gusts, and tangled rawhide rope festooned empty wooden crates. A solitary horse stood mournfully attached to a hitching post, looking as if had been standing there since the Spanish conquest. It was exactly the sort of animal Don Quixote would have ridden, thought Robert ruefully; a "Rosinante" of the pampas.

James looked around him with growing irritation. It seemed that he, too, had hoped for a semblance of a greeting from his brother Edward and their Danish manager. Kicking an empty bottle which had once contained the Anchor brand of rum, known locally as *caña*, James strode towards the wooden shack which answered for an estancia dwelling-house. He kicked open the door with his boot and marched in. Robert followed, in some trepidation as to what he might find. Had there been an Indian raid, he wondered? Or had the revolution spread from Monte Video?

Peering round him in the semi-darkness he was at last able to make out two figures slumped in basket chairs, with empty bottles lying on the ground beside their feet.

James swore loudly, and his dog set up a growling, whining sound. The fair-haired Dane opened a bloodshot eye and closed it again, as though the sight of James and Robert was too much for him.

"Edward!" shouted James, angrily shaking his brother's arm as he strode up to the second man.

The slumped shape gradually seemed to come alive, and a strange lop-sided grin adorned his drunken face.

"Welcome home, my fren's. I'm getting the drinks out for you, Don Diego. Mus' have a celebration." He struggled out of his chair and lurched towards Robert with an outstretched hand. Robert shook it politely and found that he was being used as a support, as Edward clung to him for dear life.

"Been waiting for your arrival," Edward murmured, "Hope you've brought some rum with you?" James caught his brother by the shoulders and shook him.

"Rum? Rum! Is that all you can think about? What's happened to the place? Where are the cattle and the horses?"

Edward murmured something about them being in the pastures, which made James even more angry.

"Who's out there herding them, may I ask?" He strode out of the shack, beckoning Robert to follow him. Round behind the dwelling house were the stables, and there had gathered the *peóns* (ranch-hands), playing *truco* – a card game – to while away the time until their masters sobered up. Their own horses were tethered nearby. James had a long conversation with the *capataz*,[35] in gaucho Spanish, and it transpired that some of the horses had already been stolen, but the rest were still grazing with the cattle nearby.

James, who was called Don Diego by the *peóns*, quickly mounted again, and he and Robert galloped out with them to the pastures to bring back the remaining horses and cattle.

Robert soon realised that the estancia was not only badly run down, but was going from bad to worse. Perhaps he and James could try to get the place back on its feet again, as long as James didn't fall for 'the demon drink' like his brother.

For the next few months Robert did his best to learn his new job, and to help the *capataz* and the *peónes* do to theirs. Edward and the manager were no use at all, and it was not long before James gave up trying. Soon he too was consoling himself with *caña*.

Then came the revolution, and one night the guerrillas drove off all the remaining horses.

---

[35] Foreman.

Robert wrote to his mother on 10th February 1871 to tell her about a discussion he had had with James, in one of the rare moments when the latter was sober. They were trying to think how to carry on in Entre Rios, what with the revolution and other difficulties.

"My dear Mamma,

I have been unable to get up country at all on account of the revolution, and I think the best thing I can do now is to come home, as I think I see my way to a good thing. The Ogilvys, having had all their cattle killed, herds destroyed, and lost everything, are planning to go about the country buying hides and wool, hoping to make immense profits in this way. They have proposed to take me into partnership, which might be thought of when I come home and can explain everything properly to you and Mr. Jamieson.

Will you ask Mr. Jamieson to send me out the money for my passage home, addressed to Gualeguaychú? The best way to send it is in a circular letter of credit on the London and River Plate Bank. Then I will start home immediately."

Mrs. Bontine tapped her foot with irritation. What was Robert up to? She certainly had not expected him home quite so soon, but it would be lovely to see him, for Argentina seemed such a long way off, and although he was now nearly nineteen, he was still very young for his age. She missed him dreadfully, especially now that Charlie had gone to sea. But this business about asking Mr. Jamieson for more money for his passage home was a nuisance.

She read on, "I went up to a little town in the camp the other day a good way from here. A very queer little place called Villaguay where there was a Jesuit Mission. It had been a thriving place once but like all Spanish American inland towns, is gradually falling into decay. I was riding a young horse through the town when he got frightened and began to buck. I should think the whole population of the town, about 50, came out to see the fun, and there were loud shouts of "*El Gringo sará al suelo!*"[36] But luckily I did not, as there were some uncommonly hard stones to fall on. The heat is getting a little less now, but still in the

---

[36] "The gringo will be on the ground!"

middle of the day it is very nearly as hot as ever. I generally 'siesta'
from about ten till six, as nothing is to be done in the afternoons.

"Have you heard from Charlie lately? I suppose he will soon be a fat
Admiral! When does he come home?

"I'm very sorry to see the news is going so much against the French.
Was Strasbourg cathedral much destroyed? Of course, out here, no one
knows anything about the European news, and the newspapers very
rarely come on account of the revolution.

"For the last three months there has not been a drop of rain so that the
camps are in a very bad state. At this place there is the only water for
leagues,[37] and it is a very curious sight to watch the wild horses, and
cattle and deer, come down to drink in thousands. They come down
with clouds of dust and a noise like thunder with the galloping on the
hard ground, and then they all bathe and jump about. I caught a fine
horse one evening there, a tame horse that had got away and had been
running a long time wild. I could do nothing with him, however,
owing to a trick he had of throwing himself over backwards and
refusing to get up again. I was obliged to let him go again."

While waiting for the money for his ticket home to arrive from the
Curator Bonis, Mr. Jamieson in Edinburgh, Robert mooned about the
estancia trying to tidy things up and keep an eye on the remaining cattle,
while the Ogilvy brothers continued their apparent never-ending drinking
bout. He had found in their very rare moments of sobriety they could be
delightful company, but most of the time they lived in a rum-induced
haze, and nothing got done on the estancia except by Robert. He began
to realise that they had invited him to join them at Gualeguaychú on
entirely false pretences; he had become their slave.

One day, Robert had taken some of the cattle to a pasture at quite a
distance from the house, where there was a pool of fresh water. Leaving
the beasts in their new pasture he started to canter back as evening fell.
Seeing a plume of smoke he rode over to investigate and saw a group of
gauchos sitting round a small fire of thistle stalks, with their horses
grazing nearby. He had never seen any of them before and wondered
what they were doing on the Ogilvy's land. They had not seen him

---

[37] A league is approximately three miles.

coming, and were engrossed in passing the *maté*[38] gourd to each other to suck on the silver mouthpiece.

Suddenly one of them leapt to his feet swinging his *bolas*. The next thing Robert knew was that his horse had gone down, and he had fallen awkwardly, hitting his head on a sharp stone. He must have temporarily blacked out, and when he came round he found that he had been tied up with thick ropes, and his horse had galloped off. He also found that his revolver had been taken away from his gaucho belt; he was completely defenceless.

More frightening still, one of the gauchos was standing over him with a knife to his throat. When he saw that Robert had come round, the man grinned and said in the gaucho dialect, "We took away your horse and your gun, but I shall not play the violin on your throat after all. Instead I will give you something to defend yourself with, for it is not safe in this country to be without a weapon. *Salud*!"

With that, he turned the handle of the knife towards Robert, who took it gratefully but with total surprise. Who were these men, and what were they doing here, he wondered? His question was immediately answered by another of the gauchos, a man with black hair and fierce eyes, who came across to help Robert to get to his feet.

"I am the captain of this band, and my name is Enrico. My father came here from Italy with Garibaldi, and we are called "the Colorados." We are fighting for the revolution which has been taking place since our President and general, Urquiza, was murdered. He was a great man, *muy gaucho*, and we do not like his successor. He does not understand our way of life on the pampa. Will you join our cause, and we will provide you with a new horse? We should like you to ride with us, for you are a brave young man."

Robert was astonished by this polite speech, but knew that he would not be given much option to refuse. He was their captive, in reality. Perhaps it would be rather more exciting than mooning about his friends' estancia.

"*Si, señor*," said Robert meekly, to be rewarded with a broad smile and a firm handshake and the question, "And you are called?"

---

[38] Maté is tea, the drinking of which is an essential part of the gaucho way of life. It is also a stimulant. It comes from the plant *Yerba maté*.

"Roberto, and from Escocia," said Robert.

Enrico smiled again.

"The name of a famous Scottish leader, Robert the Bruce, a man like our Garibaldi!" laughed the gaucho.

"Yes, you're right," agreed Robert, "and *I* am descended from Bruce's son, King Robert II of Scotland!"

"So we shall have a prince from Escocia in our band! Welcome, Don Roberto!"

After this exchange all the other members of the band came to shake Robert's hand. They seemed a cheerful bunch, and this might be quite a good adventure, thought Robert.

For the next few weeks Robert rode south with the guerrillas, driving off stock from each estancia they passed to provide themselves with their next meal, each man hacking off a lump of flesh with his facón, to his own requirement. Sometimes they encircled a village and watched as terrified women and children scuttled into their adobe huts, while the men drove their horses into the corral.

Swooping on the corral, the bandits selected the horses they required and galloped off again driving the horses before them. Robert found himself secretly enjoying the life; so far there had been no killing and he had soon established his prowess as a horseman when he survived a rough ride on a young, unbroken horse. He made special friends with the *payador,* or musician, who played the guitar by the fire each night. He had been captured like himself, and was called "Angel Cabrera." Angel toasted him in *caña* with the delighted exclamation, "Don Roberto, you are '*muy gaucho*'!"

Robert glowed with pride, for this was the highest praise he would ever receive from these wild people. He began to feel that this strange new life was far more fun than the daily round at Santa Anita. How horrified Mamma and Papa would be if they heard that he had become a guerrilla. Perhaps they would never know. He, for one, would not tell them. Young brother Charlie would be green with envy – this was much more fun than sitting up in the crow's nest off Halifax, shouting "Land ahoy!" Robert laughed involuntarily. It was unbelievably exciting to be alive, and to find himself galloping over the pampas with these ruffians.

Robert's job was mainly to help "Pancho Pajaró" (a young German whose real name was Heinricht Vögel) with the *caballada*,[39] made up of horses stolen from the villages they passed through. It was impossible to drive the horses forward singly so they were coupled in twos. For the weeks to come nothing interested Robert and Pancho but that "el Pangara" was lame, or "el Gargantillo" looked a little thin, or that "el Zaino de la hacienda" was missing in the morning from the troop.

They crossed rivers where the horses grouped together on a little beach of stones, refusing to face the stream. Sending out a yoke of pilfered oxen to swim first, they pressed on them and made them plunge, keeping dead silence, whilst one of the gauchos on the other bank called to them and whistled in a minor key. It was well known to the gauchos that horses swimming see nothing and head straight for a voice if it calls soothingly.

Kingfishers fluttered on the water's edge, herons stood motionless, and a vulture circled overhead.

Once they had their *caballada* safely on to dry land and had coupled them together once more for the journey, they continued to follow the river southwards. At night they would drive the horses into an elbow of the river and light great fires across the mouth, taking turns to sleep.

One evening, sitting by the fire eating their *charqui* (roasted or jerked meat) and smoking black cigarettes, Pancho turned to Robert and said quietly:

"This place is where they first captured me. The old devil Enrico was 'recruiting,' as he calls it, in these parts. My home, La Casa de Fierro, is only a few miles from here." He gazed wistfully across the grasslands to a small hill. "My father employed me as the book-keeper for the estancia. It is just over there," he said.

Robert followed his friend's pointing finger. The moon was rising over the hill, making it shine as though it were silver plated.

"Will you try and get back?" whispered Robert.

"I don't know," said Pancho, "it might be too risky."

---

[39] Herd of horses.

Robert looked thoughtfully at his friend. Perhaps he too was actively enjoying this strangely aimless life in the company of horses and wild Correntinos. Perhaps his life had been even harder at home.

Suddenly there was a shout from Enrico. He had seen some cattle grazing on the very hill Pancho had pointed out. The moonlight glinted on their long horns: here was a prize for the taking.

"My father's cattle," said Pancho to Robert, a grim look stealing over his face.

Each man swung into the saddle of his waiting horse, and soon they were flying over the ground with *lazos* whirling. The cattle turned and stampeded over the hill towards a cluster of adobe houses. The moon shone steadily, illuminating Pancho's home, as they pursued the cattle. A shot rang out and Robert saw a band of men emerge to leap on to their horses, defending their homelands from the wild Colorados. Little did these men realise that one of the sons of the house was riding with the bandits.

Pancho knew it was no good disobeying Enrico's orders if he wanted to stay alive. This was how loyalties were forged through fear and discipline. This was why revolutionaries showed more allegiance to their leaders than to their own families.

Robert could never quite remember what happened next, for a cloud suddenly obscured the moon and everything was confusion. A blaze of sound rang in his ears, shots mingled with the war cries of the Correntinos, while horseman grappled with horseman.

Suddenly it was all over and they were riding hell for leather back to their base, driving the stolen cattle before them. Wheeling his horse round Robert looked back to make sure they were not being pursued and it was then that he saw Pancho kneeling beside a figure on the ground.

"Hurry, Panchito! Leave the poor Correntino – there is nothing we can do for him," he shouted at his friend.

Pancho looked up at the sound of Robert's voice. His face was ashen as he gave Robert an imploring look. Robert turned back abruptly, realising that some ghastly tragedy had overtaken Pancho. He jumped off his horse and bent down to comfort Pancho who had a young man cradled in his arms. The boy was already dead; his hair, though matted with blood, was as blond as Pancho's and he bore an unmistakable resemblance to the young German gaucho. Pancho raised agonised eyes to Robert.

"It is not a Correntino, Roberto, it is my brother. I killed him with my own knife, thinking it was one of the *peóns*. I was trying to save my own skin."

"Oh my God!"

Nothing quite so terrible had ever touched Robert's life before. He was overwhelmed with the horror of the situation – supposing it had been one of his brothers – supposing he had struck down Charlie, mistaking him for an unknown *peón*?

Robert knelt beside Pancho, uselessly patting his shoulder. There was nothing to be done; he must get his friend away as quickly as possible. It would be even more terrible if his father appeared and Pancho blurted out the truth.

"Panchito, where is your horse?" he asked gently.

Pancho said nothing. He seemed not to hear as he gazed at his dead brother. Robert gently pulled the boy's poncho across his dead face.

"*Vamos, amigo*," he said firmly, raising his friend to his feet and taking him by the arm. "I will take you back on my own horse."

Somehow he managed to heave Pancho on to his horse, then leaping on himself, the two boys galloped after the Correntinos. Robert never forgot that evening in camp. Pancho seemed to be living an interminable nightmare, sometimes sitting gazing into the fire with blank, agonised grey eyes; sometimes snatching a moment of troubled sleep, to wake shaking and sweating.

Next morning Robert woke to find that his friend had gone, with the grey horse he loved to ride. He was not to see Pancho Pajaró again for another ten years.

After that unhappy incident, Robert turned more and more to Angel Cabrera for companionship. He enjoyed this exuberant rascal who considered himself something of a Don Juan. Once, after they had passed through a village where pretty girls peeped in terror at them from behind beaded curtains, they found Cabrera was missing. Enrico cursed him under his breath for the next two days, for the *payador* was one of his best men, especially with regard to catching wild horses.

Three days later, as they rode on through the grasslands, they heard thundering hooves behind them. The cloud of dust soon materialised into Angel Cabrera, with his guitar tied by a ribbon thumping on his back as he galloped. It was a hangdog Cabrera who returned to the fold, groaning with fatigue and cursing every woman since Eve.

Robert joined the general laughter as the gauchos teased Cabrera that night round the fire. Eventually the *payador* firmly turned his back on his companions and pulled his sombrero over his face to compose himself for the sleep he so badly needed. Next day he was back to his old self, proudly relating his conquests to his friends.

CHAPTER VIII

In the way things happen in South America, suddenly the revolution was over. Enrico's men felt ill at ease as they wondered how they were to pick up the threads of their old lives. Guerrilla warfare had become a way of life, bringing companionship, aggression, and adventure – three essentials to the male animal. It would not be easy to return to the uneventful life of a *peón*.

Cabrera sat moodily smoking a cigarette while Robert polished his Colt pistol. Enrico had returned it to him once he knew he had forged the young *gringo* into his band, as a loyal member of the *revolucionarios*.

Robert still did not know exactly what the revolution had been about, though he guessed that he had probably been on the wrong side. Jordán was a hothead who commanded the respect of the gauchos, a horseman and an estanciero, who understood their ways. Sarmiento was an intellectual with great vision, a man well able to lead Argentina forward in its basic search for a more liberal way of life than was possible in the mother country, Spain.

It seemed that Jordán had now capitulated to Sarmiento. Robert kept his thoughts to himself as he reflected that this was all to the good. He was now free to return to Gualeguaychú.

But back on the estancia with the Ogilvys, Robert felt a great sense of anti-climax. Suddenly a chance came to see more of the country. Some drovers came to buy cattle from the Ogilvys, and suggested to Robert that he should join them and give them a hand with driving their cattle to Durazno in Uruguay. Robert accepted with alacrity. He had come to respect the gauchos, and he did not want to leave Argentina for good. It was a wonderful life, perpetually on horseback.

The gauchos he rode with were rough-looking, but dignified, with the long dark hair and the colourful garb of the gaucho. They wore the *chiripa* (a sort of enveloping loin-cloth) caught in at the waist with a broad leather belt studded with silver coins, with the long-handled *facón*, or knife, tucked down their backs. Their black hats hung by silken cords from their necks, round which were tied bright cotton kerchiefs.

Robert felt they had something akin to the Scottish shepherd in the way they stood silently contemplating first the sky and then the grass, before they struck their bargains. He liked the smiles that suddenly lit their dark faces as they laughed to each other – probably at the plight of the innocent *estancieros*. It was all exactly like the Falkirk Tryst, back in Scotland. It was quite likely that these men had Scottish blood in their veins, for he had already heard stories about the *Protestantes*, descendants of those men who had lost everything they owned in Scotland, after the '45 Rebellion, fighting for their king and (ironically) for the Catholic faith. These gauchos often had names like Maldonaldo, Camerón, McIntýre, McLéan or Fergusón, all pronounced in the Spanish way, with the final syllable taking the accent, and none of them speaking a word of their ancient language, *el Gallico*.

The two drovers Robert was now riding with were the Scottish brothers, Don Guillermo and Don Tomas Witham, whom he had met when he first arrived in Buenos Aires.

Robert was paid off by the drovers in Durazno and made his way back by himself on his horse to Gualeguaychú and to the Ogilvys' estancia.

By the time he returned, Robert was now beginning to realise that there were plenty of adventures to be had, and perhaps he should stay on after all? But he had no time to write to his mother when he got back to Gualeguaychú, for he had no sooner arrived than he found an urgent message asking him to take a vital remedy to a neighbouring estancia, where the *estanceiro* lay desperately ill. It was thought he had typhus fever.

A *pampero* was blowing, for it was approaching mid-winter in the southern hemisphere, and an icy wind pierced Robert's poncho as he set out for Bland's estancia, some fifteen or sixteen leagues from Gualeguaychú. The cold rain poured off the brim of his sombrero down his neck. Reaching a small river he had to cross, he found it in flood and had to make his horse swim to the opposite bank. He was drenched to the skin by now, and freezing cold. He realised that the river was rising so fast that he would be unlikely to be able to get back across it on his return journey. He would probably have to stay at Bland's estancia until the *pampero* blew itself out, which might not be for several days.

Robert was greeted rapturously on his arrival by Bland's Indian wife, who had been beside herself with anxiety. She hurried him to a blazing fire, where he took off his dripping clothes and wrapped himself in a thick blanket. She assured him that his horse would be cared for by the *peónes*; then she hurried off to give her husband the medicine that Robert had brought.

After a hot meal, Robert was shown to a comfortable bedroom, but somehow he could not get warm. He must have been chilled literally to the bone on his ride. Next morning he woke up feeling even worse, and by the evening he knew that he was seriously ill. For four days he tossed and turned and shivered, while Bland's wife and daughters attended to his every need, with large, frightened eyes. Bland himself had made a speedy recovery once he started to take the medicine, but now they were all far more worried about young 'Don Roberto.' Robert had never felt like this before, and wondered if he was going to die.

A doctor had been summoned to see Bland, but he had not been able to reach the estancia because of the swollen rivers. He was a Scots doctor called Forbes, from Concepcion del Uruguay, some way up-river from Gualeguaychú. He could usually reach most of his patients over his huge 'parish' by river-boat and horse, but the rivers were all in flood. It was nearly a week before he finally got through, to find his original patient, Bland, already up and about, but young Robert barely conscious.

He quickly diagnosed typhus fever, probably caught when the boy's resistance was low after his exhausting ride from Gualeguaychú at the height of the storm. For the next six weeks Bland and his Indian wife nursed Robert devotedly, and Dr. Forbes stayed on through the crisis. James and Edward Ogilvy were sent for, for all they all feared they might lose the boy.

In his delirium Robert called out to 'Charlie' and 'Mal,' and talked to the dogs and ponies of his childhood.

There was one terrible night when they all feared that he would not survive. At the moment of crisis, he suddenly called out, "No, Papa! Put the sword down! No, no, no! Run, Mamma, he is after you …….. no …….. Papa …… please ….. no……no."

Just as suddenly his strange terror receded, leaving Bland mystified and alarmed. Soothingly he wiped Robert's sweating brow with a cool cloth, talking gently to him as to a child having a nightmare. Robert's fever left him that night, and he fell into a deep sleep. From that moment he began his slow recovery.

When he was better, Robert was invited to spend his convalescence at Concepcion del Uruguay by Dr. Forbes, who had treated him in his illness, and who was glad to have the young Scots boy for companionship. He found his erstwhile young patient both intelligent and amusing.

It was now 20th August 1871.

James Ogilvy sent a reassuring letter to Robert's mother.

"Dear Mrs. Bontine,

I received your letter of 7th July a few days ago, and am very glad to be able tell you that the last time I saw your son, which is about a fortnight ago, he was very much better, though he has been very seriously ill. For two months my brother and I took the best care of him we could at the estancia, and as soon as he could bear the journey we got a carriage to convey him to Dr. Forbes' house in Concepcion del Uruguay, where he is at present. I have advised him to go home as soon as he is strong enough to bear the journey, which I expect he will soon be now, as after such a severe illness it would scarcely be prudent for him to knock about any more in this country. I believe he intends returning home.

I got three letters for him the other day, which I have forwarded to him. The postmarks on the envelopes were Feb. and March, the mistake I saw was addressing them to Monte Video, which is the capital of the Banda Oriental, and as there has been a revolution there for about two years, or more, I expect the letters have lain there for some time. Revolutions in the S. American Republic are of too frequent occurrence, as my Brother and I have found out to our cost, to induce anyone to invest much capital in them, at all events in stock, and I am afraid there is no hope of getting any compensation from the Government for losses, as the Argentine Minister says he will pay no claim for any damage done by the rebels, and the same with regard to the National forces, unless you have receipts.

He also stated that he considered foreigners in some degree as rebels for carrying on business in a province which was in rebellion against the National Government.

You must excuse me as posting a letter is different to what it is in England, especially as the estancia where your son was taken ill is about 15 or 16 leagues from town. I intend going over to Concepcion del Uruguay in a few days and when I see your son will show him your letter.

Believe me,
      yrs very truly, James Ogilvy."

Meanwhile, at Concepcion del Uruguay, Robert was growing stronger day by day, and Dr. Forbes noticed that he was already growing restless, which was a good sign. It would be good for him to see a bit more of the country before he returned home, the doctor suggested. He had a friend, another Scots doctor, who would be glad to have him to stay. Stewart's brother was the Honorary Consul in Asunción, where he had a *quinta*[40]; but he also had another even more attractive *quinta* in Misiones called Potrero San Antonio, Forbes explained.

If Robert travelled by river-boat up the Uruguay River to Ibicuy, then it would be a short ride, with an Indian guide, to Dr. Stewart's *quinta*. The doctor would certainly be there, because, since the terrible war of the Triple Alliance in Paraguay, when Stewart was military surgeon to the President, he had left Asunción because it was now occupied by the Brazilians.

Robert felt the 'sap' rising again, for the first time since his illness. Here was another chance to see more of this fascinating country.

A week later Robert found himself riding up a steep banked trail that wound for nine miles until it reached Dr. Stewart's house. Small palms, known locally as *yatais*, fringed the lane, and from deep woods on either side Robert could hear the shrill croak of frogs and a great humming sound of insects. The orange trees gave out an oppressive scent as the leaves stirred in the warm north wind. Robert rode with his revolver in his hand in case a jaguar should suddenly drop from a tree.

---

[40] The Brazilian (Portuguese) word for *estancia*

Half way down the lane Dr. Stewart was waiting for them on his horse, to guide them to his home. News of travellers speeds ahead quickly in countries where every lone horseman must be investigated closely before being welcomed to the ever-hospitable hearth.

The doctor sat his horse rather stiffly, very straight in the saddle, due to his early training as a military doctor in the Crimea. He was middle-aged, dapper, alert, with reddish hair turning grey and clear, steel-grey eyes which twinkled like stars on a frosty night. When he spoke, it was with the strong Galashiels accent which he had never lost.

He greeted Robert warmly, asking whether he had regained his health, and what he thought of the dangers of life in South America? Robert told him that he was enjoying it all hugely, had never felt better, and hoped soon to have a good head of hair once again.

As they rode down the sandy lane together, Dr. Stewart talked to Robert of his own life, and of his strange part in the recent revolution in Paraguay. He had got to know the President, Lopez, and his courageous mistress, Madame Lynch (an Irish lady of good family) very well indeed. He had been deeply distressed by the various tragedies she had suffered at the end of the war.

The President had been selfish and cowardly, and the whole terrible War of the Triple Alliance seemed to have started because he imagined himself to be a sort of South American reincarnation of Napoleon. After his death, the doctor helped Madame Lynch to flee the country, but one of her brave young sons was shot as they left. She was now living in London with her remaining children, in great poverty.

The lights of the house came into view at the edge of a peach grove, and a troop of dogs rushed out barking, to seize the horses' tails as they trotted up to the verandah.

Robert was soon relaxing in a hot bath with a glass of *caña* at his elbow. Coming downstairs in a fresh shirt, with his hair well brushed in the places where it had started to grow, Robert was greeted by a beautiful fair-haired woman in her late forties, standing smiling at the bottom of the stairs. This was obviously William Stewart's wife, Venancia.

Robert was amazed by her blonde hair, for she was the first fair-haired South American he had ever met. She explained that her family had originally come from northern Spain, with some Portuguese blood added, and Robert realised that she was a perfect partner for her Scottish husband, her Latin ancestry tempered with the characteristics of the Galician race. They seemed very happy together, although they had no children.

After a sumptuous dinner with fine Chilean wines, Dr. Stewart poured out glasses of port for himself and his young guest, and they talked of a journey Robert could make to Asunción, to see some more of this fascinating country, before he returned to Scotland.

CHAPTER IX

A few days later, Robert was provided with a horse and an Indian guide to take him on his expedition to Asunción. He felt fit and strong once more, and was looking forward to a new adventure.

As they rode through the thick woods, they saw alligators lying partially submerged in small creeks; and, as they approached a dark backwater, they suddenly caught a glimpse of a jaguar stretched out on a log over the water, watching the fish below, just as a cat lies beside a goldfish pond.

On their third day, starting well before dawn, they encountered long lines of white-clad women, barefooted, marching as silently as ghosts to attend a great feast-day in Santa Maria Mayor. They were all smoking their great green cigars as they marched along, their leader carrying a torch through the darkness. As dawn broke they arrived at the crossing of a little river where the women bathed and gathered flowers to stick in their hair.

At last the procession reached the town, and the silence in the woods turned to the chattering of a thousand parrots in a maize field. Men arrived on horseback and tied their horses to the rings on wooden posts that stood in the shade of the great plaza, slackening their broad hide girths, and piling up before them the heaps of the leaves of the palm, called *pindo* in Guarani, till the horses were cool enough to eat their corn.

Sometimes the women took the little undersized Paraguayan horses down to bathe in the river, to comb their manes and tails with loving care, for horses had become most valuable now that so few were left in the country because of the war.

The square was soon filled with a seething mass of humanity, predominantly female, both women and children smoking continuously. Suddenly, some Correntino gauchos galloped into the middle of the square, wearing their national costume of loose black merino trousers stuffed into long boots embroidered in red silk; red silk handkerchiefs tied loosely round their necks, vicuna ponchos, and their saddles and bridles ornamented heavily with silver.

At noon, when the sun was almost burning a hole in Robert's head, he noticed a band getting ready in the church porch and soon they were processing round the square, playing on the strangest assortment of ancient musical instruments. They were followed by the Alcalde,[41] an ancient Indian, dressed in long cotton drawers split into a fringe that hung from his knees to his ankles, a spotless shirt much pleated and a red cloak of fine merino cloth. In his right hand he held his badge of office – a long cane with a silver head, and with this he gave the signal for the "running at the ring."

The ring itself dangled from an arch on a piece of string. The competitors attempted to dislodge it with their lances as they galloped towards it. Robert had never before seen this ancient feat performed, and he remembered the line in his ancestor Robert Graham of Gartmore's love poem, "for you I'd ride the ring." He knew it had once been the sport of kings and knights, in the days of chivalry.

Robert watched fascinated as the Correntinos gave a brilliant display of riding, passing right through the middle of the square at a wild gallop, and then swinging down sideways from their saddles to drag their hands upon the ground; back into their seats, still at full gallop, they suddenly reined up, making their horses plunge and rear and then stand quietly in line, tossing the foam into the air. This display was greeted with enthusiastic cheers from the crowd, after which everyone went to bathe in the river, or to slumber through the heat of the day in swinging cotton hammocks slung between trees.

After the event, Robert was taken off by an Italian, another Clerici, (not related to the guerrilla who had recently captured Robert) who had settled in the area to run a *pulperia*, or store, at Ytapua, and who had come over to see the fun. They drank *caña* together, while Clerici told Robert how he, too, like many other Italians, had once fought for Garibaldi in Uruguay, and the Italian's eyes gleamed as he spoke of his hero. The place seemed full of Italians who had fought with him, Robert thought, remembering Enrico, the captain of the revolutionary band who had briefly captured him.

---

[41] Mayor.

Next day, Robert and his guide rode on towards Asunción. They rode beneath the trees, looking up at purple bunches of *ceibos* where humming-birds seemed to nestle, so rapid was their flight; and over all a darkish vapour hung, blending the trees and water as one.

Several days after leaving Stewart's *Quinta*, Potrero San Antonio, they rode into a clearing where once there had been a village or Jesuit mission. There, Robert and his guide were given a meal by some of the women of the place – jerked beef stewed with rice and pepper, and sprinkled with mandioca flour, which they consumed in a cloud of insects.

Oranges and mandioca had become the staple diet of these people since the war, jerked beef being a great luxury kept for special occasions. To entertain a handsome young man was indeed a special occasion, for the female population was now roughly thirteen to every man – nearly all their menfolk having been killed in the long struggle with Brazil.

It was strange to find women doing men's jobs. In one village Robert encountered an old Indian who had been made Mayor. She wore a European footman's hat, and carried a long cane with a silver top as her badge of office. Most of the Paraguayan women wore the coarse white cotton shift known as the *tupoi*, though sometimes even these were scarce.

As they approached another village, Robert heard shrieks of feminine fluster, and saw the naked women disappearing into their houses. A few minutes later he was greeted by one who had donned the only *tupoi*[42] to be found during the preceding flurry, and who graciously invited him to spend the night in her house.

In other villages Robert found women gathering the crops, tending flocks, shooting, fishing, hunting, and doing all the tasks that their menfolk would have performed in happier times. But their *yerbales* (the plants which produced *Yerba maté*, a form of laurel*)* were left untended for trade in *yerba maté*, or green tea, had come to a standstill.

As Robert rode on, he wondered who could be persuaded to come and get this fascinating country on its feet again after the disastrous war? Scots colonists, perhaps, or maybe Yankees? On the other hand, the

---

[42] Dress.

Spanish and Portuguese seemed to adapt best of all to South America, and there would not be so great a language problem. Dr. Stewart had told him that the government of Paraguay badly needed foreign investment.

Resting a while on the river bank while his horse cropped grass beside him, Robert imagined the house he would build for himself. Perhaps he should have a little colonial house on one floor, with large, cool rooms, an oval drawing-room, and a long curving verandah. Mosquitoes sang in his ears and the parrots screeched in the trees above as he dozed off, dreaming of himself as a colonist on the Alto Parana.

Four days later, after passing Quirindy and splashing through the swamps of Acaai, Robert saw Paraguari in the distance with its saddle-shaped mountain, which stood out as a landmark for leagues upon the level plain. Here was Paraguay's only railway, known as the *Maquina-guazu*. Once the train would have been filled with rawhide sacks of *yerba*, bales of tobacco, and food; but now business was at a standstill and it puffed the six hours to Asunción packed with a human cargo in search of work.

The train stopped when Robert was sighted, but he declined the offer to take both him and his horse aboard, and headed on for Aregua, where he was given a bed for the night by a drunken Scotsman. The man seemed to have several wives, but his chief complaint was that his wives were all Catholics and now and then they trudged off to mass, leaving him without anyone to cook his food. He had never managed to convert them to the Protestant faith of his youth, he said. Robert's host was half-drunk all the time, but extremely hospitable, and soon had some women cutting *pindo* for his guest's horse, telling them to take the horse down to the water to bathe him.

Next morning, as Robert rode into Asunción, the place seemed buried in vegetation and the sandy streets ran with water after a night's unexpected rain. There were great unfinished palaces, squares with uncut grass growing five or six inches tall, donkeys straying to and fro, with women everywhere, white-robed, and with their hair hanging down the backs and cut square on the forehead. A sandy street merged into a great market full of people, the noise of their chattering startled Robert, after riding for so many days across solitary plains and dark silent woods, alone with his guide.

William Stewart's brother, George, a lawyer and the Honorary British Consul, gave Robert board and lodging for the next few weeks. In the evenings they would talk over the *caña*, while the sweat poured down their faces from the perpetual humidity, and Robert learned that the best thing he could do if he wanted to help the people of Paraguay was to go back to London and persuade someone there to invest in the neglected *yerbales*, which were still capable of producing a valuable export if properly farmed. Robert decided he would have a try. It was the only way he would ever get back to this fascinating country.

After spending a week in Asunción, Robert rode back to Potrero San Antonio to return Dr. Stewart's horse, and to thank him for giving him the opportunity to see a small part of Paraguay before returning home. Robert confessed to the doctor that the trip had made him long, more than ever, to stay in this wonderful country; but as his money was fast running out, and there was obviously no future for him on the Ogilvys estancia, it looked as though he would have to sail home again shortly.

Dr. Stewart had taken a great liking to the young Scots boy, and felt he was just the sort they needed to help colonise Paraguay and to develop the *yerbales*. Surely Robert must know some men of business in London who could invest in the country? Then he could come back and help the Stewart brothers to get concessions from the government, and bring some colonists with him. Was this just a castle in the air, Robert wondered? It was worth a try, he told the doctor, *anything* was worth a try if it would bring him back to South America!

A few days later Robert set out to return to Gualeguaychú. Dr. Stewart watched Robert cantering through the orange trees with his stylish seat, looking so much like one of the old prints of Cortez or Pizarro. No wonder his own Paraguayan wife had referred to this young Scot a "muy caballero."

"Good luck, Don Roberto!" he called out after the boy, and Robert turned to salute the old Scots doctor with a cheerful wave, before disappearing into the thick palm-woods.

CHAPTER X

Robert stopped off at Dr. Forbes' in Concepcion del Uruguay on his way back to Gualeguaychú. The doctor was delighted to see Robert looking so well. Would he like one further trip before he returned to England, Dr. Forbes asked? He needed a *tropilla* of mules fetching from Cordoba – Robert might like the opportunity to see the great Andes mountains, under which Cordoba lay.

Robert could not resist the offer. But first he must return to Gualeguaychú to tell the Ogilvys his plans, and to see if there was any mail waiting for him. Guiltily, he knew he should have written to his mother, but James had assured him that he had already written to her, to explain about his illness, once he realised she had been frantically writing to the Consuls for news of her son.

On reaching Gualeguaychú, two months after he had set off to stay with Dr. Forbes, Robert found the estancia had gone from bad to worse. 'Don Diego' (James) had been drinking so hard that he now had D.T.s and his brother Edward (who had pulled himself together somewhat, realising that one of them had to cope) suggested to Robert that he had better take James back to Scotland with him. Robert dreaded another journey like the last: perhaps James would have mended his ways by the time Robert came back from his trip to Cordoba, and then he could stay out in Argentina with Edward.

Angel Cabrera had stayed on in Gualeguaychú, and the next day he came to the Ogilvys, bringing some horses with him to sell. He offered to escort Robert to Cordoba. Robert was delighted, especially as they could now sell Angel's horses in Cordoba. Angel was one of the best horsemen he had ever known. He was an amusing fellow, too, and would be good company on the trip, for he was full of gaucho sayings and proverbs. During the revolution he had liked to sing great Argentine epics to his guitar, as they sat round their fire of thistles at night, smoking black cigarettes and passing round the *maté*.

Cabrera was also known for his talent in lassoing stray horses, and hastily branding them with the brand of his current employer. (Robert had been given his own brand when he worked with the drovers, and was proud to see that it closely resembled the brand of Urquiza, who had been the gauchos' hero until he was murdered the year before Robert's arrival in Argentina.) Robert and Angel would now have a round trip of nearly a thousand miles ahead of them, riding to Cordoba by way of Rosario, where they would cross the great Paraná river. But the strong criollo horses could easily manage fifty miles a day over the great grasslands of the pampas, though it would be slower on the way home with the *tropilla* of mules to drive to Concepcion del Uruguay for Dr. Forbes. Robert estimated that he and Angel would probably be away for a month altogether.

Before setting out, Robert put pen to paper and wrote his long over-due letter to his mother.

"Gualeguaychú. 10th October 1871.

My dear Mother

I arrived here last night and saw your letter to Don Diego. I will come home with him soon, but I cannot come until I have been to Cordoba. Horses are very scarce there. The Indians carry off all they can lay their hands on, also there is an exhibition there and great quantities of foreigners are in the city for it.

I have bought thirty or forty horses at twenty dollars apiece, and hope to sell them there for eighty to a hundred dollars each. I have also hired a man to help me take up the horses. I expect to be away a month and I will try to come home as soon as I return. Poor Don Diego, who has lost all of his cattle, horses, and everything else, with the war, has taken to drinking and is in a state bordering on Delirium Tremens. His brother and I have been trying to get him out of town, but it is no use.

I have just come from a part of the country called the Ibicuy, an old Indian camp. It is by far the most curious country I ever saw. Sometimes you have to go for miles crawling through the thick woods leading your horse. The woods are perfectly swarming with humming birds (picaflores) and there are carpinchos (water-hogs) and all sorts of 'tigers' (jaguars), some of them very fat.

I am getting much stronger again but am still a fearful object without any hair. I have got you a good many skunk skins, but not quite enough yet. I am going to bring you some 'lobo' skins, which are very pretty. I had a very bad fall the other day from a wild horse which I foolishly mounted before I was strong enough. The brute fell on top of me and squashed me a good deal. A man gave me a pair of black horses, what they call 'Seguidores' – that is, when a horse is being ridden the other runs after him loose. They are worth a good deal of money as they are very hard to train.

Give my best love to Mal, Ganama, and dear Cat.

Believe me, yr. affec. son, R. C Graham."

Amongst Robert's mail from England there was a letter from his younger brother Charlie, who was serving as a midshipman on board H.M.S. Royal Alfred, based in Halifax, Nova Scotia. The ship had recently been cruising in more southerly waters, and Charlie described 'a very jolly stay in Havana.' He had been to a Ball, and the Opera, and a bull-fight – "I do not think I shall ever go out of my way to see another, they killed six bulls, one man, and several horses."

His ship had now reached Chesapeake Bay: "the Yankee Naval Academy is here, that is why we came as the Admiral wants to see it."

His letter ended with the words, "I am very glad to hear that you are now all right again. I hope I shall see you when I next come home, which will not be till next year, I am afraid."

Robert suddenly realised how much he missed old 'Tarlee,' what a pity they could not have ridden to Cordoba together. It was strange that they were both travelling in the New World, with its many Spanish connections. How pleased Ganama Catalina must be!

Robert put aside his temporary bout of homesickness and prepared for the journey ahead. He was never to forget the month he spent in the company of Angel Cabrera as they rode across the grasslands, through an ocean of tall grass, turning yellow as the hot weather approached. A ceaseless wind stirred the waves of grass, amongst which stood herds of pale yellow deer and bands of ostriches – known by the gauchos as 'Mirth of the Desert.' Cabrera taught Robert to use the *bolas* – the three small stones wrapped in raw-hide, hanging from long hide ropes, which the gauchos used to fell ostriches, deer, and even the wild horses which would form part of their *tropilla* once they were tamed.

As they rode, the *tero-tero* bird circles above their horses' heads with its repetitive cry, and from every *monte*, or wood, flew chattering flocks of parakeets. Solemn little owls sat at the entrance to the burrows made by the *viscachas*[43] and oven-birds made small muddy nests on fence-posts.

In that great ocean of grass it was true that "he who wanders from the trail is lost," and Angel taught Robert to sleep with his feet pointing in the direction they must start next morning. Their ponchos kept them warm at night, and their sheepskin saddles made comfortable pillows.

The horses Robert and Angel were driving were all criollos, the indigenous horse of the pampas which came from the thirteen mares and three stallions which Pedro de Mendoza left behind when he sailed back to Spain after his first attempt to colonise. These were the horses that roamed the pampas now, for there had been a long interval with no horses after the Tertian eight-toed horse died out, and before the Spanish Conquistadores brought horses back to Argentina in the sixteenth century.

In Cordoba the horses were soon sold, and Dr. Forbes's mules located for the homeward journey. Angel Cabrera knew many of the gauchos who had gathered in the city for the great exhibition, and Robert joined them to drink *maté* and smoke black cigarettes once the horses were satisfactorily disposed of.

It was there that they met some Chilean horsemen who told them they would be setting off the next day to ride back over the Andes to Santiago with the horses they had bought. Would Don Roberto like to join them for the first part of the journey? It would be a great experience for him, they assured him.

Robert could not resist the invitation, and during the next few days he and Angel found themselves starting the slow and arduous climb up the rocky valleys with white peaks glittering in the bright blue sky far above them. At the height where mountain sickness was likely to strike, the Chileans gave Robert and Angel cloves of garlic to suck, and they kept at an unhurried pace so that the horses would not be affected. As the weather was clear and bright they were fortunate that there were no *viento blanco*, or blizzards.

Eventually they reached a point where a second trail made its way back down the mountains, and Robert and Angel said goodbye to their

---

[43] A type of water rodent, similar to (but larger than) a chinchilla.

new friends. Even though they would never cross the mountain pass into Chile, they both felt that this unexpected expedition had been something they would never forget. Looking back at the towering peaks they could not believe that they had negotiated the steep rocky trails with no ill effects. What a contrast to the flat grasslands of the pampas!

Robert and Angel arrived at Concepcion del Uruguay with Dr. Forbes's mules. After delivering them to him, Robert said farewell to Angel Cabrera and took the river steamer back to Gualeguaychú.

CHAPTER XI

When Robert arrived back at the estancia, Edward Ogilvy took him aside and explained that his brother now had frightful D.T.s, and must return to Scotland. Would Robert escort him, as he intended to go home quite soon? Robert's heart sank, but he agreed he would be prepared to do so if they could get James "dried out" before they left. Fortunately he found a letter awaiting him from Mr. Jamieson, enclosing the cheque for his fare back to Glasgow.

Robert started to make inquiries as to the cheapest way to get back across the Atlantic, and found that he could get a cheap ticket if he was prepared to get them both to New York and from there sail to Glasgow on board a coaling ship. Robert felt he could cope with anything after his recent adventures with the guerrillas, so was delighted to find how cheaply he could travel; he might even buy a return ticket, and sail straight back to South America with the same ship two weeks later on her return trip. That would give him enough time to visit his mother, and have talks in London with the firm of tea-importers who might commission him to do a survey of the *yerbales* in Paraguay. There was the possibility of getting a concession from the Paraguayan government in Asunción, with the help of the Stewart brothers, the Honorary Consul and the Doctor.

James was duly "dried out" and kept locked up until they sailed. The first part of the trip would be in a coaster from Monte Video to New York, where they would join the coaling ship and sail for Glasgow. James's family had been contacted to meet him on arrival, and Robert would take the train to London. The whole enterprise would only take a couple of months, and he would soon be back in the country to which he had now lost his heart – Paraguay – and with his new friends, the Stewarts.

They got James safely on board the coaster at Monte Video, but he got ashore at Rio, where they had to stop for a night en route for New York, and undid all the good of his recent "drying out" within four of five hours. Robert therefore had to lock him in his cabin for several days after leaving Rio, and even then the language that poured out in a torrent could be heard throughout the small ship.

Soon after leaving New York the full force of a north-easterly gale hit the coaling ship and Robert was immediately prostrated, unaware that his cabin was awash, with his portmanteau banging to and fro in a foot of water. On the fifth day out, the cargo of coal shifted and the ship seemed to lie almost broadside on to the huge seas for several hours on end. The timbers groaned, the wind roared, and Robert was dimly aware of the pattering of naked feet upon the deck above as he dozed fitfully; only to awake when the steward came in with a cup of arrowroot and whisky, and the news that everything was battened down and the skipper looking like Lot's wife after sixteen hours on the bridge.

The air in Robert's tiny cabin was stifling, water dripped on his pillow, rats ran across the floor and crumbs of biscuit lurked in his bed-clothes. A futile tin basin floated in the cabin and candles swung gutter-ing in the gimbels. In the fixed wash-stand a brandy bottle was wedged between a Bible and a sponge.

Robert lay in a state of suspended animation between sleeping and waking. The dense, steamy atmosphere was unbearable. Struggling on deck he was astounded to find that yards of bulwarks had been swept away, doors were torn off their hinges, the smoke-stack had fetched loose, and the rigging was a mass of tatters with halyards flying loose. The boats and the jackstaff had been washed away days earlier.

The Captain, clad in dripping oilskins, with a speaking trumpet in his hand, was practically asleep on his feet. Clutching a lifeline, Robert struggled to the engine-room, sitting awhile to listen to the yarns of the chief engineer, a bushy-bearded man from Greenock, who had "gone out east in '47, second engineer aboard the craft what took out Rajah Brook."

Then back in bed again, Robert comforted himself with his battered copy of the "Faerie Queen," and lay half awake as the ship continued to roll and pitch through the night, while he dreamt about the adventures of Sir Satyrane of Britomart, Parlante, and the Faire Florimell. The roaring of the wind and the shouting of the boatswain eventually became con-fused in his mind with the bellowing of the Blatant Beast.

When at last the ship docked at Glasgow at the end of October, 1871, James was met by his family and Robert caught the first train to London. He could only stay in London for ten days, to see his mother and to have talks with a firm of Tea Importers, Messrs. Holland & Jacques, for his ship was due to sail once more on 29th November. To his great delight he found out from Mr. Ross Groves of Holland & Jacques that they would be prepared to commission him to make a survey of the concessionary lands in Paraguay on their behalf, and would pay his fare to and from South America and any necessary expenses. He had won the first stage of the battle.

Two weeks after his arrival home he boarded the coaling ship once more, at Glasgow (where she had been refitted on the Broomielaw to repair the massive storm damage), with a sense of excitement, for the voyage back to Monte Video.

His mother knew that he had lost his heart to South America, and that his *yerba maté* project was the most important thing in his life at this moment. She felt sure it was just the thing to occupy him until he could take over the running of Gartmore. Missy only hoped he could bring it off, for she could not believe that Robert would ever be one of the world's best business men, he was far too impetuous and impatient.

The only incident on the trip back to Monte Video was when Robert nearly lost his life at the hands of an inebriated French emigrant who followed him up the rigging and drew a knife on him. Fortunately the first officer was on deck and was able to lure the Frenchman down; and, having been threatened with being put in irons, the emigrant soon sobered down and apologised to Robert. For the rest of the voyage the Frenchman seldom left Robert's side, addressing him as *mon brave,* and *mon cher.*

At New York, the Captain said he had a cargo to take from New York to Monte Video so he would be going on south. Robert was delighted, as it meant he would not need to change ships.

New Year's Eve found the ship within a few days' sailing of Rio. The Scottish crew managed to celebrate hogmanay in the traditional manner, although no one ever found out where their supply of whisky had come from. Soon both officers and men were "a wee bit overcome" – and fighting broke out.

A French steward, who had sailed with Robert on his previous journey in the "Patagonia," gave him a hand to lock the purser into his cabin, and several of Robert's emigrant friends helped to sail the ship until the Scottish crew were fit to play their part once more.

CHAPTER XII

Robert arrived back in Paraguay at Asunción, in time for his 20th birthday on 24th May 1872. It was getting dark as he dismounted at Casa Horrocks, where he had stayed on his first visit to Paraguay. He had spent three months in Buenos Aires, enjoying the summer months, and some of his old friends at Claraz's hotel.

The house stood at the junction of one of the sandy side streets and a deserted plaza, overgrown with castor-oil plants, bounded by ruined houses on one side, and on the other by a hedge of orange trees, in which the fireflies were starting to glisten as darkness fell. It was built round a courtyard with doors of solid urunday[44], studded with wrought-iron nails. Inside there was scant furniture, no beds but hammocks made of ornamental cotton with long lace fringes swinging in every room on to the pillars of the court. Enormous Spanish leather chairs were scattered around, and heavy tables, each bearing a porous jug of water, on the outside of which by night and day thick drops of moisture hung. There were no pictures or clocks, but the walls were dazzling with whitewash on the inside, and the outer walls were coated with saffron-coloured paint, so that the Casa Horrocks shone like a ripe banana.

Across the river lay the mysterious land of the Chaco, with its palms, its billows of waving pampas grass, and its are of prediluvian impregnability.

Robert stood at his window looking out across the Chaco as the last coppery light of the setting sun dipped below the waving palms. He thought of the lonely camping grounds of his last trip with Cabrera, the open plains and the wild gallops in the dark, bending close to his horse's warm coat as the animal flung out his head and streaked through the night.

In Asunción by the end of May, everything was the same as before: half-finished palaces, standing under the hot sun amongst orange groves, petty officials carrying out their bureaucracy with wholehearted self-importance, Brazilian soldiers lounging round the town, and the great Paraguay River astir with river traffic and guarded by the Brazilian

---

[44] Astronium Fraxinifolium, a highly durable hardwood

Navy. The rumours in the liquor stores were all of the coming of a new man to lead the country, the foremost hero among the handful of distinguished Paraguayans to survive the war, one Bernadino Cabellero.

Everyone told Robert that Caballero was exactly the right man to take the country out of the clutches of the Brazilian army of occupation. He was a conservative of great influence, they all said, and with his crony General Patricio Escobar to help him, he could not fail. There was a mood of great optimism abroad.

Robert's first call was on the Honorary British Consul, his friend George Stewart. Both the Stewart brothers were in the Consul's office that day, the doctor having just come back to Asunción to spend some time in another *quinta* he owned just outside the town. He had received a letter from Robert telling him of the interest of Mr. Ross Groves, of Holland & Jacques, in the *yerbales* of Alcorta, a Brazilian contractor, and Stewart wanted to be on hand when young Graham returned to Asunción from London.

The first thing Robert must do, said William Stewart, was to meet the President.

"Me? Meet the President myself?" asked Robert in surprise.

"Oh yes," said the doctor airily, "he's nothing and nobody; his name is Salvador Jovellanos, just a trumped-up Paraguayan soldier, and a puppet of the Brazilian government. If Caballero manages to dislodge him, now *there's* a man to reckon with! The Brazzies will be off with their tails between their legs as soon as he sets foot in the Presidential palace, I can assure you! But meanwhile we have to deal with this poor figure of fun! I'll make an appointment for you to call on him tomorrow, then we can start the ball rolling. There is so much bureaucracy these days in Asunción that it's bound to be several months before you can start off on the survey. If you get fed up waiting around, I'll send you down to Potrero San Antonio to fetch back a troop of mules I need up here."

Robert thanked the doctor warmly and settled down with his lawyer brother, George, to go carefully over the details of the concessionary document. He wanted to send off his first report to Holland & Jacques as soon as possible. It seemed strange to be sitting in their office in tropical heat, talking to these two Scotsmen with their strong Galashiels accents which they had never lost. If it wasn't for the fan that stirred the air, and

the strong scent of orange blossom outside, he might have been in the
office of a Writer to the Signet in Charlotte Square, back in Edinburgh!
Was he really in Paraguay, or was it all a dream, he wondered?

On 16th July 1872 Robert wrote to his mother from Asuncón.

"My dear Mother,

"I am very sorry none of the 'cruciform characters' are coming to
hand (business phrase!) as I am despatching them with a regularity and
celerity truly marvellous!   I got your last letter enclosing one from
Charlie. I was very sorry to hear of the accident to his starboard thumb,
but am glad to hear it has escaped being taken off. When this letter has
been duly read, please send it to Charlie (after having left a copy for the
British Museum!) as it would be absolutely useless posting it here. It
would be a hundred chances to one it ever reached him, and if it did so, it
might perhaps be handed to him some day when, as an admiral, he is
sitting in the window of his club! I have plenty to do here, as, hearing
that I came here on account of the Ross Groves affair, they all lie with
surprising facility and a marvellous resemblance to truth, which makes
things rather rough for me. As soon as I can get my talkings over here, I
intend to start for the survey.

"After that I shall write a long report to Holland & Jacques and, to fill
up the time till I hear from you, I am going down to Corrientes to fetch
up a troop of mules for Dr. Stewart; who, by the way, has been
extremely kind and civil to me. I am at present staying at his other
quinta, about two miles out of Asunción, which is of course a great
saving of expense to me. I am very glad I have come up to Paraguay – I
think a very great deal is to be done here. I hope to make some money
by the mules I bring for Dr. Stewart – and of course Ross Groves' people
will have to pay me pretty well for the expense I have been at, and shall
have to incur on my journey to their concession, which is situated about
80 leagues from here on the banks of the Alto Paraná.

"I am thinking of applying to the government here for some concessions to make a 'yerbale' on my own account. If I can obtain these, I
shall come home at once to see if I can get any business house in London
to take them up. However, it is not very easy to get a concession, and a
good deal depends on whether the President is in a good humour or not,

as he is almost a fool and quite in the hands of the Brazilians who still occupy the country.

"I find Portuguese very useful to me up here, as it is almost if not quite as much spoken here as Spanish. I am very glad I began to learn it. Guarani is very difficult. I have only learnt a very little of it as yet. I believe about the balance of my Guarani consists of 'Bati copa' which is said to mean 'Good Morning!' The people of the country are not gauchos like the Argentines and Orientals (Uruguayans), for otherwise, although they wear the same sort of clothes and have a fair number of horses, they are in general quite duffers on a horse and few of them throw the lasso any better than I can myself!

"I have got a very nice horse, a tordillo (grey). I paid 40 dollars for him which is very dear further south, but considered quite cheap here! He says his name is '*pingo*'[45] and I think he is the tamest horse I ever saw in South America. I call him 'Bunny' and the Brazilian sentries (who have got to know me and him pretty well as I am almost all day about the government offices, trying to see someone or other – who, of course, is always 'infermo' or 'siestiando'[46]!) call out "Olá, José Maria, acqui ven Dom Roberto com o 'Bonee'!"[47] and some fellow always answers "Si, Jose Antonio, cabalo mexito bein!"

Although not near such a pretty or lively a horse as my entrepelado I had in the Banda, he should be, I think, a very good journey horse as he is rather lazy, which is always considered a good sign of a horse's endurance in these parts. He follows me about and comes when he is called!"

At the end of August 1872 Robert set out for Potrero San Antonio, Dr. Stewart's *quinta* on the Paraná, to fetch the troop of mules. While he was there he got a sad letter from his mother, telling him that Aunt Annie Speirs had died. Aunt Annie had done so much to help them ever since Papa's illness that she would be dreadfully missed. Her death also meant that there was now no-one living at Moffat to visit Papa at Eccles. His mother told him that Uncle Tom was broken-hearted, and he had laid a single rose on Aunt Annie's grave as he mourned at his sister-in-law's

---

[45] The gaucho word for 'horse.'
[46] Ill or having a siesta.
[47] "Hey, José Maria, here comes Don Roberto with 'Bonee'!"

funeral. Aunt Helen was prostrated and had retired to bed saying she would never get up again. Annie had been so good to her husband's brother and sister that they felt they could not live without her.

Robert felt very miserable and wrote to his mother apologising for the lack of black-edged paper, "It is not rife in Mission Dolores, as of course you will understand." He would always remember Aunt Annie's extreme kindness to them all. It was 9th September and Robert hoped to be back in Asunción by the end of the month. He went on to say:

"I have not yet received any more from the firm, but I despatch letters of extreme length, dullness, and promptitude to them every week! I hope they may like them. I had just returned from a ninety-mile ride (about seven in the evening) when to my horror I was told the postman was to saddle up at daybreak. As I have thirteen letters to answer, one of them being from the firm, I shall probably, after feeding my own horse, retire to sleep on my 'recado' at daybreak – just when the infernal postman is starting for his ride of 140 miles! I have got another *pingo*, a doradillo. He is a useful beast, but a fearful kicker. He has already lamed one fellow, besides fighting with and beating almost all the other horses in this place! Bunny has turned out to be one of the best horses I ever had. I could saddle him at 9 o'clock in the evening and be 50 miles by morning. I have been offered a good deal for him several times. I have to take a great deal of care of him on account of the 'tigers' (jaguars) of which there are a great many here. One killed a bullock the other night. I think that with care I may be able to make a good thing out of this Paraguayan business, as it is just the thing to suit me."

Back in Asunción with the mules safely delivered to Dr. Stewart, Robert found a letter waiting at Casa Horrocks from Ross Groves of Holland & Jacques. Robert opened it eagerly and was delighted by the first sentence: at last they had started to take him and his project seriously!

"We cannot but express to you our very great satisfaction at the evidence of care and thoroughness in the exhaustive and valuable information contained in your first report."

This was splendid stuff and music to Robert's ears, who already thought of himself as a successful colonist, if a somewhat eccentric one, for he would never be prepared to force a new way of life on his friends the Guarani Indians. He wanted to see them happy and prosperous, but he was determined that they should not be exploited by selfish materialists, as had happened throughout so much of the British Empire.

Holland & Jacques went on to say that they would now like him to carry out his inspection of Alcorta's conceded land, "but we trust you will not be induced to do so at any considerable risk to your person or health."

They then turned to another possibility which they wanted Robert to investigate: was Alcorta's concession the only one available, or might it be wiser to break away from a man who had proved to be somewhat difficult to deal with, and to obtain an entirely independent concession from the Paraguayan government?

"It would be well if you could place yourself in communication with those who are in a position to give you trustworthy advice as to the best mode of obtaining such a concession as would enable us to be entirely independent of Alcorta, the contractor," they wrote. "Possibly it may be advantageous to make allies of Messrs Stewart and others, we leave you to judge. Our idea is that with an independent concession, and such ample authenticated information as you can supply, we should find no difficulty in placing it in the hands of large capitalists who would benefit Paraguay, the concessionaires, and themselves.

"We have again, within the last two or three weeks, made repeated but fruitless attempts to bring Alcorta into an amicable state of mind, which would have enabled us to make some working arrangements advantageous to all concerned. But it is evident that he does not wish for harmony. His motive we cannot discover. So we have determined to leave him henceforth alone and see what we can do without him. We write to Messrs. Stewart Brothers in this sense, but we leave you entirely unfettered as to your choice of allies in negotiating for another concession. Of course in taking steps to throw Alcorta overboard in his concession you are bound to Messrs. Stewart, as it was through Dr. Stewart that the concession was introduced to us.

"We do not wish you to stay a day longer in Paraguay, on our account, than may be necessary in your opinion for the furtherance of our interests and views as shown forth in this letter."

The letter showed that the tea-importers were thinking seriously of going into the *yerba maté* business on their own account. Robert was relieved that he was being given permission to push the tricky Señor Alcorta out of the boat, if the Stewarts agree. Now he had a free hand. He would set off straight away for the conceded lands, and at same time he would ask the Stewart brothers if there were any other *yerbales* they knew of, which he could investigate for them while he was doing his survey.

The doctor said he would help Robert to find a good Indian guide, and together they poured over maps once again, while William Stewart showed Robert an area on the Alto Paraná, a good deal to the north-east, where there might be some concessions available. The doctor suggested he should look at Chiriguela lands, situated in the remote Sierra de Mbaracayú, which had been the scene of Lopez's last stand, in the woods there, during the war.

To get there, Robert would first have to take the river steamer as far as the river Ipané, a tributary of the river Paraguay, and from there he could take his guide and the two horses on rafts until they reached the sierra, which lay in a curve of the river Paraná, north of the mountains of Aracanguy. He could then ride on down the Paraná, suggested the doctor, to have a final look at Alcorta's *yerbales*, before returning to Asunción.

Soon everything was arranged and the Stewart brothers finally agreed that they would waste no more time over Alcorta, but would send Robert straight off to the Chiriguela lands. It would be a long and arduous journey, but they knew that Robert liked nothing better. He was an astonishing young man, and they had come to think very highly of him – a true "man o'pairts," as he would have been described in their native Border country. By now they had found a cheerful Indian guide who was willing to go with him, and he could pick up his provisions en route. Another two days, and he should be ready to go.

That night Robert joined some of his friends at Casa Horrocks and drank a great deal more *caña* than was good for him. Later still, he found himself entwined in the arms of an attractive little mulatto girl with twinkling black eyes, who gazed at him admiringly as though he was the only man on earth, and probably a god into the bargain.

His life was taking shape at last, for all the false starts, and he knew he was now going to enjoy himself. Even if nothing materialised from the survey, he would have explored a part of Paraguay that was practically unknown to man, with a horse for company. What more could he want?

The mulatto girl eyed him with surprise as he threw back his head and laughed uproariously in the middle of his love-making. Robert slapped her affectionately on her rump, simultaneously giving her a quick kiss on her full lips. "When I come back I shall buy you a beautiful mantilla," he told her, "because, very soon, I shall have become a wealthy colonist." The little Indian looked at him in awe and adoration, believing every word, while Robert almost believed it himself.

The journey by river-boat up the Paraguay river was fascinating to Robert. He got into conversation with a young Jesuit priest as soon as he got on board, who was setting off into the jungle with nothing but a newspaper and a few cigarettes. Robert wondered quietly to himself whether even Providence might not think this action on the part of the priest to be a little rash. The priest told him that he would be quite safe with the Guaranis, whom he hoped to convert, and all he would require would be some *mandioca*,[48] a few oranges, and shelter at night. Everything he needed was available from the Indians, and he was not in the least afraid.

When Robert and his guide got off the river steamer to start their trek up the Ipané, the last person they saw was the Jesuit, who firmly struck off into the woods by himself with a cheerful wave of the hand.

The first part of the journey was by *balsa*, or raft. Bunny, tethered to a bolt on the raft, did not seem to mind gliding down the narrow river one bit. He flicked at the flies with his tail and munched contentedly at a bale of *pindo*, or palm leaves. The trees which completely concealed the hot sun were huge and, as Robert was to write in a letter home on 4th November, "the tigers and tapirs are also abundant and of a large size. I fired at a tiger three times with my revolver, quite close, but could not hit on account of Bunny expressing his strong disgust of the proceeding.

---

[48] Starchy root (the source of tapioca) from which a substance like ground rice is pounded. It is the main nourishment in poorer parts of South America to this day.

We then (I and an Indian fellow I had taken as a guide) were preparing to attack him with lances, but he walked quickly away, wagging his tail."

Once they had reached the end of their water-borne journey, the two men mounted their horses and rode through the darkness.

On evening, as they were looking for a clearing in the jungle in which to spend the night, they came upon a small wooden house with a large area of jungle cleared away around it and a small pasture. Robert's horse, Bunny, suddenly started neighing loudly, and to Robert's astonishment there was an answering neigh and a beautiful roan horse came galloping over the grass towards them.

As nearly all the horses had been killed during the war, along with the men, this was a most extraordinary phenomenon. The horses greeted each other like long-lost friends, nuzzling each other and making little whinnying noises. Robert jumped off Bunny, laughing, and at that moment a little wrinkled old man appeared at the door of the shack, smiling warmly.

"Let them play together," he said in Spanish. "My horse has not seen another for two years or more. He is so happy! Take off your horse's saddle and bridle, he will not need to be tethered, for they will play together and talk together all night, while you will sleep the night in my house." He came forward stretching out a welcoming hand and, with a broad smile he introduced himself as "José." He was one of the few Paraguayan soldiers who had escaped the enemy, and, after hiding in the woods for two years, he was quite unaware that the war was over, he told Robert.

That night, while the horses played joyfully round the little wooden house, Robert listened to the old soldier's story as they smoked on his verandah after eating their *mandioca* together. A bottle of rum from Robert's knapsack soon let the old man's tongue loose, and he told Robert of his adventures. Just as the roan horse could not stop whinnying to Bunny as they played, nor did the old man draw breath for most of that night. It was a story of great courage, typical of the Paraguayan soldiers, as Robert now knew.

The man had apparently been taken prisoner by the Brazilians and was being transported by river-boat, along with other prisoners, down the Paraguay to Asunción. While the Brazilian guards were dozing after their midday meal, the prisoners decided to make an attempt at an escape by jumping simultaneously into the river. Unfortunately one of the guards spotted the last prisoner crawling across the deck, and opened fire on the men who were swimming underwater to the shore. José was shot in the leg and all his companions were killed.

He managed to remain submerged until the boat had disappeared from sight. His dead companions had been left in the water by the Brazilians for the piranha fish to dispose of, which they did within the next few minutes, to José's horror. Fortunately for him, the piranhas had so many other corpses to devour that he managed to scramble ashore before the deadly fish smelt the blood from his own wound.

José told how he had lain in great pain and high fever for several days, hidden in the scrub on the edge of the river, until a Guarani Indian woman found him and took him back to her house, more dead than alive. Somehow he survived, thanks to the care of the woman, and after a few weeks he could manage to move around again.

By luck, a stray horse came to the woman's hovel one day, looking for food, and José managed to catch the beautiful roan. Once he had a horse to ride, he decided to set off into the jungle, heading for Corrientes on the other side of the Paraná. Somehow he had never reached his goal, for he was not sure whether even Corrientes would be safe for an escaped Paraguayan soldier, so he built himself a small wooden *rancho* by a stream, in a clearing in the jungle, and there he had stayed, alone with his horse, ever since. Neither of them had set eyes on man or horse since that day, two years ago, and always there was the fear that the war might still be raging, and that it was safer to stay hidden in the jungle.

Next morning, José saddled his horse to ride a league or two with Robert and his guide, and then they parted again, the roan whickering its farewell to Bunny, while Robert thanked the old soldier for his hospitality and wished him well. Would he now go back to "civilisation," he asked?

"Perhaps not," said the old man, "my horse and I are used to the solitude, I think we should find the world too noisy."

Robert knew exactly what José meant, he had often felt the same himself when he was riding Bunny through the woods of Morosimo,

Curupay, and Yba-hai, amongst the brilliant flowering trees, the tuneful bird-calls, and the peaceful buzzing of a myriad insects.

For the next few days he and his guide rode on alone through the Paraguayan jungle. Sometimes it rained heavily and Robert found it hard to get on his horse, after lying wrapped in a damp poncho to snatch a few hours' sleep, for his joints had swollen with rheumatism. Then the sun would come out and all his aches and pains would melt away. Streams flowed sluggishly in the primeval woods, and he saw great alligators basking, their backs awash, flamingos fishing amongst shallow pools, herons and cranes sitting on dead stumps, and innumerable vultures perched in trees above.

Here was a country untouched by human hand where a man could be happy, he thought as he rode. Was he right to be entering the world of commerce in his efforts to develop the *yerbales* through the government concessions?

He supposed it would give work to the Guaranis, so perhaps it was worth trying. Nevertheless, he felt the life they lived at present was so idyllic that it seemed almost wrong to submit them to the pressures and anxieties of agricultural development. Robert laughed at himself. He knew he was an idealist at heart, and what he really wanted was for everyone to live in a sort of Garden of Eden where "man's inhumanity to man" did not exist, and where everyone was kind, especially to dogs and horses.

He missed the dogs of his childhood. The only one left was his mother's rather dreadful little King Charles spaniel, but even that small creature had a charm of its own, and in his letters home he never forgot to send the dog his love, just as he sent it to his father, his brothers, his grandmother, and his step-grandfather Khāt. He missed his family intolerably, but now that Gartmore was no longer their home, he knew that he was happier riding through the Paraguayan jungle than being a "young man about town," living with his mother in Belgravia. He often described her smart neighbours as "flies in amber," and had always thought Belgravia was quite the most snobbish part of London, and the most disagreeable. He hoped his mother would not always live there. Most of all he hoped that one day they would be able to live at Gartmore again.

For the last few miles Robert and his guide had emerged from the jungle on to the Sierra de Mbaracayu, with huge mountains in the distance. A few miles ahead they could see the *yerbales* stretching down to the river Paraná --journey's end, for the time being. These would be the Chiriguela *yerbales* which might one day become a part of his life, if the Stewart brothers could persuade Holland & Jacques to invest in them.

On reaching the high banks of the Paraná, Robert could see great areas of white water and waterfalls. Little did he realise that he was seeing the Iguacú Falls, which were one day to be as famous as Niagara.

Meanwhile, Robert had resumed his patient knocking. At last Don Maximilio Alcorta agreed to hand over the concession, and Robert's spirits soared. He now informed Holland & Jacques of developments, and sent them the details of his 600 mile survey up the Parana River. He waited in Asunción for the next move to be taken by them. The ball was in their court. He had played his part. It was now up to them to agree to invest in the *yerbales*.

Early in December, in high summer weather which caused inertia to settle on the inhabitants, who swung sleepily in fringed hammocks under the shade of trees, General Caballero's long-awaited revolutionary forces arrived at Asunción. Robert promptly retreated to William Stewart's *quinta* two miles outside the town. He had no wish to be involved in another revolution just as he was approaching his *El Dorado*. However, within a day or two news filtered through that the whole thing had been a fiasco. Somehow their revolutionary foray was a failure and the Brazilian troops, reinforced, had repelled the strangely half-hearted attack. In the midst of all this, Dr. Stewart rode into town to make his daily visit to the hospital and was suddenly fired at by a Brazilian sentry. Fortunately he escaped with a flesh-wound to his leg.

After a fruitless meeting with Don Maximilio Alcorta, (the contractor seemed reluctant to do anything with them or to help him get the extension to the original concession) the Stewart brothers said they thought they could pull some strings to get the official approval to the extension. But they advised Robert not to apply for the exclusive right of working the *yerbale*, as the government would be sure to demand that colonists should be sent over from Europe, which would be a great mistake. They quoted the case of two Englishmen called Robinson and

Fleming, during Lopez's rule, whose colony of Europeans failed dismally owing to the climate, to the inability of the colonists to adapt to their new way of life, and to fever.

Robert explained to Holland & Jacques how ludicrously business was conducted in Paraguay, telling how he had asked a clerk to let him have a copy of the extension of the concession before he left the President's office.

"The government official to whom I applied for the copy asked me if I had any authorisation from you to make inquiries on the subject. I happened to have your letter of 1s^t March with me, which I instantly showed him. He did not read a word of English but expressed himself perfectly satisfied!"

Robert ended his letter by explaining, "I have not been able to start to inspect the concession yet, but intend doing so as soon as I can get the extension of 20 months (backdated to 11th August 1872) confirmed by Congress."

Robert was unaware that in London his letters to Messrs. Holland & Jacques were causing quite a stir. His first letter was passed carefully round the partners who all pronounced themselves most impressed. The young man was proving to be a great deal more thorough and reliable than he had at first seemed. They all admitted that his long hair, worn gaucho-style, and his strange tales of guerrilla warfare in Argentina, had made them wonder if he could be trusted with the task in hand. But the letters they had received were admirably clear, and gave vivid pictures of the political situation in Paraguay and the difficulties of doing business there.

On 8th August they wrote to thank Mr. Graham for the excellent information he had already procured.

"We cannot but express to you our very great satisfaction at the evidence of care and thoroughness in the exhaustive and valuable information contained in your report."

Robert roared with laughter as he savoured the formal language and the flowery phrases. Well, well! What a hell of a dog he had become, quite the experienced colonist, in fact! The letter went on to say that they looked forward to having his opinion as to the condition of Alcorta's conceded land, after having inspected it, "but we trust you will not be induced to do so at any considerable risk to your person or health." Robert snorted indignantly at this. The letter continued:

"It would be well if you could place yourself in communication with those who are in a position to give you trustworthy advice as to the best mode of obtaining such a concession as would enable us to be entirely independent of Alcorta."

Trustworthy advice! Robert laughed. It didn't exist in that part of the world!

The letter ended:

"We do not wish you to stay a day longer in Paraguay, on our account, than may be necessary in your opinion for the furtherance of our interest and views as shown forth in this letter."

They were cautious, smiled Robert, as he read the final sentence. In other words, these men of business had no intention of paying him another penny if the whole thing was likely to fall through! He would jolly well show them that it wasn't going to fall through.

Robert was back in Asunción by early November, staying on the Stewarts' *Quinta* once more.

"My dear Mother," he started his long letter, "I have just returned from the Alto Paraña and found your letter waiting for me. Did you ever get my letter from the Mission Dolores? I had a very interesting and pesky journey to the concessions. It rained tremendously and I had the rheumatism all the time and had to be helped on and off my *pingo*. Added to which I slept out in pouring rain every night and had nothing to eat except oranges and mandioca.

"'O Blanco' has come back in first-rate condition, but a little lame in the off-hind leg. He did about six hundred and fifty miles. I had to get him shod as his hoofs were a good deal worn away, as Paraguay is very stony. Not like the splendid turf of the Banda and Entre Rios. He spent a whole day trying to pull off his shoes against posts and things, but now is reconciled, in fact rather proud of them! The country on the banks of the Alto Paraná is magnificent, only the scarcity of food is rather pesky. If I had not met an Italian friend on the Correntino frontier who lent me a gun – of course I had left my rifle in Asunción when I wanted it most – I should have eaten very little meat. The country down there is very find; the trees, tigers, and tapirs being abundant and of large size. You would have been delighted with the ferns which were splendid (some tree ferns of enormous size). The flowers are lovely, and some of the acacias and mimosa, too. The lagunas are all covered with an immense white lily.

"An amusing scene occurred in the town yesterday: I was in a shop in a narrow street and had left "Blanco" in the middle of the street. A party of Brazilian soldiers, all black with a black sergeant, in immensely hot uniforms and very white teeth, came by to relieve the guard. The Brazilian mind is not quick at expedient – it would have occurred to most people to have led the horse to one side to let the troops by; but they considered a long time, when suddenly a nigger stepped out of the ranks with a grin that made his mouth meet at the back of his head, saluted, and said, 'O sarjiento, Bunny must not be disturbed.' The sergeant then divided the niggers into two columns and they solemnly marched past, leaving Pingo in the middle. Every nigger stopped to pat him and say, 'What a good horse you are, Bonee!' Pingo expressed his disgust by pulling off one of their hats and chewing it fearfully before I could rescue it! The United States gunboat, 'Wasp' was up here, and the officers were very funny. Dr. Stewart lent the Captain a brown horse to ride one day; however, it speedily came back without him. He afterwards said it had cut adrift from him and he preferred to veer along on foot – or words to that effect. The heat is great, but I don't mind it so much as I did before.

"I hope by this time Charlie is home? How nice it will be. I liked the photo of him pretty well but it is not very like him.

"I hope Aunt Maggy will write to me if she hears any particulars about the Menteith peerage? I care very little about it as long as no-one else gets it. Of course if I had it I should be a sort of Lord Cardross and sit at rich men's feasts in a sort of second-hand way as he does! However, as to that agreeable sort of entertainment, I would rather share a handful of maize with 'Blanco' out on the plains."

That evening, the doctor suggested to Robert that the best thing he could do now was to return to London to show his survey of the Chiriguela *yerbales* to the Tea Importers. Staying on in Paraguay would do nothing to further his project.

Robert mulled over the doctor's advice. He knew that his greatest fault was his impatience; perhaps the doctor was right – it would be even worse waiting here with the concession so nearly in his grasp and yet so tantalisingly out of reach.

A month later, on 20th December 1872, Robert wrote to his mother again.

"My dear Mother

"I am coming home at once on business for Holland & Jacques and hope to be in the centre of civilisation again in about five weeks. I think I am going to drop in for a pretty good thing with 'Mr. George' and Dr. Stewart, in this concession to make yerbales for the Paraguayan government. Bunny got his leg cut on a steamboat recently, but if it is well in time I shall be photoed with him. If not, I shall leave instructions to have him photoed without me, and the photo sent on --that is, if he approves.

"Please try to find a writing-master for me as I intend to do all I can to improve my hand when I arrive, as I expect to be only a few months in England.

"With love to all, I remain,

    yr. affec. son. R.B.C. Graham."

Just as he wrote the last words of his letter to his mother, Robert heard the doctor calling, "Roberto! The steamer goes in thirteen minutes! Borrow my horse if you want to try to catch it to send that letter!"

Robert hurtled out of the house and threw himself on to the patient horse who stood ready saddled by the verandah. It was two and a half miles to the river port, but somehow he got there in time, at full gallop, to hear the final hoots from the steam whistle, and to see scurrying figures unwinding ropes from bollards on the rickety quay. The steamer was already swinging out from the quay as Robert handed his letter to a seaman wearing a white chiripa like a gaucho. The man leapt over the guardrail to hand the letter to an office, and threw himself back on to the landing stage again as the strip of water widened. Grinning at Robert he made a low bow, like an acrobat at the circus.

"Viva!" shouted Robert, clapping his hands, and the good-humoured crowd, watching the steamer depart, roared with delight. What a strange country this was, thought Robert, who would eve know that a revolution was going on?

Cheerful passengers leaned over the sides of the departing steamer to wave and shout, while their friends and relations on the shore responded with equal enthusiasm. In a week's time I shall be on the steamer myself, thought Robert, with a mixture of sorrow and joy. It would be awfully jolly to see Mamma and Mal, and Ganama and Khāt, and perhaps old Tarlee again; but it would be winter in London and the chill winds always made him feel so melancholy. He sniffed the exotic scents of jasmine and orange blossom as he jumped on the doctor's horse to return to the *quinta*. He was already addicted to the heavy scent of South America, to the dignified Guarani Indians, and to the gloriously oppressive, humid heat. He knew that he was a different person in this strange country, more relaxed, more philosophical, and a great deal happier.

Robert spent Christmas with William and Venancia Stewart at their *quinta*, and George Stewart, the lawyer, joined them. Talk of revolution against the Brazilian overlords seemed to have subsided for the time being, and Christmas Day with his kind Scots host and his aristocratic fair-haired Paraguayan hostess was almost as much fun as being at Gartmore amongst his own family. It was one of the hottest days of the year, but in honour of their young Scots visitor, Doña Venancia insisted on providing a full-scale Christmas dinner, just as her husband and his brother had described the Christmas dinners they remembered in Galashiels before they left the shores of Scotland.

"How do you like our roast vulture?" George winked at Robert, as they tucked into succulent turkey, while the thermometer on the verandah soared to 90 degrees.

On 28th December, after a sorrowful farewell to "Bunny," Robert boarded the steamer "Guarani" bound for Buenos Aires. Bunny's gashed leg had healed well, and the promised photo was safely packed in Robert's luggage. Even more important were letters from the two Stewart brothers which he had to deliver to Holland & Jacques on his return to London, assuring them that the concession would be the best possible investment, and that they themselves would oversee the whole project. Robert tucked the letters carefully into his pocketbook, together with the latest draft of the concession.

Robert always enjoyed the river trip to Buenos Aires, but he felt sad when the steamer finally crossed the last stretch of the yellow rolling waters of the River Plate. Collecting his bags he soon found a Basque porter to carry his things to Claraz's and rejoiced to find so many of his estanceiro friends installed in the familiar old place. Here was Maxwell Witham hurrying over to shake his hand, Eduardo Peña and Estaquio Medina wanting to know all his "novedad," and the delightful French journalist Lucien Simmonet smiling from his usual corner, as though he had never moved out of it since the day Robert had arrived in South America nearly three years ago – and here, joy of joys, was his favourite character of all, one of the best fellows he had ever met, the redoubtable Cossart.

Over a glass of *caña*, Robert picked up all the gossip – how one of the Milburn brothers had died of drink, and so had Duarte; it was the occupational hazard of living on the pampas, of course. Then there was the sad story of "Charlie the Gaucho," who had been a British sailor and had settled happily with an Indian wife near Monte Video. Everyone knew how he had suddenly received word from home that he had been left a great fortune, but the night before he was due to leave, he got into a fight and was stabbed to death.

That was life in Argentina for you! Few ever survived it.

The men drank a few more glasses of *caña* in memory of their friends, and slowly the party broke up – some to wend their way to the Casa Amueblada, where the French and Hungarian women sat on their balconies in their dressing gowns with their hair most elaborately dressed; and some to the opera.

PART III
FURTHER TRAVELS – ICELAND, GIBRALTAR, AFRICAN CONGO, ARGENTINA AND PARAGUAY

CHAPTER XIII

In May 1875, Robert found himself, somewhat to his surprise, sailing down the west coast of Africa in the trading barque "*Wilberforce*," a five-hundred tonner from Bristol, painted chequer-sided, commanded by one Captain Thomas Bilson. Robert uses this name as a joke, as will finally become clear. The ship was in fact called something quite other!

Once he had reached Gibraltar, a year after his return from South America, it had all happened very quickly, and Robert still could not believe that events could have moved so fast. The new adventure suited him down to the ground. At the same time he had acquired a new and valued friend. After spending several weeks travelling through France and Spain during 1873, Robert had arrived in Gibraltar in the spring just as the Fleet sailed in with his brother Charlie's ship, H.M.S. Northumberland.

Great-aunt Elisa Guibara and her husband Francisco had insisted that Robert should stay in their house, while Charlie, who had been allowed ashore for a short spell of leave, lodged with the other great-aunt, Ana de Jimenez. On this night they were all together in the Guibaras' house for a special dinner to celebrate Robert's and Charlie's arrival in Gibraltar, and they had also invited two of Charlie's ship-mates: Prince Louis of Battenberg and a cheerful young man from Dorset called George Mansel, whose father had owned a large estate between Bridport and Abbotsbury. George's father was a soldier but had died when George was a small boy, and his mother lived on in the manor house at Puncknowle.

After dinner, Robert and Charlie walked with Louis and George back to their ship, through a throng of Spaniards, Arabs and British who were

enjoying a "paseo"[49] under a benevolent moon. The great-aunts had provided quite a banquet, with excellent wine, and the four young men felt
that all was well with the world.

As they walked, George started to speak of his ambition to travel to
the country that Robert had told them so much about at dinner. How he
would love to gallop across the pampas and drive cattle with the
gauchos, as Robert had described. Life on board one of Her Majesty's
men-o'-war was far too restricting for him – nothing to do but drink and
fight. He had been thinking for some time that he would like to take
advantage of a new scheme in operation to leave the Royal Navy with
some capital, in lieu of a pension, from their Lordships, and become a
cattle farmer. Now Robert's tales of life in Argentina and Paraguay had
finally decided him. Tonight he had made up his mind: tomorrow he
would write to the Admiralty to resign his commission.

Next morning his letter was written and posted. Mansel called on
Robert on his way back from the post to thank him for the unwitting help
he had given him in taking this difficult decision. It would probably be a
few weeks before he was finally released from the Navy, but this very
morning he had been having a chin-wag with an old friend who was captain of the trading barque *Wilberforce*.

It transpired that Captain Bilson would be sailing next day, on the
morning tide, across the Straits of Gibraltar to make a trip from Mogador
to Mossamedes, on the West African coast, and would be glad of the
company of Lieutenant Mansel and Mr. Cunninghame Graham on the
voyage. Would they like to join him for the trip?

Would they like to?   Robert's eyes lit up at the thought of a new
adventure.

On Robert's return to London he had found that the tea-importers,
Holland & Jacques, were not at all happy about the political situation in
Paraguay, especially since the latest coup had failed, and they told
Robert that no-one would be prepared to invest in Paraguay until the
country had built up its economy again and settled its political squabbles.

At first Robert felt totally shattered, but gradually he became more
philosophical, realising that commercial ventures were obviously not up

---

[49] A stroll.

his street, and that he had better stick to the things he knew about. His uncle, William Hope, was still suggesting sugar-growing in the West Indies, or coffee-planting in Ceylon,[50] but Robert could get South America neither out of his head nor his heart. He felt as though he had been jilted by a beautiful but capricious girl.

Robert's mother tried to take his mind off South America – she took him to the opera, and to concerts and plays, and she collected all the intelligent young people she knew to her house. Robert saw a great deal of a young lawyer he used to know, called Francis Adey, and he slowly began to enjoy his widening circle of friends.

By July 1875 Robert was still at a loose end; so his mother suggested that he should join Charlie, who was going to spend two weeks' leave in Iceland. The Curator Bonis authorised the money for their fares, and Robert found himself with his brother once more, in the strange land of snow and rivers, of reddish mountains, flecked with green and crowned with snow, rising above the eerie lava fields.

The two boys rode, and fished, and enjoyed the hot springs, and the carpets of wild flowers, but their holiday went far too quickly and soon it was time for Charlie to rejoin his ship. Their trip was to be the inspiration for one of strangest stories Robert was ever to write, called *Snaekoll's Saga.*

On Robert's return to London he found his wanderlust had increased, so he told his mother that he would spend some time in Spain, tracing the history of the Jesuits in Paraguay. For the next few months Robert found that he enjoyed travelling alone on the continent just as much as he had enjoyed his solitary expeditions in Paraguay. In April 1875 his brother's ship arrived in Gibraltar with the Fleet. He had recently been transferred from the *Royal Albert* to the *Northumberland.*

* * * * * *

Robert was to set off with George Mansel on board the *Wilberforce* a few days before his twenty-third birthday. It was a clear day, and Robert could see the mountains clothed with arbutus, dwarf rhododendron, and

---

[50] Now called Sri Lanka.

the kermes oak, running to the water's edge. The Straits of Gibraltar were only thirteen miles across, and it was possible to see the mountains on both sides. From both sides, too, the goatherds floated songs as wild and quavering as a heron's screams, taught to them by their remote and common ancestors.

Early that morning they had loaded a strange cargo of rum, gin, gas-pipe muskets (long as a spear, and painted red), brash dishes, musical boxes, cheap German clocks and pornographic French prints. A few beads, bells and looking glasses were added, and some well "sized" cotton, and then the *Wilberforce* was ready to sail, well equipped with goods to barter for palm-oil, ivory, kola nuts, beeswax, gold dust and ostrich feathers.

George Mansel had sailed with Captain Bilson before, and he explained to Robert that the idea was to drop into some river where no trader lived, signal to the chief of the tribe for a pilot; and, either in the chief's hut, or in the captain's cabin, "set up a trade," after a long palaver where cases of gin from Rotterdam found the chief arguments. If the interview was with the chief in his own house, then palm wine flowed, tom-toms beat and negro women danced seductively. A great banquet was usually held and presents (such as the indecent French prints) were given. George laughed as he told Robert that most of the chief's houses were furnished with three or four iron beds, a cuckoo clock, two or three musical boxes, and religious pictures on the walls depicting the Prodigal's Return, Rebecca at the Well, or Noah's Ark.

Captain Bilson was well known up and down the coast – from Mogador, through Agadir, Cape Juby, Bojador, to Bathurst, Sierra Leone, Accra and down the Gold Coast, where a white vapour hangs over everything and obscures the sun as if it were covered with a thin white gauze; right on down past Fernando Po, which rises from the sea – an offshoot from the mountains of the Cameroons, to the Congo, St. Paul's, Loanda and Benguela, until the dense bush gets more sparse and the land gets sandy, arid and sub-tropical below Mossamedes, some two thousand miles south of Mogador.

He would usually pick up a gang of "Krooboys" (pidgin English for crewmen) for the cruise at Cape Palmas. The "Krooboys" had their towns between Cape Mesurado and Cape Palmas; they were a race apart, the Lascar of the coast, who was a healthy pagan, tall, muscular and active, with his face tattooed on either temple with a triangle from which a line of blue ran down his nose from his hairline giving him, when he laughed, a look of having two distinct faces.

On this voyage they called in at Cape Palmas as usual, and Robert saw the "Krooboys" coming on board and was told that they bore such names as "Jack Beef," "Sam Coffee," "Little Fish," "Joe Brass," and other "cognomens." Amongst the "Krooboys," Robert saw a young negro girl come on board, rather to his surprise. She carried a large bundle and looked as though she meant to stay. Her clothes were stiffly starched and she carried herself with great dignity as though she held some important position.

"Who on earth is that?" Robert asked George, as they leant over the side of the ship to watch the coming and going, and to see the antics of the children who dived for coins.

George smiled, "Oh, she's known as a 'consort' – all the captains have them to act as interpreters with the 'Krooboys,' and for many other reasons too."

"Sounds convenient!" laughed Robert, "how does one qualify?"

"Strictly for captains, I'm afraid," said George. "The girls are trained at a special seminary in Accra, to keep the captain's cabin shipshape, sew on his buttons, play on the marimba, dance and act as an intermediary in their dealings with the chiefs. It's considered a very honourable and lucrative profession.

They starch their dresses with arrowroot, by the way, and if you cut their legs off their skirts would still help them to keep their balance by sheer force of starch! Of course Captain Bilson is most impressed by this neatness, for you know he likes everything to be shipshape and Bristol fashion!"

"What a horrid thought!" said Robert.

Robert was thoroughly enjoying the trip. He was interested to see the negro in his natural habitat, after encountering him so far from home in South America. The Brazilians were still shamelessly trading in "rolls of tobacco," and Captain Bilson had hinted several times that even his own ship had been used for this purpose from time to time. Slave trading was never spoken about as such, but Robert guessed that the name of the trading barque was meant as a good joke – the *Wilberforce*.[51]

It was while they were anchored outside the bar of a small river off the Congo that the event occurred which turned the captain into a raging fury. The boatswain came below while he was studying the chart, to tell him that some of the "Krooboys" had stolen one of the ship's boats and, having crossed the bar, had paddled up river and disappeared. To lose a boat at this point on the cruise was extremely serious. It would be impossible to get another till they reached a major port, and it was bound to cost a great deal of money as well as much inconvenience. The worst of it was that he had been outdone by his own "Krooboys," heathens, as he put it, who were sharp enough to leave him in the lurch.

Captain Bilson took down the Bible which always stood in its appointed place in his cabin, beside his revolver, and turned the page until he had assured himself that "eye for eye, and tooth for tooth," was God's own law, then he went on deck.

Now that Captain Bilson had got "scripture" for it, he would stick at nothing. He knew that the "Krooboys" were certain to sell the stolen boat and ship aboard the first returning vessel to Cape Palmas. The captain had thought of a way to trick them.

Robert and George were now to witness a charade which not only afforded them great amusement, but also increased their admiration of the captain's ingenuity. For five days the ship was concealed behind a mangrove swamp while great activity took place aboard the *Wilberforce*. When she put to sea once more she was unrecognisable. The chequer sides were gone and a red stripe replacing them caused her to look much higher, the cherished figurehead of Wilberforce (in the act of benediction) had been cased up in canvas and painted black, and a few heavy weights moved further aft gave her a different set. The square yards on the mainmast had disappeared and, with the Stars and Stripes flying from her peak, she looked exactly like a Yankee barquantine sailing from Portland, Maine. Even Captain Bilson had been transfigured into a Yankee captain, dressed in white drill, wearing a broad Bahama hat, his

---

[51] William Wilberforce (1759-1833) fought in Parliament for nineteen years for the abolition of the British slave trade.

hair dyed black, moustache cut off, and beard and whiskers trimmed to look like an "Uncle Sam" goatee.

On reaching the bar of the small river where they had originally anchored, Robert and George watched with delighted anticipation from behind an awning, to see if Captain Bilson's plan would work. Sure enough, a canoe put off, and as it neared the ship, one of the missing "Krooboys" called out,

"'Spose Massa Captain want Krooboy, Tom Coffee, Little Fish, Joe Bras lib' for ship one time."

Bilson answered in an exaggerated New England accent that he was shorthanded and was going north, at which the unsuspecting "Krooboys" ran their canoe alongside and came on board. As each man stepped on deck a heavy blow stretched him half senseless, and he came round to find himself in irons and listening to a torrent of abuse from his erstwhile captain before being thrown into the hold amongst the cargo.

On reaching another small river further down the coast, from where it was well known that the Brazilians shipped their "rolls of tobacco," Captain Bilson went ashore to see the local chief. Later in the same day the *Wilberforce* was approached by a war canoe manned by sixteen warriors wearing collars of leopards' claws, armlets of ivory, and armed with spears. The wretched "Krooboys" were gagged and tied hand and foot, and dumped like logs into the war canoe. Robert watched the canoe speeding towards the shore, as the warriors paddled, in unison, with frightening precision. It had been a splendid trick, but now he was beginning to feel rather sorry for the poor "Krooboys" who were un-doubtedly destined for the coffee plantations of Brazil, if they were lucky, and perhaps for the tribal stewpots if they were not. The local African chiefs were on to a good thing, as there was lots of gain to be had with this trade, and they felt no pity for their own people who were thus exploited and ill-treated.

Captain Bilson hauled in his own boat, braced round his yards, and slipped into the night. The rest of the voyage was uneventful, but Robert was never to forget his one and only sight of a war canoe manned by cannibals, selling their own brothers as slaves, in the steaming Congo.

Back in Gibraltar after the four thousand mile round trip, Robert felt as though he had visited another planet. Africa had cast its spell over him, but he knew that he would feel restricted and stifled in the African jungle, whereas in South America one was never far from the grassy plains. North Africa had appealed to him a great deal more than the Gold Coast or the Congo. In North Africa he felt a strange kinship with the Arabs, especially as he watched them whirling across the rocky desert on their "wind-drinkers" – the forebears of the *mestenos* of the pampas. He knew that one day he must return to Morocco, for Moor and Spaniard had both contributed to his heritage, along with the Earls of Menteith, one of whom (buried on the Island of Inchmahone) had left his island castle to take part in the crusade against the infidel led by St. Louis of France in 1248. It was a strangely comforting thought that he was not the first of his family to cross to North Africa.

Their last port of call had been Tanger la Blanca – whitewash and blinding sunlight on the walls, white sand on the beach, the people dressed in robes of dusky white – "Tangier the White." It had been fought for through the ages by Goth, Spaniard, Portuguese, Greek, Roman, Arab and Carthaginian, but still the city stood, enduring sun, dust, rain, wind, the lapse of time, and neglect; and although only thirteen miles from Europe, it was still utterly unspoilt by European ways.

The qualities of its people still seemed to be mainly a delight in life: tears, joy and laughter unrepressed; a simple faith, few wants, and no ambition. Robert found himself longing to stay on in Tangier where time meant nothing and men were free from care, but George Mansel was impatient to return to Gibraltar to see if his release from the Royal Navy had come through, and so they sailed across the Straits with Captain, and took their leave of the *Wilberforce* on British soil, in Gibraltar.

Robert and George had frequently discussed their Argentine project on the voyage, and by the time they crossed the Straits of Gibraltar at the end of the cruise, they were both convinced that the partnership would be a satisfactory one, and that the friendship had already been forged. George was probably to be the closest friend Robert would ever have. Once they had kicked the dust of the African continent off their heels, they could turn their thoughts seriously to their future together.

It had been a delightful and fascinating respite, and Robert left the *Wilberforce* with genuine sorrow and affection. He promised her captain that he would visit him in the West Country after his retirement, which was due the following year. Robert could hardly imagine Captain Bilson back in England, at his home in Bristol, with his respectable wife, and found himself picturing the captain off the African coast, swigging gin sweetened with marmalade, while the "Accra girl" spun round in front of him, half naked, in a frenzied dance to tom-toms and flutes. What would poor Mrs. Bilson say if she knew?

Charlie was standing on the quay to welcome them back, and to give George the news that his release was at hand. The two brothers had much to talk about, and Robert was pleased to find letters from his mother and Malise. Robert told Charlie that he would not have missed this trip to Africa for anything, and had already planned a trip with George to South America, hoping to set out by the end of the year. For the time being, George had invited Robert to be his guest at Puncknowle in Dorset, where he knew his mother would be glad to welcome them both on their return to England.

Together they made their plans, and together they discussed the best way to set about finding an estancia and stocking it. Robert had told George that he had found out that the Brazilian Cavalry were willing to pay large sums of money for Argentine horses, and it might be an idea to take a *caballada* from Uruguay to Rio. The profit they made could go towards the price of the estancia they would eventually buy. He wrote to a South American friend, Johnston, now living in London, to find out about the journey they would have to make between Uruguay and Brazil.

"I don't know any book that describes the country between Monte Video and Rio," Johnston answered, "indeed, I don't think any writing-man has gone that way. There is a good one in German about the Rio Grande by the colonists from the 'Vaterland,' and Castelnau is I think still the best for the country crossing north of that. He describes some of the mule caravans and the tracks. By far the most vivid idea of the kind of life in the camps of the River Plate is given in Head's 'Journey Across the Palmas': it is the same sort of thing exactly in the interior of the Banda.

"As to danger, I do not think there is any worth speaking of, unless there happened to be a revolution, in which case the horses would not get very far. Shortly before I returned to Monte Video in coming home, two or three fellows connected with the telegraph cable being laid along the coast from Rio to Monte Video had ridden all round the coast route from Monte Video to past the Brazilian frontier, and described it as a very jolly trip. Everywhere that they came across an estancia or rancho they were most hospitably received. There are no roads however, but the camp is open. The only trouble is to hit the passes of the rivers and to get over them if they happen to be high. In the Rio Grande I believe travelling is much the same: between Curitiba and Rio I should imagine the chief difficulty would be to get food for the horses where the country becomes thickly wooded. I only wish I was going too!

"In haste, very truly yours, K. Johnston.

"P.S. The 'mountains' are all my eye and bea'te Martine[52] as far as Uruguay is concerned, and I don't think there is anything worth the name till one gets close to Rio!"

Little was Robert to know that his friend could not have given them worse advice.

George was staying at Ebury Street with Robert for his final week before sailing, and the two men were much encouraged by this letter.

"Well, that's all right then," said George. "Let's start with the Brazilian remounts to give ourselves a little jog up to Rio and back, and then we can begin to look for our own estancia after that. You'd better write a few letters to your many horse-dealing friends, and tell them to start collecting a hundred or so nags for our arrival."

Robert laughed at his new partner's enthusiasm, and said, "They'll probably try to palm us off with all their unwanted *baguales*, so we'll have to be on our mettle, George, old man! Incidentally, I've already written to my Swiss hotelier friend, who is really a naturalist in disguise. I've asked him to find us a nice little property. He is in a good position to hear of something from all the *estancieros* who patronise his establishment in Buenos Aires."

Missy, Robert's mother, was delighted that Robert had such a good friend as George Mansel for his new venture. Lieutenant Mansel was eleven years older than Robert, a lively fellow, short and stocky with short hair that stuck up all over his head "like a dog's back" as Robert

---

[52] The expression "All my eye and Betty Martin" is well known, and means "nonsense." The spelling here indicates it may be the original source of the phrase!

was to laugh She was sure the older man would have a steadying effect on her son.

She was sad that Robert was insisting on returning to his beloved South America. He simply did not seem able to keep away from the place, and was like a lovelorn swain parted from his shepherdess when forced to return to London.

(She was also worried about Willy, for she had just heard that the specialist, Dr. Sharpe, who had looked after him so well, was thinking of retiring and moving away from Dumfries.)

But she could understand Robert's love for the countries of the *conquistadores*; his Spanish heritage was very strong and he seemed to feel totally at home in a Latin country. As he had very poor circulation, the hot sun was probably a vital element to his well-being; and he was volatile, unlike his more phlegmatic younger brother, so it suited him to be amongst people who were alternately intensely happy, deeply sad, or furiously angry, in rapid succession.

Most of all there was the pull of horses: she wondered if Robert would ever get married, he seemed to be so much fonder of horses than girls! Everything was "*pingo* this" and "*pingo* that" in his life. The affectionate word used by the gauchos for their horses had become a part of their family vocabulary; rather like the family's ridiculous nicknames for each other, all of which incorporated the word "cat."

It had started as a family joke connected with Doña Catalina's marriage to Admiral Katon. "So many cats in our family!" the young Robert had once remarked in the nursery, "Ganama <u>Cata</u>lina, Grandpapa <u>Kat</u>on – and they often call you their 'Kit,' Mamma!"

"Yes, darling," his mother had smiled, "and now I have three little kittens of my own, Bob-cat, Lee-cat, and Mal-cat!" The joke had stuck, the only difference being that Malise, now aged sixteen and firmly destined for the Anglican Church, via Oriel College, Oxford, was designated by his brothers as "the Clergy-cat" – or sometimes "the brutal padre," which was an obscure joke whose origins nobody could remember.

Nicknames had always played an important part in their family, possibly because they were none of them very good at using conventional endearments to each other, and preferred to show their affection by the use of a private pet name. Papa had always been "Strix" (nobody could remember why), Mamma had started life as "Anita" but soon became "Yitty-Missy," gradually changing to "Missy," which had been Uncle Mount's special name for her, or "Prinny," which was another name her mother called her.

Robert was greatly relieved that his mother no longer called him "Podge," now that he was tall and thin it would have been even more ridiculous! Aunt Clemmy's children were called by the most extraordinary names – Trotty, Chucks, and other variations of the nursery theme. It had been all right when they were babies, but Robert thought it was rather undignified now that some of them were attractive young ladies! He had seen a good deal of his cousins during his two years at home, and he was growing particularly fond of Aunt Maggie Hope's children, Adrian, Laura, and Charles. Unreliable as their father had been in his financial advice to the family, Robert could not help liking his children who were all intelligent and full of fun.

The day before Robert and George sailed in *s.s. Douco* from Southhampton, a letter arrived from Charlie, who had recently changed ships again and was now serving in Malta on board *H.M.S. Helicon.*

"My dear Bob," he wrote, "when are you going to start for South America with little Mansel? I wish I was in England to help to fit you out and see you off. Now I have changed my ship I shall probably stay with her until I am promoted, unless I am lucky enough to get the Royal Yacht. How jolly it would be if I could come out with you and ride 'pingo.' I like Mansel very much, we used to have a great many years together in the Northumberland.

"I came to this ship to do 1st. Lieut. Work, which you can guess is somewhat trying, as you have the whole of the arrangement of the internal economy. She is now having a thorough refit, and is being painted up very well. Our boats are painted the same as the Royal Yacht's dark blue and gold. I have a fair sized cabin on board and am rather sorry that I left all my Greenwich furniture at home, as it might be useful.

"I wish, if you had time, you would order me some things from Bowring, as I cannot get shirts and things out here worth twopence. I want 12 white shirts with collars on them, 6 of those coloured Oxford shirts, 1 dozen pairs of socks (I know you will choose nice ones), 2 black neckties, 6 pairs of drawers, and 12 white handkerchiefs. I want them all marked in simple red letters like yours are. The bill can be sent to Jamieson. I would not trouble you as I know you are busy, but you will know it is impossible to get anything of this description in foreign parts. The best way to have them shipped is by an Indian trooper.

"Please give my love to Papa. I am very sorry to hear about Dr. Sharpe having to leave. I am afraid it will be a great difficulty to get another such a good man.

"I suppose the Clergy-cat is still hard at work, assuming the 'Eastward position' – tell the padre not to forget to allow for the variation of the compass and magnetic declination when he does so!

"I have not written to 'the Kit' by this mail, as I have told you all the news. Please give her my love. I still hope for 'the Yacht' – please keep a steady strain on Cousin John Erskine, or any other influential person. Write and tell me when you sail.

"Believe me, your most affectionate brother, Lee-cat."

Robert passed the letter on to his mother, asking her to see about the clothes Charlie wanted.

"He's always been much too extravagant about clothes," she remarked, "I don't know what Mr. Jamieson is going to say about all these bills pouring in."

"Oh, Mamma, the poor chap has got to look his best if he's a First Lieutenant, hasn't he, George?" George laughed, adding with a grin to Mrs. Bontine, "It's an investment as far as young Charlie goes, Ma'am. Think how proud you'll feel when you have a son swanking about on the deck of the Royal Yacht, in the company of his good friend and shipmate, His Most Serene Highness Prince Louis of Battenberg,"

Missy tucked Charlie's letter away in her marquetry bureau, snapping, "I can't think why Charlie is so keen on our dreadful Royal Family."

Robert put his arm round his mother's neat waist.

"Cheer up, Mamma, it takes all sorts to make the world. Young Louis is a very likeable chap, and he probably wants Charlie with him for light relief from what you so unpatriotically call our 'dreadful Royal Family.' Anyway, admit it, you're only in a bad mood because 'Don Roberto el Bobo' is setting out once more to seek his fortune, and you're convinced he's going to do something stupid, like firing off revolvers, or getting in rages!"

Missy hugged her eldest son, and blew her nose hard on a fine lawn handkerchief.

"Of course I shall miss you, Bob! I sometimes wish you had settled for the law, like your friend Francis Ady[53] – I might have seen a bit more of you that way."

Robert shouted with laughter.

"Can you see me as a lawyer, Mamma? I'd let everyone off and it would no longer be safe for respectable citizens like yourself to come out of their houses! No, it's the wide open spaces for me – and what could be more spacious than the Pampas? I've found my metier, dear Mamma, and this time it's going to be far more fun because George will be with me. I can't wait to see him riding a baguale!"

"And biting the dust, you mean, while you, the horseman of all times, stands by laughing your head off," said George. "Splendidly jolly fun old man. I'm off to pack, and I shall take the precaution of putting in a few of my mother's best satin cushions to protect my anatomy during this dangerous sport. Can't think why I ever agreed to go. Well, can't back out now, must be off to the morning train, across the raging main, as your friend Francis so aptly sings," he added.

Missy smiled at the two young men.

"I *am* glad you're going to have George with you, Bob," she said, "Oh, and by the way, I've invited Francis to dinner tonight, as well as the Wrights, and a nice young American writer called Henry James who you'll like. He's been living in London for a while, but has just moved to Paris. He's back here on a visit and wanted to meet you, Bob. You can ask him all about Custer's 7th Cavalry, and Crazy Horse's Sioux stronghold at Bowder Rover which you've been going on about lately!"

"I don't suppose he knows anything about it," retorted Robert. "Anyway he won't see the Indian's point of view, Americans never do."

"I find him a very intelligent young man," said Robert's mother gently. "But perhaps he is more interested in Europe than in North America, so maybe you are right."

---

[53] A close family friend, the same age as Robert.

Next day the two "colonists" set out to join the good ship s.s. Douco, which was to take them to Monte Video to begin their new life together. Robert was flushed with excitement, he was going back to South America where he had spent five out of the past seven years, and where he knew he was happiest in all the world.

CHAPTER XIV

On 19th January Robert wrote to his mother that he and George Mansel had dined on board *H.M.S. Black Prince* at Lisbon, and next morning had steamed through the Fleet. They had passed right under the stern of the Flagship. "The last thing we saw of them they ran up 'Adios' to us in the signals." Both Robert and George had felt decidedly gulpy at the time, but were careful not to reveal their emotion to each other.

Robert's mother had given them a copy of *Omar Khayam* to read on the voyage, and Robert told her that it had been a great consolation on board ship, adding, "Mansel likes it very much, but says that the grape, as far as he knows, is not allowed by the Koran."

The two young men had kept themselves well exercised on the voyage with fencing bouts each day. They had acquired a dog to take with them to South America, but were very put out to be told that the 'dawg' was not to run about on the decks; so Robert was longing for their first port of call so that he could give the poor animal its first run for nearly two weeks.

They had made good friends with the 'familia Rocha' on board, who had "turned out great fun," and Robert particularly admired their seven-year-old son who played the piano very well indeed.

They were also vastly amused and intrigued by a large Brazilian lady who sat at their table for meals and put her knife right down to the handle in her throat at every mouthful, "this shows me what I might attain with practice!" he added.

Like all passengers travelling long distances by sea, they found that the most trivial incidents occupied much of their attention: rollicking porpoises and flying fishes were the best diversion of all, and at night the phosphorescent light on the water never ceased to fascinate them with its beauty.

The final week of the voyage flashed by with Mansel having his hair cut so short that it looked like "the top of a match," and being taught Spanish by an Andaluz bullfighter who had taken a great fancy to the ex-naval officer and declared that he would soon turn 'Don Jorge' into a complete torero. Mansel declined the invitation politely, and continued to practise his Spanish until, as he put it to Robert, he reckoned he would soon be able to make himself pretty well *misunderstood*!

At Rio the two friends went ashore, and George was just as captivated by the beautiful harbour as Robert had been on his first voyage to South America six years earlier. They were delighted to learn that they might hope to supply the Brazilian cavalry with remounts from Uruguay and Argentina at eighty dollars a horse. From that moment, not all the glories of the Tijuca with its view across the bay straight into fairyland, the red-roofed town, the myriad islets, the tall palm tree avenue of Botafogo, the tropical trees and butterflies, contented the two young men, as they counted the hours until their ship sailed. They imagined that they were millionaires already.

On their arrival at the River Plate they were kept on board for the customary week's quarantine, as a precaution

Once they had eventually been allowed to disembark at Buenor Aires, they quickly went to see Robert's friend, Claraz, to ask if they could stay at his hostelry. A bottle of *caña* was produced and the three men sat round a table in the courtyard, back at Hotel Universal – Robert felt he had come home.

"I have important news for you," said Claraz, after drinking to their good fortune in the country, "an estancia has just been put up for sale in Bahia Blanca, about 400 miles from here. It is called Sauce Chico (which means Little Willow), and I have it on good authority from my friend Martin Villalba that it would be extremely suitable for your purposes, despite raids by dispossessed Indians from beyond the Rio Negro, who have attacked isolated homesteads and driven off cattle to sell across the mountains in Chile. This means there is a great shortage of cattle. It's a bit desert-like, but the wild cattle and horses seem to thrive on the wiry grass that grows about there. It's your best bet if you want to sell cattle, to move in where there's a shortage and supply the demand. They'll be paying high prices."

"And supposing the Indians attack us, too?" asked Mansel.

"Young Graham is a known Indian sympathiser," laughed Claraz, "I expect they'll leave you in peace! All you need is a small brass cannon, and a ditch round your domain, and you should be quite safe. Some of your old friends from Bahia Blanca will be delighted to see you again, and put you up for a few days."

Robert and George decided to go and inspect the property at once, while Claraz added, "If you still want to risk your necks in the Brazilian jungle at a later date, you are perfectly free to do so!"

Robert suddenly realised how much he had missed his Argentinean friends. It would be good to see them all again, and quite an adventure to take Mansel down to 'Indian Country' before they set out on their trip to Rio. Tomorrow they would set out. Claraz said he knew of a good *restreador*, or 'track-reader,' to guide them by Azul and Tardis, and on by the trail which crosses the Tres Arroyos – a week's journey altogether. They would be able to sell their spare horses for a high price, he was convinced.

Walking across the great plaza Robert suddenly spied a familiar figure. Poncho thrown across one shoulder, guitar hanging from a ribbon, and huge silver spurs attached to decorated boots.

"Cabrera!"

The gaucho whirled round and a smile split his face.

"Don Roberto! Madre mio!"

Cabrera was introduced to George as "my old revolutionary companion!" and the three men stepped into the nearest bar to celebrate their chance meeting. When they emerged, half an hour later, Cabrera had signed on as their *capataz* for the expedition to Bahia Blanca. Robert felt a great deal happier about the whole plan; Providence seemed to have almost literally dropped Angel Cabrera into their laps at just the right moment, as though he was destined to be Robert's guardian angel in this strange, wild country. There was nothing he did not know about survival on the pampas, and if the estancia turned out to be what they wanted, he might be prepared to stay and look after it while they took their horses up to Rio.

By 3rd March 1876 Robert and George Mansel had arrived at the Fonda de los Catalenes in Azul, some two hundred miles south of Buenos Aires. To Robert's relief, he found that George was a born, if inelegant, horseman.

Cabrera urged him on with shouts of delight as he got into his first gallop, arms flapping and feet stuck out at right angles in their heavy stirrups.

"Bravo! Viva!" yelled Cabrera with joy. "It is not necessary to ride well on the pampas, only to fall well!" at which point, as though taking the hint from Cabrera, George's horse suddenly shied violently at a vizcacha which popped its head out of its hole in the ground a few feet from the horse's hooves, and George went straight over his horse's head to land nimbly on his feet. This amazing acrobatic feat earned him even more applause from Cabrera who was already 'Don Jorge's' slave for life.

Robert, too, was full of admiration for this plucky sailor, who seemed to be taking to life in South America like a duck to water. Of course, he had ridden to hounds in Dorset as a boy, and had been brought up in the country, but the province of Buenos Aires was as different to Dorset as Central Africa is to the North Pole.

The weather was getting a little cooler with the onset of autumn (George was astonished to find the seasons back to front, having forgotten that they were now in the southern hemisphere), and the nights were turning quite cold, which they soon found out to their cost as they huddled in their ponchos beside a fire of dried thistle stalks. Cabrera had shown his new pupil how to doss down for the night on his saddle: the padding which went under the saddle was spread on the ground first of all, then the cloth that covered the horse's back spread on top like a blanket, the sheepskin under the hips for softness, and the head pillowed on the saddle pommel.

It was surprisingly comfortable, as Robert was able to assure his friend from his own previous experience of the gaucho's 'camp bed.' Once you were wrapped in your poncho with your head tied up in your kerchief, you would sleep as peacefully as a baby in a cradle, he told George. But of course you must make sure that your pistol, knife, and gaucho belt (or *tirador*), and especially your boots, were kept safe under the saddle pad, in the eventuality of an attack by Indians in the early dawn. Indians never attacked at night in this part of the country, only at first light, Cabrera told them reassuringly.

At dawn he heated the *maté*, passing round the gourd with its silver mouthpiece containing the hot, bitter drink, and they were off across the pampas just as the first rays of the sun came out to melt the early frost.

On reaching Azul the whole place seemed agog with the news that a few days earlier Indians had carried off above a hundred thousand head of horses and cattle and burnt all the camp for miles. Robert and George took this information with a pinch of salt, knowing that (like all country dwellers) the local people loved to dramatise any interruption in their peaceful lives.

The *fonda* in which they installed themselves at Azul was surprisingly comfortable, and they made haste to the dining room for their first square meal for several days. George looked the bill of fare up and down, but finding the Spanish difficult to understand, he finally gave up and asked Cabrera to translate; alas, although highly accomplished in other directions, the gaucho had never learnt to read. Nothing daunted, Cabrera announced confidently that the main course consisted of beefsteaks and cutlets.

George's face of horror had them all rocking in their chairs when the *plats du jour*[54] arrived, consisting of sausages, blood-pudding and tripe. But nevertheless, he started to address himself to the somewhat unappetising meal, for he was hungry enough that day to eat anything that was put before him.

After they had eaten, Robert and George wandered round the little town. The talk was all of the recent Indian raids, or *malones*, and of their fears of the wild Indians of the Ranqueles tribe. Each warrior would carry round his wrist two or three pairs of *bolas*, as well as a sword and a long spear. Their bodies were smeared with a coat of ostrich grease, which terrified the horses by its evil smell, making them mad with fear. This was especially so when combined with fierce cries which the Indians made by striking their hands upon their mouths to produce a loud prolonged "ah, AH, Ah-h-h-h." The whole population of Azul seemed to be in a state of terror.

Later that night Robert and George were able to witness the local Mardi Gras celebrations.

---

[54] Dishes of the day.

The track-reader of the pampas had an uncanny ability to translate every sign into factual information. He could tell where a horseman had ridden ahead of them, where the man's horse had stumbled on the dry ground, and even where he had halted to light a cigarette. Their tracker was also a vital protection from Indians. Juan Maclean spoke not a word of English, in spite of his obviously Scottish ancestry.

A ceaseless wind ruffled the tall brown grass as they rode, bands of ostriches and pale yellowish deer peered at them as they passed by, like groups of loyal subjects lining the route of a royal progress. Maclean told Robert that the numbers of ostriches and deer was a bad sign, as they were only on the move because of the Indian raids.

Just before reaching the little town of Tapalque they came upon their first sight of a rancho that had been burnt and sacked by the Indians. As they rode into the plaza at Tapalque they found it full of men arming, and yelling countrymen galloping in on foaming horses as yet another scare was announced. In a cane chair in the middle of the plaza sat the *commandante* of the local militia, taking *maté*, as he reviewed his rough recruits from his chair.

Many of the inhabitants of Tapalque looked half Indian and it seemed strange that, caught by civilisation, they were now deeply afraid of their wilder brothers. That night Tapalque, too, celebrated carnival: Robert and George were fascinated to see small children, armed with the hearts of sheep and calves, squirting blood at each other from these strangely primitive 'water-pistols.' The customs of their elders were not so very different from the fierce Ranqueles, their gaucho huts not so very much more comfortable than the Indian *toldos*.

Continuing south, they followed a path of destruction and came to an estancia surrounded by a ditch, guarded by a small brass cannon, and full of women and wounded men. Robert had heard how the Indians were always on the look-out for young and handsome women on their raids. "Christian girl, she more big, more white than Indian," they would say. Of the unfortunate girls they managed to capture, the young and pretty ones were given to the chiefs, and the others were made to do the hardest kind of work in the *toldos*, being beaten and ill-used in particular by the Indian women.

At Las Tres Horquetas they came upon the body of a man, a casualty of a recent raid, and after digging a grave, gave him the most ecumenical burial ever given to a Christian, composed of stumbling attempts at the burial service by a Presbyterian, an Anglican, plus Cabrera's own colourful brand of Roman Catholicism. The latter insisted that they should all dance a *triste*, to which Robert heartily agreed, for what was a funeral without a wake? They sincerely hoped that the unknown man's spirit had appreciated their efforts on his behalf.

A week later, nearing journey's end, it was obvious that rumours of devastation by the Indians were no exaggeration. Passing horsemen shouted salutations and paused to give news of more houses burnt, men killed, and women and cattle carried off, a week before. Shortly after this, Robert and George were horrified to see a woman's body hanging naked to a post, decorated with leaves from a Bible skewered artistically where decency required.

That evening the two friends and their escort reached a *monte* of peaches, and a strong corral enclosing a small fort. Calling out "Ave Maria!" in a loud voice, Robert was rewarded with the traditional reply, "Sin pecado concebida" (conceived without sin) and the men were invited to bring their horses within and to enter the house.

Their host was a man called Eustaquio Medina, who had been wounded by the Indians. They were told that his youngest son had just died and therefore they had an *angelito* in the house.

The gaucho custom of holding a dance to celebrate a child's soul going to heaven was known to Robert. He explained to George that they would be expected to join the party, so he hoped he would not be too squeamish.

George was certainly not prepared for what he saw when they were ushered in – the *angelito* sat in a chair dressed in his best clothes, greenish in colour and with his hands and feet hanging down limply. Just below his chair sat an old gaucho playing a guitar while the guests danced *el cielito*, the *gato*, a *manguri* and *habernas*.[55] As they passed the body, the girls snatched their hands loose from their partners to cross themselves.

---

[55] These are the *tristes* which were danced at funeral wakes by the gauchos.

Robert and George escaped as quickly as they could, leaving the ghastly proceedings on the excuse that after a week's hard riding they badly needed sleep before their final ride next day to Sauce Grande. They were treated as heroes to have ridden across the Pampas at such a time of danger, and taken to a whitewashed guest room, where they slept exhaustedly.

Downstream from Sauce Grande in its clump of willows lay the smaller property of Sauce Chico – almost as Robert had imagined it, except there was no *monte* of peaches. In the pastures grazed hundreds of horses, and a large herd of cattle were watering down at the river side.

"Look, George old man!" said Robert eagerly, "The Promised Land! I'd know it anywhere from Enrique Edwards' description." As George shielded his eyes from the sun, gazing towards the two estancias, Cabrera shouted, turning his horse to slip out of sight. Robert and George quickly followed him, with Maclean and their band of gauchos at their heels. Cabrera leapt off his horse, wrapped its head in his poncho, and gestured to the others to do the same to stifle any possible neighing which might give away their hiding place.

Robert looked at him questioningly.

"*Los indios bravos*....." mouthed Cabrera, and although he stood like a statue, Robert could see his hands shaking as he held grimly on to his horse. Listening intently, Robert suddenly felt the earth throb and heard a hundred hoof-beaets. The same sound he had heard when he was captured by the *Correntinos*, but this time the horses were galloping away into the distance. Cabrera's quick action had prevented them from being spotted.

The men waited in the hollow for half an hour, and then cautiously crawled over the summit on all fours to make sure the Indians had gone. Amongst the estancia buildings smoke was rising, and where there had been cattle and mares grazing up in the pastures there was a great emptiness. It was as though the large herds had never existed. They had arrived at the precise moment of the Indian raid: the two properties were now valueless.

It was true dramatic irony, thought Robert. Was he always to be destined to fail? Were the dice so heavily loaded against him? As he gazed at the desolation a new thought came to him: he had just witnessed an

Indian raid! He had just seen something with his own eyes that most people only read about in books! Perhaps the failures in his life were not so disastrous after all?

He already knew more about the social problem of Paraguay than most of his countrymen knew about the slums of London; he had ridden with the gauchos and been accepted almost as one of them, all because of a revolution; and now he had first-hand experience of the Indians' desperate fight against extinction.

These were things no-one could learn out of books, these were facts of life which must be accepted so that relief could be brought to these unfortunate people who had just as much right to live in this world as he himself. So many wrongs to put right: the Paraguayans living in a country desolated by war, the gauchos striving to make a living in a country where the open pastures were already threatened, and the Indians dispossessed of their rightful lands and pushed further and further south to the inhospitable lands of Patagonia.

If everything had gone right for him, he would be far too busy making money for himself to take notice of these things. Someone had to stand up for the rights of these people, at least he could talk to his friends about them when he got back home – influential people who could improve their lot. Perhaps he could even try to write about what he had seen. He might never make his fortune, but his life was a great deal more exciting and fulfilling than most.

Why had he always been so interested in people like Raleigh, Cervantes, Claverhouse, and even Guy Fawkes, who had failed? Failed gloriously, even? Failure alone was interesting, and had any of his ventures turned out well he would quickly have forgotten them. But because he was gazing down at a scene of disaster he found the adrenalin suddenly flowing. Here was a part they could play instantly, in a real-life drama, instead of idling away their days playing at being *estancieros*.

George noticed his friend's burning eyes and thought he was suffering from shock and anger. This was certainly a devilish reward.

"Come on, George," called Robert suddenly, as he hurried back down the hill where Cabrera had remained holding the horses.

"We must go and give *Facon Grande* and *Facon Chico* a hand, Cabrera. The Indians have ridden off with all their stock. They'll need help. Come on, everyone. *Vamos.*"

Robert leapt on his chestnut horse and led the way. The river was low and they were soon across, within hailing distance of Sauce Grande, where the cousins came running to greet them; Edwards tall, dark and lanky with long hair and a ragged beard, and Walker of middle height with sandy hair and a short well-cropped beard.

"We saw it all happen," said Robert.

"We have not been able to give you a very good welcome, after all these years, Don Roberto," said Edwards, who still spoke English as though he had just emerged from his club in St. James's Street.

Walker looked totally dejected.

"Once you have rested, you will want to ride straight back to Buenos Aires. There is nothing for you to stay here for, now."

"Nonsense!" said Robert as cheerfully as he could, "at least we could have a shot at getting some of the stock back, couldn't we? We'll ride out with you and do what we can to help, won't we, George?"

George smiled encouragingly at the two cattle farmers.

"It's the least we can do. Just tell us the form, and we'll help in any way we can. Cabrera here has quite a reputation for collecting horses, so I'm told!" he said, grinning at Robert.

After a few glasses of *caña*, the two *estancieros* and their visitors had got over the worst of the shock and started to work out how to set about recapturing the horses and cattle.

"The Indians are bound to be making for the Andes, up through the apple forests to the passes where their kin the Araucanians will take the animals on to exchange them for silver horse-gear known as Chafalonia Pampa – much coveted because of having no alloy. The area they occupy is known as the *tierra adentro*," explained Edwards.

"Do they travel fast?" asked George.

"No faster than any other herd on the move. Robert knows all about driving cattle and horses. You can't exactly hurry them, or they stampede. I should think we could catch up with them quite easily, but I don't think four of us against those ferocious Indian braves would be much good! The trouble is, they have great courage and tenacity – and our own horses are terrified of them! They look pretty frightening with their horses painted and feathered, and they smell perfectly awful."

Edwards wrinkled up his nose at the thought.

"In other words you echo the North American sentiment that the only good Indians are dead Indians!" chuckled George.

"They've far more right to be here than we have!" exclaimed Robert, jumping to their defence.

His three friends burst out laughing.

"Oh, Robert! You rose to that one superbly, my dear chap! We all know how you respect the Indians. Perhaps you would be kind enough to go and ask your friends if we can have our ball back?"

There was more laugher at this, which Robert joined in as whole-heartedly as his friends. He knew that he had overreacted very pre-dictably and had thoroughly deserved their teasing.

Their merriment was the only possible reaction to the terrible events of the morning, and they all felt much better for a good laugh, though they each knew in their heart of hearts that what had occurred was total disaster for Sauce Grande, and that Sauce Chico was now quite worthless and there was not even any point in contemplating it as an investment for the future. To supply it with stock from scratch was quite beyond the amount of money either George or Robert could raise, even if they pooled their resources.

"Why do you think the Indians have suddenly started all this pillaging after living quietly beyond the Rio Negro for a good number of years?" Robert asked his friends.

Walker answered him gravely, lighting up an evil-smelling pipe, "It's quite obvious to us, Roberto. It's all the fault of those idiots at Washington who have messed around with the Sioux's rights in the Black Hills, or the Paha-Sapa as the Indians call them, up in Dakota.

"In 1868 the United States Government signed a Treaty with the Sioux, giving them the Black Hills territory forever, and forbidding white men to enter it without their permission. Shortly after this, some white men chanced to find gold in the Black Hills and Americans began flocking there. Naturally the Indians killed them or chased them out, partly because of the treaty, but more importantly because it was sacred ground. You see, the Indians thought the Paha-Sapa was the centre of the world, the place of gods and holy mountains, and it was there that their warriors went to speak with the Great Spirit. Because of the killings the United States government tactlessly sent a thousand soldiers to invade the Black Hills and protect the gold-hungry Americans in 1874. Even more tactlessly, the general they sent to lead the expedition was none other than General Custer who had slaughtered the Cheyennes on the Washita six years earlier. The Sioux called him 'Long Hair,' or 'Pahuska'."

Walker paused to relight his pipe, then went on.

"In October of 1874 a band of young warriors cut up a pine tree that had been selected for a flag-pole in one of Custer's army camps, and the reservation was punished for this act with even more army supervision. Throughout 1875 the Indians tried to prevent the Washington men from taking Black Hills away from them, patiently negotiating, and pointing out to the commissioners that the treaty had laid down that three-quarters of all adult male Indians in the area must be prepared to sign the treaty if any of their land was to be sold.

"Realising that there were at least twenty thousand Indians in the area, the commissioners at last realised they would never drive a bargain; but they still hoped to buy the mineral rights of the Black Hills from the Indians.

"In September 1875 – that is, *last* September, gentlemen – at a council meeting, it was made quite clear to the commissioners that the Indians would never sell the Black Hills, nor would they enter into any form of lease. On hearing this, the commissioners went back to Washington and, believe it or not, told the government that they should compulsorily acquire the Black Hills and ignore the Indians' wishes in the matter. A sum should be fixed that was a fair equivalent of the value of the hills, and the matter be presented to the Indians as a finality.

"At this point the government decided that all bands of Indians off the reservations would be hunted down and moved inside the reservations, and that all Indians should be warned to come into the reservations before 31st January 1876."

"My God!" exclaimed Robert, interrupting the story with an explosive oath, "it's unbelievable – do you realise this is exactly how Dutch

William[56] brought the Highland clans to heel, and caused the massacre of Glencoe[57] into the bargain? Exactly the same tactics – all the chiefs had to sign an oath of allegiance at certain points throughout Scotland before 1st January 1692. That was two hundred years ago, and the silly bastards are still at it. I just can't believe their idiocy."

"Well, you know the rest of the story all too well, Robert, and as you've rightly said, it's not much different to Glencoe – the Indians have simply been massacred. That's why we all agree with your own enlightened view of the Indians and their right to hold land – until they come and drive off all our own stock. Just at this particular moment I'm not sure that I don't slightly sympathise with General Custer!"

At the sound of horsemen riding into the corral, Edwards leapt to the window. Then he sighed, "I'm a big jumpy after that last episode – thought it might be our friends back again for more horses! It's our neighbours, the Millburn brothers and Don Martín Villalba. The buzz must have got around. They'll be delighted to see you, Roberto, and to meet Mansel, too."

An hour later, they found themselves riding with Cabrera and Maclean, some of the Sauce Grande gauchos, and the five *estancieros*, towards the headwaters of the Naposta river. All were armed with a strange assortment of weapons. Robert was torn between his desire for fair play with the Indians and his anxiety about the cattle and the horses they had driven off.

They were ten miles from the estancia when ostriches were sighted flying over the grass towards them and a herd of deer bounding across the skyline of a small hill in the distance. The Indians might only be about five miles ahead of them if they were driving the herds of cattle and horses; or they might even have stopped to let the animals graze for a while.

Robert rode on beside Facon Grande and Don Martín until they reached a small rise in the ground. As they rode over the crest of the hill Robert saw down below them a small monte, and beyond that, by a fork

---

[56] William of Orange, who was crowned King of England on 11th April 1689.

[57] The infamous massacre at Glencoe took place on 13th February 1692. Over three dozen MacDonalds, suspected of being Jacobite supporters, were brutally killed by soldiers commanded by Captain Robert Campbell of Glen Lyon.

of the Mostazas river, the herds from Sauce Grande were indeed grazing. Round a fire sat the Indian *bravos*, obviously having something to eat after all their exertions.

The sun was beginning to go down, and Don Martín told his friends there was only one possible chance. If they could approach the Indians from the west, in other words from the opposite side of their temporary encampment, the Indians would have their eyes blinded by the rays of the setting sun. One of Don Martín's party must then gallop in and lasso the bell-mare, and then go hell for leather downstream in the hope that the horses would follow and that they could turn the herd in the direction of their homelands at Sauce Grande. Meanwhile the reset of the men must try to turn the cattle, who might well stampede at this point. It was a dangerous plan, but the only chance they had.

Don Martín looked around the men, who were all eager to go.

"Facon Grande had better lasso the bell-mare – he's her owner, after all, and she knows him. I'll ride behind to cover him in case of an attack by the Indians. You, Facon Chico, can take the reset of the men to do what you can with the cattle.

"Don Roberto, you can go with them to help him: you've driven cattle I know. And if your friend Mansel cares to wait in this region with one of the Millburns, they can ride for help if we get overpowered by the Indians. The two sailors can rush to the rescue with the channel fleet if all else fails!" he laughed mirthlessly.

"Delighted, I'm sure!" said the elder Millburn, known as 'the Captain.'

Robert felt extraordinarily elated, as the body of men rode one behind the other down a narrow valley to skirt around the Indian encampment. Cabrera and Maclean rode behind him, and he could sense their excitement. He hoped their horses would not start to play up, sensing the disturbing currents from their riders. Don Martín had worked out his plan to perfection, the sun would be just at the right height when they swung round towards the encampment, still high enough to give out blinding rays when you looked straight into it, as the Indians would be forced to do once the alarm was tiven.

They had now skirted the encampment and Don Martín signalled for them to turn. They paused for a moment while he slipped from his horse and crawled over the skyline to reconnoitre. Robert had ridden quietly up beside Don Martín's horse to hold the rawhide rein. Don Martín was back on his horse in a moment and whispered to Robert that it was now or never. The horses and cattle were still grazing peacefully, so they were not aware of the arrival of their previous owners; but the Indians had obviously finished their meal and were beginning to move about as though preparing to set out again.

The men loaded their various weapons, old and rusty as some of them were, and Don Martín gave another signal. This time they were all galloping towards the river, over the hill, in a mad rush towards the grazing heards. Heads had lifted, and Robert knew that any minute now there would be a stampede. They simply had to get amongst the animals before the whole lot bolted, probably in the wrong direction.

Don Martín was galloping hard towards the horses, and Facon Grande had now got ahead of him, whirling his lasso round his head. Robert and his colleagues were making for the cattle, with Facon Chico leading their charge, lasso at the ready. Robert felt his horse bunch up underneath him and then streak ahead in a gallop that was faster than anything he had ever experienced. There was no motion in it, it was as smooth as the flight of an arrow, and almost as fast. For some extraordinary reason Robert did not even feel frightened, the speed was so exhilarating that he wanted to shout for joy, but he knew that he must continue to be in control, he must be ready to slow down when they reached the cattle, and ready to speed on again if they stampeded, to turn them in the right direction. There would be no time to get into the traditional positions of point, swing, counter, and drag, but somehow he was sure that they would instinctively do the right thing.

It was at that moment that it all started to go wrong. Don Martín had been unable to pick out the bell-mare and had lassoed the wrong animal, which had given the Indians time to jump onto their own horses bare-backed, and ride off the herd who were posed ready to stampede. They were already shouting their spine-chilling "Ah-Ah-h-h," and for a moment Robert had a glimpse of their strange yellow coppery bodies, not tall, but well proportioned (all but their legs, which were bowed from lives passed on horseback since their youth), their black hair, long, cut square across their foreheads and hanging down the back; and their faces, flat and brutal, with restless eyes as though they lived their lives in constant fear.

Then they were off, galloping like the devil, each warrior with a spare horse, which had been taught to run easily beside him and leave his hand free for the spear. But now they were only anxious to escape with the herd. They did not want a confrontation with the Alcalde (whom they knew of old) and his men. Robert watched fascinated as the Indians somehow managed to drive the frightened cattle before them, at the same time urging the bell-mare ahead, so that the horses had soon surrounded her and were pushing forward without outstretched necks, anxious not to be left behind. The shouts and the dust created a scene that made Robert think of Dante's *Inferno*, and when it cleared the Indians had vanished into the dying rays of the sun, with the cattle from Sauce Grande and Sauce Chico driven before them.

A curl of smoke twisted slowly from the fire the Indians had left behind them, and a breeze bent it sideways as the sun finally slipped down below the edge of the pampa.

Don Martín sat on his horse in a dejected position, while Facon Grande held on to the only horse they had saved out of the whole herd, a *Tedomon*, or half-tamed mare who happened to be the same colour as the bell-mare, which was why the whole plan had failed. Nobody was going to blame anyone for that, the important thing was that there had been no bloodshed. But it was humiliating to think that these men, who were so careless of life and so contemptuous of death, the rightful owners of the pampas, had shown in less than five minutes that they were still the best equipped to cope with life in the Tierra Adentro – Bahia Blanca.

Slowly the *estancieros* and their gauchos made their way to the fire which still smouldered. It was too late to ride back to their homes tonight, so they might as well use the fire of their victors to warm themselves as the sun disappeared below the horizon.

Somehow or other none of the men felt like sleep that night. It may have been that they were hungry, or it may have been from sheer disappointment that their well-conceived plan had gone awry, and that the Indians still had the upper hand. They had failed to retrieve the valuable heads of cattle and horses, the livelihood of el Facon Grande and el

Facon Chico. Mansel and Milburn had seen it all happen from their hiding place, and had now joined their friends at the fireside.

To while away the night, somebody produced a copy of *Martin Fierro* by José Hernandez, and, it being an appropriate story, the men decided to take turns in reading a hundred lines or so each, so that they could all hear the story of how Cruz and his friend took refuge with the Indians. The fire was fed with cow-dung and thistles, and gave out a fierce, transient flame. Someone heated the maté, and Robert handed round cigarettes. A few strips of *charqui* were produced from someone else's pouch, and the men settled round the fire for the night, huddled in their ponchos. They would not be disturbed by the Indians again: the Indians had everything they wanted, and were heading home for their own encampment where they would feast on mare's flesh, and the *caña* that was never wanting in the Indians' *toldos*, or tents.

Next morning they agreed that George Mansel should go to see the lawyers in Mar del Plata, to talk about whether it was worth putting in an offer for Sauce Chico under these unfortunate circumstances.

Robert let George go on his own, so he would feel free to make his own decision. With his own more slender resources, if Robert wanted to go into partnership at a later date, that could be arranged later.

While George and Walker were away, Robert decided to ride down the coast towards Bahia Blanca, with Cabrera and Maclean. He was anxious to see something more of the country. Midwinter had arrived in the southern pampas, and the chill winds froze him to the marrow. Sauce Chico was far too near Patagonia for his liking, almost as bad as being in Scotland; he preferred Paraguay where frost was unheard of, he thought as he wrapped his poncho closely round him.

Later that day, Cabrera suddenly leapt off his horse to lead them quickly down into a boggy hollow, with their ponchos muffling their horses' heads. They hardly dared to move. Robert could hear the thunder of the Indians' horses' hoofs not far off, mingling with the thumping of his own heart. Silence at last, and Cabrera peeped stealthily over the brow of the hill.

"Another cattle raid. I never thought they'd come as far east as this."

"We'd better get back to the fort," said Robert. "I'm not going to walk straight into an Indian skirmish like this. We're not even armed!"

Juan Maclean agreed with Robert, and they persuaded Cabrera to return to Mar del Plata. The wind was against them on their ride back so they never heard the sound of hoofbeats following them. Cabrera was well ahead, and Juan Maclean was lagging behind on a lazy horse when they were attacked.

Robert tried to remember afterwards if he had heard anything, but all he could think of was the shout of warning from Maclean, and a quick glimpse of three Indians galloping after them at breakneck speed, bare-backed, and with lances made of bamboo. These were fifteen to twenty feet in length, the shaft joined by a piece of a cow's tail and decorated with a tuft of horsehair under the blade, which looked, at a distance, exactly like a human scalp.

Robert did not wait for a second glance, whipping up his horse and digging in his spurs, his one idea was to put as much distance between himself and the three *bravos* as possible. Fortunately he was riding one of the fastest horses from Sauce Chico, and his steed wanted nothing more than to beat Cabrera's horse in a wild life-or-death race.

He streaked past Cabrera, urging him to flee, and the two horses flew on together mile after mile like the wind. Suddenly Robert found that the dreadful sound of pursuing hoofbeats had stopped. The Indians had given up the chase, but he still dared not look round in case it was an illusion. He continued to dig his spurs into his horse's flanks until he was safely through the gates of the little fort on the outskirts of Mar del Plato where they were staying.

It was only then that the appalling fact dawned on his that the Indians must have caught the young *restreador*, which was why they had broken off their pursuit of Robert and Cabrera. There was no sign of Juan Maclean. As Cabrera slid to the ground he, too, realised that their young friend must have been captured. What should they do? How could they rescue Maclean?

"I will tell the men here, perhaps they will get up a search party. We can only hope that Juan's skill as a *restreador* may help him to escape – that is, if they have not killed him instantly," said Cabrera.

Robert kicked the corral gate viciously with his boot.

"Damn and blast this appalling country. It's bad enough having our stock driven off, but when one of our best men is taken – that's the final

straw. I'm not staying another minute in Bahia Blanca. This land be-
longs by right to the Indians and they are not going to let us forget it. I
don't blame them, and I don't intend to trespass any longer. I'm going
back to the Banda, and if Don Jorge wants to stay here, he won't have
me for a partner."

When Robert confessed that his heart wasn't in Sauce Chico, George
nodded gloomily.

"I was a fool to think we could make a go of it. I suppose it's really
my fault about poor young Juan. If I hadn't been an obstinate fool and
wanted to stay on down here, it would never have happened. It's just
pouring money down the drain to try and run a property in this area. I've
realised this now, and I can only say how sorry I am about everything.

"We'll ride north as soon as we get some definite news about Maclean. I suppose there's still a chance that a bright boy like that, with so
much experience of the pampa, might manage to escape?"

"Not much chance of that," said Robert, "Cabrera tells me hardly any
white man has ever got away from the Indians once he's been caught.
They'll probably have scalped him by now. It's too awful to think
about."

Next morning the two men were woken early by a great commotion
in the courtyard, and Robert was astonished to see Juan Maclean standing in the midst of an admiring circle of militiamen. The boy looked
exhausted, but quite uninjured, and was grinning from ear to ear.

The militiamen had been out the whole night searching for Maclean
and for their stolen cattle. They had just come upon the whole herd,
grazing peacefully, not far from the town, when they saw a lone horseman galloping for dear life towards them.

After a short, sharp skirmish with the Indians they had driven them
off, rounded up the cattle, and brought young Juan safely back to the fort.

"Come inside, Juan, we'll get hot water and food for you," said
Robert. "Juan! I *am* glad to see you – are you *sure* you're not a ghost?"
he asked the tracker in Spanish.

Juan laughed. The Indians had taken him to an encampment some
miles away which they were using as a base for their coastal raids. He
had been stripped and searched, and then staked out on the ground,
spread-eagled. He could see various things going on around him. It got

cold and dark and no one came near him, but he was secured in such a way that it would be impossible for him to escape. His horse was tethered quite near and a guard was set over Maclean to keep watch over him through the night.

Then, like a miracle, when he moved during the night he found his hand resting on a penknife that had fallen out of his pocket when he was stripped. A finger tip hold, and then he slowly eased it into his hand. After nearly an hour of perseverance he finally severed his bonds. "When the alternative is death, Don Roberto, one is not only given super-human strength, but immense patience too!"

Robert and George remained silent while Maclean finished his story.

"Just before dawn," he went on in Spanish, "I finally broke my bonds, throttled my sleeping guard, untied my horse, and galloped as fast as I could towards the coast. The Indians nearly caught up with me again. They must have heard my escape, and it was the most terrible ride I have ever had in my whole life. I kept thinking they would catch up with me, but luckily I was able to ride straight here, as you say 'like the crow flies,' thanks to my training as a tracker. Although they had blindfolded me when they captured me, I knew exactly where they had taken me to, so it was no problem for me to find my way back.

"Not many men escape from the Indians, and I still don't know why those savages did not kill me or scalp me as soon as they caught me. I am a very lucky man!"

After Maclean had fed and bathed, Cabrera fetched him to take him back to the militiamen's quarters for the sleep he badly needed. But he showed no signs of a reaction to his terrible ordeal, and assured Robert and George that he had been greatly revived by his large breakfast, and that after a rest he would be as good as new.

"Just as well, Juan," said George in his halting Spanish. "We're going to need your services again soon! We'll be setting off back to Buenos Aires in a day or two, leaving this place for good."

To Robert he added, "I've been talking to Facon Chico and he's deci-ded to buy Sauce Chico for himself. He is going to ride into town this morning to make the deal. He says we can come and stay with him there whenever we like!"

Robert roared with laughter.

"Now that's what I call real hospitality," he chortled, "but we'll only accept if he'll promise us at least one Indian raid every day!"

Winter was drawing on, and George had caught a bad cold which had developed into a severe attack of bronchitis. There was nothing for it but to stay until he had recovered, although Robert was beginning to get impatient about the delay in getting organised for their original plan of selling horses to Brazil.

At Azul, there was an unexpected bonus waiting for them in the shape of a packet of letters from home. Robert found time to write his mother a long overdue letter.

"I have got some rather curious silver earrings for you, made by the Pampa Indians. Yesterday we celebrated the anniversary of the Independence by all sorts of games on *pingo*, 'running at the ring,' etc. I got a ring, and was the only foreigner that rode! I had a splendid horse, but he was very wild, or else I would have got two or three rings.

"I see by the English papers that our Prince (!!) has been tiger shooting in India[58] and achieving great feats of daring. Caractacus, I believe, fought in the arena against a gladiator with a wooden sword, also I believe Nero and several others fought in the arena with wild beasts – so why not our future Emperor? Apropos of emperors, what an absurd fuss seems to be going on about the Queen's title. I can imagine the articles in the French papers!"[59]

---

[58] The Prince of Wales was disapproved of by the general public for going tiger-shooting – not because they worried about the *tigers* in those days but for the safety of the Prince.

[59] Queen Victoria was made "Empress of India" and some other countries (like France) felt that the British Empire was moving a bit too fast!

CHAPTER XV

Robert and George arrived in Monte Video in June after spending a few days in Buenos Aires en route. It was nearly five months since they had arrived in s.s. Douco, and George Mansel was beginning to feel as though he had lived in South America for most of his life. The first four months had, without any doubt, been the most exciting he had ever experienced. He was determined to settle and was now even more of an *afficionado* than his enthusiastic friend.

Back in the Banda Oriental, Robert regained his high spirits. Although it was still winter, they were no longer subjected to the icy winds of the southern pampas which had blown straight up from the freezing wastes of Tierra del Fuego. Monte Video was a real centre of culture compared to Bahia Blanca, or Mar del Plata. Robert and George celebrated their return to civilisation with a visit to the opera.

The audience consisted mostly of gauchos, in from the camp, and they went wild with delight when a horse was brought on to the stage during one of the scenes. At the end of the opera the horse was brought in front of the curtain to take a special bow with the prima donna and other principal singers, while the gauchos yelled and clapped in a frenzy of rapture. Suddenly the horse broke away from a trembling French tenor and escaped behind the scenes, the audience aghast as they heard loud crashes and sounds of splinter wood, and muffled shrieks from the wings. Robert and George laughed until their sides ached and the tears poured down their cheeks. How typical of this extraordinary country, to let a horse steal the show from the prima donna!

Several ships of the Royal Navy were anchored at Monte Video, and George found some old friends on board H.M.S. Beacon and H.M.S. Volage. The two young men spent some happy drinking bouts with the young Naval officers, many of whom also knew Charlie. One young lieutenant, called Huntingford, had even known Malise, having met him when he had done a short spell of schoolmastering before joining the Navy.

Writing to his mother from Monte Video on 21st June, Robert described their visit to a photographer who doubled as a shoeblack, and how he had insisted that Robert should wear his gaucho hat jauntily tilted to one side for the photograph because he felt it to be *muy artistica.*

Robert found a large packet of mail waiting for him in Uruguay. He had occasional bouts of homesickness, and his mother knew so well how to cheer him up by keeping him in touch with events at home and by giving him all the family news.

By the end of July Robert and George had arrived in Durazno, to lodge with Robert's old friends, Don Guillermo and Don Thomas, a league outside the town in a wooded elbow of the river Yi. Robert remembered helping the two men to build their house, four years earlier, while resting between journeys when they were driving cattle to Pelotas, before his capture by the Correntinos.

For a week or two Robert and George scoured the surrounding country to inquire where suitable horses could be bought. Gradually the word got around that two crazy *gringos* were buying up horses to drive to Rio for the Brazilian cavalry, and all the dead beats, buck-jumpers, wall-eyed and broken backed *pingos* in the neighbourhood were brought for them to view.

Obviously they were going to get nowhere this way, but fortunately Robert's friend Witham suggested that they should move their head-quarters to his house so that he could put them on to some more reliable sources.

Within a few days they had collected seventy horses of every shade and hue, wild and tame, with tails sweeping the ground, manes to their knees, trembling and wild-eyed as they were driven into Witham's corral. Delayed a week by incessant rain, at last they were ready to go.

On the last night before they set out, 5th August, Robert scribbled a letter to his mother.

"A Scotchman called Graham stole my horse and my saddle the other day! I had to pay thirty dollars to the Alcalde before I could get it back again. A fellow here murdered an Italian the other day, they were going to let him off but everyone went and petitioned to have him shot!

"One of our friends is a curious fellow who lives by himself, having lost his brother of whom he was very fond, and has a cat that reminds me of Tom Quattz in Mark Twain.

"Decidedly it is reserved for me to be the Bret Harte of the South, but in Spanish or in English?

"With best love to all. Believe me your affec. son,

R. C. C. Graham."

Witham's house seemed to be devoid or writing paper so Robert wrote his letter on a piece torn from the estancia's account book, heading it in bold letters "Colonists letter to his Mother."

That night he retired to bed early, revelling in the warmth and comfort of his bed as he contemplated the journey ahead and the fact that they might not sleep between sheets again for at least two months. He gave a shiver of excitement. Whatever disasters befell him on his expeditions, there was something about riding over the pampas in the Banda Oriental, or through the jungle further north, that was quite unique. To be out in the wild with his horse was the best thing in the world! How lucky that George Mansel enjoyed it so much; it was luck that he had found such a perfect companion and such an entertaining fellow, all thanks to Charlie really.

Next morning their friends insisted on riding the first mile or two with Robert and George and their peons until they came to the *balsa*[60] where they must cross the Yi. Just before they reached the river, they said their goodbyes. Robert watched them fading out of sight, tall, lithe figures dressed in loose black merino trousers, tucked into boots, hats tied beneath chins, wearing Pampa ponchos. By degrees the motion of their right arms touching their horses, gaucho fashion, at every step, grew slower, then stood still and lastly vanished with the swaying of the riders, out of sight.

The *balsa* was drawn across the river by stout ropes, on either side of the river stood *pulperias* where gin and sardines, Vino Carlon, *yerba*, and all the necessities of frontier life could be procured. Horses and cattle, mules and troops of sheep, passed all day and gamblers plied their trade, while the local "china" girls loitered in deshabille[61] before their mare's hide doors in their little huts, singing to a guider, or calling out encouraging remarks to the gauchos who passed.

---

[60] Ferry.
[61] Half-dressed.

The ferry was owned by Eduardo Pena, whom Robert had known in the old days; he was still the same robust character who could not understand the virtuous, or the bigoted, feeling that bigotry is, after all, not so much excess of faith or want of tolerance, but a neglect to fall into the vices of one's friends.

Once across the ferry, the *caballada* headed north-west for the Paso de los Novillos. On the way, at the Paso de los Toros, the horses bunched together on a little beach of stones and refused to face the stream. A yoke of oxen was borrowed from a local rancho and sent out into the river to swim across it, while a naked man upon the other bank called to the horses and whistled in a minor key, having swum the river himself first. At last the horses plunged into the water, while the rest of the gauchos splashed water in the faces of any who tried to turn back. All went well until a favourite grey roan mare put up her head and snorted, beat the water with her feet, and then sank slowly, standing quite upright as she disappeared.

The sun beat down on the river bank, bringing out the scent of the flowers; kingfishers fluttered on the water's edge. Herons stood motionless and great vultures circles overhead while Robert and George mourned the lost of their first horse.

During the next weeks they crossed mountains and plains, rivers fringed with thick, hard, thorny woods, and undulating seas of grass. They sweltered in the sun, shivered on their horses during the watches of the night, slept fitfully by turns at the camp-fire, ate *charqui* and drank *maté*. The two men had been short-handed from the first, and they soon found that this did not pay, for the *caballada* soon got into bad ways, a group of wildlings causing most of the trouble as they repeatedly bolted at the least little disturbance, wasting hours of time while the *peons* rode after them to drive them back.

A *caballada* that has once bolted is easily disposed to run, so everyone was given strict orders to hobble his horse if he had to get off it for any reason.

At last they got near the Brazilian border and camped in an idyllic spot on a river bank. The weather was still extremely cold, and after a particularly chill night, Robert and George and their *peons* huddled round a fire of leaves, cooking sausages flavoured with Chile pepper.

One of the men (who had been on horseback that night to watch over the *caballada*) drew near the fire, and fastened his horse's reins to a heavy-handled whip, squatting on it as he tried to warm his hands at the fire. Just at that moment a water-rat dived into the river with a splash from the bank, startling the horses. In a moment the horses all took fright, and, separating, dashed to the open country with heads and tails erect, snorting and kicking. The horse that had been attached to his owner's whip soon freed himself and joined the others; but Robert managed to calm his own horse which was plunging furiously with its reins attached to a big stone.

For five hours they chased the horses through the great grassy plains until at last the animals tired, and they were able to round them up and bring them back to their camp, driving them into an elbow of the river and lighting great fires across the mouth of it.

Next day they rode the final five leagues to the frontier. At this point their guide, a half Indian fellow called Fruitos, told them to wait while he fetched the man who would guide them across the frontier at a special place where there were no guards to obstruct their progress. Fruitos's friend turned out to be a noted smuggler, and he led them by devious paths through a thick wood to a ford, known only to him, which was only just practicable.

Passing across the ford by swimming, wading and struggling through mud, they found themselves in Brazil. Robert was amazed to find that it suddenly seemed as different as the country at Gretna or Carlisle appears to the southbound Scot.

But their troubles were still not over; for they had to ride a league or more through a thick cane-brake. Because it was impossible to pursue the horses through this thicket when they straggled, the men finally had to leave several of their best horses who had disappeared amongst the towering bamboo. Robert and George listened intently in case they could hear the horses in the undergrowth, but all they could hear was the strange creaking like the timbers of a ship groaning in a storm, and realised that it was the sound made by the giant bamboos when they swayed in the wind. It was a strangely ghostly sound and they could not wait to get out of the cane-brake, even though it meant that their *caballada* was now down to sixty horses – nine lost today, and the mare drowned at the Paso de los Toros.

Next afternoon they came to a small rancho and were welcomed by a friendly Spaniard, originally from Navarre, who had married a Brazilian woman and settled in this place. He had never managed to learn Portuguese, so was delighted when he found that his guests could speak Spanish.

The *peons* were in a bad mood after the misfortunes of the last few days' march. Robert ordered one of the men to catch and tie up a horse that was playing up, and might cause a stampede. The man merely glowered at Robert and sat stubbornly by the fire. These men were being well paid for the work and Robert would stand no nonsense.

"*Apresuramiento!* Hurry, Pablo!"

The man did not move, but flung curses at Robert, snarling, "I am not a *domador* – horse-breaker, Señor. If you wish that wild horse to be caught you can do it yourself."

Robert caught the horse himself. Suddenly Pablo leapt to his feet, and in one movement he had drawn his knife, ready to attack the caballero who had caused him to lose his *machismo* in front of his friends. Fortunately George had watched the scene developing, and quickly pulled out his pistol. Suddenly the other *peons* appeared from everywhere, and after crowding together to have an angry discussion, they rode off, leaving the two friends with sixty horses on their hands and not a single hand to work them. The only one who insisted on staying with them was the Indian guide, Fruitos.

"Blast it," said Robert, turning woefully to George, "that was entirely my bloody fault. Sorry, George, old man. I just got so damned angry with that son of a bitch that I had to put him in his place. I should have known it was a stupid thing to do. What a fool I am!"

George assured his friend that he would probably have behaved in exactly the same way. The old Spaniard offered them some Brazilians who had been working for him and were now looking for new work.

Next day a bullock was procured and the meat 'jerked.' A pack-horse was bought to carry the panniers of beef and they were soon ready to set off again with their new Brazilian *peons*. The walk-out of their gauchos had been a blessing in disguise, for the Brazilians were far better acquainted with the country and also proved to be very handy with their *lazos*.

They were also full of interesting local knowledge. One day they came upon a deer jumping up and down on the same spot, and were told that it was killing a snake. Snakes were afraid of deer, which was why all the *peons* wore deerskin boots and rode, like Fruitos, with a deerskin laid on their saddles.

By the middle of October they had reached the little town of Cruz Alta. Winter had turned to spring, the sun was scorchingly hot in the middle of the day, and the rains were diminishing. Most of the time they could now ford the rivers with the water barely covering the horses' hoofs instead of forcing their *caballada* to swim the rivers.

Cruz Alta was a small, flat-roofed town, straggling along three flat and sandy streets, the little tree-lined plaza serving as a lounging-place by day, and by night a caravanserai for negroes. When it rained, the streets were turned to streams and the plaza became a lake.

There were three shops in the place: the barber, the chemist and Cardozo's emporium, which was store, mart and meeting place for the inhabitants of the little town and passing travellers. This small metropolis lay half way between Santa Maria to the west and Porto Alegre to the east, in the area of Brazil known as the Rio Grande do Sul. The quiet, sleepy place was situated in the midst of forests, noisy with many coloured parrots and macaws, herds of peccaries, bands of screaming monkeys, bright striped tiger-cats, and flaming creepers with brilliant flowers. Beyond were the grassy plains.

George remained outside the town with the *peons* and the *caballada* while Robert rode to the plaza to get some local knowledge about the best route for the next stage of their journey to Rio. He felt strangely flamboyant standing in Cardozo's store in his gaucho clothes, for when he looked around him he saw that the Brazilians were all garbed in subdued off-the-peg trousers and jackets, and elastic-sided boots.

The shop-keeper, Cardazo, threw up his hands in horror. "It would be madness to try to go by land," Robert was told. "It is five hundred miles from here to San Paulo, and after that the forests are impenetrable."

Robert was not going to be put off so easily.

"Well, if we cannot get to Rio, can you suggest where we could sell the horses for a profit between here and San Paulo?"

"You cannot sell horses in Brazil," said the man, "for everyone in this country uses mules. Only the cavalry use horses and they are based in Rio; it will take you a year to get there! Any profits you might make would be lost in buying feed for the animals on the way."

"How about shipping them from San Paulo?" asked Robert, thinking the store-owner was like some of his fellow Scots who particularly enjoyed putting up obstacles to any new plan that was suggested.

"It would cost a lot of money, and you would have to get a very big price for your horses in Rio to make any profit after so terrible a journey. There is a malign quality in the pastures over the next range of mountains. The horses and mules get very sick. They must be taught to eat salt, for only salt can cure this terrible disease. Should you decide to go, I could sell you salt at the best rate in town."

The businessman had taken over from the geological expert, and Robert saw that the store-owner would soon be encouraging them to make the trip when he realised he could sell vast quantities of salt.

Robert returned to George and the horses with his gloomy tidings. The horses were beginning to look decidedly out of condition. With an arduous trip ahead they had best find an enclosed pasture where they could be fattened up for a few days before resuming their expedition.

Inquiries revealed to Robert that grazing could be obtained from a retired slave-dealer and mule-dealer called Xavier Fernandez. His house stood on the edge of a thick wood; on one side were the corrals for the horses and cattle, and on the other the slaves' quarters. The house itself looked like a flattish haystack thatched with reeds and with a verandah rising round it, supported on strong posts. One end was used for a kitchen and a negress was squatting by the fire baking thin girdle cakes of maize. Slave girls of several hues lounged about, chattering volubly.

Xavier Fernandez wore an old straw hat, bedticking trousers and leather slippers with an iron spur attached to one of them. His untidy wife and two thin, large-eyed, yellowish girls were introduced. They seemed to be wearing garments like pillowcases, tied around the middle with string. Over a glass of Malaga, Fernandez regretted they had not brought mules to sell, a more valuable commodity than horses in this part of the world. Robert was getting rather tired of being told this, but listened politely.

Fernandez told them how a really good mule must be mouse-coloured, large-headed, long and thin, with ears erect, round feet – and that when it was spurred it should never be seen to whisk its tail. Obviously Fernandez considered himself to be a world expert on mules – and Robert wondered if he was also a good judge of 'slave-flesh,' as the cynical thought crept into his mind.

Never mind, here was a valuable pasture for the horses.

Terms were soon arranged and the horses were let loose in their new fenced paddock, with rock-salt laid out in lumps. Some of the tamer horses had pieces forced into their mouths, after which they taught the other horses. The *peons* were paid off, and Fruitos said he would be free to rejoin the two men whenever they required him.

Then began a time of total inactivity for Robert and George. They drank innumerable glasses of sweet Malaga in Cruz Alta, joined in cattle markings, races, and attended all the local dances, near and far, where they met the prettiest of the local señoritas. Sticky cakes and wine circulated amongst the female guests at these dances, whilst the men drank gin, ate bread and sipped their *maté*.

Robert was persuaded to dance a Spanish *pericon*, waving his handkerchief about as he had seen the gauchos do in Entre Rios, hoping that his feet were performing the right steps, his partner gazing admiringly at him throughout.

At the end of the dance Robert remembered a previous experience when he had found it was the custom for the cavalier to present his handkerchief to the girl with whom he had danced. This time he had no intention of allowing his silk handkerchief to pass to the hand of the mulatto girl. After a brief compliment and a bow to his dusky partner, Robert hurried quickly off.

At the *fazenda* of Xavier Fernandez they got to know some of the slaves. Luis, who had been born in Angola, became their special friend. After being baptised, he had spent his whole life with Fernandez. He told Robert that he had been on many trips into Uruguay with his master when he went to buy mules or cattle. When Robert asked him if he did not know that he was free as soon as he stepped on Uruguayan soil, he said,

"Yes, but as I have been brought up here since I first came from Africa and they have been kind to me, it is like the horse's *querencia!*[62] So I stay here because I love the place."

He seemed almost proud of his title when he referred to himself as 'Luis a Captivo.' He was a very upright, gentle person, and Robert and George soon became devoted to him.

By December Robert and George had become so used to their life of leisure at Cruz Alta that their enthusiasm for the trip to Brazil was waning fast. They decided to cut their losses, sell most of the horses for what they could get, and ride back to Uruguay by way of Robert's old Paraguayan haunts. But selling the horses proved to be more difficult than they had imagined. Two of them died of snake-bites.

Robert had been fascinated watching the people making their little *pesebres* or cribs for Christmas, with ox and ass, and the infant Jesus lying in a manger filled with straw. Just as he and George were about to give up hope, the miracle occurred, appropriately enough on Christmas Day.

They had stayed in the town to watch a firework display that was to be held as part of the Christmas celebrations. It was while they were drinking a glass of Malaga outside that Robert and George encountered their own particular 'saviour.' He was a pawnbroker who had a house full of silver horse-gear, and was prepared to take the horses off the two men's hands, half for money and half for barter. After much bargaining they closed for three hundred dollars and a lot of silver bridles, spurs, whips and other stuff, also reserving the six best horses for their return journey and, of course, the pack-horse.

Two days later they paid their debts, and said goodbye to Xavier, his wife, his two sallow daughters and their friends the slaves. At daybreak they set out, accompanied by the faithful Fruitos.

Robert wrote to his mother while they were packing up. He had not written to her for over two months, and she might well be worried about him. He liked to give her good news in his letters, so was rather apt to

---

[62] Homing instinct.

wait until he had something worth while to tell her about. He did not like to admit to failure nor frighten her with some of his more dangerous exploits, or his lack of money. Now he could write optimistically.

Cruz Alta, Rio Grande,
Brazil
27th December 1876

"My dear Mother,

"Mansel and I have just succeeded in selling the last of our horses, and are just going to start the 'back trail,' cheerful but flat broke, but with six 'pingos' and a pack horse!

"It is exactly four months since I have looked on print, except an old almanac in Portuguese that I know by heart now. Of all the people in the world (the Scotch not excepted) the Brazilians are the most disagreeable, mean, thievish, mendacious lot of brutes I ever came across. Cruz Alta of itself is lovely but the pomposity of the people surpasses all belief. Tell Grandmama that although I now speak Portuguese well and quite as fluently as I do French, she shall never hear any more of it from me.

"Who of note are married or dead at home?"

"Last week we had nine days of praying and singing to herald the anniversary of our blessed Lord's birth, it was rather amusing as all sorts of old 'pingos' turned up. Here the people are so ignorant that what they don't know would fill a library. (One of those with the books in glass cases and brass wire in front of them!) I wish I had my Shakespeare with me, but I did not anticipate being so long away. Our clothes are like Robinson Crusoe's, but the horses are in 'grate estate.' We could do nothing but smoke, sleep, bathe and walk, and could not get through the days. I never was so glad to leave any place. It is raining for the first time in months."

Robert tried to think what else his mother would like to hear about. Perhaps he had exaggerated the bit about being so bored in Cruz Alta – it had really been rather pleasant to be able to loaf for once, but he was glad to be moving on even though the rain had started again. He picked up his pen once more.

"How is Mala-Kat, and Lee-Kat too? He ought to be promoted soon, Mansel thinks. What is his present grievance?

"A lawyer died here the other day, as is usual they placed his body in an open coffin before the altar; in the morning his body was missing. The people thought the devil (here there are no doubts of his probability) had taken him to himself. In the mean time it turns out he owed a lot of money, shammed dead, and bolted out of the coffin in the night!

"With best love to all, Believe me your affec. son,

R. C. C. Graham"

Their friend Luis the slave promised to post the letter, and stood waving sadly as the two men set out for Paraguay.

For five or six days Robert and George rode towards the river Uruguay, camping at lonely ranchos inhabited in general by free negroes, and living on jerked beef moistened with orange juice, and a vile-tasting brew of tea made of birch leaves. The horses were going strongly all day long, for the two friends had taken the trouble to give them plenty of Indian corn during their last few days at Cruz Alta, blistering their hands as they husked eight cobs a day for each horse.

They crossed the Uruguay by ferry into Corrientes, and on the third day's riding came to the great river Paraná and to the little Jesuit town of Candelaria. It had been founded on Candlemas Day in 1665 by the Jesuits as the chief town in their missions, but now it had fallen from its proud estate and had become a little gaucho country town, with sandy streets and horses tied at every door, with a barren sun-burnt plaza. The blue and white barred flag of Argentina hung listlessly down from a flag-pole outside the Alcalde's office, which was housed in the old Jesuit college, now turned into the town tall.

The fine church seemed deserted and uncared for by the godless, careless, semi-gaucho population. Robert and George took themselves off to a building called "El Hotel Internacional" where they were given their first regular meal since leaving Brazil, accompanied by some wine of a suspicious kind. The change was so great from their wild camps that they almost felt as if they had arrived in Paris!

Next day Fruitos bade them farewell, for he now wanted to make his way back to Durajno, having been away from home for more than four months. They paid him, and sold their spare horses. Then they had their remaining horses shod, for Robert remembered how stony the ground could be in Paraguay.

After riding through the woods of Morosimo, Curupay and Yba-hai, the two friends arrived at a village where Robert had found an old Paraguayan who looked after the remnants of the Jesuits' library. He poured over the books all morning, absorbing himself in the gentle priests' activities in Paraguay which had lasted from 1604 to 1786. Robert thought their rule was a little like dropping down a diving bell in the "flood of progress," to keep alive a population which would otherwise soon have been suffocated in its muddy waves. Now the muddy waves had rolled over their heads, and the Paraguayans were helpless and bewildered as the tide started to sweep them along. Gone were the happy days when the Jesuits looked after them with music and singing in their Reductions like one enormous Sunday school, and, except in backwaters like Santa Rosa, life was becoming very hard for the Paraguayans.

On reaching Asunción, Robert heard that the steamer to Monte Video was delayed owing to low water, and somehow he did not want the adventure to end quite yet. He had a premonition that this might be his last one in South America. Meanwhile they could stay at Casa Horrocks, and pay their respects to the Stewart brothers.

Ten days later word came that the boat would arrive in Asunción within twenty-four hours. Dr. Stewart was to buy their horses from them, so Robert went for a final gallop on the beach on his faithful skewbald, or *pateador*. He remembered to well his last gallop on the beach three years before, on old Bunny, but Bunny had not survived his return and was now galloping in *Trapalanda*, the heaven to which all horses go.

Suddenly he remembered it was 24th May, and his 25th birthday! He had reached his "legal majority." Perhaps the lawyers would now let him go to live at Gartmore where there would be plenty to do running the estate, and plenty of space for more horses. He could not live without horses!

All their friends came to see them off next day, and as the vessel swung into the stream with her paddles turning, the town dropped rapidly astern. A little way downstream they passed a narrow tongue of land covered with grass on which two horses fed. As the ship drew nearer, Robert suddenly realised that they were their own horses – jumping on the taffrail he shouted "Adios!" at which the horses raised their heads.

Robert never knew whether they had heard his voice or whether they had merely raised their heads at the snorting steamer.

Looking back for the last time, he could see their heads down, grazing once more in the reddish haze, and the grand, half-finished imperial buildings of Asunción piercing the skyline.

These, the dreams and follies of Francisco Solano Lopez, reminded him of a child's toy building-bricks, as they broke the skyline, finally disappearing from view as the paddle-steamer swung round another bend in the great Paraguayan river.

Gartmore

Charlie and Robert Cunninghame Graham
at Finlaystone in 1863 (aged 9 and 11)

"Robertito" (aged 10)

Admiral The Hon. Charles
Elphinstone Fleeming, M.P.
(Missy's father and Robert's
grandfather)

Charlie (the author's grandfather) aged 6
with his mother, Missy

Major William Bontine (Scots Greys)
Missy's husband and Robert's father.

"Bob as he will appear when
ready for the road" – drawing
by James Katon, Robert's
step-grandfather – 1870

Charlie (Robert's brother)
in 1880

The Countess Teleki (née Langdale)

White Pingo "Bunny" at Asunción.

Malise Cunninghame Graham, Robert's youngest brother.

Robert in 1869 (aged 17) back from his "finishing school" in Brussels.

Uruguay – Tropa de Ganado
Cattle being moved by gauchos, 1870.

James Ogilvy and his dog,
"Curd" – 1870

Robert, aged 17, wearing
Gaucho costume – 1870

George Mansell, Durazno, Uruguay, 1876

Robert in Durazno, Uruguay, 1876.

The Alamo – 1880

Setting off from San Antonio to Mexico City - 1880

(The two photographs above were taken by Gabrielle with her "Kodak")

The wagon train with which Robert and Gabrielle travelled
from San Antonio to Mexico City in 1880.

Jack in Texas, 1880

La Graña (Vigo) "Chid" – 1881
(Caption in Robert's own
handwriting)

Gabrielle de la
Balmondière – 1885
*Portrait by Jacomb Hood,
Hands by Whistler*

Robert by Gabrielle, his wife
Drawn in Galicia at La Graña.

Ardoch – 1901

Robert at the age of 34, standing for Parliament in Lanarkshire – 1886

"The Fencer" – Robert, shortly after his return from Mexico and Texas, c. 1885 *Portrait by Sir William Rothenstein* (now in the Dunedin Art Gallery, New Zealand).

Gartmore exterior – 1884

Gartmore interior - 1884

These two photographs taken by Gabrielle.

Robert in prison garb,
Pentonville prison – 1887
From a sketch by Tom Merry

Robert at the age of 40 – 1892

Ardoch

Right: The window of the study
at Ardoch, where Robert wrote
most of his books.

Robert riding in Rotten Row,
London – 1925

Robert with Missy, c. 1925

Speaking in Scotland. Seated, the Duke of Montrose, the Clan
Chieftain of the Grahams of Menteith, c. 1930

www.horsetravelbooks.com

Above: The last equestrian portrait taken in Rotten Row, London, in 1935.

Robert in Buenos Aires a few weeks before his death – 1936.

Bust by Jacob Epstein (now in the National Portrait Gallery, London).

www.horsetravelbooks.com

Mancha and Gato, Aimé Tschiffely's famous horses, following
Robert's hearse in Buenos Aires, March 1936.

Caricature by Tschiffely – Don Quixote and the windmills!

PART IV
"LA BELLE EPOQUE" – 1877
CHAPTER XVI

It was a cold afternoon, and a pale wintry sun shone on the Seine so that it looked like a silver scarf binding the hair of the goddess that was this great throbbing city, Paris. Robert walked across the Pont St. Michel, and halted in the middle of the bridge to look across to Notre-Dame. The grey façade of the cathedral glowed softly pink in the afternoon sunshine, as the sun itself turned into a glowing red ball shrouded with wisps of grey cloud. Paris was beautiful even in late January, thought Robert.

Next day, he decided to hire a horse and ride in the Bois de Boulogne. He enjoyed watching the Parisians walking in the park, and admiring the pretty outfits of the ladies, their coloured parasols, their fur-trimmed capes, and their beribboned bonnets. On one of the garden seats a young girl seemed to be deep in a book, as she sat quietly with an older lady. She looked up as he rode past, and he noticed that she had a delicate white skin, soft dark hair straying out from under her bonnet, and huge black eyes. She looked very young, but there was a strange sense of maturity about her, as though she already knew a great deal about life, but looked upon it with a special sort of serenity, almost with a sense of detachment. She made him think of a young nun, and yet she was not wearing the habit of a 'religious.' He was intrigued by her, and he was sure that the flicker about her lips when their eyes met for a second, was almost a gesture of welcome or even invitation. He could not get her out of his head.

That night, Robert and John Lavery joined their friends at Gambrinus. There was a great sound of good-humoured chatter from the diners, and after dinner the young men moved on together to a night club they knew for a further drinking session.

The girls from Bullier's were singing a song when they arrived. It was a song that everyone seemed to know and the audience had joined in

the chorus, something about "Vous met la tête en feu." Robert thought
the words were very appropriate as he thought about the girl in the Bois,
so different to these girls with their trim, tight little figures, their black
silk stockings with scarlet clocks and the white diaphanous frills under
their demure black skirts. They wore scarlet slippers, and slender red
velvet ribbons round their throats. Once their song was finished they
began a wild dance, kicking higher and higher, pirouetting and tossing
their hair, while the young men in the audience shouted and yelled; their
swift whirlings produced an impression of flashing red, white and black
until one's eyes were dazzled, but they still danced, faster and faster and
faster, till suddenly – zip! – down they all slid on the floor in the "grand
écart,"[1] smiling calmly up at their audience as the students thundered
"Bravo! Bravo! Bis![2]"

Next morning Robert went for his usual fencing lesson to the
Academie where the classes were held. He was considered one of the
best pupils and was told that he might take part in an international
competition that was to be held that day. He had a natural talent for the
movements of attack and defence, with reactions so quick that they
seemed almost automatic. To his utter astonishment, Robert came fourth
against one of the most brilliant of international fencers. He thought it a
splendid joke, for he had always considered himself a "Jack of all trades,
master of none."

At dinner that night Robert's friends emptied their pockets to see if
their combined resources could rise to a bottle of champagne. The bottle
was bought and everyone's spirits soared.

After the fun was over, Robert strolled back to his rooms. A moon
shone on the Seine as though a ribbon of light was threading its way
through the great city of Paris. He was happy here, for the first time
since he had returned from South America.

As he walked through the cobbled streets, Robert could not get the
thought of a young girl out of his head. Twice when he was riding a
horse in the Bois de Boulogne he had seen her sitting on a seat under the
trees. She still looked like a little 'religious' in her dark dress, with her

---

[1] The splits.
[2] Encore!

dark hair and eyes and the whitest skin he had ever seen. As she turned the pages of her book, he noticed that she had beautiful hands, too.

Next morning the sun was shining and it was a golden May morning; perhaps she would be there today, he thought. It would be a perfect morning for a ride in the Bois de Boulogne. He was soon cantering down the rides in the beautiful park beyond the Arc de Triomphe, on a quiet mare from the livery stables.

There she sat, on her accustomed seat, reading her book.

This time, greatly daring, Robert got off his horse and bowed. He had learnt that, in Paris, it was not always necessary to be introduced by someone else. Social conventions were far freer. He hoped the girl would not think him too bold. In his confusion he found himself talking Spanish, not French.

To his surprise, the girl answered him in Spanish – but he could tell it was not her own language, she must have thought him a Spaniard. He quickly turned to French, apologising for his lapse. She laughed. Shyly.

"Vous êtes Français, alors, pas Espagnol?"[3] she asked in surprise. Again Robert detected that she spoke the language with a slight accent.

"Pas vraiment Français – je suis Ecossais!"[4] he laughed.

She joined in the laughter, and her pale skin flushed like a white rose that gradually turns pink as its petals open.

"How very confusing!" she said in English "A Scotsman who looks like a hidalgo and speaks French!"

"Well, you see, my grandmother is Spanish, and we all learnt to speak French when we were children – it was part of our education. The Scots *like* the French you know! – in fact, you probably know about the 'Auld Alliance'? But tell me about yourself. I've seen you here before, sitting reading."

The girl smiled.

"Not exactly reading!" she laughed. "Learning my part for the next play, in fact. My family live in Yorkshire, but I've always wanted to go on the stage. I got the chance to act with a French company."

"And *you* can speak all three languages – French, Spanish and English?" he asked her admiringly.

---

[3] "So you're French, not Spanish?"
[4] "Not really French – I'm Scottish!"

The girl lowered her long eyelashes, then looked up at him hesitantly. "I think you will be a little shocked if I tell you that I am an actress, perhaps? I work for a small company here, and we do plays in French and Spanish and English. They call me 'Gabrielle de la Balmondière'!" she laughed.

"Your *nom-de-guerre*?" asked Robert with a twinkle in his eye. This was a girl after his own heart. She was a real flesh-and-blood actress. He had met plenty in his life, but none of them had looked so gentle and so finely drawn. He felt greatly attracted to her, and continued boldly, "But you still haven't told me what nationality you are!"

The girl laughed. "You are very persistent, sir! But I think I like you, so I'll reveal all to you. I come from Yorkshire, near Bedale, and my father is a respected surgeon at Masham. I have twelve brothers and sisters, I ran away to join the stage when I was 16, and my real name is Carrie Horsfall."

Robert roared with laughter. "Who on earth would have guessed it! Well, after telling me all that, I think you must give me the pleasure of your company to dinner one night! What about tomorrow? Tell me the name of your play and I'll come and fetch you at the stage door. I suppose I'll have to remember to call you 'Gabrielle,' Miss Carrie Horsfall?"

Perhaps she would not want him to see her on the stage, he wondered, but she smiled with pleasure.

"Of course you can come," she rummaged in her handbag. "Here is a ticket for the first night, tomorrow. They always give them to us, but I can never think of anyone to invite!"

Robert looked at the ticket. It was for a very small theatre he had once noticed on the Left Bank.

Gabrielle could not believe that this handsome young man in his smart clothes would want to dine with her. She was not even sure if she had a grand enough dress for the sort of restaurant he would take her to.

But it would be exciting to see him again.

He lifted his hat formally to her.

"And my name is Robert Cunninghame Graham, but I'm sometimes called Don Roberto!" he smiled.

"A demain, Don Roberto!" said the girl.

"A bientôt, Miss Horsfall!" said Robert. "And, by the way, the Scots and the people from Yorkshire have always got on rather well, too!" he laughed as he jumped on his horse.

Next day, after the play, Robert took her to his favourite restaurant to tell him all about herself.

"Mamma and Papa wouldn't let me be an actress, so I ran away to London – and now I'm here, with this small repertory company. It's good for my French – we have to act French farces! Can you imagine?"

The words had come out in a rush, as though she had been longing to confess it all to someone kind and understanding. Her still-white face had become flushed and animated, and Robert thought he had never seen a prettier girl in his life. From Yorkshire! He could hardly believe it. And an actress. That was extraordinary, too. She had looked just like a 'novice' in her black dress.

As they drank wine together at supper, the girl and the young man both realised how homesick they were, and how good it was to find someone to talk to in English. Robert thought that he had never talked to a girl this way before. Having no sisters, he had never had the companionship of anyone of the opposite sex before. There had been animal desire in South America, where the *chinas* (so called from their slant eyes, for most of them were of American Indian extraction) were readily at hand.

In England there had been cousins, Aunt Clemy Elphinstone's bevy of beautiful daughters who had been photographed for posterity in various classical postures by their Mamma, who had become a talented amateur photographer as Clementine Hawarden (married to Viscount Hawarden).

And there had been the smart and petulant young heiresses, in whom Mamma had tried so unsuccessfully to interest Robert, with an eye to recouping their financial losses at Gartmore.

Next evening Robert dined again with his usual friends at Gambrinus. He wanted to tell John Lavery about Gabrielle. Everyone seemed cheerful, and Robert was introduced by Lavery to a young French writer called Guy de Maupassant; Robert Louis Stevenson and George Moore had also joined them and they chose what they would eat. None of them were exactly wealthy, but at Gambrinus it was well known that you could get a good dinner for quite a reasonable price. That was why so many of the young students ate there.

Soon the conversation turned from polite preliminaries to a discussion about what they were all doing in Paris. It seemed that they had all come there for the same reason: to catch glimpses of the new forms of art that were emerging and that were freeing them from the meshes of traditional literature and painting. It was an exciting time to be alive, they all agreed.

Robert told the others that he and his mother had been to an exhibition of the American, James Whistler's, work at the Grosvenor Galleries the year before, and had admired his clever way with colour and shade very much. They were furious when they read that Ruskin had heartily condemned the painter and had said he was "flinging a pot of paint in the public's face."

"I want to be able to *write* like Whistler paints!" said Guy. "Light and shade, just the way life *really* is!" he added.

"Tell us about this new movement of naturalism, George," asked Robert.

"Well, it's a sort of revolt against the escapism of the Romantic School, I suppose," said George Moore. "We want to show what everyday life is like, just as Guy has said, and we particularly want to show that there is a great deal of misery in the lower strata of society – in fact, the de Goncourt brothers have done something like that already, but with a sort of 'cold analysis.' Flaubert treats it a bit differently, and concentrates on a minutely descriptive style, on aesthetic grounds; and I think Zola's driving force in the movement is a passionate zeal for social reform. Perhaps we all came to it for different reasons, but our technique is roughly the same: a sort of objective, detached method of narration, meticulous accuracy of detail, and scholarly care in the documentation of historical background. We have a great respect for the individual experience, so we can write about the seamy side of life, or the hypocrisies of society; or perhaps even the behaviour of the bourgeoisie; or of soldiers, in a war."

"That's very well put, George," said Guy de Maupassant. "We want to write about things that *really* happen in our lives, unglamourised – not about romantic ideals!" he laughed.

Robert Stevenson had sat quietly while they were talking, he had strangely burning eyes in his dead-white face.

"I think I'm the odd one out in this conversation," he smiled. "It all sounds a bit clinical to me, I think I'll stick to travellers' tales and perhaps some historical romances one day!"

"Quite right, Stevenson," laughed Robert. "Every man should write the way that comes most naturally to him. I've never written a word in my life, but a lot of the books I enjoy most are tremendously romantic, like Spenser's 'Fairie Queen' and Cervantes' 'Don Quixote'; however, you know, I am most terribly interested in what George and Monsieur de Maupassant have been saying, because I think there's a great need for this new movement in literature. I've seen some really tragic things on my travels, and I'd really like to write about them one of these days."

Robert's new friends asked him to tell them about his South American adventures. They themselves had never been further afield than the Bay of Biscay, they laughed. Robert's tongue had been loosened by the Pernod, and he started to talk to the three men about his passion for South America. He told them of his recent expedition into Brazil and Paraguay with his friend George Mansel, of the estancia they were going to buy in Bahia Blanca which was sacked by Indians; and how, when they got back to Monte Video and were just about to start up a horse-dealing business in Uruguay together, he had received an urgent summons to return home to Scotland. His father's severe mental condition was apparently supposed to be deteriorating.

Added to this, Robert had come of age (according to Scots law) on his twenty-fifth birthday, which had been on 24th May 1877, and his mother's cousin, Admiral Erskine, who had a house near his home in Scotland, Gartmore, had suggested that Robert should come straight home to stay with him and to lay claim to his family estate. Robert had suddenly realised that Gartmore meant far more to him than South America, so he had packed his bags, left George Mansel to find a new partner for his droving enterprise, and caught the next ship home.

"You'll certainly have plenty to write about!" smiled Robert Stevenson, rather enviously.

Soon the five young men were occupied with mounds of delicate pink *ecrevisses*, a bottle of Loire wine, and all conversation temporarily stopped.

Later in the evening a party of rather older men came into the restaurant and John Lavery got very excited.

"I say, look who've just come in!" he said, as the other four looked at the group who were arranging themselves round a snowy tablecloth, examining the menus. "Those are four of the great masters: Camille Pissarro, Edouard Manet, Degas, and Renoir; and the teacher Gleyre – and the other two who've just joined them are Gauguin and 'Le Douanier'!"

Robert gaped in admiration; here were some of the great artists whose 'Impressionist' exhibitions had been causing such controversy; aged between forty and fifty by now, they were still developing new ideas all the time.

"Who is 'Le Douanier,' as you call him?" asked Stevenson. Lavery laughed.

"Oh, he's really Henri Rousseau, he does those strange primitive paintings. He works as a minor customs official, so he's always known as the 'douanier'!"

"Gauguin looks an interesting fellow," said Robert. "He's almost got the same features as a South American Indian!"

"You're right on target," said Lavery. "His mother was half Peruvian, a Creole. He has spent a lot of time at sea, I believe. Only came back to Paris six years ago to settle down. I gather he's got a Danish wife and lots of children."

"Pissarro was born in the West Indies, too," said Guy de Maupassant.

"Perhaps he's a descendant of Francisco Pizarro, the conquistador?" laughed Robert. "In fact, he might even be related to Gauguin! Don't you remember, it was Pizarro who conquered Peru, in the fifteenth century?"

"This is where you come into your own, Don Roberto," said Lavery. "I don't think any of the rest of us could give you the history of the conquistadores. You know, old man, you even *look* like one now I come to think about it! You must let me paint you one day."

"My grandmother comes from Andalusia, so I suppose I've got quite a splash of Spanish blood in my veins," explained Robert.

Steven looked at him with great interest.

"I'm just setting off on some more travels through France and Spain for another book, perhaps you would be good enough to tell me where I ought to make for in Spain?" he said.

"I hardly know the country at all myself, yet," said Robert. "In fact, I hope to go down there later on in the spring. I have something I want to research – it's a thing I got interested in when I was in Paraguay: how the Spanish Jesuits had such a good influence on the Guarani Indians in the seventeenth century."

The next evening, Robert went to watch another French play in the seedy theatre where Gabrielle was acting. At the end of the performance he waited outside the stage door for his lady-love, for this was how he already thought of the beautiful girl he had addressed for the first time in his life only two days before. That evening they found out even more about each other, and Robert decided that he would like to see a good deal more of Gabrielle.

For the next few weeks Robert took Gabrielle out to supper every night. He was entranced by the little Yorkshire girl. She was two years older than Malise, his youngest brother – nearly twenty now. She was all alone in the world, for her family had felt utterly disgraced by her decision to go on stage, and she could never go back to them in Yorkshire.

"Not all alone in the world, Gabrielle," said Robert impulsively. "You have me. I love you, and I want to look after you."

Gabrielle looked at him with brimming eyes over her glass of champagne. "Do you really mean it, Robert? Or are you just being kind?"

Robert took her long, thin fingers between his own and kissed them gently.

"Fetch your things, Gabrielle. I am going to take you straight back to my lodgings. I have a motherly landlady, and I know she will look after you very kindly. I just know already that I love you, Gabrielle."

Gabrielle put up a hand to touch his cheek.

"Oh Robert, you are like one of those knights or princes in a fairy story. I can't believe this is true. Am I dreaming, Robert?"

Robert laughed and helped her to her feet.

"No, but at last I've found my 'damsel in distress.' Now, we'll go back to your lodgings to collect your things and move them into mine. You can pretend I'm your 'long-lost cousin,' if you like!"

Once they had settled into his lodgings, Gabrielle and Robert soon knew that they wanted to spend the rest of their lives together. In between their love-making, Gabrielle drew from Robert the story of his life. She was still puzzled by his sudden decision to move from South America to Paris. Why had he left George Mansel in Uruguay instead of staying on to sell cattle and horses as they had planned?

It was all so complicated that Robert did not know where to begin. Gabrielle would not understand the ins and outs of land ownership in Scotland, after such a sheltered upbringing in Yorkshire. Neither could she possibly know how he was bound to Gartmore heart and soul, and that when his mother's Elphinstone cousin, John Erskine, had written to him in Monte Video to remind him that he would officially come of age on 20th May 1877, Robert had packed his bags and taken the first ship home. He had suddenly realised that nothing in the world mattered more to him than Gartmore, and that the fascination of the pampas had been a mere mirage.

When Robert got back from South America he was introduced to a new friend of the family, the lawyer, Mr. Wright, who had been advising his mother in London in his absence, and was obviously her close friend. He had already been given almost too much advice by his Graham relations, but Mamma's new lawyer friend seemed so sensible and down to earth.

Robert would always be grateful to the three men who had his interests so much at heart: Mr. Wright, Mr. Jamieson and cousin John Erskine. But he was not so happy with some of the suggestions Uncle William Hope had offered. Aunt Maggie's husband, a VC from the Crimean War, had always been full of hare-brained schemes, many of which his father had fallen for, to his subsequent financial detriment. Robert decided to listen politely to his uncle's advice, and quietly to go his own way. He had not the least intention of planting sugar in Jamaica, tea in Ceylon[5] or building railways in Russia.

"So you came to Paris!" laughed Gabrielle, stroking his thick red-brown hair tenderly. "Wasn't that lucky for me?"

Robert took her in his arms.

"The best thing I ever did in my life, ma chère," he whispered into her hair. Smoking a cigarette, half an hour later, Robert wondered what had really made him come to Paris. He seemed to remember Mr. Wright suggesting that it would be a splendid contrast to life on the pampas; and Mamma had once got him on the raw by telling him that he had become very uncouth since his latest foray to South America. But perhaps most of all the idea had come from Lavery, when they were fencing together at Angelo's in St. James's Street. His friend had told him that lots of young men had crossed the Channel recently to savour the new ideas blowing round the French capital. Lavery was going there himself to study art with the great Impressionist masters, and would enjoy Robert's companionship. Robert could attend fencing classes, and meet a great many interesting people.

Now he had to think how he could afford to go on living there with Gabrielle. Perhaps he had better go to London and explain it all to Mr. Wright. The lawyer was the most understanding man he had ever met. Gabrielle assured him that she would happily stay in Paris till he came back. She knew he had just received a letter from Charlie suggesting he should go to Vigo[6] for a few days, as the fleet was putting in there. She suggested it would be a very good thing for him to see his brother again after such a long parting, for she already knew how devoted they were to each other. Robert was longing to tell Charlie about his new love, but he hated leaving Gabrielle for so long. However, she implored him to go and insisted she would be all right. The landlady was most motherly and kind; and Robert's friends would look in on her from time to time.

Robert crossed the Channel the next day. Over dinner at the Devonshire Club, Mr. Wright listened sympathetically to his tale of his "damsel in distress." If the girl was really alone in the world, the best thing to do

---

[5] Now called Sri Lanka.

[6] An important port and fishing centre in North-West Spain, where nearly all ships called in en route for South America.

would be to make her Robert's ward, so that she could receive some maintenance. It was a delicate affair but it could certainly be organised, he told Robert. He suggested that Robert should go and visit his father, briefly, at Moffat and then spend a month in Vigo with Charlie. By the time he got back to Paris again in a few weeks' time, he would hope to have everything sorted out for him.

Robert decided this very human lawyer was the kindest and most broad-minded man he had ever met. Over their glass of port Mr. Wright asked Robert whether he might one day wish to marry Gabrielle. It seemed that he did, but he knew his mother wanted him to marry a wealthy and well-born heiress, if possible.

"You must marry the girl who is going to make you happiest, Robert, my dear boy," said Mr. Wright kindly. "This strange Scottish anachronism of 'arranged' marriages is an appalling thing. If Gabrielle is really the girl you are going to love for the rest of your life, then you must marry her."

How sensible this man was, and how clever of Mamma to have found such a good friend for her sons, thought Robert gratefully.

"I'll think about it!" grinned Robert. "Thanks awfully for all your help, sir; I'll go back to Paris after I've been to see Charlie at Vigo, and perhaps the next time you see me I shall have married my 'damsel in distress' – but please don't say anything to Mamma about it. I'll tell her everything in due course. I just want to have a bit more time to think about it."

"Mum's the word!" said Mr. Wright. "Now let's have another glass of this excellent port."

Robert decided to take the night train to Scotland and go to Gartmore first of all. There was nothing to stop him visiting his friends the Gartmore employees, and the village people. They were delighted to see the laird's son back amongst them, and hoped he would soon settle there for good.

Taking the train from Buchlyvie to Glasgow, and then on to Beattock Junction, where he changed to the little Moffat branch line, he got himself to the pretty Dumfriesshire house at Penpont and found Papa surprisingly well and lucid this time. While they walked together over the springy turf of the great Dumfriesshire hills, he told his son about the poems he was writing. It was a good visit, and Robert felt cheered. Papa seemed wonderfully happy, and the faithful Italian valet still attended to his every need.

That done, he set off for Vigo to join Charlie and his ship, H.M.S. Northumberland.

From Vigo, Robert not only wrote daily to Gabrielle in Paris, but also to his mother. He was thoroughly enjoying being with Charlie again.

"H.M.S. Northumberland, Vigo, 21st June 1878.

"My dear Mother,

"The Fleet is still here waiting to hold a regatta. It is a very pretty old place and I think must have very little altered since Drake's time. The bay is quite lovely surrounded with steep hills and pine woods down to the water's edge.

"We have been away on several boat excursions, one to a place called Bayona where there is a fine old Moorish castle, with, of course, a Spanish church built in the middle of it, and also in ruins.

"The fleet is to go on to La Coruña, from there I think of going to Santiago (Compostela), and then to Madrid, and home by Barcelona.

"This is one of the great places that Spanish emigrants go to the River Plate from, one of the Pacific steamers is expected in today."

As Robert knew his affairs at home would take some time to sort out it seemed sensible to take the opportunity to travel round Spain. But he missed Gabrielle intolerably and wished he could have afforded to bring her too. At least he was not having to pay for her lodgings meanwhile, for his kind landlady had said Gabrielle could help with some housework in lieu of rent until he came back. Gabrielle was only too pleased.

Robert's letter to his mother continued.

"After seeing the North of Spain, I begin to understand Pizarro and Cortes better than I did. America was not conquered or colonised by Andalusians. The northern Spaniard, though not nearly so amusing, is much more of a man for a colonist or a soldier than the southern.

"A French company is making an aimless sort of attempt to pick up the treasure sunk in some Spanish galleons in Drake's time. I do not think they will make much of it – dive they never so wisely.

"I dined with Admiral Beauchamp on board the Agincourt the other day. He was very civil and desired to be remembered to you. Spring-

Rice still continues to be 'resembling Mr. Charles' – in Lisbon he was taken for my brother! He and I are great friends. We went on an expedition up the Bay the other day, and after lunch we were throwing the lazo with a piece of rope when, to my amazement an old Spanish countryman who was standing by remarked that he had not seen that done since he was in Monte Video. It turned out that he had been in a Spanish frigate in the River Plate! I told him that I had been too in Monte Video.

"Believe me, your affectionate son, R. C. Graham."

By the end of June the fleet had sailed back to their base at Gibraltar, and Robert took himself off on his journey through Spain to fill in the next few weeks until he was due back in London, to receive Mr. Wright's answer to his financial problems.

It was the first time he had penetrated northern Spain, and he was soon wandering happily through Galicia, watching endless hay-making in operation, and finally emerging into the great golden square of the Hostal de Los Reyes Catolicos, in Santiago, founded as a hostel for pilgrims by Isabel and Ferdinand.

Then on to Salamanca where in a library Robert was able to find some ancient documents which showed that the early Jesuits had taken part in the curious experiment of introducing semi-communism to the Guarani Indians in Paraguay in the seventeenth and eighteenth centuries. As Robert had seen with his own eyes, these people were able to enjoy a half-arcadian, half-monastic life with their kind priests to rule over them, until the Jesuits were finally expelled by men who considered them to be too powerful. (*"Jesuita y se ahorca, cuenta le hace"* meant that even if a Jesuit is hung he gets some good out of it, in the old Spanish proverb.)

Robert wanted to find out why the Jesuits had been so unpopular, when to his mind and in his experience they had been the only truly enlightened missionaries. His researches took far longer than he had expected, and the days slipped by unnoticed as he sat poring over old books in the cool libraries.

At 32, Ebury Street, Missy had devoted the summer to Malise. It was his last term at Winchester, and he had distinguished himself in his own quiet way at the school. Apart from being a good scholar, he was also one of the best musicians in the school.

Mother and son had a very close relationship, for they had been left on their own together so much since Papa went to live at Penpont in Dumfriesshire, and the two older brothers had gone out into the world. Malise had the same quick wit and pronounced sense of humour as Robert and Charlie, and Missy much enjoyed his company; but his health gave her great anxiety. For the past few winters she had taken him abroad to keep him away from the chill, damp weather of England and Scotland. Once or twice the doctors had murmured the dreaded word 'tuberculosis,' but Malise always seemed to be so fit once the weather turned warmer again that she could not believe they were right.

Now he was to have a few months at home before going up to Oriel College, and they had already been on two delightful visits: to Leamington, to see Aunt Helen, and to Cortachy to see his mother's childhood friend, Lady Airlie. Charlie wrote regularly and was enjoying his time in H.M.S. Northumberland, having just returned to the Mediterranean.

Robert wrote less frequently, and had apparently been all over the place – first to Lisbon to meet Charlie, then to Vigo, then La Coruña, then Santiago, and then Salamanca, and now back again in Paris. He had written to say that he had done a great deal of research on the Conquistadores.

But he had particularly enjoyed taking Malise to meet their Fitzwilliam relations at half term (his Cunninghame Graham grandmother was the grand-daughter of Lord Fitzwilliam and had been brought up in a very "horsey" family.) Robert rode a delightful mare called 'Luna' but he knew that he had much preferred his gallops on the pampas to 'the Hunt' in England. He missed all the fun of his gaucho friends.

Back in London at the end of July, Robert saw Mr. Wright and was given the good news that a sum of £256.6s.11d had been awarded for the maintenance of his "ward." He dined again next night with Mr. Wright at the Devonshire Club and they discussed his future. Mr. Wright came straight to the point and asked whether Robert wished to marry Gabrielle. He did, but he knew that his mother wanted him to marry a conventional Scottish heiress. What should he do? He had no wish to upset his mother.

Mr. Wright repeated the advice he had given Robert at their last meeting. "You must marry the girl who is going to make you happiest, my dear boy. If Gabrielle is the girl you are going to love for the rest of your life, then you must marry her."

* * * * * *

When Robert walked into the London house on 25th October 1878 his mother was quite astonished. From his last letter, it had sounded as though he intended to spend several more months in Paris, on his way home from Spain, for some fencing competitions.

"Darling Bob!" she cried in delight. "What a lovely surprise!" and threw her arms round his neck. "Where's your luggage, darling?"

"Mamma – I've come to tell you that I've just got married," said Robert quietly.

Missy sat down heavily on the nearest chair, looking as though she was not sure if she had heard her son properly.

"Married, Bob? Did you say married? What do you mean?"

Robert shifted from one foot to the other, just as he used to do when his mother scolded him as a small boy.

"I've met a very beautiful and marvellous girl, Mamma. Her name is Gabrielle. We decided we didn't want any fuss, so we got married yesterday in a registry office in the Strand. I think you'll like her, Mamma," he said.

"But Bob, you mean you got married just like that? Without bringing her to see me first? Without asking any of us to the wedding? What can you be thinking of?"

His mother looked very strained and Robert knew she was trying to control herself. She was both hurt and angry. He had been so passionately in love with his beautiful Gabrielle that, for the first time in his life, he had quite forgotten his mother's feelings. How awful, what had he done? Perhaps he should have asked Mr. Wright to break the news more gently to his mother. He remembered his father's words, so long ago:

"You'll break your mother's heart with your impetuosity one day, Bob."

"Oh Mamma!" he cried, kneeling down beside her, "I didn't realise you'd be so upset. I've got so used to having to make my own decisions and having to look after myself, I didn't think about you . . . . I forgot that you might like to meet Gabrielle first . . . . perhaps I was frightened that you mightn't like her or something . . . . and Mamma, I can't live without her, really I can't."

Missy had regained her control. She took Robert in her arms just as she used to when he was a small boy, and said, "Bob, I'm being very selfish and silly! Bring your Gabrielle to see me, and I'll try to love her, for *your* sake, darling."

"I hope you'll come to love her for her *own* sake, too, Mamma. She is only nineteen, and she has no family, and I want her to have *my* family to love her now."

"And you are a 'verray parfit gentil knight,' as our friend Chaucer would have said!" and she gave him a loving smile; Robert knew that he was forgiven. But he still had to bring Gabrielle to be vetted by his mother, which would be something of an ordeal. He tried to laugh and answer his mother's quip with the same light touch.

"She can speak Spanish, too; and she loves reading just as much as we do, Mamma!" he said, determined to show his mother that his wife had all the right attributes.

"Can we come to tea this afternoon?" he enquired tentatively.

"Of course, Bob. We'll have a 'wedding tea' – but alas, there's no time to produce a proper wedding cake!"

"Never mind, Mamma. If Gabrielle had wanted all those fripperies, she wouldn't have been prepared to marry me in a registry office, would she?"

"Is she a Catholic, Bob, by any chance?"

"Yes, Mamma, she is. Perhaps that's why she didn't see much point in a church wedding. You see, I told her I could never become a Catholic – I just couldn't come round to all those bells ringing, cocks crowing, incense, and things. I'm not really a very good Christian at the best of times, Mamma."

"No worse than most people, Bob. Anyway, let's make the best of it now. I'm quite looking forward to seeing this new little daughter! Poor thing, tell her I promise I won't eat her," said Missy.

Robert kissed his mother and said goodbye.

* * * * * *

It suddenly occurred to Missy that if Gabrielle was a Catholic and they had been married in a registry office, then, in the eyes of her Church they were not truly married. But that was not much comfort to her real feeling of shock.

Gabrielle was dreadfully nervous, and Robert could feel her thin little hand trembling as it lay on his arm when he took her to Ebury Street that afternoon.

"She'll love you, darling petite femme!" he whispered. "You look entrancing in that suit and bonnet. Just try to stand up to her – I know Mamma so well, she is a strong character herself, so she respects boldness in others. Don't worry, we'll soon be over this hurdle, and then I shall take you to dinner at the Ritz!"

Gabrelle managed a bleak smile, and clung harder than ever to Robert's arm. Her first impression of Mrs. Bontine, as she was ushered into the drawing room, was of a very beautiful woman who exuded tremendous energy and vitality, just like Robert. In fact there was quite a similarity in their looks – the same dark eyes, the same determined chin, and the long aristocratic nose which Robert said they had both inherited from his Elphinstone grandfather.

It was the first time Gabrielle had ever met anyone like Mrs. Bontine. She had spent a quiet childhood in Yorkshire and then acting in seedy theatres in London and Paris. Here was a great lady who had been brought up and educated to play a special part in the world, to be the capable wife of a wealthy landowner, to entertain in her conversation, to run a large house with lots of servants and to bring up her sons so that they, too, could play their part in the world with distinction. Gabrielle already knew, from what Robert had told her, that his mother had not only had to do all these things, but had also had to be both father and mother to her three boys. She knew too that Robert was deeply devoted to his mother, and that she would always have to share his love with another – suddenly she felt a strong resentment for this woman who seemed to have so much while she, Gabrielle, had so little.

Robert noticed with anxiety that a strange look had come over his wife's face. She was not smiling, she seemed to have withdrawn into herself, and her beautiful little flower-shaped face looked almost sullen and obstinate. This was terrible, his mother would never understand what it was he loved so intensely about her if she could not project herself more amiably.

"Mamma – may I present my wife?" he said, using the formal words to cover up his own agony.

Missy took the cold little in both of hers, smiling with a big effort and saying warmly, "You are my first daughter, my dear! Welcome to our family!"

Somehow Gabrielle found herself unable to respond to the kind smile; she did not want to be a part of this woman's family, she did not want to be gobbled up by these people who seemed to think that they were so important. She just wanted to be Robert's 'chère petite femme' – to live alone with him in their own private love-nest, isolated from people who seemed to feel they had as much claim on him as she had. Without speaking, she sat down on the sofa beside Robert, and drank tea from a Minton cup – pale China tea that tasted of damp straw. Robert and his mother tried to draw her into the conversation, but her answers were monosyllabic.

Robert saw that this first meeting was a disaster, his mother's warm welcome had been rejected so plainly by Gabrielle, and now his mother would take against her. He knew Missy so well: she did not forgive people very easily if she felt they were unprepared to co-operate. She did not suffer fools gladly. She had strong feelings about the unity of a family, the sanctity of relationships within it, and if Gabrielle was ignorant of the rules of the game, or, worse still, refused to obey them, then there could be no meeting-point for the two women.

Robert's heart sank, he could never have imagined that the two women he loved best in the whole world could possibly dislike each other. It did not occur to him, who had never been given to that particular emotion, that there could be an element of jealousy in their attitudes to each another. All he could do was to remove Gabrielle as quickly as possible, and do his utmost in the future to keep them apart. He would always love his mother very deeply; he needed her cheerful courage, her funny words, that had become so firmly incorporated into their family vocabulary – he wished so much that she thought Gabrielle was 'pet' – her wisdom, and her great appreciate of art and literature and music, and above all, her *belief* in him – her eldest son.

But now a new element had flooded his life, he had found his own helpmeet, his manhood was fulfilled as never before by his intense physical love for this adorable girl, Gabrielle was his chosen partner for life. If only they could have loved each other, Gabrielle and his mother, how much easier his life would be. Why was there always some terrible snag to everything he undertook? Why was life so impossibly difficult?

In the cab on their way back to the hotel, Gabrielle suddenly burst into tears.

"She was horrible to me, Robert. She hates me, I know it. I'm not grand enough for her. She wanted you to marry The Honourable Miss Somebody or other, and I'm just Miss Nobody. She doesn't think I'm good enough for you."

Gabrielle sobbed as though her heart would break, and Robert pulled out a large handkerchief. He found this all very upsetting and undignified, and he felt thoroughly angry with the two women he loved so much. He would have liked to have banged their heads together and said, "Love each other, for God's sake!" But it was no good, he must accept an added problem in his life and try to make the best of it.

Meanwhile, if his marriage was going to succeed he must somehow try to comfort his poor unhappy little wife. If only she knew how unattractive all this crying made her look, her face was all swollen and blotchy, and she had lost the serene composure which had first attracted him to her so magnetically.

"It doesn't matter, ma chère. You need never see her again if you don't want to. All that matters is that you and I are together for the rest of our lives, and that we love each other! Now, dry your eyes, and when we get back to the hotel you are to put on your prettiest gown so that I can take you to the Ritz for a proper celebration. Then tomorrow we will catch the train to Dorset. I want you to meet my friend George Mansel's mother – she is quite different from Mamma, and she will make you very welcome, I know. Then we'll find a nice little lodging by the sea for our honeymoon!"

He was soothing her with words, just as he remembered his old Ninny doing when he was a small boy who had suffered a disappointment. Slowly the sobs and sniffs subsided, and Gabrielle leant against his shoulder as the old cab horse trundled along Pall Mall. He could smell that strangely sweet scent of violets that always seemed to linger about her, and the warmth of her was like a kitten curling round his neck. Giving her nose a final blow, she looked up into his eyes with her own big dark eyes, and a beautiful smile spread over her face, lighting it up in the way he knew so well – the way she had refused to smile for his mother. She would always keep that special light for her beloved, alone.

"You are a kind old Lob!" she smiled, as he put his arm round her.

Robert and Gabrielle were always to remember their honeymoon in Dorset. They were blessed with a St. Luke's summer, and rambled happily in and out of the coves, watching the leaves turning golden and scarlet and the bright blue sea washing pale yellow sands at Golden Cap as the autumn sun shone warmly upon them. On the green downs, the white sheep were scattered like small fluffy clouds, and on the waves at the foot of steep slopes bobbed gaily painted boats.

They stayed in a cottage suitably wreathed in late autumn roses in the village of Chideock, three miles west of Bridport. Robert teased Gabrielle and called her 'the lady of the Manor,' or 'the countess of Chideock.' This soon turned into the nicknake 'Chid' which was to become his special pet name for his adored wife for ever more.

They often visited George Mansel's mother at Puncknowle and, as Robert had predicted, she soon struck up a firm friendship with Gabrielle. She was not, after all, Robert's own mother, so she did not have such impossibly high expectations of his choice of a wife. She found Gabrielle to be an attractive little thing, who soon came out of her shell if treated kindly and gently.

The child was totally lacking in self-confidence, which was not surprising when you thought about how she had been rejected by her own family, but she had been brave enough to pursue the career of her choice.

Mrs. Mansel loved to watch Gabrielle blossoming as Robert's love touched her heart. She was a perfect companion for him, very well-read and intelligent, an accomplished linguist, and full of physical courage –

ready to gallop up and down the steep Dorset downs on some horses Mrs. Mansel had lent them, as she followed Robert willingly to the end of the earth if need be. They were so happy together it was a joy to watch.

By the end of November the weather had changed. Storms blew from the west, down the Channel, and Robert and Gabrielle stood hand in hand to watch huge waves breaking on rocks out to sea, sending spume flying into the air in clouds. It was growing cold, and the leaves were being torn from their twigs by the relentless west wind.

Robert wrote to the Curator Bonis to ask if there were any shooting tenants at Gartmore. If not, could he bring his wife there for a few weeks over Christmas? He longed to show his family home to his wife. He knew should would love Gartmore.

To his delight, Mr. Jamieson wrote back to say there were no tenants at Gartmore at present, so they could come for four months. Robert and Gabrielle were overjoyed.

Just before they left Dorset Robert got a sad letter from Uncle Bobby to tell him that his mother, Grandmama Cunninghame Graham, had died on 30th November at her house at 35 Thurloe Square. "The last person she mentioned was your father," he wrote.

At the funeral he spoke to all his relations, who begged him to bring Gabrielle to see them.

A week later, Robert and Gabrielle, en route for Gartmore, stopped off at Leamington so that Gabrielle could meet the Graham great-aunts, who were delighted with Robert's wife. Aunt Helen Speirs received her very kindly, too, once she had discovered that Gabrielle was a competent horsewoman. Robert was relieved, for he knew that Gabrielle was vulnerable about his relations since his mother had apparently rejected her. He watched her blossom under the warmth and friendship offered by the old ladies, and all three of the aunts told Robert that they were pleased to find he had acquired such an enchanting little wife – so intelligent and scholarly, too. The success of the visit put new confidence into Gabrielle, and when they finally arrived at Gartmore she was able to walk into the house to greet the servants just as though she had been born to it.

The four months at Gartmore sped by far too quickly. Gabrielle was immediately accepted by the people both on the estate and in the village. The undemonstrative Scottish farm-workers liked her quiet ways for they understood diffidence, and were apt to be suspicious of extroverts. Gabrielle shared their qualities of quietly restrained friendship, and they respected her for it. The young laird had done well in his choice of a wife. She and Robert visited each one of them in their houses as they rode round the estate; and Gabrielle was soon playing on the floor with their children, or telling an elderly incapacitated grandmother about life in Paris. They liked the strange way she spoke, with the merest hint of a foreign accent, acquired in Paris when French became her everyday language. Knowing that Robert's maternal grandmother was Spanish, they presumed that the young Mrs. Bontine must have come from the same country. She became known as "the Lairdie's wee Spanish wife," and Robert did not try to correct them, for he knew that Gabrielle had acquired for them a special aura of romance under this title.

They spent Christmas by their own fireside, content in each other's company, and on Boxing Day they went to dine with the Erskines at Cardross House. Gabrielle was soon taken to their hearts, and found she had yet another new family of cousins to get to know. The old bachelor Admiral, John Erskine, brother-in-law of Keithy Erskine, was particularly pleased that Robert had found himself a wife, for he knew that the Curator Bonis would now be a great deal more willing to allow Robert to take up residence at Gartmore, with a wife to help him run the place.

The Christmas and Hogmanay festivities at Gartmore lasted well into January, and Gabrielle was introduced to several of the neighbouring landowners and their wives and families: the Stirlings of Garden, the Murrays of Polmaise, the Grahams of Rednock and of Glenny, the Graham-Stirlings of Duchray and Auchyle, and the Forresters of Polder. Gabrielle also met Robert's favourite neighbour, old Mr. MacLachlan of Auchentroig; then there was James Graham of Leitchtown to call on, and old Mrs. Eastmount of Invertrossachs. She had never met so many people in her life before.

She was glad to find that Robert treated them no differently to the farm-workers or the village people, and she was much interested in this natural feeling of equality between the landowners and the working

classes in Scotland. There seemed to be little resentment on the part of
the estate workers, for each one felt that he was vital to the overall
running of the estate, and that he had just as much right to be there as the
laird himself. No wonder there had been no equivalent of the French
Revolution in Scotland; though Gabrielle had heard it was different in
the Lanarkshire coal mines and in the shipyards of the Clyde. Like other
victims of the industrial revolution, these men were beginning to feel that
they were being exploited by capitalism, and there had already been one
or two ugly scenes.

Robert told her that he had read in "The Scotsman" about a severe
depression in the western coalfields, with falling wages; and that a man
called Alexander McDonald had just formed the Lanarkshire Miners'
Union and was urging his men that the only feasible basis for a stable
wage was to reduce output (as had been done in South Wales in 1875) in
the hope that a sliding scale might be accepted.

The newspaper article went on to say that a bright young man had
been appointed agent in the Hamilton district of the new Miners' Union:
his name was James Keir Hardie. He was becoming one of the leading
young organisers (at the age of twenty-two) for the Good Templars, and
his activities were apparently strongly geared towards the temperance
movement, telling miners to "drink less, read more, and think more."

"Sounds quite a character," smiled Gabrielle. "Shall we offer to lend
the miners some books from the vast library here, Bob?"

"Can you see them enjoying the 'Red Book of Menteith' or 'Biggar,
and the House of Fleming,' Chid? I should think those books would
produce a revolution on the spot!"

"Don't be silly, Bob. I meant things like translations of Russian
authors, Turgenev and Chekov!"

Robert was fascinated to find that Gabrielle was as interested in the
politics of reform as he was beginning to be himself.

During one particularly cold week, Gabrielle had an attack of bronchitis, but she soon threw it off, especially once the mists of Menteith
lifted and a frosty spell made everything sparkle again.

It was a happy time and they thought of little but each other and their
plans for the future. When they dined with their neighbours they found
there was much talk about the large amounts of money to be made from

cattle "ranching," as it was called, in Texas, since the end of the Civil War. Apparently there was a great shortage of meat up in the northern states, and a man called Chisholm had been driving cattle up to Abilene where Mr. Coy, an Illinois cattle dealer, had built shipping pens beside the railroad, so that the cattle could then be shipped on north.

It was said that between 1868 and 1871 nearly 1,500,000 Texas long-horns had passed through the yards at Abilene. Those men down in Texas must be making a lot of money for themselves! Their friends went on to talk about the new breed of men known as "cowboys who had learnt the art of driving cattle from the Mexican vacqueros, and how they had spread their techniques all over the Great Plains, to which so many settlers from England, Scotland, and Ireland were flocking. There was a mighty cattle boom going on in Texas, so it seemed.

Gabrielle turned to Robert.

"That would suit you down to the ground, Robert! You could teach them a thing or two from your beloved gauchos, couldn't you?"

Everyone laughed, and looked at Robert, who sent into an imaginary rope-spinning act.

"You should have heard the stories that were going round the first time your husband came back to Gartmore from South America, Gabrielle!" laughed Horatia Erskine. "You'd have thought they were describing General Custer instead of a harmless gaucho. Long hair down his back, outlandish clothes, and riding round the farms smothered in lassos and knives!"

"They loved it, Horatia," said Robert, "it gave them something to talk about!"

He turned to Horatia's husband.

"But David, seriously, do you think there's any money to be made in this Texan cattle business? Gabrielle and I can't go on living at Gartmore once the new tenants moves in, so we've got to find something to do. Perhaps with my experience in Argentina and Uruguay this *might* be just the thing for us?"

"I believe it might," said his cousin, David Erskine, "my friends in the City tell me that a lot of investment is going into the cattle business in Texas from this country – it was the Scots financiers who led the way in the first place, and I gather one or two Scots have bought ranches near

Corpus Christi, around the Nueces River. That might be a spot to make for. I'll make some inquiries for you, if you like, Robert?"

David Erskine was true to his word, and Robert soon had enough information about Texas to put a proposal to the Curator Bonis, so that he could go through the now familiar process of petitioning the Court of Session for a grant from the family funds, in order that Robert and Gabrielle could set out for Texas.

The young couple found themselves getting more and more excited. This project sounded exactly the sort of thing Robert liked best, and Gabrielle thought it would be a great adventure. She would miss Gartmore terribly, for it was already becoming home to her; but as the Curator Bonis insisted that it must be let for the shooting and that it would be impossible for them to live there all the year round, they might just as well go and seek their fortune in Texas.

Gabrielle went to a local dressmaker to make her a serviceable riding habit, and together they chose strong leather boots. Robert got out his Winchester rifle and oiled it carefully, while Gabrielle worked grease into his raw-hide lasso which he had brought back from South America. He wrote excitedly to tell George Mansel his new plans, and promised to keep a lookout for any new markets in North America for River Plate horses.

Malise came to spend a few days at Gartmore with the newly marrieds, and found that he got on well with Gabrielle. Then Charlie came on leave and hurried north to see his brother and to meet his sister-in-law for the first time, before they set out for Texas. Charlie could see why his mother had reservations about Gabrielle for he, too, found that his new sister-in-law did not give out very much of herself unless you worked hard on her. To such generous natures as Missy and her second son, to be "withdrawn" was an incomprehensible trait. But he liked her well enough, and he could see that Robert was happier than he had ever known him. They were obviously well suited to each other.

In London, Missy felt desperately lonely for the first time in her life. Robert was far too occupied with Gabrielle to want to come and see her, and now both her younger sons had rushed north to Gartmore to be with the young couple. She knew she had not handled the situation right, hard as she had tried.

Fortunately she now had a delightful young girl living with her as a companion. Her name was Blanche Fane, and she had already become like the daughter Missy had never had. Missy had got to know her family well during their winter in Florence in 1866. Blanche had never married, and was devoted to Mrs. Bontine. She had a wonderful sense of humour and had become like a sister to Charlie and Mallie. It made it so much easier to go about in society when she had a companion to accompany her, and Missy thought the arrangement was perfect. Robert liked Blanche, too, and Blanche was often able to tease him out of his moods. But for the time being Robert was completely taken up with Gabrielle.

The Curator Bonis, Mr. Jamieson, was delighted to hear that Robert had at last found a metier that would suit him so well. On making his own inquiries about the cattle trade in Texas, the accountant found the market was still growing and it seemed to be one of the best investments going. The Curator Bonis knew that many Scots financiers who had put money into the enormous new Texas ranches (particularly a substantial and profitable one, the "Matador" Ranch) and they would give Robert several introductions. The Court of Session readily agreed to a grant of £400 a year, and an extra sum for sailing tickets for the young couple. Robert felt confident that he would make a vast fortune in Texas, and that he would soon be able to send something home to put against the Gartmore debt. What a relief it would be to have the debt finally paid off, and to be able to live at Gartmore for the rest of their lives. He was so delighted that Gabrielle had taken to the life there so happily, and that she had made friends so quickly with their friends and neighbours.

Leaving Gartmore was more of a wrench than they had realised. They spent February and March exploring Spain and southern Italy, for Robert wanted to get his wife to a milder climate. She had thrown off her attack of bronchitis at Gartmore quite quickly, but she still had a persistent cough and looked far from well. She would get used to the mists of Menteith in time, he was sure, but the harsh climate on the edge of the Highlands had a bad effect on her chest, which had been weakened by long working hours in the theatre and poor food – for she had been badly paid, like all actresses.

In Barcelona, Robert took part in another fencing contest and very nearly beat the reigning champion of southern Spain. Gabrielle had yet another bout of illness while they were there, and he had to write and ask his mother for some money to be sent out to pay the doctor's bills. She sent the money immediately, but in her letter he found no reference to Gabrielle. Missy did not even inquire after her health. This was very unlike her, and Robert realised that she was still feeling deeply wounded by her daughter-in-law's rebuff. Their relations were worse than before. Well, it was no good rubbing salt into the wound; for the time being, he would leave Gabrielle's name out of letters he wrote to his mother. She obviously did not want to hear of her existence.

When Gabrielle had fully recovered, they moved on to Gibraltar so that Robert could introduce his wife to his two great-aunts, Aña de Jimenez and Lisa de Guibara, Doña Catalina's sisters. This visit was a great success, and Gabrielle became quite vivacious once she found that the Spanish great-aunts obviously approved of her. The fact that she spoke Spanish was a special delight to them, for their own English was almost non-existent. After the young couple left, they wrote to Missy to tell her how glad they were to find that Robert's little wife was so "animada.[7]" Missy received their enthusiastic letters with surprise, for she had never really thought of Gabrielle as "animada."

The young couple returned from their tour of Italy and Spain to spend their last two weeks in London. Gabrielle spent the final days shopping, and Robert decided to spend as much time as possible with his mother and Malise, for he knew that he might not see them again for several years. Malise was looking forward to Oxford, and to the High Anglican set, the disciples of Cardinal Manning. Robert was somewhat sceptical of this new development in Malise's life. He promised to take photographs of any interesting churches they saw, especially the old missions in Texas, and send them back to Malise. Gabrielle had been very handy with their new Kodak in Spain, and she was becoming quite a talented photographer. He was careful not to talk of Gabrielle when he was alone with his mother, and was relieved to find that their own unique relationship had survived intact.

---

[7] Lively.

Missy was as entertaining as ever, full of the latest gossip about politicians, artists, authors and musicians. Since settling in London, she had got to know a good many of them quite well. Robert was so glad to find that his mother had this interest in her life; she was creating quite a little "salon," and was considered a constructive support to the artistic set, who valued her advice and criticism. She was already considered quite a "catalyst" as she helped the young men to meet each other and to stimulate each other in their work, he found.

Four days before Robert and Gabrielle were due to leave London, "Ganama" Catalina suddenly fell ill. Old Khāt was also laid low with his particular plague, the gout, so Missy had to hurry off to look after them both at Ryde. It would now be impossible to take Gabrielle to meet his Spanish grandmother before they sailed, which was a great sadness to Robert.

On their last night in London, Robert accepted an invitation from Mr. Wright to dine with him at the Devonshire Club. A great friendship had now grown up between the young man and the lawyer. Robert talked excitedly of his Texas venture, and hoe he had heard that violence in the country had been considerably reduced since Governor Richard Coke was elected by the people in 1874. The Texas Rangers were doing a great job quelling the bandits down near the Rio Grande, and there must still be land to buy, for he had heard that one of McNelly's young sergeants, a man called John B. Armstrong, was now negotiating for some land next to the great King ranchlands.

Mr. Wright watched Robert's eyes light up as he spoke of these things; he only hoped that poor little Gabrielle knew what she was in for. From what Robert had been saying, it sounded as though Texas was a pretty dangerous place.

Robert had mentioned the rift between his mother and his wife, and the lawyer smiled kindly and told Robert not to worry too much. It was a natural reaction from a mother whose son meant so much to her, and if he could be patient, Mr. Wright was sure that it would not be long before Mrs. Bontine started to look more kindly on her daughter-in-law. Gabrielle would be sure to respond in due course, and they would come round to each other in the end, he was convinced.

When Robert got back to Morley's Hotel in Trafalgar Square, he found Gabrielle fastening the straps of their steamer trunks. She looked happy and excited.

"I thought you were going to have an early night, Chid!" laughed Robert, "and here you are, still packing!" He caught her round her narrow waist, and whirled her into a spinning dance.

"Do you know what Charlie's friend and shipmate Francis Spring-Rice used to sing when he was going to sea? It was a silly song with a chorus that went:

"I'm off by the morning train, across the raging main,
I'm off to my love, with a boxing glove,
Ten thousand miles away!"

CHAPTER XVII

On 17th May 1879 Robert and Gabrielle arrived in New Orleans. Robert wrote next day to tell his mother that they had not had a rough day on the whole passage. It was very hot and he thought New Orleans was a particularly attractive city, with its French and Spanish influence and huge shady trees. But it was unfortunate, he said, that as soon as a rich citizen wanted to build a new house, "the old Anglo-Saxon vulgarity steps in, and Ionic columns with Doric capitals, the whole finished with a Gothic (strangulated) spire, is the order of the day!"

He went on to tell his mother that New Orleans had been completely ruined by the Civil War – previously it has been the rival of New York with about six hundred thousand inhabitants. Now the population was less than a hundred and fifty thousand.

"I think here one realises the south more than anywhere," he went on. "I mean, as in opposition to the Northern States: long lank faces abound, feet are elevated (on chairs!) high above the head, and everyone chews. To speak to they are decidedly better than the Northern people. (There is no enormous quantity of 'nigs' to be seen in the streets.) Quite as much French as English seems to be spoken.

"'The Brownsville boat, Sir, sails on Thursday, Sir, and takes three days' – hence I think my next move will be to Hidalgo, about eighty miles off. Pingo is not very good here, but the mules are very fine. I should like old pingo out here, as it is too hot to walk. I saw a Chinaman and two Indians (not 'red') this morning.

"The British Sabbath reigns here with all its accustomed horror and want of charity: when I add that the principal church (I have not seen the Roman Catholic Cathedral yet) has a yellow pine gothic door, with sham iron clasps on it, I think you will understand the extreme respectability of the city.

"With best love to all, especially Clyta dog,

"Believe me, your affec. son R. C. Graham Bontine."

Robert kept to his vow not to mention Gabrielle's name in the letter, out of respect for his mother's feelings, and realised for the first time in his life that love for a person sometimes means telling small white lies – or, in his case, omitting certain important aspects of his life. He found it hard not to write in the first person plural, when Gabrielle and he had already become so much of a partnership. She had taken to life on board ship like a duck to water, and was now as curious as he to explore this exciting new world. The camera went everywhere with them, and they sent home several photographs of the vulgar New Orleans churches to amuse Malise.

The trip to Brownsville was as rough as their passage to New Orleans from Bremerhaven had been smooth. They sailed down the Gulf in a small flat-bottomed steamboat which rolled like a Russian doll, and were both violently seasick – Robert even more than Gabrielle. They both began to wish they were dead. Coming ashore at Brownsville the ground still seemed to be swooping and swaying, and the nausea remained for several more hours until their legs got used to terra firma again.

But Robert soon cheered up when he saw horses all around him. It was almost as good as the River Plate, except that the horses were not nearly so fine as the Argentine mustangs.

Robert's letter to his mother from Brownsville, on 2nd June, told her that he had managed to buy a black horse for £4, and that he was trying to get a small place for breeding mules, from an old vacquero who spoke just like a gaucho.

"There is a good wooden house and a garden, which is a great thing."

He described the people in the area as being "a little like the gauchos, but they do not wear their hair long or dress in any particular kind of costume. The only curious thing they wear is a hat with a large band of silver and silver flowers embroidered on it." He went on to tell his mother that "there is a large contingent of Texas Rangers here, they are well mounted, but about as effective here as the Trades Union in Zululand."

But the brave Texas Rangers who had formed such a successful band under the inspired leadership of their commander, Captain Lee Hall, were more effective than Robert knew, and were already stamping out much of the cattle-stealing and banditry on the Rio Grande, to the relief of the great cattle men like King and Kenedy.

One day Robert and Gabrielle went across the Rio Grande from Brownsville to the Mexican city of Matamoros, only a mile across the river. It was like stepping into another world. There the people all rode about on good horses with silver mounted saddles, just as they had done in South America. The population of Matamoros was around fifteen thousand; it was very picturesque, and the plaza and streets reminded Robert and Gabrielle of Spain.

Aimless soldiers in red trousers wandered listlessly about with a burnt-out cigarette hanging from their lips, occupied with their thoughts as they wondered whether the Mexican government would ever come round to paying their eighteen months' arrears of pay, or if they might meet a friend with a match about him. In either case quite resigned to steal the first box of matches they could find, or to ask the first person handy for "a dollar, for God's sake."

Robert had wondered whether they should first of all look for property in Mexico, but he soon realised that it would be a certain way of losing the small amount of capital he had brought with him. So they returned to Brownsville.

But by the middle of June, Robert and Gabrielle decided to move from Brownsville further north to Corpus Christi. They had discovered that Brownsville was much too near the Mexican frontier to be a safe place in which to settle and that there was plenty of land available in Nueces County. Taking a final look at the little wooden house and garden that had been their temporary home in Brownsville, they sadly told the old vacquero who had rented it to them that they would not need it any more as they were moving further north.

The ride to Corpus Christi took them through desert country for a hundred and sixty-five miles, past great sand dunes, with sand flying off the tops as a gentle breeze blew, like spray from a wave. There were brilliant wild flowers growing in the wiry grass, and small turtles plodded over the sandy ground with determination as they looked for more greenery to eat. Great herds of cattle grazed in the pastures, and vacqueros rode stiff-backed upon little prancing horses with their high pommelled Mexican saddles, and reins held high as though holding a cup to the lips.

In Brownsville they had acquired a delightful stray fox-terrier from the Lost Dogs' Home: he was christened Jack, and had already become their devoted companion. The little dog trotted happily along behind them, never seeming to grow tired.

For most of the way they were riding over the property of one of the biggest landowners in the area, Richard King, the son of an Irish immigrant, who had been born in New York fifty-five years ago. He had come to Texas as a steamboater, and eventually stayed as a riverman and pilot until he bought land and put a cow-camp together, in partnership with a Texas Ranger called Legs Lewis. He was still in partnership on the Rio Grande with another steamboater called Mifflin Kenedy from Downington, Chester County, in Pennsylvania, who had gained his master's ticket after a voyage before the mast to India and back. Robert was told in Brownsville that King and Kenedy had started their business on the Rio Grande working for the government to ship army stores during the long-drawn-out Mexican campaign. When King went off into the cattle business, he was supposed to have said to Mifflin Kenedy, seven years his junior:

"Land and livestock have a way of increasing in value, cattle and horse, sheep and goats will reproduce themselves into value. But boats, they have a way of wrecking, decaying, falling apart, decreasing in value and increasing in cost of operation."

In 1852 (the year Robert was born in Scotland) King had acquired a piece of land by the Santa Gertrudis Creek, forty-five miles south of Corpus Christi, where the grass grew stirrup-high and there were shady trees bordering the flowing creek. Two years later, King had added the La Garza property. He had bought the fifteen thousand five hundred acres at a price that worked out at two cents an acre. Robert felt encouraged by this story and told Gabrielle that they would soon be in the ranching business, growing richer every day!

Robert wrote to describe the journey from Brownsville to Corpus Christi to his mother, and told her that the vacquero who had been their guide on the journey had said that Robert looked like a member of the Spanish royal family, and had asked if he was a cousin of the La Garza family who had sold land to Richard King?

Gabrielle was amused to see how much Robert enjoyed the compliment, and how he sat even more regally on his horse for the next mile or two! He was endearingly vain, she thought with a fond smile; he loved compliments, especially when they referred to his noble birth.

This was Gabrielle's first taste of "pioneering." They rode north-wards for four days through the brittle grass over the sand; to their right lay the sea, and the strange long island known as Padre Island. Antelope and deer bounded away through the scrub as they approached, turkey flocks and quail coveys whirred out of the mesquite. They also saw a great many rattlesnakes and sidewinders, which the locals killed with a crack of a long horsewhip.

They had been warned that they might meet bandits on the road, but the journey was uneventful. After the first night, Robert stopped the stage-coach that plied between Brownsville and Corpus Christi to give Gabrielle and the tired little fox-terrier a rest from the long trek. After that Robert led Gabrielle's horse beside his own.

When she joined him again at the next stage, the vacquero pointed out King's great herd of Santa Gertrudis cattle, telling them that the man was "opulento." That evening they cantered in to Corpus Christi, their little Texan horses as fresh as the day they started out.

On 27th June 1879 Robert and Gabrielle bought a parcel of land con-sisting of a hundred acres, four miles north of Corpus Christi on the Nueces Bay, at a cost of one thousand five hundred and fifty dollars. Admittedly it did not look very prepossessing, but once it had been drained and fertilised with great herds of cattle and horses swarming over it, Robert told his wife, it would become the greatest ranch in Texas!

Robert wrote to Mr. Wright, his mother's friend and lawyer, that day to tell him that they had taken the plunge and bought some land. He had promised to keep in touch with him, and in turn Mr. Wright had said he would make sure Robert received his allowance from the Scottish Cura-tor Bonis, Jamieson. Now that he had a wife to support, it was vital that he received the payment regularly, especially having spent everything he had brought out with him on his piece of land. He could not expect Gabrielle to rough it in the same way that he used to when he travelled alone in South America for weeks on end, out of reach of a bank or a postman.

Next day Robert and Gabrielle walked round their property and decided where they would build their house. Robert remembered helping the Withams to build a house in Uruguay, and told her he was sure he could do it himself if he could get a vacquero or two to help him.

Then they must start looking round for some stock to start building up their ranch.

Gabrielle knew they had spent all their money on the land and asked her husband how he intended to pay for his stock? Robert told her gaily that he had an introduction to people called Doddridge and Davis who would give him a loan. It would all be quite easy, he said. Unfortunately it was not as easy as he had thought.

On 6th August they sold their parcel of land again, for exactly the price they had paid for it. Gabrielle chided Robert for not being more businesslike; he should have tried to make a profit, she said, but they were both so relieved to have their precious capital back in their hands that she soon forgave him.

Just before they left Corpus Christi they received a large packet of letters from England, forwarded from Brownsville. Robert decided not to tell his mother about their brief ownership of land on the Nueces Bay. It was embarrassing that his period as a Texan landowner had lasted for precisely ten days. He scribbled a letter to his mother, carefully leaving the episode out, and told her that her other suggestion, shipping, was out of the question.

"Corpus isn't adapted for shipping, so unless shipping houses were started, on very favourable terms, I don't think they would really succeed," he wrote. There was already a successful service between Galveston and New York, run by the Mallory Line, and Robert knew he would never get into the market. He went on: "Words are inadequate for the citizens about here, their meanness, hypocrisy, and assassination being beyond bounds. I don't believe in Italy, in the Middle Ages, there was so much assassination as there is in Texas today. Every day there is one or two; such a thing as a fair fight is unknown and if you enquire how so-'n-so was killed, 'I guess, Sir, they waited for him in the chaparral and shot him in the back, Sir.'

"The Baptist is the most prevalent form of Christianity here.

"Two Texans called respectively 'Broncho Bill' and 'Sam' (cognomen unknown, Broncho is only an agnomen!) meeting on opposite sides of a river and being unable to shake hands, Broncho remarks, 'Say, Sam, it's a pity we can't shake hands. Let's go down stream a bit and have a friendly shot at one another.' At the first fire, Sam called out,

'Hallo ol'man, you broke the pummel of my saddle – darn it.' Mumbled Broncho, 'You went better than that, you got about two inches into my left arm; waal, old fellow, goodbye. Tell the folks at home I met you and we had a good time together.' Mind and tell Cousin John Erskine this episode of life in a country untrammelled by an effete code of laws!

"Sarah Bernhardt indeed seems to be spoilt, I wander what language she is to act in in America, as French is not much understood, I should think, out of New Orleans. I suppose the Afghan affair is over by this time. What a curious turn things seem to be taking in Egypt.

"It is still very hot here and there is a great want of water. I am very sorry to hear poor Khāt has got the gout again.

"I have no wish to see California now – not any – 'nor go to anywhere within the territory of that great country, Sir.'

"With best love to all, Believe me, yr. affec. son

R. C. Graham Bontine.

"P.S. There is a lot of people here who have got religion (methodist form) and really seem as if they worshipped God for spite!"

Robert also wrote a quick note to Blanche Fane, his mother's friend and companion, asking her to reassure his mother and to tell her how happy he was. He still never mentioned Gabrielle to her in his own letters, and Missy never spoke of her either. Robert asked Blanche to write regularly to tell him if his mother was in good health, and also because he enjoyed Blanche's own witty letters.

The last one he had received from her had taunted him with his radical politics, saying, "I still wait for the day when you take your seat as Earl of Menteith in the House of Lords, as a prop of church and state!" Blanche loved to tease him about his aristocratic Scottish forebears, and about his own attitude to the upper classes, of whom he disapproved thoroughly, thinking them unintelligent and narrow-minded.

Gabrielle was fascinated to hear that Sarah Bernhardt was to act in New York. She had admired the great actress from afar, in Paris, hoping that her own career on the stage would eventually be as successful, while realising wistfully that it was highly unlikely. A doctor's daughter from Yorkshire was hardly the right background for that kind of thing.

In the news received in letters from home they heard that Charlie had been appointed to the Royal Yacht. Robert had reservations about the appointment; it seemed that Missy was none to happy either. Robert wrote back to his mother to say, "Charlie's appointment was a great surprise to me, as I thought all hopes of the 'Osborne' were over. The Yacht will bring him into contact with the pestilential caste of swells again – a class decidedly below the average intellectually, and resembling waxworks corporally, and therefore damaging to the artistic sense."

Charlie's friendship with Prince Louis of Battenberg was the real reason for his appointment. Prince Louis had told his cousin, the Prince of Wales, about his amusing shipmate, explaining how kind Charlie had been to him when they were midshipmen together, when Louis was being ragged in the gunroom for being a German princeling. Charlie had been the only midshipman who would speak to him when he first joined the *Ariadne*, he said.

The Prince of Wales promptly invited Charlie to a shoot at Sandringham. When the young sailor proved to be the best shot there, Prince Edward became even more interested in Prince Louis's shipmate and friend. Charlie was obviously delighted with his new appointment, especially as it meant that he would continue to serve with his friend.

On 8th August 1879 Robert and Gabrielle set out for San Antonio, a journey of a hundred and fifty miles, with all their belongings in a hired wagon. They felt exactly like the many pioneers who had been taking their household goods out west in wagon trains over the previous fifty years. Their guide was an offhand, disagreeable American who looked as though he had not washed for the past ten years. Just after they had started off, the heavens opened and the rain poured down relentlessly, as though apologising for the eight months' drought. At each river they came to, they camped for the night before attempting to cross. Several times their wagon stuck in the mud up to the axles, and they had to push and shove and dig to get it moving again.

Eventually the rain stopped, and they started to make better progress; but the next night, as they camped near a little Irish settlement called San Patricio (a grant in the time of the Spaniards to a colony of Irish), the horses managed to escape. Searching for them the next morning, Robert found himself totally lost in the chaparral area where mesquite and thorn grew like a barbed wire fence, and painful burrs worked themselves up inside his trouser legs. Luckily an old vacquero appeared out of the mesquite just as Robert had practically given up all hope of being reunited with Gabrielle and their possessions, and put him on the right road.

Robert was so exhausted by the time he got back to the wagon that they decided to stay in the area for another night and set out the following morning. However, during the night it started to rain heavily once more, and next morning the river had risen so high that they were unable to cross. They spent three days at San Patricio, waiting for the river to drop, before they could resume their journey, having managed to find their horses again.

On the seventeenth day out they saw great stands of trees on the sky-line, the spires of the churches in the far distance – journey's end was in sight at last. Robert had read the accounts of the Franciscan fathers who had set up missions in 1709, and he was pleased to be back amongst Spanish traditions – in this town that had become a meeting place between France and Spain, between the Indian and the White Man, between the South and the West, between the old and the new. Such a place should suit them down to the ground. Jack bounded ahead, barking, as if to establish territorial rights. He seemed to sense that this was to be the end of their journey.

On their first day, Robert and Gabrielle eagerly explored San Antonio. The hall-porter had given them a great deal of information. He told them that the population of the city was growing all the time, around 20,000 now and likely to be 40,000 before long, at the rate folk were flocking to the place.

Gabrielle begged Robert to take her for a ride on one of the streetcars drawn by fat little Mexican mules, and they bounced all the way from the Alamo Plaza to the end of the rails at San Pedro Springs, and back again. At night the streets were lit by gas lights and some of the richer inhabitants were even beginning to install it in their houses.

There were a great many Germans living in San Antonio, and they had built their *biergartens* and *halles* throughout the town. They reminded Robert of his visit to Homburg in 1865 with Papa, Mamma and Charlie.

On the second day they investigated various houses which were for
rent, and finally took one in Calle de las Salinas, and had their belongings installed.

Writing to his mother on 27th August to tell her of their safe arrival,
Robert said, "San Antonio is by far the most picturesque place in Texas,
and in the time of the Mexicans must have been wonderfully so. It is
intersected in all directions by the river, and by little irrigation canals,
like in Spain. A great many families were imported here from the
Canary Islands. The old missions are all in ruins, but I have not had time
to go and see them yet. The churches in the town are mostly in ruins, but
one next to this street is an old Spanish church, being restored, and a
stone tablet sets forth that it is to be 'the first Presbyterian Church.' The
cross has been taken down, and an effigy of the Rev. Samuel B. Edwards
has been placed in its stead.

"Tell Mr. Wright, who I know loves guns, that I use exclusively the
twelve-shooting Winchester, and find it a very good weapon: no-one in
Texas stirs without his rifle. I saw a Mexican methodist preacher the
other day. He was on 'pingo', of course, black clothes, white tie,
Mexican hat, and a bulge at his back indicated that he had either a bible
or a pistol there!

"Believe me, yr. affec. son, R. C. Graham Bontine."

While Gabrielle arranged their new little home to her satisfaction,
Robert spent his days investigating the possibility of some investment in
ranchland; or even the purchase of horses for export. Prices were
already rising steeply, and it seemed as though the real boom was now
over and that it was no longer possible to pick up good land dirt cheap, as
it might have been twenty or thirty years before. Robert was not likely to
be able to repeat Richard King's luck in finding land to buy at two cents
an acre. But San Antonio was hotching with lively, enterprising men,
and Robert found the best meeting place of all was the Menger Hotel.
He was sure that a hot tip would soon come his way.

Robert and Gabrielle found life in San Antonio pleasant and leisurely,
but they soon began to wonder how they were ever going to be able to
stay on in Texas if they could not quickly find some sort of money-
making enterprise. Robert still hankered after the River Plate, and often

talked to Gabrielle about the open spaces, the wild horses, and the wonderful companionship of the gauchos.

It was in January 1880 that Robert, Gabrielle and Jack, the fox terrier, got the chance to join an expedition to Mexico City. It had come about after they had spoken to one of the big cotton traders in San Antonio, who had suggested that they might like to travel with the next wagon train bound for San Luis Potosi; then they could either take the stage coach on to Mexico City, which would take four days, or they could take the train from Huehuetoca.

He warned them that the journey was often hazardous, that the occasional Indian was still likely to be encountered, that Mexico was full of thieves, and that the winter weather was now upon them and might be very cold and unpleasant. If they accepted all these facts, and also that the journey was entirely their own responsibility (or folly, as he preferred to put it), then they were welcome to ride with his men.

Gabrielle laughed at Robert's excitement – she had never seen him quite like this before. She only hoped she could cope with the dangers. Robert often seemed to forget that she was a girl, especially now she wore her hair short like a boy. Robert's black horse from Brownsville would be ideal for the expedition, and Gabrielle also had a horse from Corpus Christie which had carried her safely to San Antonio.

On the day they departed, Gabrielle wrote to Malise to describe the start of the journey, telling him she intended to keep a diary.

"The excitement is unbounded as we leave San Antonio, 'outward-bound' for San Luis Potosi; and it reminds one forcibly of a vessel clearing out of London docks. Men say goodbye to their wives, children and sweethearts, or shout and swear fiercely at the restive mules; dogs bark, and the mule-boy, a sort of savage, brown and ragged, his hair coming through the crown of his silver embroidered hat, and iron spurs on his dilapidated boots, which have evidently belonged to some bigger man than himself, drives the spare mules furiously hither and thither, to the barking of all the curs in the neighbourhood. The men have donned their best go-to-meeting clothes for the occasion, and swell about, clanking their spurs, and showing their clean frilled shirt and gaudy sashes, with great complacency.

"By the side of the wagons rides the capataz, or overseer, directing the muleteers, with much unnecessary gesticulation and cracking of a long whip. The suburbs of San Antonio are not very extensive, and we soon emerge into the flat, brush-covered plains, and the mules, of which many are half-broken, and some in harness for the first time, now steady down into a soberer pace, although one of them kicks himself free and escapes into the chaparral. After an exciting chase of about a mile and a half, he is lazoed, and brought back, kicking vigorously, and we all feel much enlivened by the incident."

They halted for the night on the banks of a small creek, the capataz having first ridden forward to ascertain if there was wood, grass, and water – the three requisites of a camping ground. It was customary to make a short stage on the first day, as nothing was in good working order yet.

The wagons were formed into a square, the interstices between them being secured by hide ropes; the harness was taken off the mules and placed neatly under the wagons. Round the inside of the square a portable manger, filled with Indian corn, was speedily erected, and the mules fell into line to eat. As it was the first night out, the grass bad, and the mules near home, they had brought hay for them, and they were not let out of the square all night.

The camp fires were then lit, then coffee boiled, beans put in a pan to stew, bacon fried, and a rough bread of maize flour mixed and baked in covered iron pots called skillets. After supper they gathered round the fire to smoke their cigarettes, and as the evening was chilly and threatened a Norther, they indulged in a stiff glass of hot toddy.

Their sleeping arrangements were simple, rolling themselves up in a blanket and sleeping where they liked – round the fire, on top of the bales of cotton with which the wagons were loaded, or underneath the wagons. Robert and Gabrielle chose to sleep by the fire with Jack curled up beside them to keep them warm. Later on in the trip, Jack was to be quite a hero, responsible for saving their lives one night when he woke them with barking to warn them of an Indian raid. Next morning they found arrows close to the wagons.

During the day Jack chased tortoises and armadillos or joyously put up coveys of quail and flocks of wild turkey rushing ahead of Robert and

Gabrielle as they rode south, with the wagon train following along behind.

On 19th January 1880 they arrived at Monterey and Robert decided they should spend a few days in the place. Robert hardly dared to tell Gabrielle that they had not even reached the half-way mark yet. Neither did he tell her that they had been in danger of their lives for the final fifty miles or so, for he had discovered that the capataz fully intended to murder them at some point on the journey and steal their money. Robert had not slept once since learning of his evil intentions, and sat over Gabrielle while she slept, with his rifle at the ready. As a result, the capataz had never found the opportunity to carry out his bloodthirsty plan, and they had reached Monterey, miraculously, in safety.

That first night in the Meson del Comercio in Monterey, Robert slept like the dead, out of relief and exhaustion, and Gabrielle began to wonder why he seemed even more tired than she was herself.

Next morning he awoke feeling renewed and refreshed, and overjoyed to find that they were now well south of the cold weather and could expect to be warm for the rest of the journey. Robert always felt he could accomplish anything as long as the sun was shining and the temperature was at least seventy degrees Fahrenheit. This was the sort of climate that brought him alive. Everything would be all right from this moment, he knew. He had brought his "fair ladye" safely out of danger to a place of pure delight. What a brave little Chid she was! She had survived the expedition with the courage of a boy.

On reaching Tula they found a livery stable whre they could leave the horses for a month. There as a train they could take to Mexico City from Tula, which was only a short journey.

On 2nd March they arrived in Mexico City having accomplished most of the journey of eight hundred miles on horseback, in fifty-eight days. After one night of extravagant luxury in an expensive French hotel, they soon found a perfectly adequate lodging at a reasonable price in Callejon del Espiritu Santo in the old part of the town where Cortes had once lived in the sixteenth century.

Robert and Gabrielle were never to forget that month in Mexico City. There was so much to see and do; the streets were full of elegant people, and the shops were the smartest outside Paris and London. Every

morning Robert went for a fencing bout at the Academy of M. Cavantous, at the end of their street, to keep himself fit.

A week before they were due to leave Mexico City, Robert was
invited to take part in an important contest at M. Cavantous's establishment, in front of some of the most distinguished ladies and gentlemen of
Mexico City. Gabrielle was extremely proud of his prowess, and even
more so when she read a description of the event in the newspaper next
morning which, being roughly translated, said that the young Englishman
had great skill, dexterity, and extraordinary agility.

M. Cavantous tried hard to persuade Robert to stay on to help him
teach at his academy, but Robert explained that he was a countryman at
heart and could never last long in a town, so must gratefully decline the
compliment. Nevertheless M. Cavantous insisted on presenting Robert
with a testimonial showing his qualification as a fencing master. It might
come in handy one day, he said. Robert was very touched.

On 3rd April 1880 the young couple set off to travel home again to
San Antonio. As their train puffed out of the city, an answering puff of
smoke came from a distant volcano beyond the father of all volcanoes,
Popacatepetl. When they arrived at their first stop, Tula, the old Aztec
capital, Robert found his revolver had been stolen at the station. Luckily
he still had his Winchester carbine, but he was particularly sad to lose the
revolver given to him by Mr. Wright. It was here that he and Gabrielle
collected the horses they had left at Tula while they had spent time in
Mexico City.

The trail home was less eventful than the journey out. Robert and
Gabrielle were expert trail-riders by now, and knew how to make themselves comfortable on the route, with Jack still trotting gallantly along
beside them.

By the time they reached Monterey, they had been on the road for
nearly three weeks. One night they camped near Villaldama, and during
the night a troop of wild horses stampeded past their camp. Robert
awoke to hear the thunder of galloping hoofs and loud neighing. At first
he thought it was "los Indios bravos" once more, but when he realised it
was only some wild horses, he turned over to wrap his blanket more
closely round him and edged closer to the dying embers of the fire.

It was only when he awoke next morning that he realised his black *pingo* had found the call of the wild too much for him, and had slipped his halter and galloped off into the night. It was no good trying to pursue him, he would probably be fifty miles away by now: they would never catch up with him. In any case, the wild horses might well have galloped up into the mountains where they could not be pursued.

Fortunately one of the muleteers had brought a spare horse with him, hoping to sell it for a good price in Texas, so he offered it to Robert. It was a nice roan, and after some haggling Robert managed to beat the Mexican down to a reasonable price. For the rest of the journey he tried to mould the new horse to his own requirements and to teach it some manners. He missed his black horse from Brownsville very badly; it was most upsetting to lose the horse that he had trained for several months, and which he had got to know well. Now he would have to start all over again.

Gabrielle, on the other hand, thought this new "pink" horse was decidedly prettier than the black, and that Robert had done rather well for himself. The horse was promptly christened Jorge, after Robert's old friend George Mansel.

Everything went smoothly after that, until they were within twenty miles of the Eagle Pass on the Rio Grande, the day before Robert's twenty-ninth birthday. They would only take another four or five days to reach San Antonio. The caravan was just about to cross the river Sabina when they came upon a shepherd with a flock of some two or three thousand sheep, who pointed to a cloud of dust across the river remarking casually, "Los barbaros con una caballada."

Nobody would have taken any notice if a small urchin had not come running out of the scrub to announce that there had been an "assasinato" nearby during the previous night.

Robert and the capataz followed the small boy and found a horrible sight on the river bank a few hundred yards upstream. Two Americans had been murdered, obviously many hours before, and beside them lay a small dog keeping watch over the corpses. The capataz murmured to Robert that the faithful watchdog had probably kept away coyotes and buzzards during the night.

The dog allowed Robert to pat him, but when he removed his hand from the animal's head he found it smeared with blood; examining the dog further he found that it had been shot through the ear. It was improbable that the murder had been committed by Indians, for they seldom used guns. It was much more likely to have been performed by bandits.

The small dog was already the hero of the hour, and some of the muleteers who appeared on the scene promised to take it back to San Antonio and give it a good home. The bodies of the two men were already terribly swollen and disfigured by vermin, despite the little dog's watch-keeping, and it was agreed that they must be buried instantly.

Robert decided to take Gabrielle back into Texas as quickly as possible, away from the murderous bandits of the Rio Grande.

They arrived back in San Antonio at midday on 27th May, just four months after they had set out on their astonishing trip of over fifteen hundred miles to Mexico City and back. It was the longest expedition Robert had ever made, even longer than his exploration up the Alto Paraná in Paraguay or his travels with George Mansel from Durazno in Uruguay to Cruz Alta in Brazil.

Gabrielle had celebrated her twenty-first birthday while they were on the trail. She told him that the whole trip had been the most wonderful thing she had ever experienced.

CHAPTER XVIII

For the rest of that summer, 1881, Robert filled in his time schooling his friends' horses; or interpreting on hunting trips for rich Europeans who could not understand the Spanish spoken by their Mexican guides. He also spent a great deal of time lounging about on the balcony of the Menger Hotel, to keep abreast of the latest news of properties being bought and sold in the area. But still nothing turned up, and at last Robert was tempted to take up an offer from his old friend, George Mansel, in Argentina, who had suggested that they might be better going into partnership with him instead of hanging around in Texas.

Gabrielle did not want to make another trip so soon, but encouraged Robert to go on a visit to his old haunts. She was sure it would cheer him up. She did not mind staying with Jack for company in San Antonio while Robert was away – especially now that she had found a small job, teaching painting and drawing to girls in one of the convent schools.

Robert received a joyful telegram from George a few days later, saying that he was all ready to "push the boat out." George had obviously not lost his nautical terminology, even though he was now a hardened cattle man. Robert countered Mansel's telegram by wiring to say that he was "coming under his own steam" and hoped to be with him in a day or two.

The two friends spent a happy three weeks together, and Robert was back to his old life on the pampas again, herding cattle with George and taking part in hectic ostrich hunts with *boleadoras* swinging. He remembered that you must never call them *bolas* in Argentina, for that word had a double meaning! *Boleadoras* was the polite word, especially if ladies were present.

Robert felt much at home in the Estancia de los Arias, for he had stayed there in 1873, long before his friends, the Fairs, had sold it to George Mansel. How he wished he could persuade Gabrielle to join him there.

On 20th August he wrote to her.

"Estancia de los Arias,
        Republica Argentina.
"My dear Chidling,

"I have long meant to write to you, but have been so much occupied I have never done so yet. This is a charming part of the country, splendid open plains for miles, all over long pampas grass, and absolutely covered with horses and cattle. In the distance there are a surge of low hills, and a very nice little river. It goes right past the house into the Paraná, about three miles below the house, where there is a shipping place for Buenos Ayres, which is about 100 miles off. The house is built round a patio in the old Spanish style, and the courtyard is planted with orange and lemon trees. The corrals are behind the house. There are about 5,000 head of cattle on the pFace, and 1,700 sheep, and also about 510 head of mares and 40 tame horses.

"Buenos Ayres is rather dull now as the Opera troupe has left and there is only the French company at the Alcazar, and a rather heavy Spanish one at the Colon. I wonder how you can still stay among those odious Yankees in Texas, when down here it is so much nicer, and we might have ostrich and deer hunts together. If you can come just send me a wire saying what steamer you are coming in, and I will meet you, with a *tropilla* of horses, and we will gallop out here! Yr. affec.

Roberto el Gaucho

"P.S. Mind and bring Jack with you)"

For several days Robert waited hopefully for Gabrielle's answer. He had fallen in love with the pampas all over again, and he did not think he could bear it if Chid refused to come. At last he got her reply. The wire said, "Prefer stay Texas. Come back soon. Chid."

George came into the large airy sitting room at that moment and saw Robert standing with the telegram in his hand, looking crestfallen. He guessed that the beautiful Gabrielle had refused to join them; women always caused trouble, that was why he had never got spliced. George produced a bottle of rum and both men proceeded to get very drunk that evening. Robert hated getting drunk, it never did any of the nice things people said it would do. It just made him feel very sick. He knew he had a head like a rock, and this was how he paid for it. He could not think why he had let George talk him into it.

Robert knew he should have not been riding the next morning; he was not completely in control and his horse sensed it straight away. It tried every trick in the book to buck him off. Normally he would have found the gallop enormously invigorating, but today he felt at odds with his horse. George had lost some *baguales*, or wild colts, and the two friends had set out together to find them with a party of gauchos. At last they saw the young horses grazing peacefully by a small wood, and Robert watched as the capataz and his gauchos circled the beasts and gradually turned them until they were able to drive them towards the estancia.

Robert did not feel up to using his lazo that morning, so he watched from a distance, enjoying the stillness as he sat on his horse and smoked a cigarette. His head was gradually clearing, and he was beginning to feel better. But he still felt upset and bewildered by Gabrielle's adamant refusal to join him in Argentina.

Letting the rawhide reins go slack, he eased his feet out of the ornate stirrups and let his legs hang down. His horse was grazing quietly, having worked off its early morning steam, and he watched the gauchos gathering the wild horses, like collies on a Scottish border hillside gathering sheep.

Suddenly, without any warning, an ostrich shot out of a tall clump of pampas grass nearby, startling Robert's horse. He just had time to catch up his reins in an instinctive grab as the horse bolted, but there was no time to get his feet back into the stirrups. Fortunately he had exceptional balance and he knew his horsemanship should help him to survive the frightened stampede. The action of his horse had set the wild horses galloping, and he could hear shouts and yells of exasperation from the gauchos as the whole herd fled in panic. Away to the right the ostrich was running with great strides, wings flapping like sails – these pampas rheas went so fast that very few horses could catch up with them.

So far, Robert had managed to stick on, and he was just feeling for the stirrups to try to get more control when his horse put a foot in a viscacha's[8] hole, and down they both went. Robert was as agile as a cat and normally he would have been up on his feet again and grabbing at the reins before the horse had even rolled over, but today his reactions were slow – that damnable drinking bout with George – and before he had time to get on his feet he felt the most appalling explosion of pain in

---

[8] A rodent similar to the chinchilla.

his back, and he knew he had been kicked by the horse in its efforts to struggle to its feet. Just before he briefly lost consciousness, he saw the capataz looking at him with his great eyes filled with concern.

Robert was taken back to the estancia by the gauchos, he could not remember how, and the bone-setter on the estancia was soon at his bedside feeling him all over to find out the extent of his injuries. All the patient knew was that he still had an excruciating pain somewhere in the region of his kidneys.

Robert was quite ill for the next few days, but eventually he was able to hobble around the house, unable to stand up straight and feeling weak and incapable.

When Robert arrived back in the stage-coach at San Antonio, and walked into their house in Calle de las Salinas, Gabrielle threw her arms round his neck and held him as though she would never let him go again. His injury was better, but he was not completely recovered yet, and he could not help letting out a gasp of pain as she pressed him into her arms, which alarmed Gabrielle greatly. She summoned a doctor from India who had been strongly recommended to them. Dr. Hadra told Robert that rest was the only cure.

Robert resigned himself to lying in bed, while Gabrielle went out to take her sketching classes. Fortunately Missy had sent him some more books and newspapers, so he had plenty to read. He had not wanted to alarm his family, so he and Gabrielle agreed they would not tell them about Robert's foray to Argentina, nor about his injury.

Dr. Hadra was most attentive, and visited Robert every day to make sure he was progressing well. To give a second opinion he brought a colleague on one of his visits. This was one Dr. John Herff, almost the same age as Robert, who had already distinguished himself by attending medical schools in Europe, although he was Texas born and bred. He was reassuring about Robert's condition, but agreed with Dr. Hadra that after being kicked in the back, it was important that Robert should take as much rest as possible. If not, he might suffer from kidney problems later in life. Nature must be given its chance to effect a cure.

While Robert lay in bed with nothing to do, he managed to write some letters to his family and friends. He decided he would only give his mother the briefest of details about his illness: "I am very ill – inflammation of the kidneys owing to pingo – and am now in bed. I cannot sit up for very long. I was very glad to get your letter and hope Homburg will do you good."

He had received a letter from Mr. Wright, who sympathised with the problems in finding a ranch, and told him he had explored the possibility of Robert becoming either an Honorary Consul in San Antonio, or a Queen's Messenger,[9] but unfortunately neither position was available at present. He had also sent Robert some copies of *The Spectator*. Robert wrote to thank him.

"San Antonio Bejar

"Dear Mr. Wright,

"Your letter arrived all right yesterday. I thought myself there would be little or no chance of a consulship, and I am afraid the messengership is more than doubtful. I am getting more reconciled to Texas, Mexico is a much nicer country, but I hate being always boxed up in a town, as one is almost forced to be.

"I believe I am probably most qualified for a Queen's Messenger as I can speak French and German (badly), ride, and have no political or religious convictions that cannot be promptly altered!

"The Spectator comes with the greatest accuracy now, since I made a row about it at the Post Office, where they used generally to steal every second or third one. I only found it out by seeing in the 'San Antonio Democrat' that 'the London Spectator says....'! On visiting the editor, who was seated in a small bullet-proof room with a Winchester rifle and a sling-shot on the table before him, he at once owned up to the fact of them being mine – the Spectators – from which he had quoted!

"Elections are going on briskly, and what are called 'shooting scrapes' are very frequent.

"Your amigo, Roberto G. Bontine."

A few days later Robert received a frantic letter from his mother, asking what was really wrong with him and if he was getting better, so he wrote again on 10th October to reassure her.

"I am alright now, the visitation was partly of God and partly of pingo, owing to the former directing pingo's near hind foot on me when

---

[9] A group of civil servants who transported Britain's most confidential messages in diplomatic bags around the globe.

thrown down. It is still awfully hot here though the nights are getting cooler."

It was only a few days after this that a packet of letters arriving bringing the sad and unexpected news of Doña Catalina's death at Ryde. Gabrielle knew how much Robert had loved his grandmother, for he had often talked about her, and although Gabrielle had never met her, she had met her two younger sisters, the aunts Ana and Lisa, with Robert in Gibraltar in the spring of 1879. Catalina had died at ten o'clock on Tuesday, 12th October, four months after her eightieth birthday.

Missy wrote a long letter telling Robert about his grandmother's last moments:

"I know how much you will grieve for Grandmamma, you will never again hear her say, 'I will not pat you, if you draw away the head,' or see her sitting working by the little table with her basket beside her and the room full of flowers. It is so very sad, and the memory of terrible sufferings will haunt me for many long days. I thought my memory was full of sadnesses and terrible recollections, but it would seem there is always room in a human heart for another bitter drop, as long as it can feel. I hope as time goes by it will efface these last weeks from my mind.

"This is a sad letter for you to read. You have the comfort of remembering her great love for you, and of knowing that she died in ignorance of anything that might have grieved her in your lot. She asked often when you were coming home.

"Poor old Khāt sends you his kindest love. It is very mournful to see him in so much grief.

"Your very affectionate Mother. A. E. Bontine."

Robert could not hide his distress. Handing over the letter to Gabrielle, he sat with his arm round her, as though physically shielding her from his mother's hurtful attitude to their marriage. To his surprise, Gabrielle turned to him with a wan smile as she put the letter down; she said that she felt strangely happy, for she felt Doña Catalina did now know about their love for each other, and approved. Robert was deeply touched.

Once Robert was up and about again, he and Gabrielle went to a circus. It was one of the best they had ever seen, and had been put together by the erstwhile buffalo hunter and Ranger, Colonel Cody, with a troupe of Indians to perform great feats on horseback. He later took the name "Buffalo Bill" and he and his Wild West show became a huge attraction, both in the States and in Europe. Robert was later to get to know Colonel Cody well, and one of Robert's famous stories was about the Red Indian in his troupe, Long Wolf, who died on the trip to London and was buried in the Brompton Cemetery. At the end of the 20th Century Long Wolf's body was taken back to America to be buried in Dakota by members of his own tribe, his descendants.[10]

A few days later Robert developed malaria. He was extremely ill again, and Dr. Hadra had to return to his bedside. The rainy weather had brought armies of mosquitoes to the surrounding creeks and to the San Antonio river banks, and Robert had succumbed to the dreaded fever. Strangely enough, Gabrielle, who always looked so delicate, was not affected. Her only health problem in the past had been a weak chest, and the climate of San Antonio seemed to suit her well. She had not felt so fit for years.

When the fever was at its height Robert received a letter from his mother (posted in November 1880), thanking him for the letters he had written to her since hearing of "Ganama's" death. Fortunately she did not realise that her son was now lying dangerously ill in San Antonio.

"Both your sad letters have arrived," she wrote, "and have touched me more than I can tell you. I do not think anyone except poor Khāt loved Grandmamma as you did. Your little note to her was most affecting. She used often to talk of you and ask when you were coming home and what you did out there.

"Your last letter to her (enclosing the photographs of the mission church) came before she was taken ill, and she said she thought, when you first came back from Buenos Ayres, you were the most beautiful creature she had ever seen."

Missy went on to tell him about a courageous exploit of Charlie's. He had jumped overboard from the Royal Yacht to save the life of a waterman whose boat had capsized. It was very likely that he would be given the Royal Humane Society's medal for his bravery. His valiant act

---

[10] The author attended the fascinating service as Robert's representative.

had helped to take their minds off "Ganama's" death, and they were all very proud of him.

"Mallie was 20 last Saturday, and is preparing for Moderations at Oxford, commonly called 'Mods,' which is to be next Monday, I think. Charlie spent a couple of hours with him yesterday on his way from Leamington, where he had stayed with Aunt Helen, on his way back from a shoot at Sandringham.

"Charlie had been to Sandringham to stay with the Probyns for the Prince of Wales' birthday festivities, and also had a very good day's hunting. He has now gone back to Portsmouth.

"Mr. Wright has been so very kind and good to me in my solitude and sadness, and the Fanes came for a week and were so kind and nice.

"Ever your most affec. Mother, A.E.B."

By Christmas 1881 Robert was well enough to go with Gabrielle to a German family they had got to know, called Vögel, out at Helotes. To everyone's amazement it snowed during the night and when they woke up next morning the whole countryside was white, just like Scotland, or Germany, as the Vögels said with delight. Everyone suddenly became very childish, rushing outside to make snowballs and throw them at each other, until they were exhausted and came back into the house to open their presents, laughing and panting.

In the evening they gathered round the Vögels' beautiful fir-tree, and tucked in to a huge banquet provided by Frau Vögel. Robert was reminded of Christmases at Finlaystone and Gartmore, and they all felt very happy. Frau Vögel confessed that she had even put her shoes outside the door last night, just as she used to do when she was a child, hoping Saint Nicholas would remember her – and guess what? When she came down to fetch them this morning they were filled with snow! What better Christmas present could she want than that? The first snow she had seen since they left Germany!

After Christmas the weather got even colder, and they heard of dreadful blizzards in the "panhandle," and cattle dying by the score. It was the worst winter Texas could remember.

In January 1882, on their return to San Antonio after Christmas, Robert received another letter from Missy. She wrote how she had gone to Ryde to help Khāt sort everything out after her dear mother's death.

"As long as I remained at Ryde I kept the grave covered with flowers. Khāt has let the house for six months to a Duchess de Choiseul. I believe she is a Yankee. Mary Anne is to stay as house-keeper. Khāt is coming here soon to look for chambers for himself; at present he is staying with Minnie[11] and Jack at Aldershot. Poor old Betsy is going to end her days at Elgin. I thought your letter to Grandmamma's sisters quite lovely. I will try to write in Spanish.

Hawarden[12] is only going to give Khāt £150 a year, which falls into them through her death. It was Clemy's dying wish that some provision should be made for Khāt. His pension is, I believe, £450, but there are some deductions for income tax, so Khāt will have £600 a year, which of course he can live on comfortably, but they might have given him £200. He was 70 today – ten years younger than Grandmamma! They were so happy together."

Just after Robert and Gabrielle had returned to San Antonio from Helotes, they received a wonderful surprise – a letter from Charlie, who had two months' leave and was proposing a visit to them!

Gabrielle was delighted to see Robert looking so animated all of a sudden. She had been worried about him since his bout of malaria, he had got so much thinner and his face looked so pinched. She knew it was partly because he was worried about their financial affairs. With no hope of ranchland to buy, they had been living on their capital, and now it was running out.

Robert laughingly told Gabrielle that they would have to get jobs as clerks in one of the big new stores, but she knew it was no laughing matter and they would very soon have to make a big decision about whether to stay on in Texas or not. She had even suggested to Robert that they could go and live in Spain and make some money by writing books, but Robert was convinced that he had no literary ability whatsoever. He had tried to write about their Mexican trip, but it was no good – he simply did not have the talent, he said.

Charlie arrived at the end of February 1882, and the two young men were so overjoyed to see each other after a parting of more than two

---

[11] Clementina's daughter and her husband Jack.
[12] Lord Hawarden, Clementina's husband. Clemy died very young – some 25 years before her Spanish mother – after having nine children.

years that they could not stop playing the fool. Gabrielle laughed till the
tears ran down her face. That first day set the scene for the whole six
weeks of Charlie's visit. They seemed to spend most of the time
laughing, and they were all three enormously happy together.

Charlie made great friends with the little dog Jack, the *pingo* Jorge,
and a foal they had adopted, which had become a special pet and which
followed him round like a dog, licking his hands to taste the natural salt
on them. Robert commented that he probably had more salt than most
people, in any case, being a sailor!

Robert decided it would be fun to take Charlie on a long expedition
on horseback out to West Texas. Gabrielle did not mind, for she knew
that the riding trip would be the best thing in the world for Robert. She
was sure he had only become ill because he had been sitting twiddling
his thumbs for so long, and of course the accident in Argentina had not
helped.

Gabrielle was perfectly happy sitting quietly in dark churches or
beside tumbled ruins with her sketchbook and her paintbox. The weather
was quite mild again, for spring always came early to Texas. The little
red buds on the bushes were bursting already, and a faint tinge of green
was spreading across the prairies.

When they came back from their expedition (Gabrielle hardly recognised them, they looked so tanned, and they had both grown their hair
much longer. She laughed and twitched her nose ostentatiously;
obviously they had neither of them had a bath since they went away.
They looked exactly like two desperados. Robert seemed much better,
and they were immensely happy and pleased with themselves.

The two brothers had covered a great deal of ground, seen some
beautiful country and met some fascinating characters, including Colonel
Cody, or "Buffalo Bill," the man who had started up the circus they had
recently enjoyed so much. He had been with a party of rich buffalo
hunters out at the Horsehead Crossing when their paths crossed, and they
had fallen in with his party for a few days, striking up a great friendship.

Robert and Charlie had also had an extraordinary encounter while
riding through the "Staked Plain." They had passed a lone horseman and
there was something about the way he rode which was familiar to
Robert, but yet he simply could not think why he should recognise a

solitary horseman riding across the prairie in West Texas. As the man on the horse came closer, Robert suddenly knew who it was: none other than the unfortunate young gaucho who had accidentally killed his own brother in one of the guerrilla raids in the Banda Oriental exactly ten years ago.

The two young men were overjoyed and astonished to see each other. Robert remembered him so well, with his German looks, and how they had called him "Pancho Pajaro," although his real name was Vögel. Of course, he now realised, their new friends the Vögels at Helotes talked of relations in Uruguay, and he had never once put two and two together. What a strange coincidence!

It turned out that young Vögel had led a sad life since the tragic episode; he had just not been able to get his unintentional act of fratricide out of his head, so he had kept continuously on the move, riding from south to north on the continent of America, both in South America and in the North.

Now he was making his way back to Uruguay, hoping that time would have healed the terrible open wound so that he could settle down again, at long last, in his own country, with no more ghosts to haunt him and no more nightmares to disturb his sleep. Robert wished him the best of good luck, and the last they saw of him was his long, lanky figure draped over his horse as he disappeared over a rocky bluff, heading for South America.

Robert could not help wishing that he was going with him. His own heart was still in South America and nothing could ever make him forget his adventures and the happiness of riding over the pampas feeling as free as the wind.

While the two brothers were riding over the prairies together they talked at length about Robert's future plans. Robert told his brother that he and Gabrielle thought they would like to go and live in Spain until they could eventually take over Gartmore. They could not take the violence of this country any longer; and Robert knew he simply could not buy a property in Texas, when all he really wanted to do was to go back to Gartmore, to run the estate, and, hopefully, to pay off the "Old Swindler's" debt. His roots would always be in Scotland, he now knew that for sure. The lure of South America was more like the lure of a beautiful mistress, he laughed.

He was even longing to get involved in the political scene at home, after all the excitement of Gladstone's Liberal Revival, and the Midlothian campaign, about which his mother had written at length. She had described how she had travelled to Scotland to encourage the people at Gartmore and at Ardoch to vote, and how Charlie and Mallie had been quite splendid coming with her to help the Liberal cause.

Good old Mamma, laughed Robert, admiring her spirit. He would have loved to have seen her chasing Charlie and Mal about and getting them to make speeches. Not many women were quite as politically involved as Missy – she was certainly ahead of her time.

No, he simply didn't want to stay here any longer, he told Charlie. Everybody in Texas was out to do their rivals down, whereas in Argentina there had been a marvellous feeling of "live, and let live." It was the difference between the competitive spirit of the Yankees, and the individualism of the Spanish, he had decided.

Charlie picked his moment to ask about Robert's marriage. Were things between his brother and his wife as blissful as he imagined? He had sensed a special something that mysteriously links a man and a woman together, drawing them to each other magnetically to seal their union in a lifelong partnership. Had Gabrielle given him the one missing ingredient that his life had lacked hitherto?

Robert smiled happily, and Charlie knew he had his answer. He knew his brother so well; when things were all right he was just like any other Scot, given to understatement and diffidence. He now knew that Robert and Gabrielle really were happy. Their marriage was indeed what Mamma had hoped for, and had so feared might not be. He could now assure his mother, on his return, that Gabrielle was truly her daughter-in-law and must be accepted into the family at once, for Bob's sake, if it could not be for her own. Mamma really must stop resenting Gabrielle's lack of "dowry," and her mysterious early life in Paris.

Encouraged by Charlie's obvious understanding, Robert told him about their one and only major disagreement, and about Robert's trip to Entre Rios – which had ended in such disaster.

Charlie burst out laughing. He felt Gabrielle had the measure of dear old Bob. She was obviously the best wife he could possibly have chosen. He decided this was the right moment to tell his brother that he, too, had fallen deeply in love with the Rector of Castle Rising's daughter, Barbara Bagot, sometimes known as "Milly") whom he had met at Sandringham. Robert was delighted.

When they arrived back at San Antonio they both felt they had blown a lot of cobwebs away, and Robert asked Charlie to explain everything to their mother as soon as he got back to London. He and Gabrielle might make a special trip to see her first, if they decided to settle in Spain. Perhaps Mamma would like to come across the Channel to meet them there? It might be best for them to meet in France, for Gabrielle would then be on comparatively "home ground," and would feel much more self-confident as a result, and more able to face her mother-in-law. It was vital that they should accept each other at long last, and try to learn to love one another. Robert could not bear this "cold war" to go on any longer, it was causing him such dreadful distress.

Charlie said he would explain it all to Missy, and reassured Robert by telling him how miserable and penitent Mamma now felt, and how he was sure she would jump at an opportunity to hold out the olive branch to Gabrielle.

Charlie wrote to their mother from San Antonio on 3rd April 1882 to tell her what a jolly time he had spent with Robert and Gabrielle, and giving a veiled hint that they were now talking of leaving Texas and coming home. He would tell her everything when he got back. He went on to say that his visit had "livened Bob up a great deal, as he is dead tired of the place. We were able to go into the interior and I have seen a good deal of the country and of the life out here. I have learnt how to throw a lasso and have seen a great many wild horses and mules tamed. The Mexican influence is by the far the prettiest element in Texas. I am bringing home a Mexican hat and Bob's Mexican saddle. It is so jolly out here and I am quite sunburnt."

Robert and Gabrielle saw Charlie off on his train to the coast the following day. He was travelling on the International Great Northern Railway, which had only just been inaugurated, and was already known locally as the "Insignificant and Good for Nothing Railway."

Back at Calle de las Salinas, they started on their own packing. The final decision to leave San Antonio had been made before Charlie left, and they had already booked their passage home. Their ship was due to sail from New Orleans in a week's time, so there was a great deal to do.

Back in Scotland, the Curator Bonis, Mr. Jamieson, had decided that the best thing to do was to keep Robert on a fairly generous allowance until Major Bontine's death, and try to restrain the young laird from entering into any further schemes which might need financial backing. Surely he could not possibly overspend in Spain? With luck they would only need their board and lodging, and a little extra for young Mrs. Bontine's clothes and for occasional visits to England. The Curator Bonis had now accepted that Robert was definitely not cut out to be a cattle rancher, nor, in fact, a businessman of any kind; but he had a feeling that Robert would make an ideal Laird of Gartmore. He knew how much the estate workers loved him and how successful the visit had been when he and his bride spent their honeymoon at Gartmore. Gabrielle was obviously a very capable young woman, and it was tragic that Willy's illness had prevented them from getting involved with the place sooner.

Robert wrote again to tell his mother that they would soon be living much nearer home, in the north of Spain, for the next few years, while his father was still alive. Missy was delighted. She knew how Robert would enjoy Spain, he had always seemed much more Spanish than her other two sons, and it was a splendid idea for him to have some time there before he finally inherited Gartmore.

When Charlie got home, he explained to his mother that he had found their marriage was a very real and touching thing. For Robert's sake, he hoped that Mamma would at last accept Gabrielle.

Robert booked their passage home in a French steamer which would land them at Dieppe, where they could make a surprise visit to meet Missy before taking the train south to Spain. They both wanted to go back to Galicia, having been so enchanted by it on their brief visit en route for Texas.

They excitedly laid their plans for their reunion on French soil with Missy. She and Malise were having a holiday in the Pyrenees and intended to travel back to Paris together. Then Malise would go on to London, while Missy broke her journey at Dieppe.

CHAPTER XIX

Missy walked into the Hotel Royale in Dieppe early in April 1882 to find Robert and Gabrielle waiting in the hall to greet her. How well they looked! Robert seemed to have become completely mature; he looked strong and handsome, with a new self-confidence. She held out her arms to them both and embraced them warmly. It was the happiest moment of her life.

The only other person who had been let into the secret was the devoted German maid, Homer, who had been with Missy since she married Willy. She too was thrilled to see Mr. Robert again, and the attractive young lady who had become his wife. More than anything, she was overjoyed that her mistress would now be really happy again, after so many tragedies. To have Mr. and Mrs. Robert living in Spain was the best thing that could have happened, almost as good as having them back in England. But she knew that would soon come. Her mistress was at last thawing out to little Mrs. Robert. High time too, thought Homer.

During their two short days at Dieppe, both Missy and Gabrielle made great efforts to understand each other, drawn together as they were by their mutual love for Robert. There was so much to talk about that their tongues never ceased.

Robert watched their reconciliation with a sense of joy. Mamma was being very kind to Gabrielle, and although he could tell that Gabrielle was still mildly on the defensive, he knew that there was at last some hope for a real friendship between the two women he loved best in the world. How pretty they both looked – just like a picture by Boudin!

On the last morning they hired a carriage to see the house in which Guy de Maupassant had been born, Château Miromesnil; Robert had totally lost touch with the young writer, but he remembered him telling Robert that his mother had rented this beautiful chateau because she wanted him to be born in a castle. It seemed so long ago since they used to meet in Paris – so much had happened since then.

Gabrielle was fascinated to find a little old chapel in the woods by the chateau, and she lingered for a while to say a prayer. The sunlit *fôret* was spring-like where the leaves were tinged pale green, and wild lilies-of-the-valley were pushing up underfoot.

When it was time to part, Missy kissed her son and her daughter-in-law with deep affection.

"Let's hope that the next time we are all together it will be at Gartmore," she said as she went on board the Channel steamer. She turned back to wave to her son and his wife, and realised for the first time how right they were for each other: it was a great comfort, and she felt happier than she had felt for a long time. She pulled her travelling cape more closely round her, blew them a kiss, and went down to her cabin, followed by Homer.

Robert and Gabrielle were on their own in their special Spanish paradise at Vigo. It was a May morning, so different from an English May morning, with its dew and freshness, mild, wet greens, and palely tinted sky. In Vigo the day awoke brilliant and hot, striking metallic gleams out of leathery leaves of big magnolia trees standing on either side of a little wicket gate across the courtyard from the old grey walls of the *grana*, or farmhouse.

Under Robert's and Gabrielle's bedroom, which was on the upper floor of the building in the old granaries, reached by an outside stair, they could hear the regular munching of fat oxen in the stable below. These were standing knee-deep in fresh clover cut by Pepa, the brown, lithe daughter of the *casera*, with hair as black as a raven's wing and as coarse as a horse's mane. The farmyard was neglected and untidy, but untidy in the most pleasing way – heaps of maize cobs piled roughly in the courtyard, a tangled garden, its sandy paths trailed over with rebellious rose shoots, and the unmolested growth of shrubs and trees providing a thick, soft curtain to protect Robert and Gabrielle from the outside world.

In the courtyard stood an old stone fountain, with stone table and benches flecked by a cool mosaic of vine leaves, hanging from a trellis, for shade. Great white arum lilies grew in a mossy nook where the water dripped into its stone basin.

A sweet odour of hay and fresh clover rose up through the chinks in the floor from the cool, dark stable below.

Across the road and over a wall and past a church and fishermen's huts, pine trees clambered up towards a high road winding, serpent-like, to Bayona, and beyond it a rugged coastline. Lying in the sea like crouched lions were the islands called Las Cies.

There was such peace here that Robert and Gabrielle both felt they would never want to go back into the "real" world again, the brash, violent world of Texas. It was the most perfect antidote they could have devised. Robert had completely thrown off his malaria at last, and Gabrielle was in her element. He had always guessed she had something of the mystic about her personality, and now it became obvious as she wandered round little churches, sitting quietly in the cool darkness, gazing at the statues and paintings of the Stations of the Cross. How strange that his first impression of her in the Bois had been that she was a "religious." Never had they been happier.

Gabrielle sketched everything in sight, from the tall yellow verbascum to the lizards that scampered in the garden with emerald, black and jewelled heads; from the blue-green aloes to the red roof and dazzling whitewash of the house itself.

Jack, too, was often captured with her pencils as he lay curled up in the sun, resting from all his months of trotting behind their horses in Texas and Mexico; and once she drew her husband as he lounged in a basket chair absorbing the notes on the Spanish conquest he had made four years before in the old university at Salamanca.

This was a good place for his first literary efforts to unfold. Both Robert and Gabrielle felt totally fulfilled; their two years of intense activity and adventure were now to be followed by an artistic interlude and this brief holiday in Galicia, before they plunged back into the life that was to be their destiny. Robert must now stop playing at being a Gaucho and turn his thoughts to the responsibility of a Scottish Laird. He also wanted to write.

Robert showed Gabrielle a few of his first scribbles, which delighted her with their wit and individuality. He was incapable of producing a cliché or a banal sentence, and he made people and places come alive with his pen. "Literary snapshots!" commented Gabrielle.

The house had been inhabited by Benedictine monks and seemed to be perfumed with the dimness of a religious life, a few little dark cells (but not many, for most of the monks here had worked on the land), big granaries above stairs for storing wheat; the refectory, windowless, chestnut-floored and chestnut-beamed, opening by two doors on to the sunlit gallery overlooking the wine press with the *lagar* still purple with the stain of last year's grapes, waiting for the riches of the coming October.

Of course there were brief interruptions to their idyllic life in Galicia, but most of them were pleasant ones. In September Malise and an under-graduate friend called Kennedy came to spend the second part of their long vacation from Oxford with his brother and sister-in-law at Vigo.

It was a happy time for them all, and Robert was delighted to find that Gabrielle and Malise had so much in common – only a year in age apart, and both so involved in religion and mysticism and a love of beautiful churches. Sadly, they also shared a less happy condition: they both suffered from weak chests.

For all Malise's seriousness about his calling, he was as full of fun and jokes as Charlie and enormously interested in people. He would be a good priest, Robert thought: it was a pity he still looked delicate, and he knew Mamma was haunted by the worry that Malise was consumptive.

Music was still his second most absorbing interest. He showed them their ancestor's poem which he had set to music. "If doughty deeds my ladye please, right soon I'll mount by steed . . ." Robert and Gabrielle were haunted by the tune as he sang his composition in a melodious tenor voice. Robert had always loved music, but he was the one member of the family who could neither sing nor play an instrument – Malise was the real musician, having been picked out when he was still a boy at Winchester to play the College organ.

After Malise and Kennedy left, George Mansel unexpectedly arrived in October off a ship, to spend a night with them on his way back from South America to visit his mother in Dorset. Mansel was delighted with Gabrielle, and congratulated Robert with his usual light touch on "his excellent taste in wives."

Robert and George talked at length about the future, and George suggested that if they buried themselves there until they inherited Gartmore, their friends and relations would be all the more inclined to gossip and to tell each other that Robert's marriage was so heartily disapproved of by his family that he had hidden his wife away in darkest Spain. Robert agreed with his friend. In any case, they had now spent an idyllic five months at Vigo, and the old restlessness was beginning to nudge Robert into action. It would be fun to take Gabrielle to see some of the relations, and it would be good for her morale to find that she was admired and accepted by them. He knew Aunt Helen Speirs and Aunt Annie would back them up; they were bound to tell the other aunts that they must be kind to Gabrielle, for Robert's sake. Also he wanted to ask Mr. Wright again about the possibility of getting a Queen's Messenger-ship, to justify his travels and to add to his limited income.

Gabrielle was prepared to fall in with Robert's ideas so long as he promised to bring her back to La Graña for the worst of the winter. She had fallen in love with the place. But she agreed that she would like to spend some time in London, for she hardly possessed a presentable dress these days, after spending so much time in boots and breeches when they were living in Texas. So it was arranged.

Their first visit to England went off more satisfactorily than Robert had dared hope. After a happy visit to the aunts at Leamington Spa, they travelled on to Scotland. The autumn weather was mild, and Gabrielle felt well. Cousin John Erskine insisted on having them to stay near Gartmore at Lochend, on the Lake of Menteith, for a long visit, and they were also bidden for a visit to some neighbours of the Graham family who also lived near Gartmore, the Stirlings of Garden. While they were in Scotland, Robert heard the sad news that his old friend Edward Ogilvy had died in Jamaica "from a complaint of the liver." Robert was not surprised, and thought James might soon be lost to them from the same illness, both brothers being incurable alcoholics.

Gabrielle blossomed under the affection and admiration bestowed upon her by their many friends and relations, who hung upon her words as she described their adventures in Texas and Mexico. What an unusual young woman Robert had married, so pretty and intelligent, so coura-geous – and what a devoted couple they seemed to be! It was delightful to see Robert looking so well and happy with his interesting young wife.

From Scotland the young couple returned south via the aunts at Leamington, and then to Dorset, where they relived their honeymoon. They could hardly believe they had now been married for four years already. It was just the same time of year, and they had golden October days, just as they had in 1878. The Mansel family did everything they could to make their visit a happy one.

In London Robert managed to find pleasant rooms for them in Green Street. There were more relations to visit, and time to spend with Mamma. Robert felt there was still some constraint in the relationship between his mother and Gabrielle, but it was no longer a state of outright war, and they both tried hard to learn to like each other, for Robert's sake.

CHAPTER XX

Early in the summer of 1883 Charlie received a Life Saving Medal at the hands of the Prince of Wales himself, which was an unprecedented honour. After the ceremony he joked with his brother and told him that the whole thing had been a bit of a lark: the old waterman he had rescued had, of course, been dead drunk! It was so like Charlie to try to brush off the heroics of the incident, thought Robert. His brother really did have a splendidly modest character.

Malise left Oxford at the end of the summer term. He had only got a third, but none of the boys had ever been very good at passing exams, so nobody worried very much. On 13th June, just after Mallie had come down from Oxford, Charlie married his beautiful Barbara. Robert decided to call his sister-in-law "Milly," for her full names were Mildred Emily Barbara, and he thought Milly suited her better than Barbara. Anyway, it was the name her own family had always called her by.

Missy was delighted with her new daughter-in-law and thought Charlie had done very well for himself. At the wedding they met the huge Bagot family from Norfolk and Shropshire and Staffordshire, and a few more from further north and south. They seemed to have even more relations than their own. Barbara had five brothers and sisters, and the one they all liked best was her eldest sister, "Constie," or Constance. The sisters were very alike, tall, with swanlike necks and beautiful creamy skins. No wonder the Prince of Wales was said to admire the Rector of Castle Rising's daughter so much. In fact, Charlie had first met his "Babs" at Sandringham, with Prince Louis of Battenberg when they shot there during short leaves from the Royal Yacht.

Missy gazed at her three sons with great satisfaction as they waited for the bride to arrive at the church. Charlie looked distinguished in his full-dress uniform and Robert elegant in a frock coat, both with the neat beards which the Prince of Wales had made the current fashion. Most handsome of all was Malise, clean-shaven, with his almost ethereal looks, Pre-Raphaelite, slightly girlish, though there was nothing remotely effeminate about his character. Malise was going through a dreadful stage of wearing very long hair and extremely odd clothes, especially the awful red socks that were his pride and joy, but Missy kept her own counsel, realising that he was out to shock, and would only go to worse extremes if she said anything. In any case, it was a healthy sign to find him so normal when he was about to take Holy Orders, at least he would be more likely to understand the weaknesses of his parishioners.

Robert was delighted when he found that Gabrielle was getting almost as much attention from his relations as the bride herself. For the first time since he had married her, he realised that perhaps he had done Gabrielle out of the best day of any girl's life by rushing her to a registry office in the Strand. But he knew they could never have had a church wedding for Gabrielle was totally committed to Roman Catholicism, and he refused to give up his own "unattached" attitude to church matters.

On to Brussels, and finally back to Vigo by December 1882, just as the cold weather was beginning to set in and Gabrielle's old cough had started to bother her. But as soon as they felt the warm sunshine of northern Spain seeping through their veins and found themselves back in the mellow beauty of La Graña, she threw off the cough again, and was happy to be alone with Robert once more in the special corner of heaven which had become their favourite place in the world.

The family continued to keep in touch with them during their temporary exile, and Gabrielle was particularly touched to receive a warm-hearted letter from Aunt Annie Erskine from Leamington, and a very kind one from Admiral Erskine, from Lochend, asking after her health and begging her to look after herself. Aunt Annie asked tenderly after the "two dear wanderers" and hoped that if Gabrielle became ill she would "return to her old aunt in Leamington" to be looked after.

Gabrielle showed the affectionate letter to Robert. She was greatly moved by it, and there were tears in her eyes as she told Robert how happy she was to be taken to the hearts of his dear old Graham and Speirs aunts.

They spent April 1883 at Dolgelly in Wales, where Gabrielle sketched and had lessons from an artist called Bernard Evans who was staying in the same hotel. Robert went north briefly to visit his father and to see Mr. Jamieson, the Curator Bonis, in Edinburgh. In Texas they had been drawing £400 a year from the family funds, but by the time they returned home in 1882 their debts had risen to £2,000, as they had spent their whole grant for capital investment in Texas on living expenses, in addition to their allowance. Jamieson agreed to give them an allowance of £500 a year to live on until Robert's father died. Robert was able to return to Gabrielle in Wales with the good news.

Although he still seemed to be waiting in the wings while his father continued his dream-like life in Dumfriesshire, he knew that his father's health was deteriorating, and that very soon he would be Laird of Gartmore.

Missy had Charlie's wife staying with her for the first few months of 1883, for she was expecting her first baby and Charlie was off on a cruise with the Royal Yacht. Missy thoroughly enjoyed Barbara's company and they spent a great deal of time calling on their friends in a brougham they had been lent and going to theatres and concerts. Missy had spent so much time alone over the years, with only Blanche Fane as a companion, that she had forgotten what fun it was to meet so many people, and her sociable daughter-in-law seemed to enjoy it as much as she did.

Robert and Gabrielle enjoyed the summer of 1883 for they had no responsibilities for the time being and their allowance seemed more than adequate for their present lifestyle. Their marriage was blossoming, and this strangely restless life appealed to them both as they moved from place to place. They were in no hurry to acquire a house of their own, for they still had La Graña in Spain, although they agreed that if Papa had not died by the following year, then they must start to look for a place of their own within reach of London.

That summer they rented an old farmhouse at Liphook in Hampshire, situated conveniently between Winchester and Portsmouth. Charlie was at Portsmouth when the Royal Yacht was in her home port, and Mallie was now a deacon at St. John's Church in Winchester. Missy was spending a good deal of the summer with Mallie, so Robert had his whole family within a small radius; and yet he and Gabrielle could still enjoy the privacy of their temporary English home.

It was a splendid arrangement. Robert hired good horses for himself and Gabrielle, and they delighted in their rides through the open country round Hindhead and Haslemere. The country was sandy, almost desert-like, with Scotch firs, and whortleberries, and there were beautiful views to the great chalk ranges of the Guildford Hills and the South Downs.

A special ride they liked to take was up Gibbet Hill, near the new village of Hindhead, and down into the Devil's Punchbowl. At Haslemere they watched the craftsmen working wood, glass and leather, producing exquisite crafts, which Robert felt proved the case against factory-made articles to those entirely manufactured by hand. It would be sad if a day was to come when craftsmen such as these were put out of work by mass-produced merchandise, he thought.

On 1st June 1883 Barbara Cunninghame Graham gave birth to a daughter. Gabrielle and Robert hurried over to the house Charlie and Barbara had rented, to inspect their new niece. To Robert's delight he found that Charlie's baby was olive-skinned with a strong look of Grandmamma Catalina about her. He had a truly Spanish niece.

Barbara was not nearly so pleased about her daughter's looks. She was an ugly little thing, she said – why did she have to have that strange sallow complexion when her own skin was always described as being "pure peaches and cream"? The baby was promptly christened Olive, which Charlie and Barbara seemed to think was appropriate, and Robert thought was an insult to the poor child. He was told her other names were to be Barbara and Clementina, an Elphinstone name and the name of Missy's older sister who had sadly died after the birth of her ninth child, in the 1850s when still quite young.

Gabrielle found the baby quite delightful and her heart ached as she watched Robert holding his niece with such pride. He seemed to have a way with babies. The child stopped crying as soon as he took her into his arms, and gazed at him with big, round eyes. It must be the same thing that made horses and dogs take to him so readily, she thought. Perhaps they knew that he made no distinctions between illustrious men and women, ordinary children or babies, horses, dogs or even small wild animals. They were all created to play an individual part on earth, so why should one be considered less important than another? It was quite obvious that he made Olive feel extremely important, as the baby stared solemnly back at him.

He handed her to her mother and took Gabrielle's hand is his, walking her through the garden to inspect the roses. He knew exactly what she was thinking, and he wanted her to know that he was perfectly content with things the way they were.

After another visit to Cousin John Erskine at Lochend in September
and October, Gabrielle started to cough again. The autumn mists were
once more shrouding the Lake of Menteith in a curtain of white, and a
dampness seemed to pervade Lochend which even roaring log fires did
nothing to dispel. Robert knew they must set out again for milder
climes. By the end of December 1883 they had reached Portugal, after a
visit to the Spanish great-aunts in Gibraltar, then to Algeciras and on to
Cadiz to see something of the town where "Ganama" Catalina had lived
as a child. They were back at Vigo by 24th January, with letters from
home awaiting their arrival.

It was most satisfactory that everyone was now rallying round both
him and Gabrielle, thought Robert. It would make the transition to Gartmore, when it came, so much easier.

It was still cold enough in the evenings to pile chestnut branches on
the fire in the refectory, as they sat together reading their letters by their
own hearth. This was where they were happiest of all, and he hoped La
Graña would always be available as their winter retreat.

PART V
LAIRD OF GARTMORE – 1884-1936
PROLOGUE

It wasn't until April 1884 that Robert and Gabrielle found themselves living at Gartmore, at long last.

"We're going to be so happy here together, Lob, darling," sighed Gabrielle happily, in agreement with his unspoken thoughts.

"Yes, Chid, we're going to bring Gartmore to life again! There's only one thing still needed – can you guess what?"

"Yes," laughed his wife, "Pingos!"

"How did you guess?" asked Robert in mock surprise. "In fact, Chid, I'm going to Glasgow tomorrow because I hear that a consignment of Argentine horses are arriving at the docks. You won't mind being left along on your first day at Gartmore, will you, dearest Chid?" he asked anxiously.

"Of course not, Lob, I shall be far too busy to be lonely. Peregrina and I will have so much to unpack, and so much to arrange."

Robert had never seen his wife so happy, even on their best days in Vigo at La Graña. She really did seem to love Gartmore.

When he got back from Glasgow the next evening he burst into the drawing room in tremendous excitement.

"Guess what, Chid? I've bought the most marvellous pingo you've ever seen. They were going to turn him into a tram horse, but he's far too good for that – a really spirited black, and believe it or not, I recognised his brand! He comes from the estancia of my friend Eduardo Casey from Entre Rios! Isn't that marvellous?"

He picked Gabrielle up and whirled her round in his arms. "A real, genuine pingo from Argentina!" he laughed. "Oh, Chid, what fun we're going to have – everything is working out so perfectly: we shall have so many things here at Gartmore to remind us of all the places we love best, or have been to together – my new pingo from Argentina, Jack from Texas, and Peregrina from Vigo!"

"Put me down, Lob, for goodness sake, you're making me quite breathless," laughed Gabrielle. "And you'd better be careful what you say in front of my maid Peregrina, I don't think she'd exactly appreciate being classed with Jack and your new pingo! What are you going to call him or haven't you thought yet?

"Oh yes, I have," said Robert. "I knew straight away, I shall call him 'Pampa' – that is what the gauchos always called a black horse with a white face – and that is what my beautiful new horse is like. You should see his lovely long tail and mane, Chid! He looks just as though he had been galloping across the Atlantic to find me. None of the men could handle him, poor chap. They were trying to harness him to a tram and he slipped on the cobbles and fell. I sat on his head and we got him up again. He was pretty frightened and angry with them all – but when he saw me I think he must have known that I was once a gaucho: he just stayed stock still until I came up to him, and let me stroke his nose. Wasn't that pet of him?"

"Lob the Liontamer, I shall call you!" said Gabrielle, "And what about a pingo for *me*, Lob?"

"That's already arranged," said Robert with a smile. "Cousin John Erskine has found two lovely ponies at the Falkirk Tryst for us, they were quite cheap so he suggests we have them both, then if one goes lame we've always got a spare. There's a Highland pony and a funny cream-coloured Iceland pony too. I remember seeing ponies like that when I once went to Iceland with Charlie, and we longed to bring one home with us in our luggage! They are quite small and shaggy, but very strong. What will you call *your* new pony, Chid, or do you want to look at him first before you decide?"

"Oh no," replied Gabrielle, "I've know for some time what my pony was to be called – he will be 'Talla' after the old Graham island in the Lake of Menteith."

Robert looked at Gabrielle very tenderly. "You really do love Gartmore already, Chid, don't you?" he said happily.

Soon everyone in the district knew the young Laird and his wife, as they rode round the estate together, Mr. Cunninghame Graham on his sturdy black Argentine, who would let no-one catch him but his master, and the pretty young Mrs. Cunninghame Graham (whom everyone still thought was Spanish) on a strange Icelandic pony of about fourteen hands. They were a handsome sight, riding together, and the people of

Gartmore congratulated themselves on their new Laird and his wife. Things were bound to improve from now on.

Gabrielle's initiation as the Laird's wife was swift, she soon found herself involved in everything from opening Sales of Work to giving parties at Gartmore for the school-children, from visiting the aged to providing food and drink for the poor and infirm on their estate. Robert often thought back to that sad moment on 6th September, 1883, eight months ago. So much had happened since then, and now he was truly the Laird of Gartmore.

CHAPTER XXI

It had been in August 1883 when Willy Bontine had suddenly taken for the worse, then rallied again, so that Dr. Sharp had thought at first that it had merely been one of his bad turns, which were undeniably becoming more frequent as he grew older. He was fifty-eight years old. But by the beginning of September he had had a relapse and it was obvious that he was dying. Dr. Sharp sent a telegram to Robert, who had hurried north with Gabrielle to be at his father's bedside for his final moments. Robert still thought constantly about that sad time.

It was now eight months ago, on 6th September 1883, that his father, William Bontine, had died at Eccles House, Penpont, in the county of Dumfries, where he had lived for the past seventeen years in sad solitude. Now that the end had finally come, Robert was overwhelmed with grief. How greatly he was going to miss his gentle, understanding father, even though they had seen so little of each other for so long. He would never forget his infinite kindness when they were boys at Finlaystone and at Gartmore, and his patient resignation to his tragic illness and exile from his wife and sons. All that was left to remember him by was a little book of poems he had published. They were simple, but charming.

Robert had stayed for the next two days at the Station Hotel in Dumfries while the necessary formalities were dealt with.

A formal letter was sent out on black-edged paper to announce his father's death:

"Eccles House. 7th September 1883

Sir

William Cunninghame Bontine, my Father, died here yesterday, and will be interred in Gartmore Cemetery.

Your company here, on Monday first, the 10th Current, at Eleven o'clock Forenoon, to accompany his remains to the Railway Station at Thornhill, will be esteemed a favour by,

Sir,

Your obedient Servant,

Robert C. Graham Bontine."

Robert had felt quite numb; all he could think of was how much he had loved dear 'Puppie.'

William Bontine finally came back to Gartmore to be buried in the family burial ground on 10th September 1883. At last he had come home, and could rest with his father Robert and his grandfather William, and with 'Doughty Deeds,' (another Robert, in the eighteenth century) in the little square patch of ground where they all lay protected from the outside world by comforting stone walls, and planted with wild roses and boxwood, a wild cherry (gean) standing sentinel on one side of the iron gate, and the scarlet berries of a mountain ash, or rowan, on the other.

Only the male members of the family and their friends had attended the burial, according to Scottish custom, but afterwards Gabrielle took her rightful place at Robert's side to dispense refreshments at the customary wake, while Missy sat in the drawing room to receive the sympathy of the many people who had known Willy since he was a boy.

It was the start of the shooting season, and the tenant, Sir Gerald Fitzgerald, was in residence; but he told them that he was glad to welcome the family back into the old house for the funeral, and did everything he could to let them feel that it was their home and he was a mere guest.

After the burial, he took Robert to one side to say, "My dear fellow, I just want you to know that I shall be perfectly happy to cut short my lease and let you move into your rightful home whenever you wish. I understand so well what you must have felt, and can only hope that my temporary guardianship of your beautiful home may have helped with the upkeep of the estate, if nothing else. I feel very privileged to have been allowed to spend so many happy times here." Robert was very touched, and thanked Sir Gerald warmly.

"It's strange," he said, "I've longed so much for Gartmore to be mine, and now all I can think of is how much I miss Papa. It's not even as though I saw much of him over the past seventeen years – but he was such a good father to us before he became so ill, and I think I shall always remember him best here – rowing us across to Inchmahome, teaching us to shoot and fish, riding in the parks with us. He was such a marvellous horseman – that's why he went into a cavalry regiment like the Greys. The best fun of all was skating on the lake when it froze over.

"He loved Gartmore, and he taught Charlie and Mal and me to love it, too. All the time I was in South America and Texas, however much fun I was having, I knew that I only wanted to live at Gartmore!"

Robert was quite exhausted by the end of the day; it had been most tiring meeting so many of the family, the tenants, farm workers, neighbours and distant relations, half of whom he never remembered seeing in his life before. at last they had all left in their carriages and dog-carts and gigs and he found himself sitting in the old library with a glass of whisky at his elbow, and the old lawyer's grandson, young Mr. Campbell, ensconced behind a table which was smothered in legal documents.

Robert laughed. "I hope you're not going to expect me to listen intelligently to the finer aspects of the law tonight, Mr. Campbell? I feel quite done up by the day's events."

"No indeed, Graham," said the young lawyer. "All I wanted to tell you was that Sir Gerald will receive notice to quit, and the property should be yours in a few months. I don't think it would be very practical for you and your wife to move in before Christmas, as there will be some repairs and renovations to be made, but shall we say, all being well, you could settle here some time in 1884?"

Robert was longing to move in straight away, but he knew that a great deal had to be settled, and there would be loose ends tied up before Gartmore could become his home at last.

There was also the whole question as to whether the estate could become a viable concern. It would break his heart to have to sell it now, but it would be far better if the men of business did their sums first. If he was never going to be able to live at Gartmore, then he would much rather that they told him first, so that he and Gabrielle could be spared the distress of moving in, then having to move out shortly after, when they found it must be sold after all.

"Do you think the whole thing is going to be feasible?" he asked the lawyer anxiously.

"I believe it will be possible, Graham," said Mr. Campbell cautiously. "The farms will have to be actively improved, of course, before you can charge higher rents. And, in fact, with agriculture so depressed at the moment, most rents seem to be going down, not up. But the very fact that you will be living on the spot should help things along greatly.

There's nothing like having the Laird living on the place – everyone's morale goes up by leaps and bounds. It's been a sad time for the Gartmore people for the past seventeen years. You're going to get a great welcome from them, and it's good to see how much they admire your wife. She'll be a tremendous asset to Gartmore! But you'll have to live very economically, of course."

Robert thanked Mr. Campbell warmly for his kind words, and particularly for the way he and his grandfather had helped to keep the family estates afloat over the years.

Mr. Campbell got to his feet and packed his papers into his attaché case. "I must be off and leave you in peace. Grant is kindly taking me to the station, so I'll see myself out. I suggest you take a breather in here, and a quiet 'dram' before facing the aunts and uncles and cousins at dinner tonight! Goodbye and good luck. It's good to know you are the Laird at last. It has been a very trying time for you all."

"Goodbye, Campbell, and thank you for all your help today. Poor Papa, how pleased he must be to be back at Gartmore at last! Gabrielle has just gone back to his grave with a bunch of spurge laurel – it's the Graham clan's badge, you know. The rascally Grahams in the days of the Earls always wore a piece in their bonnets!"

Robert saw the lawyer out of the front door and turned to survey the house that was now nearly his. Both he and Pap had come back to their childhood home at last. What a long exile it had been! He slipped back into the library for a few minutes alone before he had to face the relations once more. He looked round at the collection of fine books – Papa had called it "the library," but he thought he would revert to the old Scottish terminology and call it simply "The Book Room."

There was a tap on the door, and Charlie slipped in to close the door quietly behind him.

"Poor old Papa," he said sadly to his brother. "I do miss him, Bob, don't you?" Will you come and live here now?"

"I hope so," answered Robert, pouring out some whisky for his brother. Charlie took a mouthful and put the glass down on the table.

"Bob, I've decided to ask for a long spell of leave from the Navy. They're going to give me a year on half-pay. I want to be free to help you with all this if I can."

"Thanks a lot, Tarlee. You're a good fellow. We'll sort it out together and I'll be glad of your help." Robert smiled grateful at Charlie.

Admiral Erskine insisted on having Robert and Gabrielle to stay after the funeral; everyone else had gone back to the south, but Charlie stayed on at Lochend, too, to help Robert. There was a great deal to be done. Robert spent most days riding round the farms with Charlie, to call on the tenants, and found them all enormously pleased to have them back. Jack trotted happily behind Robert's horse as he got to know his new home.

Gabrielle, too, visited most of the women in the cottages and assured them that at last they would have people who really cared about them living at Gartmore.

The weather turned chilly towards the middle of September, and Gabrielle came down with a touch of her usual bronchitis. Robert grew anxious. How was Chid going to survive the climate at Gartmore? Her illness made her depressed and she also began to wonder if, after all, she could cope with this bleak place. She wanted so badly to help Robert with it, but it was only possible to cope if she was feeling well.

Robert decided to send her back to their rented house in Liphook while he straightened things out with the lawyers and the factor. His mother had written to say it was still warm and sunny in England, so Gabrielle would be much better off in the south.

Charlie had to go back to his wife and small daughter on the train, so he said he would accompany Gabrielle to England. After putting them on their train, Robert returned to Lochend to grapple with all the problems that were now his responsibility.

A few days later he too went down with a feverish cold – he must have grown soft, he thought crossly, living in hot climates in South America, Texas and Mexico, and then in Spain and southern England for the past two years. He was furious at having to retire to bed, and even more angry when he found that Gabrielle had suddenly gone to London, instead of staying quietly at Liphook; and was now miserably upset because she had called on her mother-in-law and her sister-in-law in Ebury Street and had not been treated as warmly by them as she would have liked. She wrote a petulant letter to Robert which arrived when he was feeling thoroughly unwell. The doctor had told him that his own fever was probably a reaction to all the stress and strain of the past weeks, possibly even a minor recurrence of his malaria, and the sensible thing would be to have a proper rest in bed for a day or two. Robert hated being stuck in bed and was more miserable than ever.

He wrote to Gabrielle on 12th October to tell her that he was "quite laid up with a violent cough and cold and a sore foot. The riding and driving in the wet, and the whisky, have brought on a feverish attack. I have had to have my "brecklin' fish" in bed, a very unusual thing for me and feel altogether very miserable this morning. I was to have gone to Ardoch tomorrow but cannot go now. I go on Monday to Edinburth (4, Stafford Street) and stay two days.

"Write a long letter to your 'petit Mari' and let me know what you think about things, and do be resolute about keeping indoors in bad weather, and think of our future.

"Sir Gerald has had notice to quit, the Duke of Montrose's shootings are given up, and I am making arrangements to let all the rest. I am in treaty for a pony, as I find I must have one. It costs me six shillings a day to hire one, and it is generally some broken down brute that takes all day to get about. I have had a whole week of going round farms, etc. and (as soon as I am out of bed) there will be two or three days in Edinburgh with Jamieson, and then back here, and a meeting with Campbell, and perhaps a new factor to look for and take round, as I am almost sure the present one will not stay without a rise in his salary that I cannot afford to give him. It is a tight fix. Do write and tell me if you got the £20 I sent you? I hope tomorrow to be better, and by Monday to go to Edinburgh, but am not sure.

"As regards Milly and my mother, do not bother yourself, and I wonder why you called at all. Both you and I are greatly liked here, and as we shall, I suppose, spend our life between here and Spain, it is all we want, chère petite femme. With great luck, towards the end of this month I may (only may) be able to run up to Liphook, but whether permanently or for only a few days I do not know yet.

"I am up to the eyes in writing all day long, about leases of farms, etc. also farming at Ardoch.

"Ton petit mari qui t'adore, Lob."

It was their first long parting since their marriage and they missed each other abominably. Robert sighed; on top of everything else, it really was too bad of Mamma and Milly to gang up against poor little Chid. He would never be able to understand why Mamma went on being so unkind – it was so unlike her.

Next morning he received another letter from Gabrielle, in which she poured out her loneliness and begged him to come back to her so they could return to Spain together. She was utterly miserable. Robert wrote again, trying to show her that their temporary parting was in their best possible interest and that she must try to bear it.

"My dearest Chid, Your letter written on the train only came this morning. It is bitterly cold her and I still have a sort of cold and bronchitis that I caught going round the farms at Gartmore.

"You had better by all means go back to Liphook and keep indoors, as London is very bad in these months and awfully dull all alone. By all means go back, as certainly Liphook is a milder climate than London.

Do try and look matters properly in the face. All our future depends on the next six months, as, if we 'play the fool' now, not even the sale of Ardoch will clear our debts then.

"Do try and keep in the house at Liphook, read and draw, and take great care of yourself. I have an immense amount to do here, still, but will be back by the end of the month, at Liphook.

"Ton petit mari, Lob."

In his postscript he stressed yet again, "I would certainly go back to Liphook – fancy how miserable you would be in town without a soul to speak to."

On top of all the work in connection with Gartmore and Ardoch, Robert was kept busy answering the many kind letters he had received on the death of his father. Mr. Jamieson, the accountant, who had been his father's Curator Bonis for the past seventeen years, was unfortunately in Paris when Willy died. He had written a typically pompous but kind letter, as soon as the news reached him, only three days after Robert's father's death on 6th September 1883.

"9th September 1883   Paris

"My dear Bontine,

"On my arrival here this morning I have learned of your Father's death: I had intended to write to you and Mrs. Bontine when I heard of his serious illness a few weeks ago, but he had rallied before I did so and I really felt it very difficult to write to offer congratulations. Nor can I offer you much condolence: the close of a life cannot be but a solemn incident to those closely allied to him who has ceased to be, but the removal from this troublesome world of one who has for so long ceased to have any part in its joys, cannot be a subject for condolence. My relations with you have been too intimate to permit of my writing stock phrases.

"Had it been possible for me to do so I need hardly say I should have asked your permission to take my place among those who were to bear your Father's remains to their last resting place at Gartmore: I should have desired to offer my token of respect to the memory of one I have long served and to the Family from whom I received so many instances of good will. But I cannot now be present if I tried, and I beg you will accept for yourself and convey to your Mother my deep regret that I was unable to be there.

"You will readily believe, my dear Bontine, that my sympathies for you are more keen in your new position than any are for the memories of the past: if during the long period of my service to your Father I have managed to mitigate to you and your brothers and Mother any of the sorrows and discomforts of your position, I will be grateful.

"I beg to be kindly remembered to your Wife and I rejoice that no difficulties now present themselves in your making your residence wherever may be most suitable for her health.

"With kind regards I remain your very trusty,

"George Auldjo Jamieson."

Robert also got a packet of letters from many kind friends, which his mother had sent on to him. She knew he would be cheered to know how many people had admired Papa, and one and all made the same observation: "one cannot but feel what a happy release it is for him, after so many years of suffering." It was nice to think that there had been all those friends silently sympathising with them throughout their troubles.

Now he must get things properly organised at Gartmore, so that Papa would be proud of his efforts to retrieve the family estates, as he watched his son picking up his inheritance on the old earth below.

CHAPTER XXII

At last Robert was free to join Gabrielle again. His talks in Edinburgh with Jamieson and Campbell had been extremely profitable, and the two men were full of admiration for the way young Graham was grappling with his responsibilities and setting everything to rights with such thoroughness during the six weeks immediately following the funeral. The tenants all expressed great satisfaction with their new Laird and the hope that he and his wife would soon settle for good at Gartmore. Jamieson and Campbell had done their sums and Robert was presented with a statement of the financial situation.

His assets came to £14,720, fourteen shillings and tenpence. His liabilities came to £94,059, eight shillings and threepence. The income from the rents was £9,700 and this was almost exactly balanced by the total expenditure of £9,040. In other words, it was costing around ten thousand a year to finance his mother, himself, and his two brothers, their wives and annuities to the Graham aunts.

There were ten members of the family in all to be supported on this income, plus interest on mortgages, taxes and the upkeep of the estate. There would, in fact, be £600 profit a year on the estate if nothing was done to pay off the final debt of £61,000 that Robert had now inherited. Of course, if the rents fell, as was likely to happen at this time of a growing agricultural slump, then there would be little profit from the rents and the debt would still hang round their necks like an albatross, in addition to the farming anxieties.

Robert was prepared to take the risk. He was convinced that he could make a worthwhile job of running Gartmore – anyway, it was the only job he had been thoroughly trained to do since he was a child, so he might as well give it a try. He could not wait to get his hands on the place once more, but he knew that it would be fatal to plunge Gabrielle straight into a Scottish winter. It would be pleasant to go back to La Graña until the warmer weather returned, and then he would take up his inheritance.

He badly needed a respite in Spain himself. He felt dreadfully tired after the events of the past weeks and was still bothered by his cough.

Robert and Gabrielle left England in November 1883 to travel through Spain on their way to Vigo. They wanted to visit some of the places in the interior that they had not yet seen. Having done a tour of the south the previous winter, they decided to go by sea to Valencia and travel right across central Spain to Vigo. This time Robert wrote to describe their journey to his mother, on their arrival at Vigo on 19th December.

"The journey through the middle of Spain was very interesting and exceedingly comfortable, and the food excellent. We came from Valencia to Alcazar de San Juan, then Cuidad Real, then Merida, then Badajos, then to Oporto in Portugal, where we stopped ten days. The cold has been awful, and since we left, there has been a foot of snow in Valencia – which I can hardly realise as there were hundreds of acres of oranges and dates when we left. But there has even been snow at Lisbon, and five degrees of frost in Seville!

"There is none at Vigo, though the wind is bitter. Though, strange to say, it is quite warm at La Graña as it is so sheltered. It looks lovelier than ever.

"We dined with the Crawfords at Oporto, they have a lovely old Portuguese house, full of pretty things, and a lovely garden. Port wine seems to be a better thing than ever judging by the merchants out here. There was a tremendous outcry in the papers in Portugal about the Queen having sent the Prince of Portugal to an hotel, instead of giving him rooms in 'old Buckingham.'

"I shall have to be made Alcalde in Vigo at the least, as this is my third visit there! The English fleet is in here, and a poor sailor was killed by falling from aloft, and was buried here this morning, it was very sad. I wrote Mallie a reverent letter this morning, I think it will arrive just in time for his ordination. Was he very pet, attired as a 'Clergy Cat'? There were some fine pictures at Badajos, but I liked a Valencian painter called Espinozas, best.

"Your 'reflejo' plate is an old one, I have also got a little funny Portuguese thing for you.

"I see by Mr. Campbell's report we should have to pay Uncle Douglas £3,000, not £500. I do not grudge it to him, but the moment is unlucky.

"Leamington must have been rather a trial. It was very pet of old Khāt to send a present to Leucha after the way her father, Lord Hawarden has behaved to him. We found a mass of letters waiting here – I was very much surprised to hear of poor old Mary's death (Grand-mamma's maid) she was quite a type of a bygone generation, I remember her well.

"I will write again soon. Gabrielle joins me in best love and good wishes for the pleasing Christmastide.

"Believe me, yr. affec. son R. C. Graham Bontine."

Mamma always kept him well up to date with family matters in her own letters. Clemy's sixth daughter, Leucha, had been married during 1883 to Sir Thomas Warner from Suffolk and the reference to Khāt's wedding present showed that her late sister Clementine's husband, Uncle Hawarden, was in Mamma's bad books.

After Christmas Robert wrote again to acknowledge another letter from his mother telling him about Mallie's ordination.

"I am glad he preaches well, but I hope he will not go beyond his pulpit for preaching!

"It is wonderfully fine here, far finer than usual. There is always a good deal of sun in the winter at Vigo. This afternoon we went in a boat to see some anchors, bullets, jars of indigo, blocks of mahogany, etc. that have been fished up from the galleons sunk by Sir Cloudsley Shovel in 1702. I have a canonball, and am going back for a great earthenware jar."

He also thanked his mother for the picture of an 'unknown dog' she had sent him for Christmas, and the 'Warwickshire engraving.' He was still signing his letters 'R. C. Graham Bontine' for he would not be entitled to use the name 'Cunninghame Graham' until he had taken possession of Gartmore.

His mother had told him that she would prefer to remain as 'The Honourable Mrs. Bontine,' the style she had used since 1860 when her brother became Lord Elphinstone. Sadly Uncle John Elphinstone had died a year after succeeding to the title, at the age of forty-two, and the peerage had now side-stepped to a cousin, William Fullertone Elphinstone, who was descended from Mamma'' great-uncle. Cousin William was now the 15th Lord Elphinstone, but Mamma retained her right to bear the style of a Peer's sister.

By the end of February, Robert and Gabrielle were already beginning to feel restless again. They had now spent more than a month at La Graña, lazily enjoying their garden, and the nearby countryside, which they explored on donkeys. But now they wanted to go further afield again, and Robert was anxious to look up a few more things about the Jesuit missionaries in Spanish America, and the early history of Spain, before settling permanently at Gartmore. He was sure there would be plenty of time to write his book once they were settled into his family home, but he must complete the research while he was still in Spain.

On 27th February 1884 he wrote to his mother (once again using the lined and black-edged paper that was customary during periods of mourning after a family bereavement) to tell her of his plans.

"My dear Mother,

"We are just in the process of starting for Madrid. I have long wanted to see it and I find the north route by Leon and Burgos takes five days and that there is a great deal of snow up there still, so on the whole I think Madrid will be the best.

"Spanish politics are very much mixed at present, and I am afraid that the look-out for the King is bad. I dare say in Madrid I shall find many books for my research.

"Mr. Gulliver (our old tutor) wrote me such a kind letter the other day: his address is, St. John's College, Auckland, New Zealand. (I find the Post Office authorities in Vigo think that New Zealand is in America!)

"What does Gordon's celebrated slave proclamation mean after he has passed most of his life putting it down? Fancy Bradlaugh elected again. I am very glad the vote of censure was defeated.

"Nothing in the world is so pesky to write on as this lined paper – I can never make the letters go near the lines, and this must look not unlike Charles II's celebrated letter to Monmouth in the South Kensington Museum, where he says, 'I would not have you take much physic, it always makes me worse.'

"Jack writes to say he is well, but found the Scotch dogs a dour lot! Gabrielle sends her best love. Believe me, your affec. son,

"R. C. Graham Bontine."

Robert and Gabrielle were back in Vigo from Madrid by the middle of March, and spent a final three weeks at La Graña, where the blossom on the trees was like a wedding, and lizards were already sunning themselves on the garden wall once more.

They made several more local expeditions on hired donkeys, and spent a good deal of time in basket chairs in their pretty garden, listening to the songs of the Galician peasants as they went about their work in the farmyard and orchards and vineyards.

Robert had found a letter from Jamieson awaiting his return from Madrid in which he told Robert that Gartmore was now ready for its rightful laird, and that they could move in any time after the beginning of April.

Robert was at last fully entitled to call himself "Mr. Cunninghame Graham of Gartmore." Robert showed the letter to Gabrielle. She knew this was the happiest day of his life. They were going to live in his childhood home at last, and she must now remember that *her* name was "Mrs. Cunninghame Graham;" she was no longer "Mrs. Bontine." (These things were much easier in Yorkshire, she laughed.)

"Lob, I'm so happy for you – it's been a difficult time, hasn't it? Now you will have more than enough to do, and I'll help in any way I can, mon cher petit mari. I'm quite good at figures, by the way, so I don't mind helping with the accounts, or the rent collection, or things like that!"

"What a useful Chid it is!" said Robert half-teasingly as he kissed Gabrielle. "Thank goodness for the ladies in Yorkshire who taught you how to do sums, good ladies that they were! By the way, we must find you a good maid, like Mamma's Homer, then you'll be free to help me with the estate, while she looks after the more feminine side of your life – like your clothes and your hair! The wife of a Scottish laird always has to have a good lady's maid. It's *comme il faut*."

"Oh, Lob, I don't really need a maid! But we might persuade Peregrina Collazo, the girl who has been helping me here, to come with us – I think she would be rather thrilled!"

"I wonder if she would survive the Scottish climate?" reflected Robert. "It would be nice if she could come – and good for us, too, to have someone to speak Spanish with, so we don't forget the language. She has such a great fund of stories and proverbs," he laughed, "we'd never be dull with Peregrina! And she could come back here every winter to see her family when we come to La Graña."

"I'll ask her," said Gabrielle.

They arrived in London at the beginning of April 1884 to stay for a few days before going north to Gartmore, and Peregrina came with them. Gabrielle needed some new clothes for the life she was going to lead as "a Scottish lady," and Robert wanted to see his mother and his brothers, so they were both very busy during their time in London.

On their arrival there Robert had written to ask old Khāt if he could pay a visit to him at Ryde. He was worried that he had neglected the old man since he got back from Texas, and since his grandmother's death. He must be very lonely – Khāt's reply was written on 8th April 1994 from the new house on the Isle of Wight to which he had recently moved. He had not liked being in London, and had moved back to his old haunts again, where he felt much happier with the Navy on his doorstep.

"St. Thomas House, St. Thomas Street, Ryde, I. of W.

"My dear old Bob,

"I am so glad to hear that you had a good crossing and that both you and Gabrielle are O.K. – So your dear Mother is going to Winchester. Dear Mallie looks very well in his parson's trappings, and is much liked. I am pretty well for an old one, occasional squeezes of rheumatics upset me, in other respects I cannot complain. I hope, dear Bob, you will be able to run down to give me a hand before you leave London, when we could talk of the probability and the feasibility of a trip to Gartmore. Mine is only a small house. I call it my 'lighthouse' from the number of look-outs it has, but tho' small there is plenty of 'good usage aboard.'

"My kind love to Gabrielle, and believe me,

"your affectionate, J. Katon."

* * * * * *

"Jack's going to *love* Gartmore!" laughed Robert, as he watched the stumpy tail wagging furiously as it emerged backwards from a clump of ferns. Peregrina was introduced to the maids and the old cook, Mrs. Boss, who greeted her kindly, though they wondered how they would get on with this tall, gaunt young woman from Northern Spain. She was shown her new quarters, and was soon unpacking her mistress's clothes in the large sunny bedroom which had been redecorated for Gabrielle and Robert.

After a cup of tea, the young couple walked round the garden in the late afternoon sunshine. The yellow petticoats of the daffodils were ruffled by the wind, a few pale green leaves were unfolding, and the birds sang as though to welcome their new laird and his wife.

The Laird and his lady had finally arrived at their Scottish home on 20th April 1884 – it was almost twenty-one years to the day since he had arrived with Mamma and Papa, and Charlie and Mallie, from Finlaystone. And yet it only seemed like yesterday!

Robert had been nearly eleven when he first came to live at Gartmore, and now he was almost thirty-two. So many things had happened to him since then, so many adventures, so many joys and so many sadnesses. Now he had brought Gabrielle to share his much-loved home in Scotland with him. Everything was going to work out, Robert was convinced, and they were so happy together now, and so miserable when they were apart.

* * * * *

Robert and Gabrielle helped to provide the pies, whisky and beer for the sheep shearings, and the new parish hall was now to be opened. A farewell party was held for a retiring tenant; and Andrew Wood's sons set off to emigrate to South Africa, so yet another party was held. There was never a dull moment.

In the few moments she had to herself that summer of 1884, Gabrielle started a collection of mosses – Gartmore standing just above the famous "Flanders Moss," which some called a Polder, from the Dutch. She had taken over the estate accounts and the rent roll, to Robert's great relief, for he did not have a mathematical mind and found them a great struggle. He was amazed to find that his talented wife knew all about accounting and that she was soon keeping the system accurately and neatly, making entries every day, and dealing with the rent roll entirely by herself.

This left Robert free to ride round the estate each day on Pampa, and to make trips to Ardoch to supervise his second estate. He had soon become the most popular laird there had ever been at either Gartmore or Ardoch – always ready for a wee 'crack' with the men, and attending the many funerals, which were considered one of the few forms of social entertainment in rural Scotland. No women ever attended and the best way you could pay tribute to the deceased was to get as drunk as possible at his wake. No-one ever missed a funeral if they could help it.

Robert enjoyed these quiet men who could tell the best jokes he had ever heard. He loved to hear their broad dialect, and he now found the farming talk enormously instructive. There was so much to be picked up from these men who had farming in their bones.

Occasionally, on the few cloudless days that came to the area that summer, Robert and Gabrielle rode down to the lake and, leaving the horses in the care of the MacGregors who owned the little hotel at the Port of Menteith, they rowed themselves across to Inchmahome. This holy place brought out Gabrielle's mystical qualities, and Robert loved to watch her sketching under her artist's umbrella in a corner of the cloisters.

"I'd like to be buried here – beside you, Lob," she said quietly one day, as they sat smoking cigarettes by the old tombstones.

"And so you shall, my darling," he said. "And whichever of us goes first, the other must promise to come and smoke a cigarette from time to time, for old time's sake."

It was unusual for women to smoke then, but Gabrielle, having caught the habit in Texas, now found it difficult to throw it off.

"That's a promise, Lob," she said, giving him a loving smile.

It was a funny thing about Chid, thought Robert. She talked about death as though it was just another expedition. He often thought she really looked forward to it, not because she was unhappy in life but because she thought it was going to be something so much better – and because she knew she would never be alone in the next world, for Lob would always be with her.

Robert was in his element. He found his tenants and employees were becoming real friends and he loved to listen to the stories they told in the accent that was so very nearly Highland, but with a subtle difference. Now that he had begun to take an interest in literary matters, he often scribbled these stories down in a notebook, and made careful note of all the bits of local history which came his way, and the myths and legends of the district of Menteith. When he had written his book about the Jesuits in Paraguay, he might even turn his attention to a book of *local* history.

Pampa proved to be the best horse he had ever had, even better than old "Pingo," his boyhood pony at Gartmore, or "Bunny" in Paraguay, or "Old Black" on whom he had ridden with Gabrielle to Mexico City from San Antonio – the horse that had escaped with its wilder kin just before they reached the Rio Grande on the way back to Texas. He was even better than "Jorge," his final Texan horse, know to them as "the pink horse."

Pampa recognised the gentle hands of a natural horseman and soon grew accustomed to his new home. What a waste it would have been, thought Robert, if this beautiful mustang had been made to pull trams in Glasgow like the rest of the shipment.

Gabrielle was enjoying her Iceland pony, too; and she liked to watch Robert breaking in the young Highland pony.

Jack thought Gartmore was the best place he had ever lived, with so many exciting scents to follow through the woods: rabbits, hares, roe deer; and the fun of putting up roosting pheasants and pigeons out of trees – and occasionally even the giant capercailzies which exploded out of the spruce and pine like gunpowder.

When Robert and Gabrielle rowed over to the islands of Inchmahome and Inch Talla, Jack always hopped into the boat so that he would not be left behind, and stood with his paws on the gunwale peering out at mallard and teal swimming amongst the yellow water lilies. Robert told Gabrielle that, in the winter, they would see the great spearheads of geese overhead returning south for the cold season. Pinkfoot and greylag were the commonest, and the air would be filled with the sound of their incessant honking, "quink…ink, quink…ink" as they grazed on the Flanders moss. He told her that sometimes the lake froze hard and the geese

walked about all over the glistening surface looking like little old gentlemen in galoshes.

Jack liked the smaller island, Inch Talla, best, with its ruined castle
and the tangle of bramble bushes and ash saplings round the stones of the
old castle. He liked to run down on to the pebbly beaches to frighten the
moorhens, who quickly put to sea like little black pirates.

One day Robert and Gabrielle rowed on to the tiny island of Inch
Cuan, which was reputed to have been the dog kennel for the Earls of
Menteith's deerhounds and "earthe dogges."

"Look, Jack!" said Robert as the fox terrier jumped out of the boat to
explore the little island. "If I had been the Earl of Menteith, you would
have spent your days on this island, except when I took you hunting. Did
you know that you are an 'earthe dogge,' Jack?"

But Jack was not listening, he had found an interesting hole and was
digging as if his life depended on it.

"I wonder what he has found?" asked Gabrielle, hitching up her long
skirt to step on to dry land. "It doesn't seem possible that any animal
could live on this minute island, Lob, does it?"

"I've heard that they swim across the lake – stoats and weasels and
suchlike – to make their burrows and holes here, Chid. Certain animals,
anyway, the ones that aren't frightened of water. And of course birds.
There used to be a lot more varieties of animals and birds than there are
now – things like pine martens and wild cats, and of course the lovely
sea-eagle, or osprey, used to build his nest in the old Spanish chestnut
trees on Inchmahome. But there are too many trippers nowadays, and
they frighten the really wild creatures away. Do you know that the last
wolf was killed only about a couple of hundred years ago, down at the
Claggans at the south-west end of the lake?"

Gabrielle shivered. "Was that why they lived on islands in those
days?" she asked.

"Partly that," said Robert, "and partly because of the 'Loose and
Broken Men'."

"Who were they?" asked Gabrielle with interest.

"The Highlanders!" laughed Robert. "You see, living on the Highland Line, our Graham ancestors didn't have much use for the wild men
from the north who came down to steal our cattle: the marauding clans

like the McGregors and McTavishes and one Ewan Cameron of Craiguchty, who came from a dwelling by the Bridge of Aberfoyle. They were just like the bandits on the Rio Grande, or the Border Reivers in Liddesdale.

"I know all about the activities of Ewan Cameron of Craiguchty, by the way, because I have a splendid bundle of papers dated 1698 in the muniments chest at home, giving an inventory of animals and possessions he and his men stole from one Isabell M'Cluckey of Gouston, at Gartmore. It says they 'Broke open her house, stript and bound herself and children contrarie to the authoritie of the nation, and took with them her whole insicht and plenishing, utensils and domicil, with the number of six horses and mares, sixteen great cows, thirty-six great sheep and lambs and hogs, and carried them all away violentile, till they came to Cameron's house at Craiguchty'."

Gabrielle burst out laughing at Robert's rendering of the old Scots documents.

"But I still don't know why you call them 'loose and broken men'?" she enquired.

"Ah," said Robert, "that comes in the next document in the stories, where it says that, not content with driving off the stock and bearing away the 'insicht and the plenishing' the complainants and their servants 'were almost frichted from their Witts, through the barbarous usadge of the said *broken and loose men*.'"

"It sounds just like Texas all over again," laughed Gabrielle. "Are there still 'loose and broken men' in these parts, Lob?"

"No," said Robert. "My great-great-great grandfather, Nicol Graham of Gartmore, strung a good many of them up from the old hanging tree on the shore over there, known as the 'Ur'; I suppose it was to *encourager les autres*! Of course in his day they would have been the men who had not been included in the general amnesty after the Forty-Five Rebellion, or the ones who had just become accustomed to a life of violence.

"I can remember my old uncle, Captain Speirs, Aunt Annie Speirs' father-in-law at Culchrech, Fintry, who had a great and violent antipathy to Highlandmen, saying to me when I was a very small boy and he was a very old man, 'When I was young, one day upon Loch Ard-side, I met a

Hielandman, and when I spoke to him he answered "Cha Neil Sasse-nach" – I felt inclined to lay my whip about his back.' A 'Sassenach' was the derogatory word they used for the men who lived below the Highland Line, you see."

"Just like the Texans and the Mexicans all over again, or like calling someone a 'gringo'!" said Gabrielle. "I suppose it happens wherever there is what the Texans call a *fronteer*!"

"Life's changing here rapidly, though, Chid," said Robert rather sadly. "All the old ways are disappearing. I believe the next thing to go will be the Falkirk Tryst; the October Tryst was an event everyone here-abouts looked forward to. I can remember seeing droves of ponies from the Outer Isles, and from the far North, being driven down the pass of Aberfoyle by the old drove road. The drover used to follow on a pony, carrying a long hazel stick, and wrapped in his plaid, with a dog or two hanging about his pony's heels. We couldn't understand a word of his language because we never had the Gaelic."

"Did they only sell ponies at the Tryst?" asked Gabrielle.

"Oh no, we used to see West Highland cattle with long curving horns and shaggy foreheads, and great flocks of black-faced sheep, and always two or three men driving the animals, dressed in homespun tweeds which smelt of wool and peat-smoke, and lean, wolfish-looking collies to turn any straying animals. We used to love watching them, but now it's all going and there are weekly sales which reduce it to a mere cattle market – an ordinary and everyday event – with trains to bring the animals in from outbye."

Gabrielle loved to hear Robert talk of the things he remembered about Gartmore as a boy, and she liked listening to his voice which changed as he told her these things, the old lilt of the local dialect slipping in unawares. He had told her that most Scotch children, from the "big hoose" in every area, had several forms of speech – the pure English they talked with their parents, the local accent picked up from playing with the children of the estate workers, and sometimes a more "refeened" accent, in addition, copied from the local schoolmaster or schoolmistress who might have hailed from Edinburgh or from the more prosperous suburbs of Glasgow.

She was sure Robert had no idea that he slipped effortlessly into the Scots tongue when he talked to his tenants. She had listened to him that very morning when they called upon the farm called Offerance, and heard him discussing repairs with the farmer.

"Ye ken your grips are wasted?" she heard him say, and the farmer answered, "Aye, Laird, and ma stickling's flure's fair boss." She had not had the least idea what they were talking about, but it was a delightful language to listen to.

"Come out of it, Jack!" shouted Robert at last to Jack, who was half-way down his hole, tail wagging like a metronome. "We must go home."

They rowed the boat back across the smooth lake, watching rings spreading as an occasional trout jumped lazily in the dusk, breaking the surface of the mirror-like expanse of water with its three dark islands.

Malise arrived to stay for a few weeks' holiday at the end of June. Robert thought he looked pale and drawn after his first few months as a parish priest. Gabrielle was sure he had been working too hard. He coughed a lot, and his pale, transparent skin took on an unnatural flush at times. He did not look at all well.

Robert and Gabrielle planned to give him a really quiet time at Gartmore, and, as the weather was good, they spent a great deal of time wandering peacefully amongst the ruins of the abbey on the island of Inchmahome. The two brothers and Gabrielle were fascinated by the inscriptions on the tombs of the Stewarts, Drummonds and Grahams of Menteith, especially one on the tomb of the Drummond whose effigy was in full armour with a device on his shield showing St. Michael and St. Colmac trampling on the dragon, the lines reading rather curiously, "John of Drumod son of Malcolm of Drumod. His widow that she may loose their souls from punishment and the sting."

On Midsummer Day all three of them went up to the top of the wild Pass of Glenny in the evening, to the well called "Tobar-na-reil" (the well of the star) to wait till the star Canopus began to shine straight down into the well itself. Robert and Malise had been told about this when they were boys and had always wanted to see the phenomenon for themselves. Sure enough, at last darkness fell, around midnight, and there was the star shining into the dark peaty water of the well, like a diamond lying in a crystal bowl. It was very beautiful.

"Doesn't it ever get dark at midsummer?" asked Gabrielle with amazement, as they picked their way back to the road, a luminous light making the path quite clear although it was now twelve thirty at night.

"This is the land of the midnight sun, Chid, didn't you know?" laughed Robert as he stopped to listen to a curlew calling.

"And there's no sun at all in the winter, worse luck," said Malise with a sigh. "I might have joined the Church of Scotland instead of the Anglican Church if it hadn't been for the dark, cold winters!" he smiled.

"Nonsense, Mala," said his eldest brother, "you never liked the Kirk. I can remember you fidgeting like anything while the Minister droned on, and we all had to play things like 'Up Jenkins' with you under the pew to keep you quiet! You've always liked the ritualism of the High Anglican Church, admit it!"

"Yes, I suppose you're right. It was the music, too," added Malise. "They sang the hymns and psalms so dreadfully slowly in the Kirk, didn't they? And those awful paraphrases used to make me giggle, the way the words got twisted round to fit the tune! Anyway, Bob, you forget I was only six when we left Gartmore and went to live in London – after Papa went to Eccles House. I don't really remember an awful lot about living at Gartmore, except that I always used to have dreadful colds – and I remember having whooping cough once, and going to Largs with Aunt Annie Speirs and old Ninny. They took me on a paddle-steamer, I remember, to Wemyss Bay, or somewhere!"

During the summer of 1884 the family all came to Gartmore in turn to visit Robert and Gabrielle, even several of Gabrielle's brothers and sisters, the Horsfalls, from Yorkshire. Missy was particularly delighted at the competent way Gabrielle carried out her duties as the Laird's wife; and was filled with admiration when she found that Gabrielle had taken over the estate accounts. She was a dark horse, this strange little wife of Bob's, he had been much cleverer than she had realised, marrying the girl.

Missy was still rather horrified at the way Gabrielle chain-smoked, and wore her hair bobbed, but she could not complain about the way the two young things were looking after Gartmore. The house felt cosy and lived-in, and the grounds were gradually beginning to look less neglected. Gabrielle told her mother-in-law that the only really sad thing was that she had had to give up the walled garden, because they found it was costing £350 a year to keep up. She was perfectly miserable about it, because she knew she had green fingers and she had quite an extensive knowledge about horticulture – another of the useful things that the Yorkshire people had taught her!

Gabrielle was now making a serious study of the mosses of the area, and was in correspondence with a professor at Glasgow University who was interested in her findings.

Just before his mother went back to London they all went to Buchlyvie where Robert was to open the new village hall. It was the first time either his mother or his wife had heard him make a public speech, and they were both struck with his easy manner and the way he could make everyone laugh and hang on his lips. The audience, made up of local farmers, landowners, village tradesmen, shopkeepers, and the farm labourers, were delighted with their new Laird's speech, and the whole affair was a huge success.

Gabrielle watched him with tenderness and pride – her handsome hidalgo, so tall and elegant, taking their homage like a king. Yes, he really did seem to have an aptitude for public speaking, he would find it easy to sway a mob with that strange magnetism he seemed to exude.

She watched him talking afterwards to two of his tenants, Stewart and Harvie, joking easily with them, and asking their advice about a farming problem as though they were old and valued friends. She was sure his mother was right when she said he would make an excellent candidate for Parliament; but she was torn by the thought. Of course she would be proud of him, but what of their own privacy, their own unique relationship? She would no longer have him entirely to herself. There would be few moments of happy freedom at Gartmore, or at La Graña, and their own particular idyll would be bound to suffer.

She dismissed the gloomy thoughts from her mind, and found herself pounced upon by the Rev. Malcolm McLean, the Free Church Minister, who told her he was starting up a "Band of Hope" in the village and wondered if she would honour them by consenting to be the President of this important temperance organisation? There was no escape as he talked on and on about the evils of drink, telling her that, but for strong drink, nine-tenths of the country's jails could be closed. Gabrielle found herself saying "yes" in order to escape from this persistent man, and was then able to laugh with Robert after the event when he told her that exactly the same thing had happened to him! Together they would have to go to the first meeting and sign "the pledge." They both felt rather hypocritical, because there was nothing they liked better than a glass of wine together.

While Charlie was still on half-pay he came several times to Gartmore that summer to help Robert with the many problems of running the estate. Milly and "Uff" stayed behind, for "Uff" was too young to be taken travelling. Her parents had given up on "Olive" as a name and, like all the Graham and Elphinstone children in the family, she now bore a ridiculous and unexplained nickname. Charlie was a proud father, and told Robert and Gabrielle in great detail all the latest exploits of his enchanting baby daughter. He had been on half-pay for a year now, but he had just heard of his new appointment: he was to be Flag Lieutenant to the C-in-C, The Nore, at Sheerness, on board H.M.S. Duncan. Once again, he was to be involved with the Royal Family, for the Admiral was the Prince of Leiningen, a relation of Queen Victoria's by her mother's first marriage to his father.

"You're becoming a professional courtier, Charlie!" commented Robert.

"I expect it's Cousin David Erskine's fault, now he's 'Groom of the Robes' to the Queen!" said Charlie ruefully.

"Or else your shipmate Prince Louis has been telling them all what a splendid fellow you are!" chaffed his brother. "Anyway, it will be perfect for Milly and Uff – you should be able to see quite a lot of them from Sheerness."

"Yes," said Charles, "I think I've been pretty lucky."

Charlie escorted his mother back to London at the beginning of September, and Gabrielle and Robert had Gartmore to themselves. They were happiest of all when they were alone together there, although Gabrielle and Missy now managed to get on quite well most of the time, and were beginning to appreciate each other's qualities.

Before she left, Missy told Robert that she was decidedly anxious about Mallie's health, he worked much too hard amongst the underprivileged members of his parish, whether they were church-goers or not, and he had developed a permanent cough which simply would not go away. His visit to Gartmore had done him a lot of good, but he was far from well. She had spoken to his doctor in Winchester, and it was greatly feared that he was consumptive. She hoped to persuade him to abroad with her during the worst of the winter, if she could convince his vicar to release him for a few weeks. They might go to Switzerland, perhaps, she would like to take him to a famous clinic she had heard of, and get him to take some treatment. She would go down to Winchester shortly, to be with him until they went abroad.

Robert and Gabrielle were deeply disturbed by this news. Malise was Gabrielle's favourite member of the family: such a spirited young man, full of jokes and fun, yet to assiduous in his work amongst the poor and needy, and most of all was his talent for making beautiful music. It always seemed to be the most talented member of the family who was struck down by this scourge of their age, tuberculosis. How mysterious were the ways of the Almighty.

Another sadness was shortly to touch Robert; old Khāt became seriously ill, and Robert hurried down to the Isle of Wight to be with the old man for his final moments, and to help lay him in his coffin, crossing his strong, brown hairy hands upon his breast, and wishing the old sailor could have just waited long enough to see the red Aurora Borealis which lit the sky the night of his death. Robert was sure he would have said that it was most unusual to see the Northern Lights so early in the autumn and below such and such a latitude, or something of the kind.

Charlie and Mallie arrived for the funeral at Ryde, and the cortege stretched right along the street. Khāt had been much loved in the Island. He had not, however, wanted to go on living without his beloved Catalina, and had now gone happily to join her, four years after her own death, at the age of seventy-four. The three boys and their mother mourned the old man greatly.

"He was just like a real grandfather to us, Mamma," said Robert sadly. Missy told her sons that she could not have had a kinder father, for she barely remembered her own father, Admiral Elphinstone Fleeming, being only twelve when he died of influenza. Old Khāt had been the kindest of men, and taken his wife's large family under his wings like a benevolent old eagle.

"More like an old seagull!" laughed Charlie.

PART VI
POLITICS – 1885
CHAPTER XXIII

The winter was, fortunately, very mild that year, and Gabrielle stayed remarkably fit. This was just as well, for they had agreed that they could not afford to take La Graña that year. There had been a bad gale in late October which blew off the top of one of the old beech trees, and Ben Lomond had its usual snowy night-cap. Robert wrote to tell his mother:

"The hills are white with snow now, and 'whisky' has begun and seems likely to do well this year! All the Iceland ponies and my pingo are well. Cousin John and 'Mist' are about to take their departure to the congenial gloom of London."

The new branch of the Band of Hope had not as yet had much effect on local habits, and whisky was certainly 'doing' extremely well in the neighbourhood as the colder weather approached. In January the cold and the damp drove Robert and Gabrielle to London, where they attended several of the newly-formed 'socialist' societies' meetings, out of curiosity. Robert thought the Fabians were rather 'precious' and preferred the Democratic Federation, where he made friends with an amusing fellow called George Bernard Shaw.

Marx's *Das Kapital* had not yet been translated into English, and was only available in the British Museum's reading room in Deville's French version; but all the young left-wing intellectuals in London had by now had a glimpse of it, and were becoming enthusiastic. The great point of discussion seemed to be based on the premise that 'the end justified the means.'

By February of 1885 Shaw had decided that the idea of revolution by violence simply was not on, and he had begun to urge the young intellectuals and their middle-class friends to join the Socialist movement in order to counteract the influence of "a mob of desperate sufferers abandoned to the leadership of exasperated sentimentalists and fanatical theorists."

Shaw had now joined the Fabian Society but, although Robert and Gabrielle agreed with much he said, they realised it was too extreme, and they were not prepared to join it themselves. Nevertheless, they met many of the Society's new members: Sidney and Beatrice Webb, Annie Besant, Sydney Olivier, Edward Poase, Frank Podmore and Hubert Bland's attractive wife, Edith Nesbit, who supplemented her husband's income by writing children's books. William Morris and Edward Burne-Jones had begun to take a back seat.

Just as Robert refused to commit himself to one or another denomination of the church, so did he refuse to align himself with the many socialist societies which had suddenly started to jostle for position. But he enjoyed the meetings, and found some of the members were amusing fellows, with something of his own outlook on life. Gabrielle, too, found herself stimulated by the discussions and enjoyed meeting so many entertaining people. She caused quite a stir by her unusual looks and her beauty, and Robert started introducing her to his friends as his 'Chilean wife,' because he found this intrigued them more than ever.

To give Gabrielle a short holiday, as they were not going to Vigo, Robert took her to Paris for a week, to buy her some pretty clothes and to introduce her to some of the friends he had made in 1879. They stayed at the Hotel Meurice. Robert wanted to see Guy de Maupassant again, and fortunately they found that he was in Paris. He told them that his first novel was coming out that year, called *Bel Ami*. He in turn introduced them to friends of his called Proust, who had an interesting invalid son of fifteen, with original ideas. While Robert talked with young Marcel Proust's parents, Gabrielle enjoyed listening to the boy's chatter and found him unusually intelligent.

They also renewed Robert's earlier friendship with several of the young artists in the Latin Quarter, and Gabrielle was thrilled to be intro-duced to a group of the best-known Impressionists, at a party in the Latin Quarter, given in their honour by John Lavery.

Robert took part in a minor fencing contest, and was delighted to find that he could still keep his end up with some of the French champions.

It was a cheerful visit, and the young couple returned to London in April feeling renewed and ready to go back to Gartmore.

On Robert's return to Gartmore he thought over some of the conver-sations he had had in London, and in Paris, with young intellectuals; there seemed to be a mood running through the two countries for a new radicalism – the old radicalism was entirely bound up with the individual, the new was a more collective ideology. Home, freedom, and country were the main ingredients of this ideology, but with Irish Home Rule becoming more and more a subject for passionate argument in Britain, the Liberal party was beginning to split in two – the Gladstonian Liberals favouring Irish Home Rule and Chamberlain's Liberals backing the unionist cause and calling themselves "Liberal Unionists."

Robert had thought a great deal about standing for Parliament over the past few months, and this year the first elections were to be held under the new Redistribution Act, with single member constituencies. The total number of voters this year would be over four million, because of the new franchise. "Three acres and a cow" had become the slogan, to attract votes from the agricultural communities who would be voting for the first time. Labouchere had written one of his witty articles saying that "Next time we must have an urban cow!" It was going to be just the sort of fight he would enjoy, thought Robert, and most of the people involved enjoyed a bit of wit and humour, and didn't take things too seriously. They would be quite a congenial bunch to work with.

For the past few months Robert had been much interested in articles written in the 'Cumnock News' by young Keir Hardie and, on hearing that there was to be a meeting of the Social Democratic Federation at Cumnock, with James Patrick as the speaker, supported by Bruce Glasier, Robert decided to go to it. He would like to meet the bright young spark of the 'Cumnock News' who expressed himself so well on matters closest to Robert's heart.

The two young men were instantly drawn to each other, and when Robert mentioned to Keir Hardie that he was thinking of standing as a Radical Liberal, the young 'Good Templar' eyed him with surprise and admiration. His own political ideas had not yet gone further than a cry for land reform, but he had been encouraged by the split in the Liberal Party, and often spoke at the Cumnock Junior Liberal Association's meetings on the subject, and on the subject of employers' liability, especially with regard to mines. He told Robert that he would certainly speak and write in support of him if he decided to stand. After all, they had grown up quite close to each other, on the Clyde, at Finlaystone and Govan, where young Kier's step-father was a ship's carpenter. Keir was born in Lanarkshire as an illegitimate baby in 1856, so he was four years younger than Robert.

By the summer of 1885, Robert had been adopted as the Liberal candidate for the Blackfriars division of Glasgow. It was not until a few days after his adoption that he realised he was standing against Shaw Maxwell, the candidate for the Land Restoration League. Maxwell invited Robert to a meeting he was holding, and Robert was so impressed by the case he made on behalf of the crofters that he told Maxwell after the meeting he would stand down, for he would not think of opposing him when he was doing so much for these poor people from the far north, and the Western Isles, who had been so greatly oppressed by the Highland Clearances.

Maxwell suggested to Robert that if he would take up their cause, there was another seat available on the Glasgow city boundary, in the constituency of North West Lanark. Robert was delighted to find that he could still enter the fight in spite of standing down from his candidature for the Blackfriars constituency of Glasgow.

In September he produced his manifesto, announcing that he was 'a Liberal both by descent and from conviction.' A good deal of his manifesto did in fact come from his grandfather's own manifesto of 1832. He was *against* an aggressive foreign policy and the game laws, and *for* more local self-government; a graduated income tax, reform of the land laws, abolition of primogeniture and entail, free education, and local option on the sale of liquor.

At first his constituents could not believe that this Scottish gentleman could be siding with the new Radical Liberalism, overturning all his own inherited advantages as a Scottish landowner, having come into possession of his estates through the very laws he was hoping to change. Was this a trick, they wondered, suspiciously? And yet this striking young man seemed to sincere, and they enjoyed his wit and humour in the face of heckling:

Heckler: "Are ye a descendant o' thon Robert Graham who killed oor guid Scots King, James I?"

Robert: "Go to hell and ask him yourself!"

Heckler: "What kirk do you belong to?"

Robert: Sir, I am a Christian – unattached."

Heckler: "Could ye gie' us yer views on the maintenance o' the airmy?"

Robert: "I have a hereditary regard for the ancient and honourable profession of arms; but I would like to see the time when no soldier would be seen, except, perhaps, a stuffed specimen or two in a museum."

Heckler: "Mr. Graham, might I ask if you send your bairns to the Sunday Schuil?"

Robert: "No." Uproar in the hall.

Robert: "In relation to this question being answered, may I tell you that Madam Graham here has not as yet presented me with any children." Laughter.

Gabrielle went with Robert to all the meetings, and was delighted to see that he had so much support. She admired his witty answers and the cheerful way he greeted his supporters, for she knew that underneath his exuberant exterior his heart was breaking: they had just received the news that Malise was back from Switzerland where the doctors had been unable to do anything for him. His youngest brother was dying, and was unlikely to last out another month.

On 4th December 1885 the people of North West Lanarkshire went to the polls. A week earlier Malise had died, at his mother's house in Ebury Street.

Robert sat numbly in the drawing room at Gartmore, waiting for the telegram which would tell him the election result. Somehow, all the excitement had evaporated; he did not care now whether he won or lost. Malise's death eclipsed everything else, and he felt more miserable than he had ever felt in his life before. Gabrielle, too, was in deep distress. She had loved Malise, and their strong faith had linked them even more firmly together. Robert's young brother would never come to Gartmore again. She stared out of the window at the rain which poured down as though the skies, too, were mourning Malise.

At last the telegram arrived. Robert had been beaten in the contest by an ironmaster called John Baird, his Conservative opponent, by 1,103 votes.

"So that's that," said Robert, rising to his feet to join Gabrielle at the window.

"But it's quite a good result, Lob!" said Gabrielle, secretly relieved that politics were not going to claim her husband from her side just yet. "There must be around 8,000 voters in your constituency, so at least three thousand of them must have voted for you. That's not a dishonourable defeat, Lob, is it?"

Robert managed a weak smile. "Ma très chère petite femme – now that the politicking is over, let's break that confounded pledge and open my best bottle of burgundy! I think we both need it."

* * * *

Robert refused to leave Gartmore for the next two months; he seemed to find solace for his grief in the old place, and Gabrielle could not even persuade him to go to London for a change of scene. She had kept in touch with the wife of the artist, Bernard Evans, after her painting holiday in Wales, and she wrote to tell her that she was coming, herself, for a short visit to London, because her cough had started up again and she knew she must go to a milder climate if she was to throw it off.

But Robert insisted on staying at Gartmore like a hurt animal lying in a ditch. "I don't like leaving him," she wrote, "but he will stay, and like a limpet will not be moved." A great melancholy had fallen upon him. His dear youngest brother had died, so had Papa and old Khāt, and Grandmamma; Charlie was taken up with his naval career, his elegant wife and his baby daughter; and Robert did not even have the ability to persuade an industrial constituency in the heart of Scotland's mining country to vote Liberal for their own good. He was useless.

After Gabrielle went to London, Robert rode Pampa off through the snow to the solitude of the little wood of birches called "Barbadoes" planted by "Doughty Deeds," in memory of his West Indian idyll. From there he could look across the wild and bleak Flanders Moss and watch the mists rising, or listen to the echoes of a dog parking in the ice-cold stillness of the day. He could see the firs on Shannoch Hill standing up like the masts of a ship, and he could see the three low islands crouching on the waters of the Lake, not frozen yet but deathly grey and still. It was a mournful landscape, and it suited Robert's mood.

In Robert's loneliness at Gartmore in January 1886, while Gabrielle was in London, he comforted himself by reading old letters his youngest brother had written him. Perhaps the best way to get over his death would be to think of him setting out on a long journey to a country from which he could not write letters – just like the times when Robert himself had been riding Bunny through the Paraguayan jungles and could not communicate with his family. Malise's last letter to Robert was written from Switzerland on 25th July.

"My dear Bob,

"Just a line to thank you for your two pet notes which we deciphered not without difficulty. I have been and am of course still very knocked up, but the air here is fine and we are going to have at least another fortnight. Fancy your having been here that Black Forest year of ours' in 1869. Today I went for a walk and my legs are now suffering, I find the inability to walk the greatest bore, but I must have patience. I do hope your electioneering will all be successful. I am so glad you have gone in for it.

"I often think of La Graña and Vigo, and the cake shop on the hill, and the oranges in the garden. Also of the funny little hotel which turned out so well in Oporto – and that <u>wine tasting</u>!

"Please thank Gabrielle for her kind messages and give her my love. I have been carried in a chaise-a-porteur once or twice and sometimes I am pushed in a chair to the village, like a Leamington old lady!

"Kit sends her best love and the "old Horror" (Homer) is keeping well.

"Goodbye, ever your affec. brother, Malise Graham."

Robert folded the letter carefully away, with a lump in his throat. Why had Malise written "Goodbye" at the end of his letter. Had he known in his heart of hearts that it really was his farewell letter? It was too awful to think about. Mamma had written to say she had received many letters from the boys Malise had known at school and university, all saying things like this one: "my love and friendship for him has never ceased since we arrived together at Dr. Huntinford's at Wimbledon. No-one but myself knows how good and kind and self-denying he was when I had an accident to my eyes at Winchester. He used to give up his half-holidays to come and sit with me and cheer me up and his kindness to me then I can never forget."

That was from his friend Herbert Griffith, who had also gone into the church. Then there was Henry Whitehead who described him as his 'first friend,' and wrote from South Newington Vicarage at Banbury – another Wykehamist. And his young Wykehamist friend, Lionel Johnson, had written a heart-broken letter, saying he was writing some poems in Malise's memory which he hoped to have published one day. *The Wykehamist* carried a long obituary saying that Malise had been known to younger Wykehamists as well as to his own contemporaries, for they had been able to see with their own eyes the excellent work of his clerical life carried out in Winchester since his ordination:

"His original power of discovering intent capacity in what to others would seem very unlikely places was quite unique. The musical and dramatic element which he developed in a very short time in the children of St. John's Parish was a surprise to everyone and will not soon be forgotten. His clerical work dealt much more with social topics than with ecclesiastical technicalities, and he altogether despised and repudiated the theory than social and political interests are in a different plane from moral and religious ones. In politics a strong Liberal, he held that the primary object of Christianity is to make this world a better place, and to this end he consistently devoted both his personal example and his teaching. The school which bred him may remember him as one of those who have devoted their lives in modesty and humility to the highest and best purposes."

But no-one can mourn for ever, and one day towards the end of January, when the sun was shining and a sharp frost had iced the puddles, Robert rode out on Pampa to see the Lake glinting like a mirror. He must pull himself together, he thought; Mal would not have wanted him to sit glooming at Gartmore. Mal would have said, "Why don't you get on and fight another election? Don't give up, Bob!" He had sounded so pleased in that last letter about his brother's decision to stand as a Liberal. For Mal's sake he must do something about all those people who needed a champion.

He had recently read a poem by the American poet, Walt Whitman, and the words had stuck in his mind:

"Oh wanderers from ancestral soil,
Leave noisesome mill and chaffering store;
Gird up your loins for sturdier toil
And build the home once more!
What matter if the gains are small
That life's essential wants supply?
Your homestead's title gives you all
That idle wealth can buy.
All that the many-dollared crave,
That brick-walled slaves of Change and mart,
Lawns, trees, fresh air, and flowers you have,
More dear for lack of art.
Your own sole masters, freedom-willed,
With none to bid you go or stay,
Till the old fields your fathers tilled
As manly men as they!
With skill that spares your toiling hands,
And chemic aid that science brings,
Reclaim the waste and outworn lands
And reign thereon as kings!"

That was a challenge, too, thought Robert. Walt Whitman's poem telling him to get on and do something about Gartmore, to appreciate what he had got and to make something of it – and Mal's last letter saying how pleased he was that his brother had 'gone in for' politics. Yes, he must pull himself together; there was a great deal to be done. He wanted Malise to know that he was going to go on fighting for the things that had to be done to make the world a better place, both here at Gartmore – and out in the new industrial slums, the mines, the factories, the mills, and amongst honest Scots people.

Just as Gabrielle was setting out to come back to Gartmore, having at last thrown off her bronchitis, Robert got an anxious letter from Aunt Char Woodmas asking him to go to Leamington, as Aunt Anne Erskine was very ill, having lost her power of speech and being almost paralysed by a stroke. Aunt Char apologised for disturbing him when he was in the midst of electioneering, but felt that the old lady's affairs needed looking into as she thought her maid, West, was rather unscrupulous, and as the head of the family he would be the best person to deal with things. Robert was now "the Head of the Family" and his old Graham aunts were an important part of his responsibility.

Robert wrote a note to Gabrielle as soon as he arrived at Leamington to explain why he had to leave Gartmore. "The poor old lady has just had a violent fit and may even yet not come out of it. I found Gartmore lovely, and everything is ready for your return. A laundrymaid came, but no kitchenmaid as yet. Old Campbell has really worked well. I will telegraph you about Aunt Anne."

Two days later Robert wrote again.

"23rd March 1886

"My dearest Chid,

"The doctor has just been and says that though Aunt Anne may die within twenty-four hours she still may last a few days. He says I should remain, and I think so too.

"I hope you had a good journey. Is not Gartmore looking lovely? I think you will agree with me about the flowering currant. You must have some roses planted inside the walls by the terrace and also some more flowers. Are not the snowdrops lovely?

"I am afraid the country will not follow old Gladstone. Chamberlain has made a determined revolt and seems inclined to stick to it. Take a look at the big drawing room and make up your mind about the looking glass and if you want to have it removed get the people in Stirling to send out a man. Put Sir John there instead, and we can put the picture of Aunt Erskine in his place. Jack was very well and I sent him off to be medicined. Talla said she had no shoes!

"Believe me, your affec. husband, R. B. Cunninghame Graham."

What a sad two years it had been with so many deaths in the family, thought Robert as he returned to Gartmore after Aunt Anne's funeral a week later. Gartmore still meant more than anything else to him. The old house had belonged to his family for five hundred years. Robert might be the last of the line, but he wanted his people to know that he understood their problems. He wanted more than anything to be a *good* laird at Gartmore.

From July, 1886, the new larger house Missy had recently acquired at 39, Chester Square had become the family centre in London, and both Robert and Charlie were delighted that there mother could now entertain on a larger scale. She had cultivated a large circle of friends, mostly from the artistic world, and her small *salons* on Sundays were already considered amongst the most exclusive in London. She had a talent for spotting "up-and-coming" young artists and writers, and for introducing them to each other and giving them the stimulation of new artistic friendships. With her usual courage she refused to be bowed down by the death of her adored youngest son, although her two elder sons knew that it was by far the most terrible tragedy she had suffered in her already greatly afflicted life.

Her greatest joy of all was Robert's success in becoming such a popular Laird of Gartmore. He had taken all his new responsibilities in his stride. Missy was bursting with pride in this new mature young man; how proud Willy would have been of his sons. But she would always miss her darling youngest, Malise.

CHAPTER XXIV

Now it was time to pick up the threads again and get himself elected to Parliament, for Mal's sake.

And so it was that Robert stood once more for Northwest Lanark in June 1886, the defeat of Gladstone's Irish Home Rule Bill early in the morning of 8th June having caused the downfall of the government and a subsequent general election.

Robert's meetings at Coatbridge were packed: he had caught the imagination of the voters in Northwest Lanark at his last attempt, and this time Robert spelt out in no uncertain terms how he would deal with the Irish Home Rule question. With masterly language he conjured up a great bird imprisoned in a cage in the zoological gardens, always flapping the air with its great wings and gazing into the far horizon: that bird was Ireland, denied her freedom for eighty years, denied her liberty and bound in a cage of our union laws, mad by men who were unconscious of the cruelty they were inflicting. They thought they were merely extending the blessings of civilisation to Ireland, the blessings of English rule, the Protestant faith, and three square meals a day. The key to that iron cage was Home Rule, declared Robert to loud cheers from his enthusiastic audience. He had hit exactly the right note, for there were a great many Irish labourers working in Coatbridge, and this was what they had come to hear.

Now he had said enough about Ireland; it was time he turned to Scotland, and he went on to tell his delighted audience about his own ancestor John Graham of the Bright Sword at a time when the English king, Edward, was grinding the Scots under his iron heel, and how his ancestor's heart had "bled for the people, but he did not skulk or cringe to Edward. He joined himself to a glorious and immortal man called William Wallace – (cheers) – these two men trusted the people, they fought, they conquered, and they died – (cheers) – their lives were heroic and glorious, and in their deaths they were not divided – (cheers) – with their right hands they carved out immortality, but by their examples they did better – they laid the foundations of Scottish liberty – (cheers) – and as long as the grass grew and water ran, and as long as the Bass Rock stood sentinel at the mouth of the Forth, and the seagulls circled round Ailsa Craig, their names would live in history. So will posterity deal with the name William Ewart Gladstone! (cheers)."

"Ye've done it, Laddie!" said the delighted chairman, Jimmy Allan. "Ye've got them feeding out of your haun'." He was fumbling for the telegram Gladstone himself had sent to the meeting. At last he got it unfolded and read it out.

"My best wishes for your success in the gallant contest you have again undertaken. Scotland has hitherto in her selection of representatives shown a thoroughly Liberal appreciation of the great issue now before the country. I hope Lanarkshire will maintain the record. William Gladstone."

On 9th July, 1886, the voters of Northwest Lanarkshire went to the poll and returned Robert with a majority of 332 votes over the Conservative, Baird. Coatbridge was in an uproar of delight, and one of the first men waiting to wring his hand was Keir Hardie, who had done his utmost to further Robert's campaign.

Gabrielle had been at her husband's side throughout, and now she turned to him, glowing with pride, her eyes full of happy tears.

"I'm so proud of you, Lob! You've done it! Think how pleased Malise would be." She knew that was why he had gone back to the attack, for the sake of his adored youngest brother who had so greatly wanted the world to become a better and a fairer place. Gabrielle was convinced that Malise was very much with them both in spirit at that proud moment.

"He did it, Mallie," she whispered quietly to herself, as Robert stood beside her, shaking hands with a long line of working-class constituents to whom he appeared as a knight in shining armour, ready to lead them forward against tyranny and oppression. Cheers still ringing in their ears, at last Robert and Gabrielle were allowed to catch their train back to Gartmore, where another celebration was in store for them.

Arriving at Buchlyvie Station, their first hint of the local celebrations was the exploding of fog signals at the station. Then they saw the huge reception committee of 500 villagers and tenants. As the local paper was to report:

"After cordial congratulations were over, the tenants formed themselves into a procession headed by the village piper who led the way to
the Mansion House (Gartmore). At the entrance to the Policies, the
horses were taken from the carriage – the younger men struggling
together in their endeavours to obtain a share in the honour of drawing
their victorious young laird to his house.

"The farmers lined the carriage on either side, while the tenants and
villagers preceded and followed. The piper at the head of the procession
led off to the east entrance of the mansion house to the tune of the
'Gallant Graham.' Refreshments were served upon the lawn, after which
dancing was kept up with great spirit. During the evening the
countryside was illuminated by bonfires at Gartmore and at Buchlyvie."

The account ended with the words, "We may say that Mr. and Mrs.
Graham have completely won the hearts of the tenantry and the
numerous villagers on their estates."

Next morning Robert and Gabrielle looked out of their bedroom
window to the extensive view across the moss to the Menteith Hills and
smiled happily at each other. It had been worth all the effort, just to see
how much they were appreciated at Gartmore. What an incredible surprise their people had sprung upon them – it all seemed like a fairy-tale
now, but they knew it was true. They hugged each other with delight.
Over breakfast they read the newspapers, and found more and more
glowing reports of Robert's victory; he had caused a sensation in the
press. The Pall Mall Gazette put in a short biography of each new
Member, and Robert and Gabrielle chuckled as they read what was
written.

"He comes of an old Scotch family – the Grahams of Gartmore, and
is the son of a very clever mother, The Hon. Mrs. (Graham) Bontine, a
sister of the fourteenth Lord Elphinstone. From her Mr. Graham derives
the literary tastes which lent a flavour as pleasant as peculiar to his election speeches. Not that Mr. Graham is a mere bookworm. On the
contrary he has much (literally) 'mother-wit', which enabled him to
score heavily in the heckling game, and he has seen a good deal of the
world. He was educated at Harrow, and for some years took to cattle
farming in South America. He goes the whole Radical hog, being

pledged among other things to interference with mining royalties, and to a ten hours' bill. Mr. Graham is a very handsome man, and is 34."

Another paper said, "The Grahams of Gartmore have always been on the side of the people, and several of the present laird's forefathers have done battle for the cause of Liberalism."

And yet another wrote a leader in which it congratulated the people of Northwest Lanark in finding their heart's desire – "a good all-round Liberal, one who, having faith in his principles seeks to apply them. Not just a Land Reformer, but one who is in favour of a full and ample measure of local self-government for the three kingdoms. He is in favour of free education, the extension of franchise to women, and all the prominent questions of the day which show that it is an independent and progressive Liberal."

Robert and Gabrielle sat on the terrace in the sunshine with newspapers scattered all round them.

"I don't think it can possibly be me they are talking about!" laughed Robert.

"Well, you certainly sound a great deal more respectable than that man I rode through Mexico with!" replied Gabrielle.

Jack came bouncing out of the rhododendrons to demand a walk. Robert got to his feet.

"Come on, Jack, I'll race you round the rushy park: ready, steady, go!" Gabrielle roared with laughter as she watched Robert's long legs swing into action and Jack go racing off after him, barking loudly.

He had at last got over the tragedy of his brother's death, she thought happily.

* * * * * *

July 1886 was full of news for the Cunninghame graham family – Charlie had decided to come out of the Navy, and had resigned his commission on 4t[h] July. He had been offered an interesting job as an inspector in the Lifeboat Institution, and his friend Prince Louis of Battenburg had told him that he was almost certain to get the job, as he was by far the best candidate. Now that he had a wife and a child he did not want to have to face constant partings; and this shore job, still connected so vitally with ships, seemed just what he wanted.

Missy was delighted by Charlie's news that he was leaving the Navy and would therefore be within reach whenever she needed him; and the greatest joy of all was Robert's success in winning his seat in Parliament. That meant he would be in London when Parliament was sitting, which in itself was the happiest of thoughts. Far more than that, it also meant that she herself could now have a real justification for her deep interest in politics, and he would be able to give her all the gossip from the House, week by week. What a delight that would be! She sometimes wished she had been a man and could have entered politics herself – but now she must persuade Robert to fight hard for women's votes, amongst his other priorities. Her eldest son's election to Parliament was the best thing that could have happened to dispel her sense of loss since Malise died.

In August 1886 Lord Salisbury took office as Prime Minister, and his first problem was to cope with the Irish reaction to Gladstone's failure to pass Home Rule, and to work out how the Irish landlord should be compensated for an intermediate policy of rent abatements. Meanwhile, Redvers Buller was sent to stamp out terrorism in Kerry and Clare.

Parnell was being superseded by more radical Nationalists, led by William O'Brien and John Dillon. In October the Irish National League launched their Plan of Campaign, which was a scheme whereby tenants could withhold rents less the abatements claimed and give the money instead to trustees appointed by the Plan, thus forming a fund from which evicted tenants could be subsidised. This scheme would keep the Liberal support that was vital to the Irish Home Rulers, and was the best form of anti-landlord propaganda. In December 1886 the Plan was proclaimed as an unlawful criminal conspiracy and O'Brien and Dillon were arrested.

This was the political scene when Robert rose to make his maiden speech in the House of Commons on 1st February 1887, during the debate on the Queen's Speech. It was the year of the Queen's Golden Jubilee, and as she was no longer able to attend the opening of Parliament in person, her speech was read to the assembled members of both Houses by the Lord Chancellor, setting out the policies of the Marquess of Salisbury in the coming session.

It stated that reforms were proposed in local government, land transfer, railway rates, and the paying of tithes, at home. The foreign policy of the government would be assure external and internal tranquillity in Egypt; there was to be no immediate intervention in Bulgaria against the Russians, and in Burma, troops had waged successful war on bands of up-country gangs of marauders, known as *dacoits*. In Ireland matters would be dealt with by the law to prevent relations from getting steadily worse between landlords and tenants. There was also to be a Royal Commission set up to investigate "the lamentable depression under which Trade and Agriculture have been suffering for many years."

Robert worked hard on that first speech. He was determined to show that the Conservatives only wanted to sit back in a comfortable state of *laissez-faire* and had no intention of easing the lot for the Irish tenants, or putting right the "glaring social inequalities" of their day. In foreign policy he wanted to draw the attention of his fellow MPs to the Conservatives inconsistent ideas: no troops in Bulgaria to restore Alexander of Battenberg to his rightful throne, but plenty to keep the peace in Egypt and to defend the Suez Canal.

As for their triumph in managing to suppress "marauders in Burma," it might be laughable – if it were not so tragic. Yes, he knew all about marauders being "put down" – he had seen it often. A native wounded to death and tormented by mosquitoes in the jungle felt his misery just as acutely as the most respectable gentleman in the House – but what was all that to the Government.

His final sentence brought out a flow of passion as he composed his first important speech: ". . . the injustices of a society in which one man works and another enjoys the fruit – a society in which capital and luxury makes a Heaven for 30,000 and a Hell for 30,000,000, a society whose crowning achievement is this dreary waste of mud and stucco – with its misery, its want and destitution, its degradation, its prostitution – the society we call London."

"That's good, Lob," said Gabrielle as she read his notes. "That should catch them on the raw. I'll be in the gallery, dearest Lob, and it will be the proudest moment of my life! You give it to them 'from the hip' as our Texan friends would say!"

And so Robert gave it to them "from the hip," and next day the newspapers were overjoyed to be able to report, at long last, "the advent of a wit" to the House of Commons.

The Pall Mall Gazette said, "The rising of Mr. Cunninghame Graham about half-past nine o'clock, was the signal for a mild sensation, the Hon. Member being distinguished by a remarkable, not to say, eccentric, personality. He had scarcely spoken a dozen sentences when he had secured the ear of the House, and almost every other sentence thereafter was punctuated by bursts of general laughter, and occasionally by the sound of party cheers. The speech was not unmarked by irony and sentiment, but it will be remembered by its smartness and wit."

There were many reports in this vein.

"Up to the present, the wittiest speech has been made by a Scotchman, Mr. R. C. Graham, the member for Lanarkshire. This possibly may be accounted for by his sitting with the Irish Home Rulers. Or is it the air of the Western world that has given the Hon. Member the peculiar dry caustic humour which he effects, and which greatly diverted the House for a short half-hour? For Mr. Graham has been a cattle raiser in South America, on the River Plate. On rising, he told the House that he should be brief, but tedious, and he kept the former half of his promise, but broke the latter."

And: "The really important thing in last night's debate was the discovery of a new Liberal wit, in the person of Mr. Graham, no slight acquisition in these endless nights of dreary talk."

In a leader which welcomed his remarks on Ireland, it went on to say: "Mr. Graham's description of his own qualification to speak on the Irish question was inimitable. He had never been to Ireland, but had gained something of a national colour by sitting amongst the Nationalist members, and (here the House went off into resistless laughter) he had once known an Irish commercial traveller who had imparted information to him quite unattainable by the general public. The advent of a new humorist – by newspaper readers as well as the House – must afford in these days of exhaustive Parliamentary reporting, infinite satisfaction."

Nearly all the newspapers carried articles on Robert's speech, welcoming his light touch.

Robert read them through like an opium-eater, looking more and more delighted as he read the complimentary remarks out to Gabrielle. "I've got the ear of the people, Chid! That's what I wanted to do. Now they'll listen to me. I shan't speak very often, but when I do I believe they really will listen!"

That evening Robert and Gabrielle celebrated with an excellent dinner at their favourite restaurant, Gianellas, and a bottle of champagne.

And that night William Morris wrote in his diary, "On the day that Parliament met, a young and new M.P., Cunninghame Graham by name, called on me by appointment to pump me on the subject of Socialism, and we had an agreeable talk. A brisk bright sort of young man; the other day he made his maiden speech and produced quite an impression by its brilliancy and socialistic hints."

About the same time the political correspondent of *Vanity Fair* wrote, "Advent of new man. Name: Cunninghame Graham. Description: Scotch Home Rule Visionary. Outward aspect: Something between Grosvenor gallery aesthete and waiter in Swiss café. Drawls out some deuced smart things. House kept in continuous roar for more than half-an-hour. Fogeys and fossils eye him askance, and whisper that he ought to be put down; but lovers of originality, in all quarters, hail him with satisfaction."

On 3rd April 1887 William Morris spoke in Glasgow on "True and False Society," after which he wrote in his diary: "In the evening I lectured in the Waterloo Hall to a big audience, say 1000, which was good as they had to pay. Cunninghame Graham M.P. took the chair for me, which was thought bold on a Sunday and a Socialist meeting: he declared himself not a Socialist because he agreed with the Owenite doctrine of man being made by his circumstances."

Next day, Robert went to his mother's house to give her a blow by blow account of the proceedings. She was utterly delighted, and prouder than ever of her handsome eldest son.

"How pleased Papa would be!" she exclaimed. "He was so distressed when he failed to win Dumbarton for the Liberals in 1859. He would be so thrilled to know that you had got in, Bob!"

Robert kept to his word, and made comparatively few utterances during that first session, but whenever he spoke he found that members had hurried to the chamber from the lobbies to hear him. Gradually he gave them less humour and more "meat." It was a little like giving medicine to a child, he thought. First of all you give more jam than powder, and slowly you increase the powder and decrease the jam.

He was thoroughly enjoying himself, and making a great number of new friends at the same time.

There was only one real disadvantage to Robert's new and exciting life. It meant that he and Gabrielle had to be parted for a good deal of the time. Gabrielle had agreed that it was most important she should stay at Gartmore to show the tenants and the employees that they were not going to be neglected since this new event had overtaken them.

It was the first whole winter that Gabrielle had ever spent in England and Scotland. Luckily it was a mild one on the whole, though there was an unpleasant cold spell in early April which started her cough up again. Robert wrote to her at Gartmore from his rooms at 52, Brook Street, to tell her that old Admiral Dunlop was dead. He had been married to one of the Graham great-aunts.

"17th April, 1887,

"My dearest Chid,

"Poor old Admiral Dunlop is dead. Cousin John feels it very much. He was a nice old fellow, and such a perfect gentleman.

"How is our 'Chidelin' – the garron?" Have you ridden him yet? If you ride him, don't let him gallop on the hard road or his legs will soon be ruined. On the grass he is quieter than on the roads, so take him there. The east wind beats anything I can remember, it goes through one like a knife. London is still in midwinter and very, very dull. Take care of yourself, dearest, and be a good Chiddy, and get well soon. Believe me, your affec. husband, Lob."

The next day he wrote in concern, after receiving her letter to him.

"April, 1887

"My dearest Chid,

"I am sorry to hear you are not so well. Yesterday the weather changed a little and perhaps it may get warmer, as the cold is awful. I went to see Buffalo Bill, there were a lot of Cowboys and I wondered who was to lazo, etc. when all of a sudden I saw a group of Mexicans, hats and all, I of course rushed to 'saludar' them, they were from some of the places we went to, Monterey, etc. We had a long conversation in Spanish, and talked all about Bejar, and Saltillo, and 'Don Guillermo Cody', and about the Comanches, the Lipanes, and the Mescaleros. Then they all introduced themselves to me – Diego, Pancho, Pedro, etc. and we had a grand talk!

"Take care of yourself, my dearest Chid.

"Believe me, your affec. Husband, Lob."

Gabrielle threw off her attack surprisingly quickly, as soon as the warmer weather came to Gartmore, and eventually Robert was able to join her.

She had become quite enthused with politics since Robert's election, and after a successful lecture in London to the Bloomsbury Socialist Club, at the request of Eleanor Marx Aveling, on "The Ideal of Socialism" she felt more prepared to help Robert by making speeches locally. She had now been made vice-president of the Scottish Women's Liberal Association. At the first meeting she told the members:

"I believe that the entrance of women into the field of politics, although on the outside it seems somewhat alien to their natures, it is the only means by which the poorer women of the middle and lower middle classes may be respected and treated as reasoning beings. (Applause.) I do not think that the giving of the vote to women will practically alter the issue of any election. The only appreciable result will be to increase the number of votes. But I do think it will put women in a more logical and a firmer position in society as at present constituted. And it is from this point of view that I earnestly urge upon women of every rank to join a women's political association."

The next morning there were several comments in the newspapers on Mrs. Graham's "rose pink socialism."

That summer, Robert and Gabrielle had a welcome rest at Gartmore, but they were not entirely free from political speeches and the duties connected with Robert's other role, that of the Laird of Gartmore. He was now a Deputy Lieutenant for the County of Stirling and a Justice of the Peace, both of which offices went with his new responsibilities as a landowner. Major McFarlane of the 1st Lanarkshire Rifle Volunteers, "Q" Company, enjoyed their hospitality at Gartmore when on manoeuvres with his men that April, and wrote to thank them warmly for the courtesy and encouragement they had personally afforded to all ranks of the column.

They held soirees for the various village organisations from Buchlyvie and Gartmore, and they spent a lot of time riding round the farms both at Gartmore and at Ardoch to find out if their tenants were satisfied with things, what repairs were needed, and if they had any difficulty in paying the rent; or visiting Robert's constituents.

In their spare time, they enjoyed their garden, took the dogs for walks, planted trees, rowed across the lake to Inchmahome, and spent the evenings that were not taken up with meeting or social activities, in writing and reading.

Back in London, in the autumn, Robert spoke in the House on the abolition of primogeniture, saying, "That gilded Elysium has run its course. Some are of the opinion that reform should come from within, but the House of Lords (like the Ark) is so 'pitched from within and without' with Conservative ideas, that reform from within would be a very slender one."

He also spoke on the case for the payment of members, saying, "It is the only chance that our crofters, our miners, our ironworkers and agricultural labourers will ever have to be properly represented. I would make the salary a small one, say £300 a year, but to it I would join a free pass to the constituency during the time Parliament is sitting. I would also make the acceptance of the salary compulsory."

But he spoke even more vehemently on the Eight Hours Bill.

"I have always considered that the first reform to really improve the condition of the working classes was the shortening of the hours of labour. This is a proposition that few seem disposed to deny. 'Let us shorten the hours of labour,' they say, 'especially in the mines, because the conditions of labour there are hard,' etc. Though in favour of an Eight Hours Bill for miners, these are not my reasons. Miners work hard, 'tis true, but not harder and not such long hours as railways servants and many other trades. The reason I am introducing an Eight Hours Bill for Miners is simply because they happened to be the first trade who were agreed upon the matter.

"Can you compete against the foreign miners who work longer hours? I say yes, you can, and do, and will do in the future. Our men work much shorter hours than the German miners in the Hartz Mountains, their wages are higher, their houses are no worse, their average product per man is much higher, and certainly their physique is as good. As of miners, so of all trades – restrict the hours, admit more men. Keep up your volume of trade under slightly altered conditions, employing ten men where you now employ eight; the result will be to absorb many of the unemployed, to give increased opportunities of intellectual improvement, and to allow the working classes time to combine in action, that the immense mass of wealth they make may be more equally divided between them and the capitalists."

Robert's speeches in the House of Commons were listened to with disbelief by many of the older members. Such ideas had never before been put forward. The man was an out and out socialist, they declared. So much of what Robert said was fifty years ahead of his own time, and for the most part he was dealing with men who did not have the intellect to understand it. So much of it is now being achieved, a hundred years later, in the 20th and 21st centuries.

Both Gabrielle and Missy were delighted with him. His mother told him that he was just like his Graham grandfather all over again; *his* ideas had been so progressive, when he stood as a Liberal in Renfrewshire in 1832, that he failed to get in because he was fifty years ahead of his time! Now people were saying the same things about Robert.

He just happened to have a bit of imagination and an original mind, said Blanche Fane, who was a permanent fixture now at 39, Chester Square, as companion to Missy.

"No," said Missy, "it's more than that. You see he has a very Spanish quality which helps, he knows he is right, and it simply does not worry him if nobody else agrees! He is in a very strong position."

That summer there had been a Miners Conference in Edinburgh at which it was said that it was not unlikely that a Scottish Labour Party would be formed before long, and that Mr. R. B. Cunninghame Graham M. P. would be its leader. The honourable gentleman was gaining an enormous popularity with the Scotch workers, and especially the miners. There was another reference to the possibility of the emergence of a Scottish Labour Party in the October issue of *Commonwealth*, the journal which had originally been started by William Morris's Socialist League.

Suddenly everyone was talking about this new word "Socialism" but Robert did not consider himself a "socialist." He certainly did not agree with everything William Morris had set forth, and there were many flaws in Karl Marx's theories; what he did want for the working classes was something Robert Owen had striven for: that it was better to provide the workers with relaxation, that it would be easier to lead men to "virtue and rational conduct" by providing them with "well regulated amusements and recreations than by forcing them to submit to useless restraints."

Robert had been fascinated by Robert Owen's experiment at the New Lanark cotton mills, and a great many of his theories were indeed owenite, but being an individualist, Robert did not credit any of the reformers with having particularly influenced him. They were basically his own theories, he was an *hombre de teorias*. The idea came from *Bobo el Filosofo*, he joked to his mother, explaining to her that great social reforms needed to be put into action, and since he had been elected as a Radical (or Gladstonian) Liberal, he was at last in a position to achieve something for people who could not fight for themselves. He realised there was a party programme, and there were certain catchwords that had to be repeated from time to time to show the constituents that you were paying attention to your original manifesto, so that meant making loud noises about free education, shorter working hours, the abolition of the laws of entail, etc. etc. But there were so many things that needed doing in addition, so many wrongs to right, so that everyone could enjoy being alive as much as he did, not just the lucky few.

His mother laughed at his emphatic words, but secretly she was delighted to see that the spark she had always known was flickering inside him had now started blazing. He had come totally alive in the best possible sense, and he was enjoying it wildly.

Robert and Gabrielle began to see more and more of people like Eleanor Aveling Marx, Walter Crane, and Beatrice and Sidney Webb. Robert corresponded with Annie Besant and Hyndman, and Gabrielle made several more speeches in the cause of women's suffrage.

But Robert was worried. The Irish Question was going to blow up in Lord Salisbury's face if he was not careful. A protest meeting at Mitchelstown, County Cork, had been fired upon early in September

1887, and the police were found responsible for the death of three of the men. They had been protesting over the prosecution of William O'Brien for his part in the Plan of Campaign. In London the unemployed were demonstrating daily in Trafalgar Square.

The mood of the working people of both Ireland and England (and perhaps Scotland too, for they usually sided with the Irish) was getting ugly. If reforms were not speeded up, it would soon be a case of getting out the barricades, and then the country would be in real trouble.

On 13th September, 1887, the House of Commons sat late, and at 3.30 in the morning a discussion was taking place on an amendment the House of Lords had made to the Coal Mines Regulations Bill in connection with the appointment by miners of men to inspect the mines. Robert did not agree with the House of Lords' amendment and rashly said that he hoped an assembly not elected by popular vote should not dare to dictate to the House of Commons which *was* elected by popular vote.

The Speaker promptly told him that these words must be withdrawn and apologised for; at which Robert, characteristically, said:

"I regret to say it is a matter of conscience with me, and I cannot withdraw."[13]

He apologised personally to the Speaker, and quietly withdrew, as it was later reported, "amid cheers of the Opposition members below the gangway," or "amidst Parnellite cheers" as another newspaper put it. Robert's constituency had earned him great admiration, but in the world outside things were going from bad to worse. Two months later Robert found himself at the centre of a near-revolution, something he had been convinced was almost certain to happen.

---

[13] George Bernard Shaw used this remark in *Arms and the Man*, attributing it to Robert whom he admired very much.

CHAPTER XXV

It all started when the Metropolitan Federation of Radical Clubs decided to add their voice to the protest in connection with the prosecution of the Irish patriot William O'Brian, who had been detained. The Irish Question was by now in a highly volatile state, and as demonstrations against unemployment in England were becoming more and more frequent as well, the Home Office took the unprecedented step of banning all public meetings in Trafalgar Square.

This was the final insult, the final threat to liberty, which caught Robert on the raw. Two months ago he had been forbidden to say what he wanted in the House of Commons, and now the people were being forbidden to say what *they* wanted in Trafalgar Square. Freedom of speech was in jeopardy, and he was not going to sit by and watch *that* happening.

He wrote an article in the *Pall Mall Gazette* on 12th November in which he stated, "I think it is high time for everyone calling himself a Liberal to protest against the ban on public meetings – and for that reason I intend to address the meeting in Trafalgar Square this Sunday."

Gabrielle tried to dissuade him, but he was adamant.

"I'll be all right," he said, "John Burns and I will go together, and as soon as I've had my say we'll come and join you at Morley's Hotel. You just go and wait for us there, and we'll be with you in no time at all, Chid!"

"Do take care, Lob," said Gabrielle anxiously. She had seen some of the recent demonstrations and the people were in an angry mood. Now the police were getting angry too, and Robert was still determined to go down to Trafalgar Square on Sunday, 17th November. There was bound to be a clash sooner or later. It was no good trying to persuade Robert to stay quietly at home: she knew what he was like. He was doing his "knight in armour" act, setting out on a white charger to rescue the people from a dreadful dragon! She could not help laughing at the thought, although she knew he might be in great danger. The editor of the *Pall Mall Gazette,* W. T. Stead, had told her that he was going down to Morley's Hotel to see the fun, and he would be very glad to escort her.

Gabrielle and Mr. Stead made notes throughout the incident, one that was to go down in history as the "Battle of Trafalgar Square."

On 17th November the *Pall Mall Gazette* reported:

"By nine o'clock in the morning the centre of the square was ringed with police, and by eleven o'clock it was surrounded by another large picket. By one o'clock 1,500 police were in position and, in addition, constantly riding round the square were mounted police, patrolling in couples. Another 2.500 police were kept in reserve on the approach routes to break up processions. Three hundred Grenadier Guards and three hundred Life Guards were ultimately to be called out as well, later that day.

"By 3.20 scuffles had begun to break out, and a party of mounted police galloped from Northumberland Avenue towards the centre of the square, to try to disperse the crowd, which numbered by now some fifteen thousand people, their white horses flecked through the crowd like specks of foam on a stormy sea. A skirmish broke out in one corner of the square and the crowd roared hoarsely in protest as a man was taken into custody, his stick confiscated by the police, and the men standing close by beaten lavishly with it. Gradually the police cavalry drove the crowds up the Strand, men, women and children fleeing before their galloping horses.

"By 3.45 another contingent of mounted police had arrived, to begin a series of dangerous gallops from the top of Northumberland Avenue, down the Strand and back again. The crowd started to hoot and hiss ominously, and more and more people poured into the square until the mass of people packed round Nelson's Column had risen to thirty thousand or more. While contingents of twenty mounted police abreast charged repeatedly down Northumberland Avenue, the crowds were getting extremely angry as they were pushed hither and thither. Fists were up by now, sticks and batons in use."

Suddenly a disturbance started at the corner of Morley's Hotel. Two men had emerged from Charing Cross Station and were making their way into the square, having avowed their intention to establish the principles of free speech and public meetings in the square. They were John

Burns and Robert Bontine Cunninghame Graham. As they slipped
between the police horses, they were suddenly recognised and blows
were rained upon them by police of all grades.

Robert was deliberately struck on the head by a constable with his
truncheon, sustaining a scalp wound about 1¼ inches long, and receiving
several blows from the clenched fists of others.

John Burns was knocked about and received several bruises on the
head. Even after Robert had been arrested, at least two policemen stepped up from behind, striking him on the head with great violence and
brutality. To her horror, Gabrielle, from her hotel window, saw her
husband being escorted by the police to one of the fountains with blood
streaming down his face, while Burns fetched water in his hat to wash his
friend's wounds.

At four thirty, it could be seen through the darkness that a 'thin red
line' of Grenadier Guards had arrived to line the terrace parapet in front
of the National Gallery, wearing their great black busbies, with bayonets
fixed. Each soldier had twenty rounds of ball cartridge in his pouch, and
an attendant doctor was accompanied by his splint and bandage bearer.

The moving cuirasses of the Life Guards sparkled in the lamplight as
they repeatedly rode round the square, while the police cavalry continued
to gallop indiscriminately among the people. Smash, crash, clatter as
they swung their batons, and members of the mob started to climb lamp
posts to escape their blows. Suddenly there was a great crash of broken
glass as the police forced a section of the mob back against a shop
window.

And so the police cavalry and the Life Guards continued to press the
people in Trafalgar Square that Sunday evening, while the Grenadier
Guards stood ready to play their part as a last desperate attempt to
control the crowd.

Slowly the police began to win the day, and the mob moved reluctantly out of the centre of the square. Just before seven o'clock, after a
battle lasting five hours, the soldiers and the immense body of the police
was withdrawn, and an uneasy peace fell upon the great square; the
battle of Trafalgar Square was over. Robert and John Burns had now
been cast into the police cells at Bow Street, charged with assault, breach
of the peace, and "unlawful assembly."

At ten o'clock that night Robert's uncle, Colonel William Hope, V.C., arrived with Asquith, Haldane, and another Tory member. But bail was refused, so the two men were kept in prison for fully twenty-four hours before finally being allowed out, Robert's head wound remained unattended, and he spent a feverish night in his cell.

By 19th January 1888 Robert (a Deputy Lieutenant for the county of Perthshire, and a J.P.) found himself serving a six weeks' prison sentence with John Burns in Pentonville Gaol. The jury had acquitted them of assault by the police, and causing a riot, but they were sentenced for "unlawful assembly," the third charge, after a trial which became a *cause célèbre*, with the public galleries packed to bursting.

As Robert sat in his white-washed cell, with windows of Dutch glass, and furnished with a table, a chair, a little square salt box, wooden spoon, tin pan and a Bible, picking oakum, he reflected on his strange circumstances. He was not the first of the Grahams to be detained in such a way. His ancestor Malise Graham, the first of the Graham earls of Menteith, had spent twenty-six years as a prisoner of King Henry IV of England, from 1423 to 1449, and as a hostage for the ransom of the Scottish king, James I. Malise Graham had been chosen to take the King of Scotland's place as the captive of the English because he was a great-grandson of King Robert II, and therefore one of King James's close cousins. (Admittedly he had been well treated, and ended up marrying the Earl of Oxford's daughter, Anne!)

Robert smiled ruefully as he realised that he now had a unique opportunity to take a close look at one of His Majesty's prisons.

After South America and Texas, the solitude and the plank bed were nothing to Robert. He found he could communicate through the wall of his cell to Burns with a formerly-agreed code of signals, and he particularly enjoyed the compulsory exercise, racing around in circles with his fellow-prisoners. He also found that, because he had always been a fast runner and was in any case in excellent physical shape, he could outrun all the others. He heard one of them whisper to his mate as he tore past:

"If *we* could run like this 'ere M.P. we wouldn't 'ave got in 'ere in the first place!"

They were never allowed to talk to each other, so the one great release of frustration came in the prison chapel on Sunday mornings, when the hymns were roared out with joyful gusto by petty thieves and London's most hardened criminals alike. It was a huge burst of sound, and Robert never forgot it. He was later to capture this strange pheno-menon in his story *Sursum Corda* (or "Lift up Your Hearts") describing the quivering of the chapel like a ship, and the dust flying, as the pent-up sound broke forth.

None of them liked picking oakum, or eating the "skilly" with which their daily diet of hard brown bread was supplemented, for it was usually of the consistency of glue; but worst of all were the long silent nights, which seemed to drag on for at least forty-eight hours, as the lonely men twisted and tossed on their plank beds, tortured by the thought that everyone in the world outside had long ago forgotten their existence.

Robert kept himself sane with the "official" Bible that was placed in every cell, the Book of Ecclesiastes being his favourite reading. There was one other book in his cell, Simon Patrick's *Parable of the Pilgrims*, published in the reign of King Charles II roughly eight months before Bunyan's *Pilgrim's Progress* made its first appearance. Robert found it fascinating, and it helped to while away the long hours.

Week succeeded week, but he only had to serve four in all, being given the reward for "good behaviour." On Robert's last Sunday at Pentonville, after the lusty singing in the chapel, one old lag whispered to him, "Does you good, Number Eight, the bloomin' 'ymn," and Robert dealt him a friendly kick, thinking that the sixteen verses were all too short.

During Robert's spell in prison Gabrielle became more and more lonely and depressed. Wandering miserably round London on a bitterly cold January day, she went into a second-hand book shop and found a battered copy of the life of St. Teresa of Avila. It cost her only a few pence, and as she read, she discovered a woman very like herself, who loved action, and yet was a thoughtful idealist; a woman who knew that there is something more in a man or a woman than idle dreaming and visions.

It was the action that she missed so intolerably now. When she and Robert had been riding through Mexico she had felt utterly fulfilled, for their way of life demanded all the qualities that she felt to be important: courage, constancy, tenacity, and dissimulation – for, she thought, right and wrong are not fixed, irreducible terms, but very much dependent on circumstances, often shading into one another so subtly as not to be distinguished.

The more she read of St. Teresa's life, the more she knew that this fascinating saint had been a woman entirely after her own heart. She would write a book about her. What a delightful idea! This, too, would give her a reason to travel to Spain. Gabrielle already realised that, as she got older, she would probably have to winter abroad for the sake of her health, and here at last was an absorbing project. She could do the research in Spain in the winters, and the writing at Gartmore and in London during the rest of the year. The whole plan was tremendously exciting, and she could not wait to talk to Robert about it.

* * * * * *

Robert was released in late February. He almost dreaded being reunited with Gabrielle, for he knew she had been growing even more morose and miserable since he went into prison. But when she came to collect him from Pentonville, there was a new spring in her step and a new glow in her eyes as she took him in her arms and hugged him joyfully.

Robert was delighted. Here was the Chid he had come to love so much during their two years in Texas and Mexico, and La Graña, in Spain. He wondered what could have happened while he was in prison to change her so much? On the train back to Gartmore, she told him that she now had something to live for. She now had a book to write! She kissed him for the hundredth time and told him she was going to fatten him up at Gartmore – he looked so pale and thin after his diet of "skilly"!

At Gartmore, the welcome was just as moving as it had been when he first won the seat. This time there was even a photographer to take a misty souvenir picture of the scene outside the front door.

Robert was not given much time to recover from his ordeal: he soon found he had become a hero, a "martyr" to the workers' cause. He showed Gabrielle the letters he had received while he was in prison. One was from Oscar Wilde, saying, "I wish we could meet to talk over the many prisons of life. Prisons of stone, prisons of passion, prisons of intellect, prisons of morality, and the rest. All limitations, external and internal, and life is a limitation."

Their interlude at Gartmore was all too short. Robert was receiving endless invitations from the whole world of social reform, who wanted him to take the chair at their conferences, address their meetings, and give them his political blessing. Robert even managed to publish a photograph of himself in prison garb, entitled "J.P., and Deputy Lieutenant, of the County of Stirling." The sort of joke he loved.

In August 1888 an important new party had its inaugural conference in Glasgow, with Robert in the chair. Keir Hardie had set up the Scottish Labour Party, and Robert was elected its first President. So he still had a political position in Scotland. Little did he realise at the time that this party would eventually become the forerunner of the Scottish National Party.

Robert now found that his writing had a far more long-reaching effect than speaking in Parliament, so he was now writing regularly for "The People's Press" under such headings as, "If Cock Robin is dead – who will kill King Capital?"

Writing came far more easily to him these days; he was beginning to enjoy it, and he remembered his father's remark in a letter to him when he was at Harrow: "Always remember the eagle in our family crest has a dagger in one claw, and a pen in the other." He was starting to find that the pen was indeed mightier than the sword.

He still spoke at a great many meetings, but he was getting tired of the game. He did not feel that things were moving quickly enough, and he found that Parliament was, on the whole, unresponsive to reform. He complained to John Burns that "political life in this country is a mean and dirty struggle, and results in nothing in the end." His health was suffering from five years of late-night sittings, and from the constant treadmill of attending meetings all over the country.

Gabrielle was now happily absorbed in her study of the life of St. Teresa of Avila and she spent a great deal of time in Spain; but she, too, had frequent breakdowns of health, and Robert hated not being able to look after her at such times. He was beginning to wonder if she had the same illness that his brother Malise had died of – it did not bear thinking about. He was still utterly devoted to his dearest Chid, and she to him.

* * * * * *

There was another reason why Robert was losing heart – he simply did not think he could *afford* another election campaign. Gartmore was gobbling up all his resources, and Jamieson, the accountant, had agreed with him that the original estimate of their annual living costs had been far too low. The debt was getting even larger.

Robert's release from Parliament came in April 1892. A signalman had been dismissed after giving evidence to the Railways Servants Hours' Committee, and Robert was pointing out to the House that long shift-working could cause fatigue and subsequent inefficiency, or human errors. He was tired and angry, and he spoke hastily, saying:

"I hope the House will see, as I think they *do* see, that gross injustice is being done to a helpless man by a rich and powerful Corporation."

There was laughter at this statement which made Robert more angry than ever. Then Asquith got up to speak about the iniquity of capital gains on development land, and drew a distinction between the receipt of unearned money by the landowner, and unearned money by the shareholder – this duplicity made Robert lose his temper completely and he leapt to his feet to interrupt. He refused to listen when the Speaker asked him to sit down. But Robert's blood was up and he simply did not care any more.

The Speaker had no choice but to suspend him, and Robert shouted rudely, "Suspend away!"

The Home Secretary tried to mollify him, but he had had enough.

"Oh, leave me alone, I don't care a damn," he said. His volatile temperament had given a final snort of contempt at the British Legislative machine and he was out on his ear.

He knew he had burnt his boats, but he found he had nothing but a great sense of relief that his parliamentary career was at an end, and that he was free at last to return to Gartmore to ride his horse, write the stories about South America, Texas and Mexico which still filled his head, and enjoy the peaceful life of a Scottish Laird, with Gabrielle at his side. He thought back over his achievements in Parliament: he had fought inch by inch to gain advantages for the down-trodden industrial workers of the late nineteenth century, especially in the sweat shops, and he had gained much popularity as a familiar figure riding to Parliament on his jet black horse, Pampa, a symbolic knight riding on his charger to free the world from tyranny.

It had been a struggle all the way and he often felt dismayed by his task, but he had continued to work ceaselessly. *"Y contra todos, y todos contra mi* is not a happy position," he had once written to Sir Charles Dilke. The workers needed a "cloth-cap" representative, a man like Keir Hardie, not a landowner whose every action was immediately suspect. He was tired of the whole business of being a Member of Parliament – late night sessions, listening to dull speeches made by dull men. "The National Gasworks" was how he described it. His suspension was indeed a happy release!

A month later he would celebrate his fortieth birthday, and Gabrielle had reached her thirty-third birthday on 22nd January. He might still have another forty years, if he was lucky, to devote to all the many other things he wanted to do with his life.

Gabrielle had just arrived back from her fourth winter in Spain. Her book on St. Teresa was nearly finished, and she was excited by the favourable comments she had received from literary friends to whom she had shown her first chapters, who told her she wrote like a man. This was high praise, for women writers were still in the minority.

A few weeks later they were back at Gartmore.

"The Laird's back!" the word went round. Robert had become a very important (even notorious, to some) public figure, but he was still their "laird" first and foremost.

* * * * * *

During those Spring days in 1892, Robert and Gabrielle walked over the hills, watching bumble bees tumbling through the tiny wild flowers at their feet: a peewit called to its mate. Below them lay Gartmore, the classical lines of the Adam mansion house a perfect foil for the rugged scenery, and the Lake of Menteith shining like a looking-glass.

The Laird of Gartmore looked happily at his wife as they walked arm in arm under the stone bridge that bore the two coats-of-arms for the

Grahams and Cunninghames. There was the eagle with his pen and his sword, and, there, written beneath, was the family motto "For Right and Reason."

"Yes," murmured Robert to himself, "that's why I do these things."

He looked happily at his wife and smiled.

"'What more felicity can fall to creature.

" Than to enjoy delight with liberty'

"– to quote my friend Spenser again! I'm beginning to think that Liberalism doesn't have much to do with 'Liberty' after all! Now we are going to start enjoying ourselves, Chid, I think we deserve both delight *and* liberty, don't you, ma chère petite femme? For *right* and *reason!*"

But Robert was worried about Gartmore. As he rode round the estate on Pampa he saw nothing but broken gates, tumbled walls, and fences to mend. Grass and weeds crept across the tracks, thistles ramped across the parks, and there was an air of evident neglect. The people seemed cheerful enough, but they probably had not noticed the way decay was spreading so rapidly through the estate. It was far more obvious to Robert, who saw the place with a fresh eye on each journey north. Now that he was out of politics the sensible thing would be to run the estate entirely himself.

The following week, Robert explained matters to Mr. Grant, and they agreed reluctantly that the factor must move elsewhere. This meant that Robert would have a full-time job running the estate. Armed with his experience from South America he got to work.

For the next five years Robert stayed at Gartmore with occasional visits to London to see his mother. In the coldest parts of the winter, he and Gabrielle explored more of Spain, and paid relaxing visits to Tangier, which had become a favourite winter resort for a group of young Scottish artists later to be known as "The Glasgow Boys". Crawhall – known to them all as "Creeps" and Lavery had always been Robert's special friends, and they went regularly to Tangier to join several other Scottish friends.

PART VI
CHAPTER XXVI

Now sixty years old, Missy was still attractive, lively, and highly intelligent, and did a great deal to help and encourage the young men who poured into her house. The young writers, artists and musicians reminded her of Malise. His friend at Winchester, the poet Lionel Johnson, had been one of the first to go to her for literary criticism and encouragement. Now the house at Chester Square always seemed to be full, and Robert and Gabrielle enjoyed meeting all these entertaining people when they visited her. Two young Oxford undergraduates, Max Beerbohm and Will Rothenstein, both young artists, amused them particularly with their wit; and a young publisher's reader called Edward Garnett, who worked for Fisher Unwin, was soon to become a close friend.

Robert and Garnett talked about a mutual friend called William Hudson, who had been brought up in the Argentine, and now lived with his wife in penury in St. Luke's Road, writing about birds, the countryside, and in particular his home on the pampas. Robert had first read an essay Hudson had published in 1890, and had written to tell him how much he had enjoyed it and how it had conjured up the pampas so vividly for him. After that, they met and corresponded regularly. But when Robert invited him to come to Chester Square, Hudson had replied, "I could no more dine at Chester Square with you and your friends than with the fairies or the angels! These beings do not really dine, they sup – but let that pass. The fact is, being poor, I long ago gave up going to houses and dining. One of the Apostles, a certain Paul, warned us against 'unequal' alliances, and Æsop touches instructively on the same subject in one of his parables."

Garnett suggested that Robert should come along to one of his literary lunches at a restaurant called the "Mont Blanc". Hudson used to attend from time to time, at Garnett's invitation, knowing that he would meet like-minded men, some of them just as poor as himself. Robert loved going to these lunches. He and Hudson used to sit in a corner together and exchange Argentinian reminiscences, while their friends looked on with amusement tinged with envy. Hudson, Conrad, and Robert were three of a kind: they had all travelled extensively, especially Conrad and Graham, so they had a head start over the other writers at Garnett's lunches.

Robert and Hudson loved to talk about their sea-trips across the Atlantic from Buenos Aires – Robert having crossed and re-crossed at least six times, while Hudson only had the one journey when he sailed to Southampton from Buenos Aires on 1st April 1874 with 127 passengers in a Royal Mail ship, the *Ebro*, but he remembered every detail of the journey and had written an "Atlantic Diary" in the form of five long letters to his brother Albert, the first dated 14th April 1874. He had arrived in Southampton, to set foot on English soil for the first time, on 3rd May 1874, and he had written a final letter which he posted on 8th May telling about his first impressions.

Robert was fascinated by this unusual man, whose father, Daniel Hudson, had come from Marblehead, Massachusetts, and whose mother, Caroline Augusta Kimble, came from Berwick, Maine. They had brought their children up on the pampas of Argentina at the House of the Twenty-five Ombú Trees in Quilmes – and William Henry Hudson remembered the details of his childhood just as clearly as he remembered the voyage to England when he was thirty-three years old. (He had been born eleven years before Robert, in 1841.)

The two men soon became firm friends, sharing the memories of their tortures of seasickness as the tiny vessels (steamships with sails) plied across the storm-bound Atlantic, and the strange passengers who had shared their voyages. Hudson told Robert about the gentleman from Montevideo who said he was going to Europe to buy a "Theofolite" – meaning a theodolite. In turn Robert told of the lady who used to plunge her fork down her throat with every mouthful, and of the fighting-drunk Frenchman who had chased him up the rigging.

Hudson said he was bitterly disappointed that he never heard the dulcet strains of the "Mermaid on a dolphin's back" nor had even a glimpse of a great sea-serpent. But they both remembered whales tumbling and blowing round their ships in the harbour at St. Vincent, and the awe-inspiring wild mountain coast of the Canary Islands, with snow patches on the mountain summits.

They talked together about the beautiful city of Lisbon, made more beautiful because it was their first landfall after so many weeks at sea. *Quien no ha visto a Lisboa no ha visto cosa boa* (who hasn't seen Lisbon hasn't seen a beautiful thing).

They remembered Rio, too, and Robert smiled in delighted recognition as Hudson described it as that "outlandish, queer, fantastical, hot, ridiculous, iniquitous, picturesque, carnivalesque, arabesque City of Rio."

Robert laughed as Hudson told him that it had been his captain's first Atlantic crossing and they had arrived slap bang against the rocky island of San Antonio at the Cape du Verde Islands one night, and set off round it the wrong way, until the captain realised his mistake and put his ship about.

Hudson had lingered on in Southampton after the ship arrived with a passenger called Babbage, he told Robert, staying at the Davis Hotel, for he had wanted to see "Mrs. Victoria's" great house Osborne, on the Isle of Wight. Robert tried to remember where he had been in early May 1874, and whether by chance he had been staying with Grandmamma Catalina at Ryde, also on the Isle of Wight – how strange if they had already seen each other, unknowingly!

Hudson's next pilgrimage had been to the modest thatched cottage of the great Argentine President, Juan Manuel de Rosas, who had been exiled to Southampton after his defeat by General Justo José de Urquiza in 1852. Babbage and he found the cottage beside a pretty orchard and green fields, guided to it by a local who described it as "Mr. Rose's house"!

He remembered it had been very cold but skylarks sang a sweet melody overhead and the sun shone at intervals, while scores of glossy black jackdaws cawed like Urrucas. Robert was astonished by his new friend's talent for total recall. Hudson thought privately that Robert himself had the same gift. They both suddenly felt happy, knowing they would always have each other to talk to, should their lasting homesickness for South America strike too painfully.

* * * * * *

Sometimes Robert's mother invited young artists of the Glasgow School to her house, and Robert was fascinated in their approach to painting and took a great interest in their work. Many of them had been taught by the great French masters. He made special friends with Jacomb-Hood and Joseph Crawhall, and picked up his old friendship with John Lavery again, who was now back from Paris. Whistler often came to Chester Square and particularly admired Gabrielle, telling Robert how much he would like to paint her long, beautiful hands. Jacomb-Hood wanted to paint both Robert and Gabrielle, and laughingly told Whistler he could have his wish.

John Lavery also wanted to paint Robert – as a horseman; and Rothenstein wanted to paint him as a fencer. They decided to meet at Angelo's, and Rothenstein pointed out a friend who might come and watch their fencing bouts. Aubrey Beardsley was a strange, elegant young man, Robert thought. Better keep him away from Oscar, too beautiful by far.

He had heard that Aubrey's painting were sinuous and sinister; he was known by his friends as "Awfully Weirdsly".

Robert told them that George Bernard Shaw had once said to his mother that the medieval sword and modern Mauser seemed to be, to Robert, what umbrellas and Kodaks were to him! Robert rather enjoyed being the centre of this admiring group, and was glad they seemed to find his stories so amusing.

Gabrielle, small and exquisite in a Parisian gown, had deep conversations with the Irish poet and playwright, W. B. Yeats; while Robert talked to Jack Galsworthy who was a Harrovian like himself. The couple enjoyed those evenings at Chester Square and at last Missy and Gabrielle began to develop an affectionate relationship. Gabrielle responded with many kind and thoughtful acts, and Missy realised how badly she had misjudged the girl. How ironical that she, so proud of her Whig politics and liberal outlook on life, should have been so snobbish about her daughter-in-law, but she was sad that there were no children from the marriage.

On 16th February, 1893, Charlie's wife Milly gave birth to a son. At last Robert had an heir for Gartmore! He rushed down to Hempstead to see the new baby and, after inspecting it, decided it would 'do'.

"What do you mean – 'it'll do'!" laughed his sister-in-law. "He's the most beautiful baby in the world, isn't he, Charlie?"

Charles grinned at his brother.

"They all look a bit alike – babies!" he said.

Uff, who was nearly ten, was enchanted by her baby brother and spent a lot of time lugging him round, when allowed to by "White Nurse."

"What's he called?" asked Robert.

"Angus," said Charlie. "Oh, and a few other things like Edward, because the Prince of Wales insisted on becoming his Godfather, and Malise after dear old Mal. Do you approve?"

"Yes," said Robert, "I think Angus makes a nice change from all those endless Roberts and Williams, doesn't it, Lee?"

At the christening, Uff got a fit of the giggles when the rather deaf parson proclaimed baby Angus, as he poured holy water over his fair curls, with the words "I baptise thee *Agnes* in the Name of the Father, and of the Son, and of the Holy Ghost. Amen."

"He called him *Agnes*!" Uff whispered in her mother's ear as she tried to stifle her laughter.

Robert brought his mother down to Hampstead to see her first grandson for whom she had waited so long, and the whole family was gathered together, to her delight. She was now sixty-five. What a pity Robert and Gabrielle could not have children, she thought. Robert was extraordinarily good with them.

Gabrielle had gone back to Spain to finish her book. Robert, too, had been writing steadily at Gartmore that winter, researching the history of the Menteith lands through the ages – it had been fascinating work. He had already found a local printer and was going to call the book simply *Notes on the District of Menteith*. Now that he and Gabrielle did not have to be forcibly separated, they found, strangely enough, that their brief separations were almost beneficial to their relationship. Gabrielle loved being in Spain, and Robert was always happy at Gartmore.

He had worked conscientiously all winter, but despite his efforts he realised, after his first year of running Gartmore single-handed, that it was only a matter of time before he would have to sell his family home. He would not give up without a fight for, if he did, he was sure he would

be haunted for the rest of his life by resentful ghosts of former lairds and
Earls of Menteith. He was sure Charlie also realised that his heir, little
Angus, was never likely to live at Gartmore.

Seeing Gabrielle off to Spain that winter had been a wrench for both
of them, but her chest was growing weaker with each successive winter,
and the doctor had insisted she spent it in a warm country. Robert
watched her white face peering over the side of the ship as the tugs
pulled the vessel out of the docks at Southampton. But he knew the
parting would do them no harm.

They had far fewer quarrels when they were both occupied with their
own pursuits, interspersed with repeated "honeymoons" at Gartmore.
Gartmore would always be the place where they were happiest of all –
though perhaps La Graña had been the most idyllic home of their married
life. Spain had become Gabrielle's second home – perhaps even her
first. She wrote that she was always fascinated to find in forgotten
villages a trace of the saint's footsteps, and always happy, after a long
day's ride, if she could lodge in a house where once the saint had slept,
too. She identified with St. Teresa more and more, almost as though the
saint had taken over her life. Robert realised that the mystic quality he
had recognised that day in Paris fifteen years earlier was indeed a strong
feature of his wife's character. He found it intriguing and mysterious,
and somehow it made his little Chid even more fascinating. He loved her
more deeply than ever.

During the summer of 1893, Robert and Gabrielle decided to cata-
logue the Gartmore books. Amongst them they found an old volume of
the works of Pliny translated into Spanish.

The name was written with a thick quill pen, a rose below the letter-
ing as an ornament, and a small piece of sheepskin had gone from near
the top of Volume II, leaving the threads that bound the leaves together
exposed to daylight. This book of Natural History had commentaries by
Fray Geronimo de Huerta, Familiar of the Holy Office of the Inquisition.
Gabrielle noticed that it mentioned a gold mine in Lusitania – the old
name for Galicia. And how they used to wash for gold on the sands.

Robert had great trust in Gabrielle's intuition; perhaps she was right,
this could well be the same gold – but could there possibly be any left

after all those hundreds of years? It was a long time since Pliny had been alive.

Robert went from Vigo to Orense by train, and was met by the mining engineer, Barnard, who had wandered the world so thoroughly in search of valuable minerals that he was rather apt to forget whether he was in Lima or Madrid. Nothing astonished him, and the next morning the two men jolted in a diligence on one of the hottest days Robert could ever remember towards Val de Orras, arriving eventually at their destination that evening feeling like walnuts shaken in a sack.

On the following day they reached journey's end. In the far distance rose the Asturian mountains, while a small river running near the inn tinkled amongst the stones. It was just like an idyll by Theocritus.

Everyone knew about the Roman mine, and they told Robert and the mining engineer that, after a flood, people still washed out a pan or two from time to time and got a little gold.

Barnard wandered enthusiastically about talking about paydirt, bedrock, gold in the quartz, and placer diggings.

A few days passed by, then suddenly Barnard rushed into the hotel shouting "Eureka!" and explaining that he had found a man who knew exactly where the Roman gold mines had been situated, three leagues off amongst the hills.

Barnard insisted that they should camp near the mines that night, so, after a stifling journey on mules, they finally came to the place just as it was getting dark. Everywhere was the poignant and aromatic scent of thyme and rosemary. The moon rose brilliantly.

The next morning a way had to be found into the bottom of this devil's beeftub, and Barnard enthusiastically started his search for gold. But each time he washed a pan, nothing but a fine red sediment remained, mixed with some little pebbles.

It was at this point that Robert knew he would find no gold in his old Roman mine, and yet he seemed to have caught Barnard's sense of joy that they had found a mine in which there were no shareholders, no calls for money, and no quotation of its stock. That they had worked in the moonlight with the help of Roman ghosts, and that it had yielded millions in experience and recollection which no-one could ever plunder or steal.

* * * * * *

Robert returned to Gartmore totally contented. The expedition had been a splendid one, he could not have enjoyed it more; and like his other exploits in the past, the enjoyment was untarnished by success. It had been the failure that he had always secretly hoped it would be.

Later on, back in London Robert and Gabrielle began to make new friends. Robert often wrote to congratulate the authors of articles he had particularly enjoyed, and just as he had met William Hudson in this way, so he was to meet Joseph Conrad. It was Edward Garnett who had first talked to Robert about this Polish seaman called Joseph Conrad Korzeniowsky, the son of an aristocratic father who had died young. Garnett told Robert he had just read *Almayer's Folly*, and it was extraordinary that a man who spoke Polish as his native tongue could write so superbly in English. He was sure Conrad (as he was going to be called when his book was published) would one day become a truly famous writer. At the time, however, he was talking about going back to sea.

Robert thought this Conrad sounded like a man after his own heart, but he did not yet know that he was ultimately to become one of his closest friends, nor that it would be Robert himself who would have to act as midwife for the birth of each book, for Conrad would always be a man who almost needed a "Caesarean operation of the soul" before he was delivered of one of his masterpieces.

(Robert was also to be godfather to one of Conrad's sons, in due course, and he became a great favourite to the two little boys, especially when he used to throw apples up in the air and fire at them with his revolver. They used to say "Don Roberto" *never* misses!")

Gabrielle's *Teresa of Avila* came out that summer, and Robert was very proud of his wife when he found that she was being greeted as a scholarly writer who had produced a definitive book on the life of the Spanish saint. She was kept so busy over the publishing of the book that Robert had more time than usual to spend with William Hudson.

Hudson told Robert that when he was a child he had had rheumatic fever very badly and was told that his heart had been badly affected. At this moment he was given Darwin's *Origin of the Species* and White's

Natural History of Selborne: these two books fired him with ambition to become a great naturalist.

Hudson and his wife had taken walking and bicycling tours, and he was now beginning to write about wildlife in England. He was six foot three in height, with grizzled dark hair, a curiously flat top to his head, and he always wore a rough tweed suit, with a stand-up starched white collar, starched linen cuffs, and black lace-up boots. His well-trimmed beard and brown eyes made him look like the autumn leaves he described so well, or like the brown animals of field and forest, or perhaps even a little like the small brown song-birds he loved to depict.

During 1894 Robert and Gabrielle were kept busy with the distribution, letters and review of *Santa Teresa.* There was a great deal of good will for the book, and Robert felt immensely proud of his clever little wife. But there were moments of gloom, too, when the reviews were bad, and Robert found it difficult to cheer Gabrielle at this times, for she was very vulnerable and over-sensitive. It was at these moments of misery that Missy found she could raise Gabrielle's spirits by telling her to look the world in the face with courage and to pay little heed to spiteful critics who had not understood the significance of her great book. Missy reminded Gabrielle that very few famous authors had ever been praised in their lifetime, and she must accept that her immortality and fame would come in the distant future. Gabrielle was sure her mother-in-law was right, and rather enjoyed playing the part of the wronged and unappreciated authoress.

Once all the excitement was over, Robert took Gabrielle for a holiday to Tangier. Morocco had always held a fascination for him, combining as it did the original territories of the Moors who had invaded Spain and from whom he was probably descended, and even more important, the beautiful horses, known as *wind-drinkers.* The weather was perfect, and they enjoyed wandering amongst the orange groves and cantering along the white sands. They also found they could buy exquisite carpets for a small sum, and were delighted to think that here might be another source of income for Gartmore, if they took them home and sold them at a large profit.

They both found they were getting quite good at justifying their passion for travel; books, carpets, goldmines – what next could they think up? Robert wondered whether it might be possible to trade with some of these people? Perhaps he could negotiate trading agreements with one of the semi-autonomous sheiks of the Sus – the province of Morocco which ran along the southern edge of the Atlas from the barren coast in Agadir. In Tangier, Robert and Gabrielle made friends with the Times correspondent, Walter Harris, who encouraged Robert's plans, and offered to get some information about the area for him.

Robert and Gabrielle returned slowly through Spain, and Robert spent some time at Salamanca, near Valladolid, a hundred miles north-west of Madrid, where he was able to inspect the most important documents for his South American research, the Archive of the Indies.

He came south again to meet Gabrielle in Madrid, where he wrote to his new friend, Will Rothestein, to tell him, "Goodbye, I am just starting for a delicious day of doing nothing, with alacrity." No-one who has not run an estate of ten thousand acres, such as Gartmore, could appreciate what Robert meant by "doing nothing."

He received a letter, forwarded from Gartmore, from a group of Labour supporters in Aberdeen, asking if he would stand again for Parliament as their candidate. He quickly wrote back, "It is very kind of the Aberdeen people to object to my retiring into private life. Still my mind is made up. I diagnose the Labour or Socialist movement in England and Scotland to be very near collapse, the same vices, foibles, and failings which it has taken the Whigs and Tories many generations to become perfect in, the Labourists and Socialists have brought to perfection, and with apparent ease, in six years."

Robert found the warmth of Morocco and Spain helped to oil his pen, and he wrote prolifically for many journals and pamphlets while travelling with Gabrielle that summer. The British Empire was worrying him more and more; in one of his articles he wrote: "Our flag waves on over an empire reaching from north to south, from east to west; it will soon wave over every island hitherto ungrabbed, on every sterile desert and fever-haunted swamp as yet unclaimed; even over the sealer amongst the icebergs."

Now he started to write in earnest, and as soon as he had got back to Gartmore he returned to his book on the district of Menteith. Gabrielle was anxious that Robert's first should be a success, for she was convinced he could write exceptionally well, with a style that was all his own, and, if he did well with this book, he would have a settled literary career. He might even turn out a book a year.

The book *was* a success; Robert and Gabrielle had both finished writing about the two things most dear to each of them, and now they were at a loose end.

That winter they wrote a joint book of their recent adventure and in 1896 Adam and Charles Black of London published *Father Archangel of Scotland* by G. and R. B. Cunninghame Graham. Their styles were amazingly complementary; Gabrielle providing a soothing narrative which dripped like honey from her pen, while Robert always seemed to be telling his readers a funny story, just as a raconteur at a dinner makes witty remarks to his fellow-guests after the port. His story had frequently interrupted asides, for his mind would wander as he scribbled and, with a chuckle, he would suddenly think "Why shouldn't I share that with the people who are going to read the book?"

Robert's literary friends loved the book, but the general public was not so sure. Gabrielle's essays were more in keeping with what they usually read, and did not offend their own thoughts on life in general. Robert, on the other hand, would lead them gently along the same path, and then suddenly rush them up a mountain of controversy or into a forest of thorny criticism and across a frozen waste of irony. They were not quite sure that they really liked this new writer who almost seemed to be teasing them. And yet he also teased himself, for he said in his preface, "The articles which follow resemble a crowd of people at a railway junction, all rushing to and fro, without connection save only the labels on their luggage. But these articles have something in common after all, for they treat chiefly of Spain or Spanish America. Both Spain and Spanish America are little written of in England."

From this first book of essays published in 1896, Robert was to go on writing a book nearly every year for another forty years, and this preface set the style in which he would always write – a style which showed a strange antagonism towards his readers, making the reading public ill at east, and delighting his fellow writers.

Garnett collected some of Robert's essays for Fisher Unwin's paperback series called *The Overseas Library*, and he was determined to have

John Lavery's equestrian portrait of Robert as a gaucho, riding his Argentine horse Pampa, for a frontispiece in the new book, *The Ipané*.

But Robert could not give himself entirely over to writing. He was still far too active. Gabrielle had gone back to Spain for more research, and he needed a final adventure, and he already had an idea for this adventure.

His literary friends were overjoyed that Graham was quite blatantly writing in his essays and prefaces about "you, the readers" and "us, the writers," but they knew that his attitude was not likely to endear him to his public, so they were not surprised when his book sold only reasonably well, and was not exactly acclaimed by the public as a masterpiece.

The writers themselves had no doubt that Robert Cunninghame Graham wrote better than any of them. He was the greatest of them all, they said. Ford Madox Ford was later to say of him, "He was the most brilliant writer of our day." Frank Harris, the editor of the *Saturday Review*, who had already published a good many of Robert's articles, said of him, "In his stories are the painter's eye and a superb painter's talent. One or two of his sketches of Paris life de Maupassant would gladly have signed, but in spite of their mastery, his best work is found in pictures of Spanish South America or of Scotland, the land of his heart and home."

CHAPTER XXVII

In October, 1897, Robert was getting ready for what was to be his final adventure on horseback before the end of the century. This time he would be riding through the rocks and sand of the Atlas Mountains instead of the pampa or the chaparral. His destination was to be the 'forbidden' city of Tarudant, and the first part of his journey was to be by sea to Mogador. From there he would go on horseback through a mountain pass, starting at a place called Imintanout, and going to Tarudant by Bibouan.

Tarudant was a city in the province of the Sus, rarely visited by Europeans and of which no definite account existed by any traveller of repute. All Robert's friends in Morocco told him that it would be quite impossible to reach Tarudant in European clothes, for the Ruler would never allow him, a Christian, to enter the Moslem city. It was agreed that Robert should don the disguise of a Turkish doctor, travelling with his *taleb*, or scribe. If he was to be a doctor, then he must have medicines, so his stock was made up for him by a local chemist, who provided quinine, mercury, some Seidlitz powders,[14] eye wash, laudanum and calomel.[15]

Robert's two companions on the trip were Hassan Suleiman Lutaif, a Syrian who was to act as interpreter, and Haj Mohammed el Swani, a Moor of the Riff pirate breed, short, strong, black-bearded, and with a turned-up moustache. El Haj was to be Robert's guide.

They acquired some mules and a muleteer called Ali, who had no idea where they were going, and when he was eventually told, took fright, but was eventually persuaded to travel with them in order to keep an eye on his mules to ensure that they were well treated.

Before leaving Mogador they tried on their Moorish clothes, which made the Syrian look exactly like a biblical figure on the front of a missionary journal, and transformed Robert completely into a man from Fez. This being so, they decided to drop the idea of his being a Turkish

---

[14] A laxative.
[15] A fungicide and insecticide.

doctor, and say nothing about who he was, as the passers-by would probably think he was a travelling *Sherif*. Looking at himself in the looking-
glass, Robert was much amused to see that he really did look completely
Moorish – it was not just the clothes, but it seemed that his type and
colouring were exactly right for the role too.

For twenty-nine dollars Robert purchased a good horse with saddle
and bridle thrown in, and was ready to set out.

He was dressed all in white, with a blue cloak to cover it all, a fez and
turban, head duly shaved, yellow slippers, a pair of horseman's boots
(called *temag* by the Arabs) buttoned up the back with green silk buttons,
embroidered down the side with silk and silver thread, and a leather bag
to sling across the shoulders and act as a pocket.

A little tent was packed on a mule, and their cooking utensils consisted of a kettle, an iron pot, a brass tray, a pewter German teapot, and
six small glasses from which to drink the green tea flavoured with mint
and made as sweet as syrup. They left Mogador on 12th October and
rode two hundred miles into the mountains. It had taken them eight
days. Suddenly, just as they were almost in sight of the pass through the
mountains to Tarudant, a troop of well-armed tribesmen came galloping
down from the Caid of Kintafi's castle, to seize their bridles and to take
them prisoner.

At first Robert thought they might manage to bluff their way out of
the situation, but it soon became apparent that the Caid had no intention
of letting them go until he had made sure why they were heading for the
forbidden city of Tarudant. During their long wait they were well fed
with couscous and meat cut up and stewed with pumpkins. For the first
few days the rain poured down incessantly, which added to their feeling
of failure and misery.

At last the rain stopped and Robert was able to stroll out of the tent
and sit on a large stone under an olive tree to think about the situation
and enjoy the view. They were in a magnificent amphitheatre of hills
with snowy mountains towering overhead and, just at the angle which the
Wad el N'fiss made (after the first five miles of its course) lay the Azib
of El Kintafi.

On one side the castle wall ran sheer down into the stony riverbed. From the top of Ouichidan there was a spring held sacred by the Berbers, and a view of a distant Tarudant and Morocco City.

Three other captives were camping in large ornamented tents on the castle M*aidan* besides them. They turned out to be three Caids from the Sus who were also waiting for an audience with their captor.

Seeing how patient the three *Sherifs* were, Robert felt he must be equally patient, but he found that he was getting more and more frustrated.

One evening the Caid's secretary came to see him; a quiet, handsome, literary man, who sat and talked about books for a long time in a most civilised manner. Several more days followed, while they walked up and down the *Maidan*, smoked, wrote, read the poetry of el Faridi and an Arabic version of the Psalms, and watched the Caid's horses being driven to the water to bathe and drink.

Robert was never dull as long as there were horses in sight, but he began to wonder if the Caid was playing with them, and intended to have them killed eventually.

At last, after waiting for ten days or more, Robert was shown into the presence of the Caid and found him sitting on a red saddle cloth, with his legs resting on a sheepskin and cushions at his back, in a room containing a small trunk-shaped box (presumably stuffed with gold), a Belgian single-barrelled nickel-plated breech-loading gun hung upon a nail, and a double-barrelled English gun from the city they called Londres, or Windres, in the "Isle of Mists."

The Caid himself was about forty years old, thick-set and dark-skinned, with a close black beard trimmed to a double point, and rather small eyes.

By race and language he was a Berber, but he spoke Arabic tolerably fluently and wore the clean white garb of an Arab Sheikh, made of the finest wool.

The audience lasted for two hours, during which time everything was discussed by both sides with perfect courtesy and long flowery speeches. It seemed that the Caid was suspicious of Robert's trip to Tarudant, and wondered if he was spying for the Globe Venture Syndicate, who were

known to want to open up direct trade in that area.   Why had they
dressed like Moors, why had they no letter from the Sultan?

After talking round the subject for a while longer, Robert let slip that
he reverenced all governments, having once been a member of the great
council of "our Empire," which statement impressed the Caid enormously. From that moment Robert knew that the Caid would, all in his
good time, come round to releasing this important traveller from
Londres. First, however, the Caid was not going to lose a captive
audience to whom he could relate the story of his latest exploits against
rebel tribes in the Sus, in the process of which he had been badly
wounded. Robert now saw that the Caid did indeed have a severely
injured leg.

In the mountains near Thelata-el-Jacoub, at the height of a foray
against wild tribesmen who were in revolt, the Caid's beautiful white
horse had been injured, and the Caid had dismounted and walked through
a rain of bullets to take his horse to safety, even though he was now
wounded himself. Robert could not but respect a man who had not hesi-
tated for a second to sacrifice his life to save his favourite horse.

The Caid was still suffering, for he had received a ball in the thigh.
He suddenly asked Robert if he could remove the ball, so that he could
ride his horses once again. Robert longed to be able to say yes, and give
himself the chance of becoming a hero, but he knew the operation would
be totally beyond him. Instead, he suggested contacting a good English
doctor he knew in Morocco City, who was a qualified surgeon. The Caid
accepted Robert's offer gratefully.

Suddenly there was a change in the treatment they received from the
Caid's minions. They were now guests of honour, Robert had passed the
test with flying colours, and in the process had learnt a great deal of
interest about this horseman and fighter, half-independent of the Sultan,
leading his own troops and dispensing his own justice. He was a descendant of those great Arab Emirs who sprang from the sands of Africa and
of Arabia, who built the Alhambra and the Alcazar, who gave the world
the Arab horse and the curb bit, and who kept alive the remnants of
Greek philosophy in Cordoba and in Toledo when all the rest of Europe
had lost its way and grovelled in darkness.

That evening, the Caid sent a sheep to be barbecued for Robert, Swani and Mohammed-el-Hosein. The Caid had not allowed them to pursue their journey to Tarudant, for he said he felt responsible for their safety and feared for their lives. But now that Robert had spoken to this great chieftain, he felt that in itself had made the journey worth while.

As he wrapped himself in his djellabah to sleep that night, gorged with mutton, Robert smiled wryly as he realised that, yet again, his adventure had ended in apparent failure.

First there had been the trip to Argentina as a boy, when he thought he was about to make his fortune as an *estanceiro*, but found himself driving cattle across the pampas as a gaucho while his partners happily took to the bottle.

Then Paraguay – his dream of the *yerba maté* trade, and the colonisation of an area beside the river Paraná (a dream extinguished by men of business in the City of London, who sat in stuffy rooms and demolished young men's enterprises).

Next his plan to sell horses from Uruguay to the Brazilian cavalry and his cattle-farming project in the Bahia Blanca – two more failures.

Finally the trip to Texas with Gabrielle in the hope of buying a ranch – failure once more. Was his whole life a failure? Surely if it was, he would not be feeling so contented. What was "failure" anyway? Did every project have to have an "end-product" to succeed? Perhaps not. Through these adventures he had learnt so much about life, far more than most men of his age. Practically every year of his life since the age of ten had been filled with new experiences, new relationships, new sadnesses and new happinesses.

Next morning Robert rode out proudly across the desert with an escort of Berber horsemen who had been sent to escort the Caid's honoured guest safely on his way.

Soon he would be back again with Gabrielle and his mother, the two people he loved best in the world. Soon he would see Charlie and his children, little Uff and four-year-old Angus, who might one day inherit dear old Gartmore, if Robert could keep the place going for him. But first there were farewells to be made to the faithful pair who had shared his adventures, Swani and Mohammed-el-Hosein, who were riding ahead of him on their mules towards the flat white roofs of Mogador.

As they clattered over the cobbles into Mogador that day in November 1897, Robert was unaware that his capture by the Caid of Kintafi was already being spoken about in London clubs, with an occasional sigh of envy, by desk-bound men. He was also unaware that his friend, G. K. Chesterton, was telling his literary and artistic friends that Robert Bontine Cunninghame Graham, traveller, politician and writer, had no need for conventional achievements, for his whole life was about the "adventure of being Cunninghame Graham." That in itself was enough, an inspiration to young men of the future, a link with the chivalrous figures of the past. Robert, when he later heard of Chesterton's remark, agreed entirely.

CHAPTER XXVIII

On 24th May 1900 Robert was forty-eight years old. He still felt in his prime of life, fit, active, with a mind brimming over with ideas. But he knew that failure still dogged his footsteps, and he was still smarting from the most painful failure of them all – he had been forced to sell Gartmore. All his brave ideas had come to nothing; the castle in the air which he had pursued throughout those early years had melted into vapour. For Gartmore had indeed been his castle in the air, and it was only when he thought he had it in his grasp that it had begun to slip away from him.

Since 1884, he and Gabrielle had worked hard to save the old place which they loved so much. But he soon began to realise that it was not just a matter of hard work, or even leadership. It was all about mending fences and roofs, about getting the best prices for animals at the auction marts, about rents, and, most of all, about getting ends to meet so that they could go on living at his favourite house of all, Gartmore. Robert was still burdened with the debt he had inherited from his father and grandfather, and an enormous amount of the income he received from both Ardoch and Gartmore seemed to disappear in allowances to all his Graham relations.

Fortunately he still had Ardoch, his ancestors' "neat wee house on the Clyde," to which they could move. It was small and elegant and would be perfectly adequate, this *cottage ornée* that was built in 1790 as a guest-house for Jamaican friends.

Gabrielle looked up from the farm accounts and sighed unhappily.

"We can't do it, Lob. It's no use. We'll just have to put Gartmore on the market. We could do up "Doughty Deeds"' little house at Ardoch and live there instead. After all, there are still seven farms at Ardoch, and we get far higher rents from them than we do from the Gartmore farms. We'll have enough to live on, and we'll be free of all this worry."

Robert was not sure he wanted to be free of what Gabrielle described as the "worry" of Gartmore. It was his heritage. It would be like turning a difficult child out into the snow. He would be abandoning the home of the Grahams of Gartmore, the place that meant stability for the family, even when they travelled abroad. It was their HOME.

Gabrielle was far from well, and he did not want her to know that this was the most agonising decision of his life. He knew that she needed all her will-power to keep the flame burning that would flicker on even when she was dragged down by debilitating coughs and fevers. This had to be his own decision, and his alone.

Robert touched her cheek, as he rose to his feet. He would go for a ride. He could always think more clearly on horseback. Jumping on Pampa, Robert rode off through the snow. The black Argentine whinnied to Gabrielle's Iceland pony, Talla, as they trotted past a rushy park where the pony was grazing.

Cantering in the cold wind Robert could imagine he was back on the pampas. That had been the best time of his life, with no worries or responsibility, and no terrible decisions to make.

* * * * * *

A year later Gartmore was sold. Robert received £126,000 for the estate and, ironically, this was exactly the same figure as the debt he had inherited on his father's death. At least he no longer had this particular albatross round his neck. The Caysers, who had bought the place, seemed nice people. Old Mr. Cayser had started life as a cabin-boy and had risen to be a great shipping man in Glasgow. They were *nouveau riche*, but thoroughly respectable and with a great sense of responsibility about their commitment to the tenant farmers at Gartmore. Robert knew they would improve the place and look after his people kindly.

Missy and Charlie had been very sympathetic and understanding when he told them about the terrible decision he had to make. Gabrielle wrote to her mother-in-law to say she had tried her hardest to keep their dear home going, and that she was heart-broken that they had failed. Missy and Gabrielle were now the best of friends, and Robert often remembered the wise words of the old judge, Mr. Wright, who had told Robert to be patient, that they would eventually learn to love each other, for Robert's sake.

In 1901, Robert and Gabrielle moved into the house at Ardoch, which they had managed to take back from its tenant. After "Doughty Deeds'" death at the end of the eighteenth century, the little *cottage ornée* had passed from one tenant to the next, and Robert was the first Cunninghame Graham laird ever to live there.

Gabrielle thought the house was delightful, with the lawns sweeping down to the shore of the Clyde, and a beautiful garden which she was longing to get round to improving. At Gartmore they had to give up the old walled garden, and Gabrielle loved gardening and was very knowledgeable about plants and flowers.

For Robert the two things he liked best about Ardoch were that he could see his childhood home, Finlaystone, straight across the river, and that he could watch the ships gliding down the deep-water channel from the Broomielaw, just as he had done as a little boy. There was always something to watch from the windows of Ardoch.

For a time, Gabrielle's health seemed to improve. Every winter, from January to March, Robert and Gabrielle went to Spain and on to Tangier, which was rapidly becoming a popular wintering place. It was a great deal cheaper than the South of France, to which the rich people were now flocking, or Biarritz, which the Prince of Wales had made so fashionable, and Robert and Gabrielle knew a great many of the artists and wirters who went there each year. Robert had been painted by both Lavery and Rothenstein, who were now close friends and thus often travelled out there together.

Charlie had now been made a groom-in-waiting to the King. As Prince of Wales he had always had a soft spot for Milly when her father was their local parson at Sandringham. He was a regular visitor to their house, as well as being godfather to young Angus. Queen Victoria had died in 1901, having been on the throne since 1819.

Charlie knew that their friendship with King Edward VII (as he now was) was entirely thanks to his old friend Prince Louis of Battenberg, who had been particularly helpful ten years earlier, just after Charlie's marriage, when Louis had promptly recommended him for the post of Deputy Chief Inspector of the Royal National Lifeboat Institution after he came out of the Navy. This job was to give Charlie another twenty years of involvement with the sea, and he found it much to his taste.

It was in 1906 when Gabrielle decided to go for a short trip to Spain with Peregrina after a very wet, cold July at Ardoch, hoping the break would do her good. Robert was deeply worried. Gabrielle had not been at all well all summer, which was unusual as she normally seemed to be so much better in the summer months, when the sun shone from time to time. Robert knew that the Scottish climate had never suited Gabrielle, and now they were living at Ardoch it seemed to rain even more than it had at Gartmore. They had laughed together over the solemn remark made by one of the Ardoch tenant farmers, "If yez can see doun the Clyde tae Greenock, ut's gaen tae rain; and if yez can *no* see Greenock, ut's rainin'."

Robert was busy on his next book, *A Vanished Arcadia*, about the Guarani Indians in Paraguay, so he did not miss Gabrielle as much as usual. He had not heard anything from her, so hoped that "no news was good news."

It was therefore even more of a shock when he received a telegram from Peregrina, asking him to come to Hendaye, where Gabrielle was dangerously ill. Robert arrived a day later, after a frantic journey by train, channel steamer, and another long train journey through France to Hendaye, on the border of France and Spain.

He arrived late at night and took a cab to a small hotel where Gabrielle and Peregrina were staying.

His beloved Chid was barely conscious when he arrived, but she was able to give him a faint smile before sinking into a coma. Robert knew she was dying, there was nothing he could do. At least she now knew he was with her, as he stroked her limp, cold little hand. How could he stop her from leaving him? He was distraught.

The faithful Peregrina had been attending her since she fell ill, and together they nursed her for her final hours. Robert had known for the past few years that Gabrielle's chest was giving her increased trouble every year, but it had never occurred to him that she was so near the end. She was only forty-eight.

The doctor's certificate announced that she had died of dysentery and diabetes. But Robert knew that her body had finally collapsed under the strain of the activity she subjected it to, being far from strong and with regular attacks of bronchitis. Smoking cigarettes had not helped, for she had become a chain-smoker since her days in the saddle in Texas and Mexico. There was probably an element of nicotine poisoning in the final breakdown of her physical health, perhaps even cancer.

It was early September when her body was brought back to Inchmahome, where she had always asked to be buried. The trees were glowing with colour on the island, and the grass was covered with fallen chestnuts from the old stag-headed trees.

Robert rowed across to the island with the old grave-digger to give him a hand. He knew Gabrielle would have liked that. When the grave was dug, in the ruined cloisters of the old abbey, Robert sat and smoked a cigarette. He remembered Gabrielle laughingly saying, many years earlier, "If I die before you, Lob, come and smoke a cigarette on my grave *de cuando en cuando*!"

The next day was the funeral. Robert had managed to get Chid's brother, the Rev. Francis Horsfall, to come and take the service on the island in the Lake of Menteith. For the past few years they had been in contact with some of her brothers and sisters again, and they often saw her sister, Grace, who wrote novels under the name "George Stevenson." Chid had told Robert how she and her brother had made a first attempt at running away together from home when they were quite small. But it had poured with rain, and they had only got a few miles before their father came riding after them, and they were "recaptured", dripping and in disgrace!

It was not that life at home was unhappy, although the surgeon, their father, was a typically Victorian parent, strict and forbidding; it was more that Gabrielle loved adventures, and her younger brother was often press-ganged, quite willingly, into her various enterprises.

Francis Horsfall, this younger brother who had joined in her child-hood adventures, was now a clergyman, so it was right and proper that he should take his sister's funeral service. Missy came up from London to be there, with Charlie and Milly. Robert, in his inconsolable grief, was comforted to know that they had all come to accept Gabrielle in the end, and that Missy had grown to love and admire her daughter-in-law.

Robert was astonished at the enormous throng of Gartmore emp-loyees and other local people who attended the funeral, and by the many obituaries in all the newspapers. His beloved Chid, always so unsure of herself, had become a celebrity in her own right.

CHAPTER XXIX

The next few years were desperately lonely ones for Robert. He and Chid had been everything to each other. It was this certainty that they were right for each other, especially in their middle age, that had made it possible for them to go on trips alone, one without the other. For there always seemed to be a strong spiritual closeness, even when one of them was in Scotland or London, and the other in Spain. That was the essence of their marriage.

Missy, his mother, became quite worried about Robert. He looked thin and miserable, and was so debilitated by his unhappiness that he did not even have the energy to travel, or to write books, something that he had been doing extremely successfully since he came out of Parliament.

The year after Gabrielle's death he went down with diphtheria, and was extremely ill. But his strong constitution pulled him through. Missy took him off to Rome with her for the winter, where he was able to convalesce in the warm sunshine.

By now Robert had already published eleven books, mainly reminiscences and histories of South America and Spain, and quite a number of Scottish sketches and stories, which appealed particularly to his writer friends. Heinemann had also published his three full-length books, two South American histories, *A Vanished Arcadia* and *Hernando de Soto*; and his book about his adventure in the Atlas Mountains, which he had called *Mogreb-el-Acksa*. This was the book which his friend Joseph Conrad liked best of all. In writing to thank Robert for the copy he had sent him, Conrad said:

"The book arrived by the evening post. I dropped everything, and rushed at it, paper-knife in hand. A man staying here" (later identified as H. G. Wells) "has been reading it over my shoulder. We have been shouting, slapping our legs, leaping up, stamping about. The individuality of the book is amazing – I do not know how really to express the kind of intellectual exultation your book has awakened in me, and I will not stay to try – I am in too much of a hurry to get back to the book. My applause, slaps on the back, salaams, benedictions, cheers.

Take what you like best of these, what you think most expressive. Or take them all. I can't be too demonstrative.

"Ever yours with yells – Conrad."

At the same time, Robert received two more letters, both brief and to the point: one from his friend Max Beerbohm who said he had just finished reading the book and "I firmly demand another." And one from Arnold Bennett from Paris, which merely said, "Dear Mr. Graham. You do me good. Thank you. Yours sincerely, Arnold Bennett."

George Bernard Shaw was already talking to him about his idea of turning this marvellous story into a play. *Captain Brassbound's Conversion* was soon to follow, with Shaw's explanation of its origin in his preface to *Plays for Puritans*.

In one of Robert's first collections of stories he had included one or two that were being favourably compared with Maupassant's *contes*. Robert was gradually gaining a reputation as one of the most talented short-story writers of his day. Frank Harris, the editor of the *Saturday Review* for which Robert wrote regularly, said of his writing:

"In his stories are the painter's eye and a superb painter's talent. One or two of his sketches of Paris life de Maupassant would gladly have signed, but, in spite of their mastery, his best work is found in pictures of Spanish South America, or of Scotland, the land of his heart and home."

John Galsworthy wrote to tell Robert that, "your philosophy is one of the most valued things walking, or rather, riding about amongst us nowadays." Perhaps it was Robert's philosophy of life they all envied after all.

But this was surely an inherited thing, the combination of the Spanish and the Scots outlook on life. All these men seemed to want to draw on Robert's inner strength and vitality. He was far too kind and courteous to turn them away, so his correspondence daily grew larger. Sometimes he laughed, realising that all they really seemed to need was to unburden themselves, for they could hardly get much comfort from his brief replies in handwriting they could not even decipher!

There were in addition still many radical politicians who wrote to him and kept in touch. Nearly all the Fabians admired him greatly, although he had never been one himself; and the remnant of William Morris's disciples were still looking to him for a lead. Walter Crane had written to Robert when Gabrielle died to say, "I remember Mrs. Graham's spirit and courage in the stormy times of the late eighties when the Socialist movement was struggling for life. The part you played will never be forgotten."

Other friends from his political past continued to keep in touch – Hyndman, Nevinson, and most of all Keir Hardie, who had, too, written on Gabrielle's death to say, "We have been through so much together, and in the days gone by have been so much to each other, that a feeling of kinship has grown up in my mind, which almost makes your griefs mine also."

His political colleagues, Hyndman, had grown as disillusioned as Robert himself, and wrote in 1911 to say, "I do not mind confessing to you that, between ourselves, I do at times feel saddened and discouraged at the outcome of all our efforts in the direction of improving the lot of the great mass of our people."

The only man amongst the writers and politicians of the day who did not thoroughly appreciate Robert's vital personality and humour was Henry James. Robert had gone to see him in Rye one day, and told the great man on his arrival that he had been quite unable to find anyone who could direct him to his house. Henry James was not amused. Robert could not bear smugness, and probably made the remark on purpose to annoy the intense American writer.

Robert still kept in touch with many of the young writers and artists he had met at his mother's house in the 1880s and 1890s. Ford Madox Ford was one of these, also the two young artists Will Rothenstein and John Lavery, both of whom often travelled to Spain and Tangier with him in the winter, to paint landscapes and to enjoy the amusing life of the English and Spanish community in Tangier.

Joseph Crawhall often joined them. Like Lavery, he was another of the artists of the now-famous "Glasgow School" most of whom had been in Paris with Robert in the late 1870s, many of them studying with the distinguished Swiss teacher, Gleyre, who had numbered amongst his pupils Monet, Sisley and Renoir.

Rothenstein and Lavery had both painted superb portraits of Robert, as a fencer and as a gaucho respectively; and Crawhall gave Robert two delightful sketches in watercolour showing a polo-player before and after death – first taking part in a chukka on *earth*, and then in *Heaven*, with winged horses and even a winged ball!

Robert continued to go regularly to Tangier with his friends from 1907 (when he was recovering from his serious attack of diphtheria) until 1911 when he first met Toppie Dummett.

Nineteen hundred and eleven was also the year his famous black Argentine horse, Pampa, died – another heartbreak for Robert, who loved that horse better than any horse he had ever owned.

Robert already knew most of the residents in Tangier, and liked them for their eccentricities. His favourite was the man they called "Bibi" Carleton, the son of a good English family living in Tangier in reduced circumstances, who had sent their son to a Franciscan school in the town. Being brought up in Tangier, Bibi had acquired Arabic so perfectly that, when dressed as a Moor, the Arabs themselves thought he was one of their own race.

But when he wore his cord riding breeches, a white silk shirt, brown leggings and a broad-brimmed grey felt hat, he looked entirely English. Often he would be absent from the town for days on end, and Robert knew he was off on his iron grey horse, given to him by a well-known cattle stealer, to visit his friends, the many important Kaids, who ruled their own little kingdoms in the Atlas Mountains. Everyone knew Bibi. Eventually, by some enlightened stroke of genius from a maverick at the Foreign Office, Bibi was appointed British consular agent in Alcazar-el-Kebir, and was consequently known as "Consu" by one and all, as he sat at the door of an old Moorish house, suitably dressed in a brown jellaba, his bare feet shoved into yellow Moorish slippers, administering justice.

Another friend was Walter Harris, the Times correspondent, who knew the area like the back of his hand, and had helped Robert to plan his own adventurous, if unsuccessful, expedition to Tarudant.

A third man Robert got to know and like in Tangier was Bernadino de Velasco, Duke de Frias, hereditary Grand Constable of Castile, Count of Oropesa, of Haro, and a Grandee of Spain. Robert used to say that when his friend walked into a room, he looked like a young thoroughbred amongst a bunch of carthorses. He had started life with great estates stretching half over Spain from Cordoba to La Rioja, with a palace in

Madrid, a villa in Biarritz, and the beautiful old La Casa del Cordon in Burgos.

"Dino," as his friends called him, had an Irish mother, the daughter of Michael Balfe who had composed the *Bohemian Girl* in 1843, and he had been sent to Eton, where he spoke both English and Spanish indifferently, but French, Portuguese and Arabic superbly. He played the violin with talent, having inherited his grandfather's gift – Balfe having been a child prodigy – and was the best horseman Robert had ever known, "with hands that only nature gives and that no teaching and all the practice in the world cannot supply."

He was also a good shot, an excellent fencer, and a tireless walker. But, as Robert was later to say, "With all these gifts, nature had omitted to endow him with a sense of responsibility." He had soon got rid of all his inherited wealth and possessions at the gaming table. Old-fashioned Spaniards would say of him that it was lucky El Duque had not been born a woman for he was unable to say "No."

Dino married an English wife, eventually, who was head over heels in love with him and was to remain so, in spite of his many infidelities, his long absences and his perfect disregard of everything that marriage should imply. Both he and his wife were brilliant riders, and his wife would often join him when he went out pigsticking.

They lived in the New York Hotel on the beach at Tangier, a hostelry that had all the discomforts of a Spanish *fonda,* and whose proprietor got used to being promised their rent when the Duke "received his olive money from his Spanish estates," which, when it did arrive, went of course straight to the gaming tables instead.

Dino was always taking part in mad schemes in many different countries, convinced that this time he was going to make his fortune. Eventually his wife decided to go back to Spain to "shepherd" his estates. In due course he joined her at Madrid, where he became a close friend of King Alfonso XIII. But his wife hated Madrid and eventually returned to England to educate their daughter, leaving Dino to live at one of his decaying family properties called El Deheson, with a girl inappropriately called Modesta, whom he had met on a street corner one night in Toledo. There he ended his days, still speaking of his wife and daughter with respect and affection, living much as Don Quixote had lived, with a thin horse, plenty of equally thin greyhounds and a brace of ferrets.

To Robert, the Duke de Frias was always to be his idea of Don Quixote – a nobleman with a leaky house who kept his looks to the last, proving the truth of the old Spanish saw, "Figure and genius to the grave." Robert was to love the man because he glimpsed a mirror image; in his own case he was the man who might have been Earl of Menteith, living in his leaky castle in Scotland, the last of his race, passing the remaining years of his life, if not exactly happily at least (to a great extent) absolved from care. Robert always thought of the Duke de Frias as his Spanish counterpart, although in many ways their lifestyles were totally different.

* * * * * *

For three years after Gabrielle died, Robert found himself unable to write a thing. He had lost his inspiration. His life became aimless as he travelled from place to place in search of some new purpose in life. Both Ardoch and his house in Basil Street, which he and Gabrielle had acquired after the sale of Gartmore, were lonely and depressing after Chid's death. He could not settle.

But in 1909 Edward Garnett, Robert's literary mentor, persuaded him to publish another collection of stories, to be called *Faith*, and to be followed in quick succession by two more volumes, in 1910 and 1912, *Hope* and *Charity*, all three published by Duckworth.

Garnett knew that Robert was still grieving for Gabrielle, and probably for Gartmore, too. But he wrote encouraging letters to Robert to get him to start writing again. He had so much talent that he must not let it go to waste.

"I admire. I admire fully and deeply! Your method is so much your own that nobody will ever come after you – and you will remain alone. I see the artist you have concealed so long under the man of action, the artist that is most important now."

Another word of encouragement came from Robert's Argentine friend, W. H. Hudson, who dedicated his book *El Ombú* to him, calling him *Singularisimo escritor ingles* and going on to say, "...who has lived with, and knows, even to the marrow, as they themselves would say, the horsemen of the Pampas: and who alone of European writers has rendered something of the vanishing colour of that remote life."

Conrad dedicated his book *Typhoon* to Robert, with a letter to him in which he said:

"Don't let your dedicatory obligation interfere with your peace of mind. Frankly I am more than repaid by the satisfaction of seeing your name at the head of my book. It is a public declaration of our communion in more perhaps than mere letters, and I don't mind owning my pride in it. I want to talk to you of the work I am engaged in now. I hardly dare avow my audacity – but I am placing it in South America, in a republic I call 'Costaguana'." This was Conrad's first reference to the most famous of all his novels, *Nostromo*. Much of it was to be drawn from Robert's own experience in Asunción, as Conrad always freely admitted.

Garnett was still trying to persuade Robert to write from the heart. After receiving a letter about Gartmore from Robert, he wrote back:

"Your words about Gartmore give me all that feeling of those things in side you which you find it so impossible to express. It is an instinct in you perhaps not to express those depths, but Turanev did, and that is why we love him."

Many other writers were attracted to Robert's personality, and he was invited to visit Thomas Hardy, John Galsworthy, and all the litterati of his day. Oscar Wilde clung to Robert as being a fellow "jailbird," slightly to Robert's embarrassment, as Oscar's wife and children had been kindly looked after by Robert's own first cousin, Adrian Hope, while he was in Reading Jail. Oscar obviously thought of Robert as a 'part of the family'. (Adrian's mother was his father's sister.) But Robert wished Oscar would learn to stand on his own feet, instead of moping round wanting sympathy from all his friends.

In 1911 Robert's mother introduced him to two young women who were friends of hers, a delightful pair of sisters, Mrs. Dummett, a young widow, and her sister Louisa Mieville. Missy was sure that these two charming young ladies would give back to Robert some of the female companionship that he had so greatly missed since Gabrielle died. Robert was soon riding in Rotten Row with the attractive Mrs. Dummett.

Her father was French, Jean-Louis Mieville, and her mother Scots, Elizabeth Roberts.

Missy was delighted that her idea had worked and, being a family who always gave each other silly nicknames, especially when they were fond of each other, Missy was even more delighted when Robert came to her one day in his riding clothes, happy and flushed after his ride in the park, laughingly telling his mother, "I really do like that girl, she rides so well. She looked very sweet this morning wearing a smart little top-hat. I told her I shall call her 'Toppie' from now on!"

And so she became 'Toppie' Dummett and a friendship started which would last for the rest of his life. They told each other later that neither of them would ever remarry, they had both had such very happy marriages before they met. Toppie's husband had been killed in the Boer War, and she was exactly sixteen years younger than Robert.

She was just the person to cheer him up at a sad and lonely time in his life, while he was still handsome and immensely attractive to the opposite sex.

They quickly found that they had mutual friends in Wilfred and Lady Anne Blunt, who bred Arab horses, and this is where Toppie had learnt to ride lively horses with such great style. They frequently went together to stay at the Blunts' Sussex stud-farm, and all four became close friends.

They soon found they had many mutual friends in London, too.

It was to be shortly after they had met that Pampa had died, having been given a happy retirement by Robert, 'out to grass' on farmland near Liphook where he and Gabrielle had once lived. That was another sorrow for him; Pampa would always be the best horse of his life. But Toppie was now a great comfort to him; realising what Pampa had been to him, she helped him through this new sadness.

When the war started in 1914, Robert was sent for by the War Office and asked if he would be prepared to go back to South America to buy up horses for the British Army? Robert knew exactly what that meant, and could hardly bear the thought that beautiful horses from the pampas would be exported as 'remounts'; in other words, they would be replacing the horses that were to be killed on the battlefields in this terrible war. The same fate would almost certainly befall the horses he selected for Europe before long.

Nevertheless, it would take him back to his beloved Argentine and to Uruguay, and he would, once more, be among horses, so he was very tempted. The retired cavalry officer at the War Office said kindly to him, "Mr. Graham, we think you are the only person who is exactly cut out for this job, and we would be greatly obliged if you would take it on for us? You will, of course, be working for the British Army, so you will be made an Honorary Colonel."

Robert smiled to himself. Charlie was only a Commander, and he had already served for well over thirty years, in the Royal Navy and the Lifeboat Service, the RNLI. Now Robert was being promoted to Colonel without any service behind him at all! It was a bit ironical, he thought, especially as poor Charlie was not going to be allowed back to sea for the war, having just been told by the doctors that they had discovered that "Commander Cunninghame Graham has a slight heart defect."

He would have to remain a courtier which would please Milly no end. She simply loved their rather grand life, and they had just heard that King George V wanted them to spend some time at Barton Manor, beside Osborne House, so that Charlie could carry out his duties when the Royals were on the Isle of Wight. It was the house which the new king had lived in, as Prince of Wales, with his family before his father, King Edward VII, had died.

Milly was very thrilled at the thought, especially because it had a lovely garden which they would all, including Uff and Angus, enjoy; although Angus was now in the Royal Navy at the age of twenty, and knew that he would soon have to join his new ship, H.M.S. Agincourt.

Angus's sister Olive had now changed her name to the more attractive Olave, but he still called her Uff, or sometimes Wouse. She was now madly in love with another young sailor, Basil Brooke, and they were going to be hastily married before Basil, too, went to join his own ship. Charlie was delighted that his grown-up children were both to be a part of the Royal Navy, in the family tradition, and only prayed that both Angus and Basil would come safely through the war.

* * * * * *

Robert was to spend the whole of the war back in South America, based mainly at Fray Bentos, where horses from all over the pampas were driven, to be inspected and loaded on to cargo ships to join the cavalry regiments in France. Robert could not help thinking sadly that it was to be the horses' *Calvary* (not just the *cavalry*).

In 1917 he was moved to Columbia to find sources of meat for the British Government to be exported to starving Britain. At Cartegena, in Columbia, he received the heartbreaking news that Charlie had died very suddenly in his London house in Warwick Square, of an aneurism of the heart. Robert wrote a distressed letter to his mother next day, knowing that Charlie had been warned about possible heart trouble only a few years earlier when he was turned down for war service with the Royal Navy.

". . . . all I hoped for," he wrote, "was that Charlie might have lived till I got home. He was indeed my 'Pylades,' so different to me – so much better, and yet we understood one another so well. I had no-one here to speak to but a Spanish bullfighter, who was with me when I opened the telegram. I went and walked on the walls at Cartegena and thought of all our life from boyhood at Dr. Bickmore's, and even before that, with Mr. Gulliver, and all kinds of things. Poor dear Lee-Cat, to think of him lying dead in Warwick Square, and me so far off."

His heart lifted somewhat when he received a letter from Colonel Theodore Roosevelt a few days later, addressed to him in "Cartogena de Indias" asking if he would write the life of Colonel Cody, "Buffalo Bill"? In the end Robert's decision was "no" for he knew he could not afford to travel so extensively to complete the necessary research, especially to such a cold country as Canada, where Bill Cody came from. However, he was flattered to find that Theodore Roosevelt had read and enjoyed his own books.

Robert had already met Roosevelt and had even asked him if he could join his Rough Riders a few years earlier, but was told that he was unfortunately slightly too old!

* * * * * *

Robert returned from Colombia at the end of 1917, and a year later the war was over. He moved from his own house in Basil Street to a new house near his mother's in Chester Square, at 79A Elizabeth Street. He wanted to be close to her for the final years of her life, for now he was her only remaining son. She was nearly 90 and he was 65.

During the next eight years he wrote a book a year, partly at Elizabeth Street and partly at Ardoch, where he returned every summer. In the winter he resumed his travels with the Mieville sisters, sometimes taking his niece, Charlie's beautiful daughter 'Olave.' She and Basil Brooke had a small son called 'Bil' (short for Basil).

Robert's nephew, who was his heir, served throughout the war in the Royal Navy, mainly in H.M.S. Agincourt, taking part in his first major combat at the Battle of Jutland. Admiral Jellicoe had a Flag Lieutenant at the time called Commander Herbert Fitzherbert, whose wife was called Rachel. In 1924, Angus married Rachel Fitzherbert's younger sister, Patricia Hanbury.

1925 saw the death of Robert's mother at the age of ninety-seven, and the birth of Angus's son (another Robert, but to be known during his childhood as Robin.)

Robert mourned his mother's loss deeply – she had been a strong and lasting influence in his life, so intelligent, so full of fun, and such a "catalyst" as she brought young writers, artists, musicians and delightful friends like the Mieville sisters together in her house.

She had kept up her interest in the development of the arts right up to the day of her death. Only four years earlier she had given her granddaughter, Olave, a book of contemporary poetry which contained the controversial war poetry of Wilfred Owen, Siegfried Sassoon and Robert Graves, together with the "sea poetry" of young John Masefield. Robert remembered that she had given him a copy of *Omar Khayyam* to take on his voyage to South America with George Mansel in 1876. He laughed as he recalled how George had enjoyed it, probably the first book the bluff sailor had ever read in his life!

The Manchester Guardian of 21st March 1925 carried an obituary of The Honourable Anne Elizabeth Bontine (for she had never changed her name back to Cunninghame Graham after Willy had died).

"Most of the experience possible to women in mortal life had been hers," the author wrote. "We who were enriched by her quality and beauty may linger in admiration that a life exempt neither from sorrow nor shock, nor call for endurance, should have left her in the end with that rare and beautiful presence, that serene courage and understanding. It was upon my first visit to her in Rome years ago that I first found a meaning in the phrase 'a lady of quality'. She maintained at the same time the dignity and poise of an outlived generation, and a welcome and sweetness towards an oncoming and different culture. There was a delicate shrewdness in her gaiety and kindness of conversation, and an innocent pleasure in herself too, and the fact that you found her pleasing. She would tell with enjoyment of her birth at sea on board her father's Flagship, H.M.S. Barham, and how the sailors had said, when her father left his wife and baby ashore at Caracas, 'Aren't we going to be able to keep the *baby*?' She told of the advent of gummed envelopes and how an old Scottish lady of her acquaintance had refused to use 'those *spit-upon* things'; while she herself kept the custom of sealing her envelopes with a little purple wafer. She counted among the chief gains of her life the admiration bestowed upon her by her sons. The tenderness between the beautiful old mother and her son, Mr. Robert Cunninghame Graham, has been among the lovely things which this generation will have to remember."

Another newspaper wrote incredulously, "Does it seem possible that only the day before yesterday died a woman who was the intimate friend and niece of the woman whom William IV wanted to marry? The mother of Mr. Cunninghame Graham had inherited her graceful picturesqueness of speech and manner and bearing, without doubt from her Spanish mother. The cousin and friend of Mrs. Bontine who won the affections of the Sailor King was Baroness Keith and Nairne, who was attached to the household of Princess Charlotte. She married the Comte de Flahaut, aide-de-camp of Napoleon who later became the French Ambassador in London, and she became the grandmother of the present Marquis of Lansdowne. Mrs. Bontine was an Elphinstone of that Scottish family whose first peer fell at Flodden Field, and she married into a family fully as proud and old."

Missy very nearly had her wish to live to be a hundred years old; her second wish was to be buried beside her beloved youngest son, Malise, at Winchester. This request Robert was able to carry out, faithfully and lovingly, in the Churchyard at St. John's, where her mother, Doña Catalina, was also buried.

To hide his own sorrow, Robert immediately set out upon a pilgrimage to the country in which his mother had spent her early childhood, Venezuela. Although he himself was now seventy-three, he still felt young at heart and wanted to have one final adventure on horseback. He knew he must truly look like "the knight of the sorrowful countenance" as he rode upon a skinny, but strong, grey pony; but the old twinkle did not take long to emerge, and he insisted on being photographed in Caracas with his podgy and diminutive Venezuelan guide – Don Quixote and Sancho Panza! Riding over the *llanos* of Venezuela reminded him of the great Argentine pampas, and he vowed to return there within the next few years.

From Venezuela he moved on to Jamaica, to inspect the old Graham plantation at Roaring River which had belonged to "Doughty Deeds" in the eighteenth century, for he now wanted to write the life story of this former laird of Gartmore, with whom he felt so much in common.

In the grounds of the 'great house,' beside a purple bougainvillea, Robert discovered the simple stone which covered the grave of his ancestor Robert Graham's agent, Angus MacBean. MacBean had continued his faithful stewardship of the pimento-producing estate long after Robert had returned to Scotland to take up the reins of his three inherited estates, Gartmore, Ardoch and Finlaystone, and to stand for Parliament as an ardent Whig in support of his friend Charles James Fox. The gravestone in the garden warmed Robert's heart, as he remembered other faithful family servants who had died at their posts, some at Gartmore during his own years as laird.

On his return to Scotland in 1928, Robert found that Angus and Patricia now had a small daughter, Jean, born four days before his own seventy-sixth birthday. He also found an invitation waiting his return, asking him to stand as the Scottish National candidate at the election of the Rector of Glasgow University, against Stanley Baldwin. He had already stood against him once before, in 1914.

Robert's politics had continued to absorb him as they evolved throughout his life. Since 1892 he had twice been asked to stand as a Liberal candidate. He had quickly become disillusioned with the Labour Movement, realising that it was unlikely to achieve his radical ideas, for its members were far too busy bickering amongst themselves.

In 1920 he became President of the Scottish Home Rule Association, but sent a letter of resignation to the secretary, R. E. Muirhead, later that year when he heard that the association had condemned reprisals in Ireland by the Black and Tans.

"Policemen and soldiers are only human," he wrote, "and it is, though not admirable, still not *unnatural* that, when they see their comrades and officers basely assassinated from behind hedges and points of vantage that they occasionally hit back. The recent horrible and cold-blooded murder of fourteen young men, unarmed, in bed, and in some instances under the eyes of their wives, is enough to fill any decent man with horror and indignation. As a Scotchman I detest assassination and despise those who resort to it. I believe no nation was ever freed by recourse to such dastardly methods."

Robert was referring to the "Red Sunday Massacre" of 21st November, 1920, in Ireland.

He soon made his peace with the association once more, however, and was to remain its President until his death in 1936. He felt strongly that Scotland needed to regain her sense of identity if she was to compete in a modern industrial world, and also to raise her morale at a time of looming financial problems in the Depression of 1929.

"The enemies of Scottish Nationalism are not the English," he said, "for they were ever great and generous folk, quick to respond when justice calls. Our real enemies are amongst us, born without imagination."

In company with his fellow nationalists he campaigned for a national parliament, but was heard to mutter with a smile, "Yes, one day we shall have the blessings of a national parliament, with the pleasure of knowing that are taxes are wasted in Edinburgh, instead of in London."[16]

---

[16] Author's note: This has now happened – in my lifetime! The Scottish Parliament was opened by The Queen ("Queen of Scots") on 9th October 2004.

Robert's kinsman, the Duke of Montrose, and he were probably the wisest of the nationalists of the day, realising that although it was desirable to give Scotland a pride in herself through nationalism, this was only a means of making Scotland truly *international,* the goal of all right-thinking men.

Robert was much in demand at the nationalist rallies, and on one occasion he shared a car with a starry-eyed lady who cooed at him, "Is it true, Mr. Graham, that you are the strongest claimant, through your descent from King Robert the Bruce, to the Scottish throne, and might one day be King of Scotland?"

The wicked twinkle came into Robert's eye, and he bowed politely to his companion, saying, "Yes, I believe that is true. And *what* a three weeks that would be!"

Robert lost the election as Rector of Glasgow University by a small minority chiefly, as he told his friends ruefully, because the women all voted for Baldwin as he was known to be a champion of women's rights. They were too young to know that Robert himself had been the first champion of women's suffrage, and women's rights, as early as the 1880s.

"What is important," he once wrote, "is not the actions of a man, which may be caused by circumstances and which, rightly considered, are as immaterial as the atoms dancing in a sunbeam, seen by the eye and not collated by the brain, but what he *thinks,* and more important still, that which is *says* and *writes.*"

One of the earliest things he wrote was the story, published in a collection by Fisher Unwin in 1899 called *The Ipane,* which he called *Un Pelado.* It was the description of the hanging of a Mexican vaquero in La Salle County, Texas, based on a true account he had read in the *San Antonio Daily Express* on Saturday, 15th July, 1886. (He had continued to have the newspaper sent to him, long after he and Gabrielle had returned home from Texas, so as to keep in touch with the 'goings on' in San Antonio.)

The moral to this tale was that the vaquero died with absolute courage and dignity, transcending the dirt, rags and meanness of his earthly

---

This was the superb new building at Holyrood in Edinburgh – we watched the ceremony on the television at Lochinver, Scotland.

existence. All Robert's geese were swans and he was determined that the world should recognise them as such.

Robert was to add at the end of his story, "He was not the first citizen of La Salle who has gone up the golden stair with the assistance of a half-inch rope. Back at the Maverick House, all over now. He had looked pale but showed grit, and in a neat fitting black suit (Dollar Store cut) made an elegant appearance. José stood mighty quiet, and as the City Marshal finished reading the warrant, he slightly shrugged his shoulders and said, "*Muy bien.*"

He was probably the first person (with the exception of Bret Harte) ever to write a "Western", long before the cinema had been invented, or had appreciated the public appeal of "cowboy stories." Robert had been there and had seen many similar incidents, so the story of *Un Pelado* was just another way of showing how the ordinary man often has a far nobler character (apart from a few lapses, like theft or rape) than the men who go down in history.

Robert was still writing a book a year, and he wrote numerous prefaces to other people's books these days, too. He had got 'preface-writing' down to a fine art. It was the one place in the book where, if they were your own books, you could get really personal with your readers and say exactly what you thought. They probably would not read it anyway, so it did not matter much if you offended their prejudices. A preface to a friend's book was a different matter altogether; it was like sending a friend off abroad with introductions, or putting your name to his cause. Robert never said no, when asked, for he was far too courteous.

Some of his best writing came out in his prefaces, and some of his most ironical comments on civilisation: "He who wishes to see Christ's kingdom upon earth, the Rule of the Saints, or the Fifth Monarchy in operation, is almost certain to be an anarchist."

Or this: "All men are equal, each inferior to his brother."

Or this: "I mean no disrespect to kings or beachcombers. Each of them probably have their uses in a civilisation that appears to me to be founded on mud, cemented with blood, and sustained precariously upon the points of bayonets."

Robert always wrote with the underdog in mind, and by using his pen he defended in turn the Indian brave, the Argentine gaucho, harlot and hawker, poacher and post-boy, showing the world their underlying qualities which might otherwise have been obscured by their various sins of commission or omission.

Robert's final book was published by Heinemann's, and called *Mirages*. He had now published thirty-one books since he started to write at the age of forty. In his preface he wrote his final commentary on his own stories. "Virtue in them is quite as rarely rewarded as it is in real life, nor is vice especially triumphant. But then, although they tell us that death is the wages of the sinner, as far as I can see, it seems to be not very different for the saint."

Death was already on his mind when he wrote those words late in 1931. His doctor had warned him against a final trip to Argentina, but Robert felt that although Scotland was his home, it would be quite romantic to return to South America to die!

Robert had frequent attacks of bronchitis during his final years at Ardoch, but he knew he could only write his books in the peace and quiet of the book-room there.

In 1932, Dr. Humble came on regular visits to his friend and patient at Ardoch. As his car crunched off over the gravel of the front drive after one of these visits, Robert walked out on a winter's afternoon to stand on the lawn at Ardoch under the old weeping ash where he had buried several more of his dogs since the valiant fox terrier from Texas, Jack.

He gazed across the river towards his childhood home, Finlaystone, and thought of the many ponies on which he had cantered over the tidal sands when he was a small boy, and of the many horses he had ridden since then. How extraordinary it was to think that he was now eighty years old. He really did not feel any older than the ten-year-old boy at Finlaystone, he chuckled to himself.

Pampa, the finest of all his horses, had died in 1911; now he had a beautiful Argentine called Chajá, who carried him as gently as though it knew its master was no longer the agile gaucho he used to be. He often rode over the firm yellow sands that seemed to stretch almost to Finlaystone at low tide. A friend had brought her child to see him recently, and the small boy had been entranced by the view across the river. Pointing to the opposite shoreline, the child had said with awe in his voice, "Is that America, across there?"

Robert recalled instantly how he, too, had thought America must be just around the Tail of the Bank, when his nurse, old Ninny, had told him that the ships sailing downstream on the tide were going to America.

He remembered the small book of adventure stories given to him by Doña Catalina, his Spanish grandmother, for Christmas 1862, seventy years ago, when he was ten years old and living at Finlaystone.

Most of all he remembered the story of Tom Bainbridge, which had seemed to be his own personal signpost to the Americas, so long ago; and he smiled to himself as he thought of G. K. Chesterton's apt comment that "Cunninghame Graham has achieved the adventure of being Cunninghame Graham."

Yes, his life had certainly been an "adventure," he mused.

CHAPTER XXX

It always seems as though Robert had known the young Swiss horseman and schoolmaster for years and years, their names became so inextricably entwined. But it was not until 1932 that they came into each other's lives, Robert already eighty years old, but still amazingly young in heart, and active, although he only had another four years to live.

Seven years after Aimé Tschiffely had achieved his astonishing adventure with his ride from Buenos Aires to Washington, with his two famous horses, Mancha and Gato, he decided to write a book. It was to be called simply *Tschiffely's Ride*. But nowhere could he find anyone to publish it. Eventually he decided to come to London to see if he could find a publisher there.

When he arrived in London he had no idea that his story had already been published in a book called *Writ in Sand* by R. B. Cunninghame Graham, just brought out that very year by his own publishers, Heinemann. Robert had read of Tschiffely's amazing feat in a newspaper article some years before and had decided to write a short piece to go in his latest book, a collection of short stories and essays.

His very first sentence said, "Tschiffely, Mancha and Gato. The three names are as indivisible as the three Persons of the Trinity." At the bottom of that first page there is a footnote, *"I did not know Tschiffely when I wrote this sketch, taking my information from Argentine papers and magazines." He goes on to say, "Tschiffely, a Swiss long settled in the Argentine, a famous horseman, is a man of iron resolution and infinite resource, as his great feat, perhaps the greatest that man and horses have performed in all the history of the world, is there to show, having travelled fifteen thousand miles during their three years' ride."

Little did Robert know as he wrote those words that Tschiffely had just reached London with his manuscript under his arm. After fruitless knocking on doors to find a friendly publisher he was just about to give up the task and return to Buenos Aires. He had even booked his passage home, and thought he should go and say goodbye to the Argentine Ambassador, Dr. Manuel Malbran, before sailing back to Argentina.

When he was ushered into the ambassador's private office, there was a young Scot sitting by the desk. Tschiffely was introduced to Colin Paterson, who was in charge the embassy's finance department. Colin listened to the sad tale of Tschiffely's failure to find a publisher for his unique story, and said, "But you can't go home till you've met my famous countryman, Mr. Cunninghame Graham! He'll help you to get your book published, I'm absolutely certain. I know him well, and I'll telephone him as soon as I get home tonight."

Tschiffely had already read several of Cunninghame Graham's books, but said he could not possibly disturb such a great man with his own affairs; it was very kind, but he really did not want to bother him.

That evening Tschiffely received a telegram from Robert, inviting him to lunch with him the next day at Martinez's Spanish restaurant in Swallow Street, near Piccadilly Circus. Colin Paterson had been as good as his word.

In Tschiffely's later book, *Bohemia Junction* (his own autobiography), he describes his first meeting with Robert.

"From the moment I met him and his friend Mrs. Dummett (née Mieville), the exquisite horsewoman, things began to happen to me with lightning speed!" He had taken his manuscript with him to the restaurant and Robert bore it off after lunch, suggesting they should meet again at Martinez for lunch the next day.

The following day, there were Robert and Mrs. Dummett at their usual table, smiling kindly when Tschiffely came in.

"I have spent the whole night reading this," said Robert, "and it must be published! In fact, it *will* be published. I have already made an appointment with my publishers for us to meet them after lunch!"

After the successful meeting with Heinemanns, Robert persuaded the disbelieving and joyful Tschiffely to stay on in London until his book was published, and to cancel his voyage home at once.

Aimé soon realised that this modern Don Quixote was going to make life come alight, and that a new and close friendship had started between the eighty-year-old horseman and an obscure young Swiss, who just happened to have completed a long ride that would have been exactly the sort of thing the elderly Don Roberto would have eaten his heart out to have achieved. There was to be admiration on both sides in this special friendship.

In *Bohemia Junction* Aimé goes on to say, "I saw a great deal of Cunninghame Graham after that. He took a great interest in my activities and one day I asked him why he wasted time on me. He told me that since his friend, Hudson, had died, until he met me there had been no-one with whom he could talk about gauchos and the pampas, which had once been his spiritual home."

Soon after that Robert took him to several parties given by Mrs. Dummett at 17, Walton Place, near Harrods, where he met a wonderful mix of interesting people. There, on different occasions, he met Max Beerbohm, H. G. Wells, Dr. Axel Munthe, Compton Mackenzie, Dr. Cronin, Sir John Lavery, Ramon Perez de Ayala, as well as many beautiful society ladies.

Then one day Aimé was invited by Mrs. Dummett's sister, Louisa Mieville, to a party in her own house, where he was introduced to a beautiful girl called Violet Hume. She had been born in Buenos Aires of Scottish and French parents, and she was a talented singer and linguist. Her singing teacher in London was Mme. Blanche Marquesi, who got her the part of Lucy Lockit in Sir Nigel Playfair's original production of *The Beggar's Opera*, and her stage name, given to her by her teacher, became "Violet Marquesita."

For Aimé it was love at first sight, and within a very short time they were married! The two witnesses at their wedding were R. B. Cunninghame Graham and Admiral Sir Frederick Fisher, better known as "Uncle Bill."

Over the weeks while Aimé was waiting for the publication of his book, Robert had begun to learn a great deal about the origins of the young Swiss.

It transpired that he was born quite near the French border with Switzerland, at Neuville, an old-fashioned little town on the southern shore of the Lake of Biel, which the French-speakers called Lac Bienne. The lake was to the west of Berne and north of Geneva. His childhood was a very happy one, and he had a brother and two sisters. He did remember, however, that he had always been terrified of the dark, a fact that he now found quite amusing, since he had made the longest journey on horseback ever with only his two horses, Mancha and Gato for company, and many nights spent in dark and dangerous places!

Another story he told Robert showed that he had been born with a strong 'bump of locality', a gift that was to stand him in very good stead on his great adventure more than twenty-five years later. Apparently he had been taken to Paris at the age of three by his parents, and they had all gone to some great public event. Somehow he became separated from them. Finding himself alone amongst a mass of strange people, little Aimé toddled back, some three miles, to the house in which they were staying with relatives. Everybody being out and the place locked, he sat down on the doorstep and waited.

It was getting dark when his mother and two other ladies arrived in a cab. They all screamed at him as if he had done something wrong, and then, to his astonishment, his tearful mother hugged and kissed him until he thought she would never stop.

Later, when his father arrived, Aimé was taken, to his great joy, for a ride in a horse-drawn *fiacre*; when the horses stopped he was taken in to a gloomy police station. He was frightened to death and wondered what they were going to do about him. The policemen did a lot of scribbling in notebooks, wherafter they departed.

At the time he did not realise that he had been reported "lost", and he had been taken to the police station merely to prove that he had been found. Ever since that evening he had privately continued to dislike policemen.

A very small boy of three years old walking three miles, quite calmly, in a strange city, to a house he hardly knew, shows that not only did Aimé have his 'bump of locality' but also that he was brave, calm, resolute and enterprising, even as a child! No wonder he had completed a fifteen thousand mile ride as though it was a canter in the park.

After he had left school, where he says he did not particularly distinguish himself, Tschiffely decided that he wanted an independent life, beyond Switzerland, and so travelled to England. In due course he managed to get a job as an assistant master in a private preparatory school in the New Forest. There were only twenty-five boys in the school, and several of them were young foreign princes. His friendly nature made him very popular with the young boys, and the headmaster gave him a glowing reference when he decided to move on.

Aimé had been able to do a great deal of riding in the New Forest, so already knew that his destiny was to be with horses. Because of this he decided to try his luck in Argentina, knowing there would be plenty of horses there. He was soon engaged to teach at St. George's School, the "Eton" of Buenos Aires, and found that he could spend most of the school holidays out on the pampas riding with the gauchos. And so it was that he finally decided to undertake his tremendous adventure with two almost wild horses, Mancha and Gato who became, as Robert was to write, "almost as indivisible as the three Persons of the Trinity." The year was 1925.

Robert continued to spend much time with Aimé and Violeta during his final years. Aimé always remembered, when they first met, that Robert had quizzed him on the pronunciation of his name, and he had explained that he came from a very ancient Swiss family, centuries old. The name had at times been spelled in various ways – Tschiffely, Tschiffeli, Tschiffeling, Gifelli and Chifelle. All these spellings seem to come from the French or Italian languages, but this was not surprising as the borders of those two countries were geographically "next door." There had never been any German influence on the family as far as he knew.

Robert was very intrigued, and said, "Good! I shall call you Tschiff**ely**, with the emphasis on the final syllable, as they would in Spain – or Argentina!"

Aimé was delighted, and so was Violeta.

Aimé had one final duty to perform for his dear friend Don Roberto in 1936. Because Robert died in Buenos Aires, a huge funeral procession was arranged by the local people, who had always admired him, to take his coffin to the docks. His body was to be taken back to Scotland on the *Almeda Star* (the very ship his passage home had already been booked in) to be buried in Scotland next to Gabrielle on the island of Inchmahome in the Lake of Menteith near Gartmore.

The day before he died Robert went with Toppie Dummett and Louisa Mieville, who had accompanied him on what was to be his final visit to Argentina, to give Mancha and Gato some oats out of a little bag he had brought out for them from Aimé. The horses had been put out to grass in their old age only a short distance from Buenos Aires, and Aimé had planned to join Robert for the journey home by sea.

At Don Roberto's funeral procession, it was Mancha and Gato who walked behind the ornate funeral carriage, as his "spare horses," with his reversed boots in the stirrups.

Behind them walked their master, Aimé Tschiffely, with the British Ambassador.

EPILOGUE
FOR RIGHT AND REASON
THE MOTTO OF THE GRAHAMS OF MENTEITH

At the end of my chronicle of my great-uncle Robert's life, I need to emphasise the fact that all I intended to do is to tell the "true story" – I have not tried to analyse his character: better writers and academics than I am have already done so and the best of all is the book *Cunninghame Graham: A Critical Biography* by Cedric Watts (Lecturer in English, University of Sussex) and Laurence Davies (Professor of English, Dartmouth College, New Hampshire) published by the Cambridge University Press in 1979. They, far more than me, were able to explain the contradictions in Uncle Robert's personality. Anyone who has developed an interest in this man, who was "larger than life" can continue to learn more about him in their brilliant book. I admit I frequently consulted it myself while writing this book.

A third book, *Don Roberto* by A. F Tschiffely, was the first of many biographies, published by Heinemann in 1937, the year after his friend's death.

Robert had always said that he did not want a biography written, but he knew that Tschiffely's unique horsemanship and his gentle nature would describe him in the only way he could recognise himself. Tschiffely had started to write it even before Robert died in 1936.

Robert had already made it clear in several prologues to his many books that everything he wrote was autobiographical, or inspired by a fascination with South American and Spanish history, and a deep love for his own native land, Scotland. He knew that he was telling about his own life in the best way of all – in his own words – so I have unashamedly used his own writing as the basis for my chronicle of his life. Many paragraphs are taken wholesale from his superb prose, which was so admired by the great writers of his day: his friends Conrad, Hudson, Galsworthy, Thomas Hardy, and many others whose names are now remembered today with great distinction. Robert Bontine Cunninghame Graham has faded into the past, as he seemed to hope he would. I apologise to him if I have brought him back unwillingly into the public arena – but he was too much of a "renaissance man" to be simply forgotten.

Everything he wrote seems to impinge on our new century; indeed he was almost prophetic: "The wickedness of war is a reason for keeping out of war; but the field once taken, it is not a practicable reason for betraying your allies and your country by throwing down your arms." (As I write this, the Black Watch have moved into dangerous territory in Iraq – Robert would have been proud of them.)

Argentina became his spiritual home at the end of his days, when he went there to die. Cedric Watts says, "It is clear that the mature Cunninghame Graham's compassionate view of humanity was shaded by his early knowledge of violence and semi-anarchy on the pampas of Argentina."

Adios, Uncle Robert!

Jean Polwarth
(née Cunninghame Graham)
Wellfield Parva – 2004

POST SCRIPTUM

By Murray Grigor, Film Maker, Hon. FRIAS (1994); Hon. FRIBA (1999); Hon Chairman, Edinburgh International Film Festival (1991-1994), Rodin Prize, Paris Beinnale 1992. Films made in 1981 and 1986: "Frank Lloyd Wright's Architecture," and "Eduardo Paolozzis's Sculpture."

> *I'll ha'e nae hauf-way hoose, but aye be whaur*
> *Extremes meet.*
> Hugh MacDairmid

'Your next film should be on Cunninghame Graham, a real fighter for working people,' urged Hugh MacDairmid. Then he added with a wry smile, 'and a true aristocrat.' Scotland's radical national bard, and the Marxist politician who was descended from the ancient kings of Scotland, revelled in each other's contradictions. Although both Robert and Karl Marx *himself* had been heard to declare firmly, 'I am *not* a Marxist.'

So there we were having lunch celebrating Trapalanda – a madly ambitious film company which my late wife Barbara and I had just set up in the hope of bringing the extraordinary life of Robert Bontine Cunninghame Graham to the screen. Jean, his great-niece, welcomed us to the Gothic extravagance of the House of Lords dining room. 'Oh, how uncle Robert would have loved to see us here,' Jean laughed. 'It's the place he spent a life time attempting to abolish.' Her great-uncle Robert may have left no offspring, but Jean is the living proof that her family's sense of fun continues.

As the ideas for our film began to take shape, Jean always had the ability to bring her extraordinary great-uncle back to life for us. To celebrate her sixtieth birthday, Barbara had found a tea-towel based on the membership card of the first Scottish Labour Party. As it dropped from Jean's outstretched arms, there were its two founding members proudly facing each other for the whole room to see. Over a cameo of the aristocratic Robert was the slogan 'No Privilege.' For his co-socialist friend, the Lanarkshire coal miner Keir Hardie, the banner ran 'No Monopoly.' The gasps of Tory disbelief from all around us were lost as

Jean's infectious laughter ricocheted round Edinburgh's New Club, that august retreat of the Scottish Establishment.

It was a scene that would surely have delighted the hero of Jean's *Gaucho Laird* – a book which switches us so wittily through the many paradoxes of an extraordinary life. Her title says it all. Don Roberto was at once a Long Rider of the New World's purple plains, and the impoverished Scottish laird, struggling to run his Old World country estate, as he fought for workers' rights and under-dogs everywhere.

Over the years many have wondered who the exotically named Gabrielle de la Balmondière, the love of Robert's life, really was, or even where she had come from. When their marriage certificate was held up at a Cunninghame Graham conference by the scholar Cedric Watts, delegates were amazed to hear that this primary source of historical evidence bore not a single fact of truth. So much for her Chilean ancestry recorded there, or her Spanish manner, which fellow socialists, writers and artists like Walter Crane so much admired in Gabrielle. Jean has finally solved the mystery, as these racy pages now reveal.

Much to the disapproval of Robert's mother, the formidable Mrs. Bontine, once described as a Scottish deity of longevity, the couple eloped to begin a life of adventures together and apart. Driven by a deep belief in the vulgarity of success their first ventures as ranchers in Texas ended so catastrophically that it made a headline in a San Antonio newspaper as a 'Colossal Failure.' Recently Jean found that inscribed in the local museum, appropriately close to that other monument of heroic failure, the Alamo.

Sadly the progress of our film to the screen became thwarted at every turn. Mrs. Thatcher's invasion of the Falkland Islands co-incided with our scouting trip to Argentina which had to be cancelled. A Hollywood producer told Barbara that there was now not too much top spin for socialism and failure in America today. Television executives accused our screenplay of being too picaresque, a hardly telling objection since we were inspired by the greatest novel ever written, *Don Quixote*. But that was fiction and Don Roberto was fact, or mostly so. His windmills were very real and many of his battles have since been won, such as Irish Home Rule, an eight-hour day and women's rights. The recent return of the Scottish Parliament would have given him, as he said, 'the particular pleasure of knowing that the taxes were wasted in Edinburgh instead of London.'

'Now there's a true socialist, unlike Tony Blair,' said Sean Connery. And who knows, Don Roberto may yet right out in our forthcoming television series of Scottish themes, hosted by Scotland's international super-star.

In *Gaucho Laird* Jean has triumphed over failure. Let's hope it now edges towards *Success* – the title of one of Robert's most successful collection of short stories. If Don Roberto ever reached Trapalanda – that Gaucho heaven of men and horses, I'm sure that he'll now be reading his great-niece's witty unfolding of his adventurous life with more than a wry ancestral smile.

Murray Grigor
December 2004

INDEX

OUR CURRENT LIST OF TITLES

Abdullah, Morag Murray, *My Khyber Marriage* – In 1916 Morag was living a quiet life in Scotland until she married Syed Abdullah, a student at Edinburgh University and went to live in the war-torn North-West Frontier Province of India.

Abernathy, Miles, *Ride the Wind* – the amazing true story of the little Abernathy Boys, who made a series of astonishing journeys in the United States, starting in 1909 when they were aged five and nine!

Beard, John, *Saddles East* – John Beard determined as a child that he wanted to see the Wild West from the back of a horse after a visit to Cody's legendary Wild West show. Yet it was only in 1948 – more than sixty years after seeing the flamboyant American showman – that Beard and his wife Lulu finally set off to follow their dreams.

Beker, Ana, *The Courage to Ride* – Determined to out-do Tschiffely, Beker made a 17,000 mile mounted odyssey across the Americas in the late 1940s that would fix her place in the annals of equestrian travel history.

Bird, Isabella, *Among the Tibetans* – A rousing 1889 adventure, an enchanting travelogue, a forgotten peek at a mountain kingdom swept away by the waves of time.

Bird, Isabella, *On Horseback* in *Hawaii* – The Victorian explorer's first horseback journey, in which she learns to ride side-saddle, in early 1873.

Bird, Isabella, *Journeys in Persia and Kurdistan, Volumes 1 and 2* – The intrepid Englishwoman undertakes another gruelling journey in 1890.

Bird, Isabella, *A Lady's Life in the Rocky Mountains* – The story of Isabella Bird's adventures during the winter of 1873 when she explored the magnificent unspoiled wilderness of Colorado. Truly a classic.

Bird, Isabella, *Unbeaten Tracks in Japan, Volumes One and Two* – A 600-mile solo ride through Japan undertaken by the intrepid British traveller in 1878.

Bosanquet, Mary, *Saddlebags for Suitcases* – In 1939 Bosanquet set out to ride from Vancouver, Canada, to New York. Along the way she was wooed by love-struck cowboys, chased by a grizzly bear and even suspected of being a Nazi spy, scouting out Canada in preparation for a German invasion. A truly delightful book.

de Bourboulon, Catherine, *Shanghai à Moscou (French)* – the story of how a young Scottish woman and her aristocratic French husband travelled overland from Shanghai to Moscow in the late 19th Century.

Brower, Charles, *Fifty Years below Zero* – In 1883 Charlie Brower arrived in Alaska. The native Inuit people taught him how to hunt seals on the ice, caribou on the tundra, and whales out on the sea.

Brown, Donald; *Journey from the Arctic* – A truly remarkable account of how Brown, his Danish companion and their two trusty horses attempt the impossible, to cross the silent Arctic plateaus, thread their way through the giant Swedish forests, and finally discover a passage around the treacherous Norwegian marshes.

Burnaby, Frederick; *A Ride to Khiva* – Burnaby fills every page with a memorable cast of characters, including hard-riding Cossacks, nomadic Tartars, vodka-guzzling sleigh-drivers and a legion of peasant ruffians.

Burnaby, Frederick, *On Horseback through Asia Minor* – Armed with a rifle, a small stock of medicines, and a single faithful servant, the equestrian traveler rode through a hotbed of intrigue and high adventure in wild inhospitable country, encountering Kurds, Circassians, Armenians, and Persian pashas.

Carter, General William, *Horses, Saddles and Bridles* – This book covers a wide range of topics including basic training of the horse and care of its equipment. It also provides a fascinating look back into equestrian travel history.

Cayley, George, *Bridle Roads of Spain* – Truly one of the greatest equestrian travel accounts of the 19th Century.

Chase, J. Smeaton, *California Coast Trails* – This classic book describes the author's journey from Mexico to Oregon along the coast of California in the 1890s.

Chase, J. Smeaton, *California Desert Trails* – Famous British naturalist J. Smeaton Chase mounted up and rode into the Mojave Desert to undertake the longest equestrian study of its kind in modern history.

Clark, Leonard, *The Marching Wind* – The panoramic story of a mounted exploration in the remote and savage heart of Asia, a place where adventure, danger, and intrigue were the daily backdrop to wild tribesman and equestrian exploits.

Cobbett, William, *Rural Rides, Volumes 1 and 2* – In the early 1820s Cobbett set out on horseback to make a series of personal tours through the English countryside. These books contain what many believe to be the best accounts of rural England ever written, and remain enduring classics.

Codman, John, *Winter Sketches from the Saddle* – This classic book was first published in 1888. It recommends riding for your health and describes the septuagenarian author's many equestrian journeys through New England during the winter of 1887 on his faithful mare, Fanny.

Cunninghame Graham, Jean, *Gaucho Laird* – A superbly readable biography of the author's famous great-uncle, Robert "Don Roberto" Cunninghame Graham.

Cunninghame Graham, Robert, *Horses of the Conquest* –The author uncovered manuscripts which had lain forgotten for centuries, and wrote this book, as he said, out of gratitude to the horses of Columbus and the Conquistadors who shaped history.

Cunninghame Graham, Robert, *Magreb-el-Acksa* – The thrilling tale of how "Don Roberto" was kidnapped in Morocco!

Cunninghame Graham, Robert, *Rodeo* – An omnibus of the finest work of the man they called "the uncrowned King of Scotland," edited by his friend Aimé Tschiffely.

Cunninghame Graham, Robert, *Tales of Horsemen* – Ten of the most beautifully-written equestrian stories ever set to paper.

Daly, H.W., *Manual of Pack Transportation* – This book is the author's masterpiece. It contains a wealth of information on various pack saddles, ropes and equipment, how to secure every type of load imaginable and instructions on how to organize a pack train.

Dixie, Lady Florence, *Riding Across Patagonia* – When asked in 1879 why she wanted to travel to such an outlandish place as Patagonia, the author replied without hesitation that she was taking to the saddle in order to flee from the strict confines of polite Victorian society. This is the story of how the aristocrat successfully traded the perils of a London parlor for the wind-borne freedom of a wild Patagonian bronco.

Farson, Negley, *Caucasian Journey* – A thrilling account of a dangerous equestrian journey made in 1929, this is an amply illustrated adventure classic.

Forbes, Rosita, *Forbidden Road: Kabul to Samarkand* – One of the most delightful journeys of the adventure-filled 1930s. The author spoke to nomads, dined with royalty, and uncovered enough stories to fill two books.

Forbes, Rosita, *Secret of the Sahara: Kufara* – The intrepid female explorer decided to penetrate the infamous wastes of the Libyan deserts. At stake was an interview with the mysterious leader of an obscure Muslim sect. Yet more important to Rosita was the need to discover, not some minor potentate, but the legendary lost city of the Sahara, Kufara.

Fox, Ernest, *Travels in Afghanistan* – The thrilling tale of a 1937 journey through the mountains, valleys, and deserts of this forbidden realm, including visits to such fabled places as the medieval city of Heart, the towering Hindu Kush mountains, and the legendary Khyber Pass.

Galton, Francis, *The Art of Travel* – Originally published in 1855, this book became an instant classic and was used by a host of now-famous explorers, including Sir Richard Francis Burton of Mecca fame. Readers can learn how to ride horses, handle elephants, avoid cobras, pull teeth, find water in a desert, and construct a sleeping bag out of fur.

Galwan, Rassul, *Servant of Sahibs* – The remarkable true story of a native of Ladakh who early on in life became a trusted assistant to various nineteenth century European explorers such as Sir Francis Younghusband. This utterly delightful book is a first-hand account of the most famous Central Asian expeditions, as seen by Galwan and the natives involved.

Glazier, Willard, *Ocean to Ocean on Horseback* – This book about the author's journey from New York to the Pacific in 1875 contains every kind of mounted adventure imaginable. Amply illustrated with pen and ink drawings of the time, the book remains a timeless equestrian adventure classic.

Goodwin, Joseph, *Through Mexico on Horseback* – The author and his companion, Robert Horiguichi, the sophisticated, multi-lingual son of an imperial Japanese diplomat, set out in 1931 to cross Mexico. They were totally unprepared for the deserts, quicksand and brigands they were to encounter during their adventure.

Halliburton, Richard, *Flying Carpet* – This describes the famous explorer's epic adventures flying a bi-plane through remote parts of the globe. It recounts how Halliburton landed in Timbuctoo, passed over Mt. Everest, flew over the Taj Mahal upside down, and dropped down into the jungles of Borneo to visit native head hunters.

Halliburton, Richard, *The Glorious Adventure* – The intrepid American set out to follow in the path of Ulysses, that royal vagabond who mirrored his own restlessness. This book doesn't lack for excitement as it details how Halliburton roamed the Mediterranean Sea searching for adventure and romance, both of which he was happy to report were still in abundant supply.

Halliburton, Richard, **New Worlds to Conquer – A knapsack full of that adventurer's gold: dreams brought to reality by the alchemy of his courage and daring. Halliburton set off for Latin America in search of adventure, and find it he did.**

Halliburton, Richard, *The Royal Road to Romance* – Halliburton's first book describes how he visited a vast array of countries from England to Japan. During the course of these travels he undertook every sort of madcap adventure that he could find, including swimming the famed Hellespont and exploring the jungles of India.

Halliburton, Richard, *Seven League Boots* – In this, his last book, America's favorite adventure writer dined with Emperor Haile Selassie in Ethiopia, interviewed the infamous assassin of Czar Nicholas II in Russia, tried to sneak into the forbidden city of Mecca, and finally, rode an elephant over the Alps in the tracks of Hannibal.

Hanbury-Tenison, Robin, *White Horses over France* – This enchanting book tells the story of a magical journey and how, in fulfilment of a personal dream, the first Camargue horses set foot on British soil in the late summer of 1984.

Hanbury-Tenison, Robin, *Chinese Adventure* – The story of a unique journey in which the explorer Robin Hanbury-Tenison and his wife Louella rode on horseback alongside the Great Wall of China in 1986.

Hanbury-Tenison, Robin, *Fragile Eden* – The wonderful story of Robin and Louella Hanbury-Tenison's exploration of New Zealand on horseback in 1988. They rode alone together through what they describe as 'some of the most dramatic and exciting country we have ever seen.'

Hanbury-Tenison, Robin, *Mulu: The Rainforest* – This was the first popular book to bring to the world's attention the significance of the rain forests to our fragile ecosystem. It is a timely reminder of our need to preserve them for the future.

Hanbury-Tenison, Robin, *Spanish Pilgrimage* – Robin and Louella Hanbury-Tenison went to Santiago de Compostela in a traditional way – riding on white horses over long-forgotten tracks. In the process they discovered more about the people and the country than any conventional traveller would learn. Their adventures are vividly and entertainingly recounted in this delightful and highly readable book.

Hanbury-Tenison, Robin, *Worlds Apart – an Explorer's Life* – The author's battle to preserve the quality of life under threat from developers and machines infuses this autobiography with a passion and conviction which makes it impossible to put down.

Hanbury-Tenison, Robin, *Worlds Within – Reflections in the Sand* – This book is full of the adventure you would expect from a man of action like Robin Hanbury-Tenison. However, it is also filled with the type of rare knowledge that was revealed to other desert travellers like Lawrence, Doughty and Thesiger.

Haslund, Henning, *Mongolian Adventure* – An epic tale inhabited by a cast of characters no longer present in this lackluster world, shamans who set themselves on fire, rebel leaders who sacked towns, and wild horsemen whose ancestors conquered the world.

Heath, Frank, *Forty Million Hoofbeats* – Heath set out in 1925 to follow his dream of riding to all 48 of the Continental United States. The journey lasted more than two years, during which time Heath and his mare, Gypsy Queen, became inseparable companions.

Hedin, Sven, *My Life as an Explorer* – The author was one of the greatest of the nineteenth century explorers, and a brilliant storyteller.

Holt, William, *Ride a White Horse* – After rescuing a cart horse, Trigger, from slaughter and nursing him back to health, the 67-year-old Holt and his horse set out in 1964 on an incredible 9,000 mile, non-stop journey through western Europe.

Hopkins, Frank T., *Hidalgo and Other Stories* – For the first time in history, here are the collected writings of Frank T. Hopkins, the counterfeit cowboy whose endurance racing claims and Old West fantasies have polarized the equestrian world.

James, Jeremy, *Saddletramp* – The classic story of Jeremy James' journey from Turkey to Wales, on an unplanned route with an inaccurate compass, unreadable map and the unfailing aid of villagers who seemed to have as little sense of direction as he had.

James, Jeremy, *Vagabond* – The wonderful tale of the author's journey from Bulgaria to Berlin offers a refreshing, witty and often surprising view of Eastern Europe and the collapse of communism.

Jebb, Louisa, *By Desert Ways to Baghdad and Damascus* – From the pen of a gifted writer and intrepid traveller, this is one of the greatest equestrian travel books of all time.

Kluckhohn, Clyde, *To the Foot of the Rainbow* – This is not just a exciting true tale of equestrian adventure. It is a moving account of a young man's search for physical perfection in a desert world still untouched by the recently-born twentieth century.

Lamb, Dana and Ginger, *Enchanted Vagabonds* – One of the greatest adventure travel tales ever to emerge from the action-packed 1930s. The newly-married couple set off on a 16,000 mile journey in a tiny canoe. Their adventures included shooting through mountainous surf, landing on fabled islands, weathering nearly a dozen fatal wrecks, and getting caught in quicksand, trapped inside an extinct volcano, and lost in a shark-infested lagoon.

Lamb, Dana, *Quest for the Lost City* – The story of how the Lambs returned to their old Spanish speaking haunts. Only this time they were not roaming in general. They were seeking in particular for the source of a legend, the fabled lost city of the Mayas. Travel adventure at its best!

Lambie, Thomas, *Boots and Saddles in Africa* – Lambie's story of his equestrian journeys is told with the grit and realism that marks a true classic.

Landor, Henry Savage, *In the Forbidden Land* – Illustrated with hundreds of photographs and drawings, this blood-chilling account of equestrian adventure makes for page-turning excitement.

Langlet, Valdemar, *Till Häst Genom Ryssland (Swedish)* – Denna reseskildring rymmer många ögonblicksbilder av möten med människor, från morgonbad med Lev Tolstoi till samtal med Tartarer och fotografering av fagra skördeflickor. Rikt illustrerad med foto och teckningar.

Leigh, Margaret, *My Kingdom for a Horse* – In the autumn of 1939 the author rode from Cornwall to Scotland, resulting in one of the most delightful equestrian journeys of the early twentieth century. This book is full of keen observations of a rural England that no longer exists.

Maillart, Ella, *Turkestan Solo* – A vivid account of a 1930s journey through this wonderful, mysterious and dangerous portion of the world, complete with its Kirghiz eagle hunters, lurking Soviet secret police, and the timeless nomads that still inhabited the desolate steppes of Central Asia.

Marcy, Randolph, *The Prairie Traveler* – There were a lot of things you packed into your saddlebags or the wagon before setting off to cross the North American wilderness in the 1850s. A gun and an axe were obvious necessities. Yet many pioneers were just as adamant about placing a copy of Captain Randolph Marcy's classic book close at hand.

Marsh, Hippisley Cunliffe, *A Ride Through Islam* – A British officer rides through Persia and Afghanistan to India in 1873. Full of adventures, and with observant remarks on the local Turkoman equestrian traditions.

MacCann, William, *Viaje a Caballo* – Spanish-language edition of the British author's equestrian journey around Argentina in 1848.

MacGregor, John, *The Rob Roy on the Jordan* – Nineteenth century adventure and exploration at its finest. MacGregor paddled his way through Palestine, Syria and eventually into Egypt, making his way through both the Jordan and Nile rivers.

McGovern, William, *To Lhasa in Disguise* – One of the most intriguing tales of travel ever penned. McGovern, an American scholar of Buddhist thought and prayer, determined to get into the forbidden Tibetan capital. He made his way over dangerous mountain passes, avoided prowling Tibetan patrols, and finally reached his goal, only to be recognized and arrested!

Muir Watson, Sharon, *The Colour of Courage* – The remarkable true story of the epic horse trip made by the first people to travel Australia's then-unmarked Bicentennial National Trail. There are enough adventures here to satisfy even the most jaded reader.

O'Reilly, CuChullaine, *Khyber Knights* – Told with grit and realism by one of the world's foremost equestrian explorers, "Khyber Knights" has been penned the way lives are lived, not how books are written.

O'Reilly, CuChullaine, (Editor) *The Long Riders, Volume One* – The first of five unforgettable volumes of exhilarating travel tales.

Östrup, J, (*Swedish*), *Växlande Horisont* - The thrilling account of the author's journey to Central Asia from 1891 to 1893.

Patterson, George, *Journey with Loshay: A Tibetan Odyssey* – This is an amazing book written by a truly remarkable man! Relying both on his companionship with God and on his own strength, he undertook a life few can have known, and a journey of emergency across the wildest parts of Tibet.

Pocock, Roger, *Following the Frontier* – Pocock was one of the nineteenth century's most influential equestrian travelers. Within the covers of this book is the detailed account of Pocock's horse ride along the infamous Outlaw Trail, a 3,000 mile solo journey that took the adventurer from Canada to Mexico City.

Pocock, Roger, *Horses* – Pocock set out to document the wisdom of the late 19th and early 20th Centuries into a book unique for its time. His concerns for attempting to preserve equestrian knowledge were based on cruel reality. More than 300,000 horses had been destroyed during the recent Boer War. Though Pocock enjoyed a reputation for dangerous living, his observations on horses were praised by the leading thinkers of his day.

Post, Charles Johnson, *Horse Packing* – Originally published in 1914, this book was an instant success, incorporating as it did the very essence of the science of packing horses and mules. It makes fascinating reading for students of the horse or history.

Ray, G. W., *Through Five Republics on Horseback* – In 1889 a British explorer - part-time missionary and full-time adventure junky – set out to find a lost tribe of sun-worshipping natives in the unexplored forests of Paraguay. The journey was so brutal that it defies belief.

Riley, James, *Sufferings in Africa* – The incredible story, based on fact, of a young sea captain and his crew who were shipwrecked off the coast of Muslim controlled Morocco in 1885. The battered survivors were pounced upon by local natives, ensnared, enchained, and marched off into the horrors of African slavery. The conditions were so barbaric, the food so scanty, and the beatings so regular that Riley dropped from 240 down to 90 pounds!

Ross, Julian, *Travels in an Unknown Country* – A delightful book about modern horseback travel in an enchanting country, which once marked the eastern borders of the Roman Empire – Romania.

Ross, Martin and Somerville, E, *Beggars on Horseback* – The hilarious adventures of two aristocratic Irish cousins on an 1894 riding tour of Wales.

Ruxton, George, *Adventures in Mexico* – The story of a young British army officer who rode from Vera Cruz to Santa Fe, Mexico in 1847. At times the author exhibits a fearlessness which borders on insanity. He ignores dire warnings, rides through deadly deserts, and dares murderers to attack him. It is a delightful and invigorating tale of a time and place now long gone.

Schwarz, Hans (German), *Vier Pferde, Ein Hund und Drei Soldaten* – In the early 1930s the author and his two companions rode through Liechtenstein, Austria, Romania, Albania, Yugoslavia, to Turkey, then rode back again!

Schwarz, Otto (*German*), *Reisen mit dem Pferd* – the Swiss Long Rider with more miles in the saddle than anyone else tells his wonderful story, and a long appendix tells the reader how to follow in his footsteps.

Scott, Robert, *Scott's Last Expedition* – Many people are unaware that Scott recruited Siberian ponies for his doomed expedition to the South Pole in 1909. Here is the remarkable story of men and horses who all paid the ultimate sacrifice.

Skrede, Wilfred, *Across the Roof of the World* – This epic equestrian travel tale of a wartime journey across Russia, China, Turkestan and India is laced with unforgettable excitement.

Steele, Nick, *Take a Horse to the Wilderness* – Part history book, part adventure story, part equestrian travel textbook and all round great read, this is a timeless classic written by the foremost equestrian expert of his time, famed mounted game ranger Nick Steele.

Stevens, Thomas, *Through Russia on a Mustang* – Mounted on his faithful horse, Texas, Stevens crossed the Steppes in search of adventure. Cantering across the pages of this classic tale is a cast of nineteenth century Russian misfits, peasants, aristocrats—and even famed Cossack Long Rider Dmitri Peshkov.

Stevenson, Robert L., *Travels with a Donkey* – In 1878, the author set out to explore the remote Cevennes mountains of France. He travelled alone, unless you count his stubborn and manipulative pack-donkey, Modestine. This book is a true classic.

Strong, Anna Louise, *Road to the Grey Pamir* – With Stalin's encouragement, Strong rode into the seldom-seen Pamir mountains of faraway Tadjikistan. The political renegade turned equestrian explorer soon discovered more adventure than she had anticipated.

Sykes, Ella, *Through Persia on a Sidesaddle* – Ella Sykes rode side-saddle 2,000 miles across Persia, a country few European woman had ever visited. Mind you, she traveled in style, accompanied by her Swiss maid and 50 camels loaded with china, crystal, linens and fine wine.

Trinkler, Emile, *Through the Heart of Afghanistan* – In the early 1920s the author made a legendary trip across a country now recalled only in legends.

Tschiffely, Aimé, *Bohemia Junction* – "Forty years of adventurous living condensed into one book."

Tschiffely, Aimé, *Bridle Paths* – a final poetic look at a now-vanished Britain.

Tschiffely, Aimé, *Mancha y Gato Cuentan sus Aventuras* – The Spanish-language version of *The Tale of Two Horses* – the story of the author's famous journey as told by the horses.

Tschiffely, Aimé, *The Tale of Two Horses* – The story of Tschiffely's famous journey from Buenos Aires to Washington, DC, narrated by his two equine heroes, Mancha and Gato. Their unique point of view is guaranteed to delight children and adults alike.

Tschiffely, Aimé, *This Way Southward* – the most famous equestrian explorer of the twentieth century decides to make a perilous journey across the U-boat infested Atlantic.

Tschiffely, Aimé, *Tschiffely's Ride* – The true story of the most famous equestrian journey of the twentieth century – 10,000 miles with two Criollo geldings from Argentina to Washington, DC. A new edition is coming soon with a Foreword by his literary heir!

Tschiffely, Aimé, *Tschiffely's Ritt* – The German-language translation of *Tschiffely's Ride* – the most famous equestrian journey of its day.

Warner, Charles Dudley, *On Horseback in Virginia* – A prolific author, and a great friend of Mark Twain, Warner made witty and perceptive contributions to the world of nineteenth century American literature. This book about the author's equestrian adventures is full of fascinating descriptions of nineteenth century America.

Weale, Magdalene, *Through the Highlands of Shropshire* – It was 1933 and Magdalene Weale was faced with a dilemma: how to best explore her beloved English countryside? By horse, of course! This enchanting book invokes a gentle, softer world inhabited by gracious country lairds, wise farmers, and jolly inn keepers.

Wentworth Day, J., *Wartime Ride* – In 1939 the author decided the time was right for an extended horseback ride through England! While parts of his country were being ravaged by war, Wentworth Day discovered an inland oasis of mellow harvest fields, moated Tudor farmhouses, peaceful country halls, and fishing villages.

Wilkins, Messanie, *Last of the Saddle Tramps* – Told she had little time left to live, the author decided to ride from her native Maine to the Pacific. Accompanied by her faithful horse, Tarzan, Wilkins suffered through any number of obstacles, including blistering deserts and freezing snow storms – and defied the doctors by living for another 20 years!.

Wilson, Andrew, *The Abode of Snow* – One of the best accounts of overland equestrian travel ever written about the wild lands that lie between Tibet and Afghanistan.

de Windt, Harry *From Paris to New York by Land* – The author dined with political exiles in Siberia, almost starved in the Arctic ice fields, and lived through more dangers than a dozen men.

de Windt, Harry, *A Ride to India* – Part science, all adventure, this book takes the reader for a thrilling canter across the Persian Empire of the 1890s.

Winthrop, Theodore, *Saddle and Canoe* – This book paints a vibrant picture of 1850s life in the Pacific Northwest and covers the author's travels along the Straits of Juan De Fuca, on Vancouver Island, across the Naches Pass, and on to The Dalles, in Oregon Territory. This is truly an historic travel account.

Younghusband, George, *Eighteen Hundred Miles on a Burmese Pony* – One of the funniest and most enchanting books about equestrian travel of the nineteenth century, featuring "Joe" the naughty Burmese pony!

We are constantly adding new titles to our collection, so please check our website:

horsetravelbooks.com